W9-AOP-823

RAFFAELE MATTIOLI LECTURES

In honour of the memory of Raffaele Mattioli, who was for many years its manager and chairman, Banca Commerciale Italiana has established the Mattioli Fund as a testimony to the continuing survival and influence of his deep interest in economics, the humanities and sciences.

As its first enterprise the Fund has established a series of annual lectures on the history of economic thought, to be called the Raffaele Mattioli Lectures.

In view of the long association between the Università Commerciale Luigi Bocconi and Raffaele Mattioli, who was an active scholar, adviser and member of the governing body of the University, it was decided that the lectures in honour of his memory should be delivered at the University, which together with Banca Commerciale Italiana, has undertaken the task of organising them.

Distinguished academics of all nationalities, researchers and others concerned with economic problems will be invited to take part in this enterprise, in the hope of linking pure historical research with a debate on economic theory and practical policy.

In creating a memorial to the cultural legacy left by Raffaele Mattioli, it is hoped above all that these lectures and the debates to which they give rise will prove a fruitful inspiration and starting point for the development of a tradition of research and academic studies like that already long established in other countries, and that this tradition will flourish thanks to the new partnership between the Università Commerciale Luigi Bocconi and Banca Commerciale Italiana.

THINKING ABOUT
DEVELOPMENT

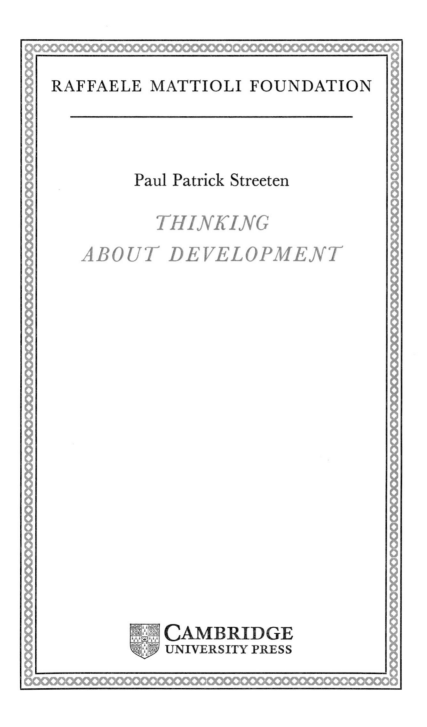

RAFFAELE MATTIOLI FOUNDATION

Paul Patrick Streeten

THINKING ABOUT DEVELOPMENT

CAMBRIDGE
UNIVERSITY PRESS

Published by the Press Syndicate of the University of Cambridge
The Pitt Building, Trumpington Street, Cambridge CB2 1RP
40 West 20th Street, New York, NY 10011-4211, USA
10 Stamford Road, Oakleigh, Melbourne, 3166, Australia

Edited by Alessandro Pio

First published 1995

Printed in Italy

Library of Congress Cataloging in Publication Data
Main entry under title:
Thinking about Development
(Raffaele Mattioli Lectures)
At head of title: Raffaele Mattioli Foundation.
Includes bibliographical references and index.
ISBN 0-521-48276 3

1. Economic Development

2. International Economic Relations

1. Raffaele Mattioli Foundation.
II. Title.   III. Series.

HD 75.5813   1995   338.9   dc20
94-39949 CIP

A catalogue record for this book is available from the British Library
ISBN 0-521-48276 3

CONTENTS

PREFACE

It is a great honour to have been asked to deliver this years's Raffaele Mattioli Lectures. I am deeply grateful to the Banca Commerciale Italiana and to Luigi Bocconi University for having invited me.

I have not had the good fortune to know Raffaele Mattioli personally, but I can claim to be only one handshake away from him, for I have shaken the hands of Piero Sraffa, Richard Kahn, Franco Modigliani and Charles Kindleberger, each of whom has shaken the hand of Dr Mattioli.

Keynes once said that he could hear more of what was going on from my tutor and friend, the late Thomas Balogh, in an hour or two, than he himself could pick up during several days in London. Similarly, Franco Modigliani learned more about the Italian banking system by talking to Mattioli than from all his reading.

As I learned from Innocenzo Gasparini, late Rettore of the Università Luigi Bocconi, the complementary relationship between the history of economic thought – a subject sadly neglected at American universities today – and our present concerns, between pure historical research, economic theory and practical policy, between our culture, our ideas, our institutions and our behaviour, was at the heart of Raffaele Mattioli's personality. It produced the partnership between a prestigious bank, the Banca Commerciale Italiana, of which he was Manager and Chairman, and a distinguished university, Luigi Bocconi University.

He contributed to the legislation that divided investment from deposit banking, helped to finance the great Italian public enterprises, and saved the prison manuscripts by Gramsci, handed to him by Piero Sraffa, by putting them into the bank's vault.

Charlie Kindleberger said Mattioli "collected" economists, which is an honour, though, he added, it is a relief not to be pinned like a butterfly or stuffed like a bird.

Bankers, it must be admitted, have not had a good press. But the strictures they have been subjected to surely do not apply to Italian bankers, if Raffaele Mattioli can be taken as their model. His openness to ideas, his vision, and his sense of history combined with practical policy can serve as an example to bankers, and, indeed, to all of us, in the rest of the world.

It was my grandparents' greatest wish that my mother should marry a banker. She never did. But they seemed to have had a better sense about bankers than the critics of the banking community.

I must finally mention that Mr Sergio Siglienti, the President of the Banca Commerciale Italiana, presided over a memorable dinner during these lectures. I am very grateful to Professor Alessandro Pio, of Bocconi University, who has edited these lectures conscientiously and imaginatively, and has become a friend in the process. My admiration and thanks go to my old friend Sergio Steve, who has inspired my work and set an example of what a humane economist should be.

THINKING ABOUT DEVELOPMENT

The *Raffaele Mattioli Lectures* were delivered by
Paul Patrick Streeten at the Università Commerciale Luigi Bocconi,
in Milano, from 18th to 20th November 1991.

INTRODUCTION

My argument in these lectures has several strands. The principal focus is the eradication of poverty in the world. Some time is devoted to a discussion of the concept and measurement of poverty and hunger. I try to show that a liberal framework of prices and markets requires an active and efficient state, larger and more active than exists now in most developing countries. How is the agenda of this state determined? State action is needed in order to stimulate private action through complementary public services, or "crowding-in". These services will go beyond the provision of a framework of law and order and security, to the conduct of economic policy, the construction of infrastructure, the financing of research, and institution-building. They will also comprise policies to make large, formal-sector firms symbiotic to small, informal-sector micro-enterprises through the "judo trick". Above all, state action is needed to provide or finance social services – nutrition, education and health – for the poor, where private provision or finance are absent or inadequate. What is the optimal mix of private and public action, and how does it determine the division of the gains from growth between rich and poor?

It has been said that the state has become too big for the small things, and too small for the big things. Delegation downwards and organization of the poor is needed in order to mobize action against poverty. As a result of the absence of any one dominant economy, delegation upwards to global institutions is needed in order to avoid mutually destructive action by governments. I propose some of these institutional changes, paying particular attention to mobilizing and bringing together underutilized resources in different parts of the world, and protecting the physical environment. Alternative, less attractive but more probable, future scenarios are outlined.

I try to sketch the basis for a normative political economy of reform: how can the political base for reform be constructed? Several possibilities are discussed at the sub-national level, such as commonality or mutuality of interests, compensation of losers, differences within the ruling group, pressures arising from groups

3

of the civil society and from outside the country, and empowerment of the poor. I then examine the relationships between
national sovereignty and the achievement of certain widely
accepted objectives, in situations that give rise to Prisoners'
Dilemma type outcomes. How can defection and free-rider
problems be avoided? This examination points to the need for
international cooperation or transnational institutions, for which
I give several illustrations. A special section is devoted to exploring the institutions for protecting our physical environment.

FIRST LECTURE
The Evolution of Development Thought

1. Introduction. – 2. Does It Pay To Be Late? – 3. The Three-Ring Circus. – 4. Unemployment. – 5. Population Growth. – 6. Human Development. – 7. Poverty: Concepts and Measurement.

1. Introduction

I have, in the past, written on the evolution of development thought from different perspectives. Several early essays are on the historical evolution of our thinking.[1] A later one took various dichotomies as a starting point and examined how they fit together.[2] A subsequent essay combined history, analysis and policy by trying to show how the successful solution of one set of problems leads to new problems to be investigated.[3] In this lecture I want to trace some ideas according to their scope and limitations of applicability.

In this post-Keynesian, post-industrial, post-ideological age, the field of development is very wide; indeed, it is much wider than economics itself. My survey will therefore have to be highly selective. I shall not say anything about the economics of information and communication, rational expectations, the service economy, game theory, asset pricing, taxation, public economics or the important subject of participation.

1. PAUL STREETEN, 'Development Ideas in Historical Perspective', in *Toward a New Strategy for Development, A Rothko Chapel Colloquium*, New York, Oxford: Pergamon Press, 1979; PAUL STREETEN, 'Development: What Have We Learned?' in *The Relevance of Economic Theories*, Proceedings of a Conference held by the International Economic Association in Warsaw, Poland, edited by JOSEF PAJESTKA and C. H. FEINSTEIN, London: Macmillan, 1980; and PAUL STREETEN, 'From Growth to Basic Needs', *Finance and Development*, vol. 16 no. 2 June 1979; reprinted in *Poverty and Development*, the World Bank, 1979 and in *Development Perspectives*, London: Macmillan, 1981, chapter 18.

2. PAUL STREETEN, 'Development Dichotomies', *World Development*, vol. 11 no. 10, October 1983, also in *Pioneers in Development*, edited by GERALD M. MEIER and DUDLEY SEERS, Oxford: Oxford University Press, 1984.

3. PAUL STREETEN, 'A Problem to Every Solution', *Finance and Development*, vol. 22 no. 2, June 1985 and 'Suffering from Success' in *Development, Democracy and the Art of Trespassing, Essays in Honour of Albert O. Hirschman*, edited by ALEJANDRO FOXLEY, MICHAEL McPHERSON and GUILLERMO O'DONNELL, Notre Dame, Ind: University of Notre Dame Press, 1986.

5

Sometimes one is asked to peer into the future and predict the next intellectual breakthrough. But such requests are asking for the logically impossible. For if I knew what the next breakthrough was going to be, I would already have accomplished it, and it would be the latest breakthrough. I shall therefore refrain from such forecasts, although I shall occasionally point to areas in need of further research.

There is apparently much that is new in economics, particularly if we go by the self-styled titles. There is the new growth theory, which permits increasing returns, focuses on technological innovation and human capital as endogenous, and reinstates policy as a source of long-term growth, which had been thought impossible since Robert Solow; there is the new theory of international trade, which permits protection; the new institutional economics, which permits economists to investigate institutions, and incorporates in the analysis the costs of information and transaction costs. There is even the new development economics. Much of this amounts to endogenizing previously exogenous variables. The new political economy has endogenized politicians. Some of these new developments tackle ancient difficulties, like monopolistic competition, uncertainty, politics. Many of these new theories put new in quotation marks. They are more elegant, though sometimes less realistic, formulations of ancient verities. Old doctrines never die; they just add the prefix "new" or "neo".

In the early days we thought of development theory as a special field, applicable to the low-income countries of Africa, Asia and Latin America. But two tendencies have been at work to destroy this view. On the one hand, as developing countries became more differentiated, it became clear that different principles apply to different countries. As we shall be examining labour markets, an important difference, for example, is that between economies with unskilled labour surpluses, like those of India, Indonesia or Bangladesh, and those with labour scarcities, such as Taiwan or South Korea. Another is that between large economies, where foreign trade plays a comparatively minor role, and who may therefore be able to influence their terms of trade, and small economies, in which trade is very important, and for which the terms of trade are given; or between land-surplus and land-scarce economies; or between exporters of manufactures and of primary commodities. Some would wish to add cultural and religious differences. Such differentiation points towards the need for a typology of countries, which would depend on the purpose of the analysis and the design of strategies.

On the other hand, it was found that principles initially thought to apply only to developing countries, applied to the whole world community: to advanced and developing countries alike. In the golden days of the 1950s and 60s, it was thought that the advanced countries knew how to eradicate unemployment, and that it was largely a problem of underdevelopment. But with the rise of widespread unemployment and stagflation in the advanced countries of the North in the 1970s and 80s, some of the employment analysis of segmented labour markets that had been conducted for underdeveloped countries seemed to apply nearer to home. Similarly, the informal sector, first discovered in countries such as Kenya, seemed to have a parallel in the "parallel" or underground or black economies of Europe and America. One could mention many other ideas that, first elaborated in a development context, found fruitful application in the advanced countries. Theories of structural inflation, first formulated for Latin America, found application in industrial countries. To those of us who thought that neoclassical economics does not apply to developing countries, it did not come as a complete surprise to discover that it did not apply to our own, advanced, countries either.[1]

2. Does It Pay To Be Late?

One question that has been found of great interest, and to which the differentiation of the subject of development studies has been fruitfully applied, is whether it pays being a latecomer in the development game. The question directs our attention to the need to look at the consequences of the coexistence of countries at

1. There has been a similar reunification in the neoclassical camp, in which authors assert that the same principles that apply to our countries also apply to the developing world. This movement has been called the neoclassical resurgence.

7

different stages of development, and to abandon the linear view that ignores both the positive and the negative impulses propagated by this coexistence.

There is the worm's eye view and the bird's eye view. The worm is close to the grass roots and looks at the world from the bottom up. The bird is high in the air and takes a global view. It is said that it is the early bird that catches the worm. But we might shift viewpoint and say it is the early worm that is caught by the bird. Is it an advantage or a drawback to be late?

As David Landes has said, there are two schools.[1] According to one, we are rich and they are poor, because we are good and they are bad. According to the other, we are rich and they are poor because we are bad and they are good. Many years ago, I analysed the reasons why lateness can be a handicap in catching up.[2]

Brain drain and capital flight deprive developing countries of two important sources of development. Though it is true that the accumulation of knowledge means that the developing countries do not have to reinvent the wheel and more modern technologies, the advanced, esoteric knowledge of the advanced countries called for by modern technology is a discouragement. And the frontiers of knowledge in the industrial countries move outwards continually, so that having caught up is not enough. The latecomers have to keep moving. Even if percentage growth rates of incomes per head are larger in some middle-income countries, the absolute gap is large and continues to widen, since even 10 per cent of a low income is much less than only 2 per cent of a high one. Hiring foreigners is expensive, and training your own people at advanced countries' universities can lead to brain drain. Modern technology, by inventing substitutes for the primary commodities on whose sale many countries depended, has knocked out their export earnings. The rich blame the poor for bad government, but part of the trouble is the impatience of

1. DAVID S. LANDES, 'Rich Country, Poor Country', *The New Republic,* November 20, 1989, pp. 23-27 and 'Why Are We so Rich and They so Poor?' *American Economic Review,* vol. 80 no. 2, May 1990.

2. PAUL STREETEN, 'More on Development in an International Setting', *Development in a Divided World,* edited by DUDLEY SEERS and LEONARD JOY, Harmondsworth: Penguin Books, 1971 pp. 34-44 and 'Development in an International Setting', *The Frontiers of Development Studies,* London: Macmillan, 1972, pp. 3-12.

politicians caused by watching the large and widening gap in levels of living. The poor may be getting better off, but when they compare themselves with the rich happiness is elusive.

But not everything is gloomy. There are clearly also advantages in being late. International trade and the stock of technical knowledge and ideas that can be imported from those ahead, raise the productivity of the assets of the poor, and speed up development. It took Britain 60 years to double real incomes per head after 1780; America 50 years after 1840; Japan 35 years after 1885; Turkey 20 years after 1957; Brazil 18 years after 1961, South Korea 11 years after 1966, and China 10 years after 1977. This is good news.

On the other hand, disparities within the so-called Third World are great. Between 1950 and 1989 income per head grew by 3.6 per cent in East Asia, by 1.2 per cent in Latin America, and by only 0.8 per cent in Africa, where it actually declined in the last two decades. I remember once chuckling over a newspaper headline, saying "Stagnation in Developing Countries". Today, we should cry when we have to say "Regress in Developing Countries". "Developing" has become a word describing aspirations rather than facts.

There are also disparities within regions. In Asia between India and South Korea; in Latin America between Bolivia and Argentina; in Africa between Botswana and Chad. And there are disparities within countries. So the answer to the question, does it pay to be late? is: it depends.

3. The Three-Ring Circus

One problem in attempting a realistic and relevant approach to policy problems in development is that the development community consists of three or four different groups, each with its own experience, approach and ideas, its own culture, but among whom there is little communication. It is rather like one of those peculiarly American institutions, the three-ring circus, where acrobats, clowns and animals perform their tricks simultaneously in three separate rings.

9

The first is the academic and research community of writers, teachers and scholars. Here novelty and originality are at a premium. Rigour in analysis, simplification, abstraction and publication in refereed prestige journals are the emblems of achievement. The limitation of this group is that a model can be a blinker and it may miss important features of reality. It draws on two distinct traditions: (1) that of moral philosophy and the humanities, going back to Aristotle; and (2) the mathematical, engineering approach, going back to Petty, Quesnay and Walras. The two have quite different inclinations.

The second group is the community of officials in the multilateral and bilateral institutions concerned with development. The various UN agencies, including the World Bank and the International Monetary Fund, and the aid ministries of the OECD countries are their pastures. Their task is partly financial and technical assistance, partly documentation, partly propaganda and public education. Perhaps one might add some of the executives of the large multinational corporations, such as IBM, Shell or Unilever, whose approach is not very different from that of some aid organizations.

The third is the large community of practising development workers: the field workers, extension workers, social workers, agronomists, teachers, animators, project officers, engineers, health officials, midwives, organizers of cooperatives, members of non-governmental organizations (NGOs) and action groups, etc., who are doing the groundwork of development. They are the foot soldiers. They have no time to read the volumes produced by the other two groups, or listen to their speeches, and would perhaps not find them very useful. Their relation to the other two rings is reminiscent of an old *New Yorker* cartoon. Two cows stand on the verge of a highway, on which a large tanker lorry passes. On the lorry is written in large letters: "homogenized, pasteurized, vitamin-reinforced, rehydrated, reconstituted, guaranteed germ-free milk". One cow says to the other, with an incredulous look: "To think that all this comes from us!"

Technical assistance presents particularly tricky problems to any critical attempt to evaluate its impact on national capacity-building. There is normally no independent measure of its output; this value is measured by its inputs: so many man-years, costing so many dollars, hence, it is assumed, the result must be worth at least as many dollars. This measure conveys a deceptive impression of achievement, when in fact nothing may have been achieved. In addition, there are powerful vested interests at work, both on the donors' and the recipients' side, and among the experts themselves, to inflate its value. To the recipient government the services are free, and therefore preferable to employing a domestic expert, whose knowledge and experience might have been more appropriate. But he would have to be paid, and therefore becomes or remains unemployed. Donors, particularly multilateral donors not subject to political control, also have an interest in inflating the assistance. Having a valuable impact on the aided country would mean showing up domestic shortcomings, hurting interests, annoying people and upsetting things. The foreign expert, as long as he has little impact, adds prestige to the host country without upsetting things.

The foreign experts themselves can live in luxury unattainable at home. They too, unless exceptionally self-critical, have no interest to probe too deeply into the question whether their presence is justified. But by their example, employing servants, dressing and eating differently, and keeping their own company, they reinforce the difficulties created for policy makers by a dual economy and society. Tact, diplomacy and delicacy reinforce these vested interests and it is therefore very hard to get an independent, objective assessment of the value of these services.[1]

Moreover, the "absorptive capacity" of developing countries is limited not only for capital, but also for technical assistance. To teach skills effectively, much more is needed than teaching. Human attitudes and social institutions in a complex social system may have to be changed if the teaching is to have an impact. Teeth-gritting humility, patience, curiosity and independent thinking are called for in learning how superior foreign technology works and how it can be improved. Without these conditions the technical assistance "does not take". The cut flowers wither

---

1. DUDLEY SEERS' well-known article on 'Why Visiting Economists Fail' needs a companion piece on 'Why Failed Economists Visit'.

and die because they have no roots. The United Nations agencies, including the main technical assistance agency, the United Nations Development Programme, have, as a result of their constitutions and their attempts to preserve and enlarge their frontiers of competence, a technocratic bias which tends to emphasize technical "solutions" without regard to their social and cultural setting, and their administrative feasibility. An Indian, who might be competent and make a valuable contribution in his own country, is recruited, at a salary substantially higher than he would earn at home, to give technical assistance to Nigeria, where his productivity is likely to be lower, and a Nigerian for Somalia.

Yet, it is of the greatest importance to know what types of technical assistance help countries to become self-reliant and to acquire the necessary skills, and which are ineffective or actually counter-productive, prolonging and perpetuating dependency. The need for an objective, critical form of appraisal and evaluation is urgent. This analysis should form the basis for making constructive proposals as to how the value of technical assistance can be improved and how the capacity of the developing countries can be strengthened.

The cartoon mentioned above, poking fun at the value of technical assistance, points to the need for a fourth group, whose function it is, or should be, to mediate between the others: the media. They include the press, radio and television. Journalists have to write in clear language and should communicate the ideas and experience of one group to the wider public. Rarely are they wholly successful in this. Having to use their eyes and ears, they are often ahead of the academics in perceiving problems (such as corruption, nepotism, environmental damage, the importance of climate, the difficulties of dismantling a state apparatus), but not having rigorous models, their observations remain ephemeral. They can exercise considerable influence on the policy makers. When I joined the Ministry of Overseas Development, in my naivety I was astonished to see a cutting from *The Times* marked "confidential". It was explained to me that the interest of the officials in this cutting must be kept secret. Amartya Sen has attributed the avoidance of famine in India since independence partly to a free press, and the presence of a famine in China to its absence.

The higher ranks of the policy makers in the developing countries fall into the group of officials, negotiating with aid donors. The lower ranks belong to the community of workers and practitioners. I will try, as best I can, to combine the best in the approaches of the three rings. But one important task is to improve the lines of communication between them.

Some pervasive ideas will be briefly examined: first, the notion of unemployment and underemployment and that "distortions" in the economy prevent the full utilization of resources; second, population growth; third, the idea of human development as a successor to basic needs; and fourth a more thorough analysis of the concept of poverty.

4. Unemployment

One of the biggest problems in development policy is how to provide productive and remunerative jobs for the rapidly increasing labour forces of the developing countries. It is not enough to provide high-wage jobs for a small group of workers, but the need is for satisfying jobs for large and growing numbers. Small countries that rely heavily on international trade can engage in labour-intensive exports. But large countries have to raise the labour productivity in industries producing products for the domestic market. This means adopting, adapting and inventing appropriate technologies.

The existence of unemployment can be regarded as a special case of distortion, a deviation from the optimum, perhaps due to a distortion in the labour market, but it is worth looking at it separately, if only because the labour market is concerned with living human beings, to whom different principles apply from those relevant to goods. Unemployment and inefficiency present policy makers with both a problem and an opportunity for substantial gains in production and welfare that would not be open to an economy that uses all its resources optimally. Since much of the inefficiency in developing countries springs from and reinforces dualistic economies, dualism is another element that the two issues have in common. But again, while it was first thought that dualism is a characteristic of underdevelopment, many features of dualism, and of segmented markets, are now noted for advanced economies.

The analysis of unemployment and underemployment was conducted by two non-communicating groups, one for advanced countries, the other for developing countries. On the one hand, going back to Cairns's analysis of non-competing groups, there was a growing literature on dual labour markets, mainly in the USA. On the other hand, Arthur Lewis's seminal article on economic development with unlimited supplies of labour[1] spawned a large literature on dual labour markets in low income countries. Only quite recently have the two met.

When Joan Robinson wrote her essay on disguised unemployment, she did not have underemployment in developing countries in mind, and in a later edition said so explicitly.[2] She was writing about the experience of the Great Depression in the thirties in England and thinking of match sellers in the Strand, who had been thrown out of a job and were seeking to eke out an existence by working in a low-paying substitute activity. The model underlying her analysis is that of two sectors: one a sector in which incomes are rigid for downwards movements, and which shows high productivity; the other a sector in which incomes (mainly from self-employment) are flexible downwards. We might also say that the fixed wage sector is demand-driven, while the flexible income sector is supply-driven. When aggregate demand declines, production, capacity utilization and employment drop. The dismissed workers seek to survive by taking up low-productivity jobs at lower incomes. In this model all that is needed to raise efficiency and employment is to increase demand. The equipment, the management, the skills and the motivation are all there, and will respond to the incentives to relocate.

In spite of her disclaimer, Joan Robinson's model can be ap-

1. WILLIAM ARTHUR LEWIS, 'Economic Development with Unlimited Supplies of Labour' *Manchester School*, vol. 22 no. 2 May 1954.

2. "Disguised unemployment as I conceived it, had nothing to do with the question of surplus labour in what is nowadays called an underdeveloped economy. At that time [ca. 1937], there were no ex-colonial nations clamouring for 'development'". JOAN ROBINSON, 'Disguised Unemployment', *Collected Economic Papers*, vol. 4, Oxford: Basil Blackwell, 1973, p. 175.

plied, with some modifications, to developing countries.[1] There we also witness dual economies, divided between organized and unorganized, formal and informal, modern and traditional sectors, large-scale and micro-enterprises. But to raise efficiency it is clearly not enough to raise aggregate demand. Depending on the particular circumstances, capital, both fixed (in the form of equipment and plant) and working capital (in the form of inventories and work in progress) will have to be generated; management will have to be trained and motivated; institutions, such as labour exchanges will have to be created; people may have to be transported; and possibly cultural attitudes, as well as industrial aptitudes and skills, will have to be changed. While in the depression of the thirties the shadow wage of labour was zero, in the developing countries it is positive, and can be quite high. But the common feature is differential productivities in two sectors, with accompanying differential incomes, and the opportunity for gains. One of many important differences is that the attack in developing countries can be two-pronged. One way is to remove the capital constraints and to construct more machines for workers to work with and thereby raise their productivity; the other is to raise the productivity of the workers in the informal (traditional, non-organized, micro-enterprise) sector, by providing them with credit, education and training, market access, inputs, information, technology, etc. The difficulty is to do this with no or with minimal sacrifice of the resources needed to expand the high-productivity sector.

In dual labour market models it is usually assumed that wages in the high-productivity sector stay constant until all workers from the low-productivity sector have been absorbed. But as experience has shown, wages rise long before that turning point. There is again a parallel to Keynes's analysis of the path towards full employment. Wages in advanced, industrial countries are supposed to be constant until full employment is reached. In fact, they rise long before that. The reasons why they rise in developing countries before all spare labour has been absorbed are related to the reasons why they are higher in the modern sector than

1. See PAUL STREETEN, 'Disguised Unemployment and Underemployment', chapter 27 in *Joan Robinson and Modern Economic Theory*, edited by GEORGE FEIVEL, London: Macmillan, 1989, pp. 723-726.

in the others. They are institutionally determined, and depend upon the bargaining and political power of trade unions, and there may also be good reasons on the demand side. Higher than equilibrium wages can elicit greater efforts and loyalties from workers. The efficiency wage literature has brought out some of these reasons. Originally based on the experience of developing countries, in which, for example, better nutrition resulting from higher wages leads to higher productivity, it has found application in the advanced countries.[1]

It is interesting to note that most analyses take the (downwards) wage rigidity as given and design policies on that assumption. But it is not obvious that the removal of wage rigidity would by itself equalize productivities in all sectors and produce full employment. There may be structural constraints, in the nature of the technology, or in skills, which would impede the better allocation of resources, even if wages were completely flexible.

Differential wages in agriculture and industry are the result of imperfect markets. First, individual incomes on family farms are determined by average productivity, industrial wages by marginal productivity. Second, transaction costs of migration from the country to the town, lack of information, and uncertainty of getting a job prevent some workers from moving to industry. Third, industrial workers are organized, raise their wages by collective bargaining, and put up obstacles to the entry of newcomers.

5. Population Growth

Rapid population growth has been a major concern of the development community. Robert McNamara, when President of the World Bank, equated population growth with nuclear war. Yet, we have no clear answer to the question why rapid population growth is harmful. When Malthus wrote, he feared an imbalance between people and food. Malthusians think that the growth of population is bound to outstrip the limited capacity of land to

1. On the other hand, the efficiency wage literature has not dealt with the problem that higher than equilibrium wages and the resulting unemployment will tend to raise resistance to the introduction of labour-saving new technologies.

grow food. Yet, since the days of Malthus nearly 200 years ago food production has increased more rapidly than population.

Next, it was thought that rapidly growing populations reduce savings and investment, an important source of economic progress. Yet, according to some theories (such as the life cycle theory of savings) rapid population growth (though not accelerating growth) should raise savings ratios.

Then it was thought that while total savings ratios may not be reduced, it is the allocation of savings between productive equipment and social unproductive investment in schools and hospitals that would be changed unfavourably in the direction of the latter. But then it was discovered that education and health contribute to human capital formation and are also productive.

Now some writers complain that rapid population growth promotes income inequality. But this depends on policies with respect to prices, wages and technology. Others charge that rapid population growth destroys the physical environment. But it is well known that damage to the global environment arises from the high incomes in the advanced countries, not from the low incomes of the developing countries; and damage to the local environment, to land and water, arises from poverty, not from population growth. Other writers have argued that rapid population growth gives incentives to technical innovation. Some innovations respond to the scarcity of land and are land-saving; others to the surplus of labour and are efficiently labour-using.

We know more about the causes than the effects of population growth. And we are beginning to know how to reduce population growth. Large and sustained reductions in infant mortality, combined with other measures, particularly female education, together with the provision of cheap and effective methods of family planning, reduce fertility rates by more than infant mortality rates, because parents tend to over-insure against the death of their children.

6. Human Development

Sometimes one gains the impression that the development debate is just a succession of fads and fashions. But the evolution from economic growth, via employment, jobs and justice, redistribution with growth, to basic needs and human development represents a genuine evolution of thinking and is not a comedy of errors, a lurching from one slogan to the next.

Economic growth was never regarded as the objective of development but rather as its principal performance test. Poverty reduction was always at the heart of the concern. The link was based on any of three assumptions. Some thought that economic growth, by raising the demand for labour, upgrading its rewards, and lowering the prices of necessities, would "trickle down" or "spread" to the whole population. Alternatively, it was thought that if this does not happen, if the benefits of growth turn out to be concentrated on a few, the government will take corrective action through taxation, subsidies, and social services, so that again the benefits are spread to the poor. A third, gloomier, assumption was that early concern in the development process for poverty reduction and equality is misguided. Development is a long and hard slog, in which entrepreneurship and savings have to be encouraged, and this means concentrating its benefits on the few.

As it turned out, none of these assumptions was universally warranted. Trickle down did not happen where assets and power were concentrated. The government did not act like Platonic guardians but reinforced the accrual of wealth to the rich and powerful. And it was found that investing in the developing countries' most abundant resource, its masses of poor people, could be a paying proposition.

There was a move to "dethrone" GNP, and the International Labour Organization organized employment missions to many countries. It was then discovered that employment and unemployment are concepts that could not be readily transferred from advanced to developing countries. And that their problem was often not unemployment, but long hours of hard but unremunerative work by the "working poor".

This turned attention to income distribution, and two questions were asked. First, how can the productivity of the informal sector (discovered by the ILO employment mission to Kenya) be raised? Two, how does economic growth affect distribution? The recommendation was made that redistribution should occur out of the extra income generated every year. But it was discovered that the results of such redistribution are very modest. The debate then shifted to meeting the basic needs of the poor. This was considered, rightly, as more important than promoting greater equality in income distribution. After the dead end of "employment" as interpreted in advanced countries, and the limitation and irrelevance of egalitarianism, basic needs was the next logical step in the progress of development thinking. But the discussion of basic needs was sidetracked both by the industrial and by the developing countries. The rich used it as an excuse to reduce development aid; the poor, or rather their governments, regarded it as intrusive on their domestic affairs and diversionary from their concern with a New International Economic Order. Some ruling groups in the developing countries had no real interest in doing much for the basic needs of their poor.[1]

In 1990 the United Nations Development Programme came out with its first *Human Development Report*, which has become an annual publication. It began with reminding us that the purpose of development is the full flowering of human beings. "So act as to treat humanity, whether in thine own person or that of any other, in every case as an end, never as means only", wrote Immanuel Kant in *Fundamental Principles of the Metaphysics of Morals*. Human development returns to the end of economic development.

There are at least six reasons for human development and poverty eradication. First, it is an end in itself, indeed it is the whole purpose of development. Second, it contributes to higher productivity. Third, it lowers reproductivity and therefore population growth. This may seem odd, for lowering infant mortality rates would appear to accelerate population growth. But families try to over-insure against infant deaths. Reduced child mortality leads to the desire for smaller families.

Fourth, poverty reduction reduces the degradation of the environment from soil erosion, deforestation and desertification. (The impact of lower population growth on the environment is more controversial.) Fifth, the growth of a civil society and democracy leads to greater social stability. And sixth, its political

---

1. For a full discussion see PAUL STREETEN *et. al.*, *First Things First*, Oxford: Oxford University Press, 1981.

appeal is that it reduces civil disturbances and increases political stability.

Of course, human beings are both ends in themselves and means of production: human resources or human capital. (It is, however, odd that beer, television and Hondas, because they are consumption goods, are regarded as needing no further justification, whereas education and health have to be justified on the ground that they raise productivity.)

At first blush, there would appear to be a harmony of interests between the humanitarians, who are concerned with people as ends, and the human resource developers, who treat them as productive means. We might expect them to embrace each other and proceed to promote a common cause, better nutrition, health and education. Such common ground would be reinforced by the faith that "all good things go together, and by the fact that the means are means towards the same ends of those who stress the ends".

This would be the case if there were rigid links between economic production and fuller lives. But GNP per head (an indicator of economic performance) and the human indicators of education (literacy rates) and health (life expectancy, infant mortality) are not very strongly correlated.

The data reaffirm the idea that economic performance can diverge widely from human development. Indonesia, Sri Lanka and Yemen have roughly the same income per head, but life expectancy is 51 years in Yemen, 60 in Indonesia and 70 in Sri Lanka. Sri Lanka has a GNP per head of $ 380 and an average life expectancy of 70 years; Oman $ 6,730 and 54 years; South Africa $ 2,010 and 55 years. Adult literacy is lower in Saudi Arabia than in Sri Lanka, in spite of an income per head which is 15 times as large. Jamaica's infant mortality is one quarter that of Brazil, though its income per head is one half. Life expectancy in Costa Rica is 75 years with incomes per head of only $ 1,600. A child born today in Harlem has a lower life expectancy than one born in Bangladesh; one born in Washington, D.C. a lower one than one born in Sri Lanka.

Differences in income distribution are, of course, part of the explanation. But they are not the only one. The ability to convert income into a good life varies according to the level and content of education, the health services and healh status, and other conditions, to which social services and working conditions contribute.

Humanitarian and human resource developers have areas of common concern, but also differ in some respects.

First, some of the groups at which policies are aimed are different. Humanitarians are concerned with the unemployables, the old, the infirm, the disabled, the chronically ill. It is true that concern for the old and disabled has an effect, if not on productivity, then on reproductivity. If it is known that the community will look after you in need, one important incentive for large families and many sons is removed. But the humanitarian concern is wider and deeper.

Second, the ability to convert means into ends, resources into worthwhile or satisfying activities, varies widely between different people. Even such a basic good as food meets the needs of nutrition differently according to the rate of metabolism, the sex, the age, the work load of the individual, to the climate, to whether she is pregnant or lactating, to whether she is ill, has parasites in her stomach, or needs the food for other uses than her own consumption, such as entertainment or ceremonies.

Third, the resource or means approach lends itself to treating individuals as passive "targets"; the approach that sees them as ends regards them as active, participating agents. Its adherents would be more reluctant to talk of "target groups" for policies, and appeal more to people's full participation.

Fourth, the two have different target groups. Resource developers aim at productive adults, humanitarians also at children, irrespective of their future productive potential.

Fifth, the two have different time horizons. Humanitarians may take a longer view than resource developers.

Sixth, sectoral priorities will be different. Housing is least linked to production, although the Soviet Union kept housing scarce, and used its location to attract workers to areas in which they were most needed. Education is most closely linked to productivity, and nutrition and health are in the middle.

Seventh, the content of the health and education programmes will be different. Should the curriculum aim at general education or vocational training?

21

Eighth, humanitarians and human resource developers will have different answers to the type of activity allotted to women: whether they should freely choose to become members of the labour force or whether they should be trained in becoming good mothers, nurturing children.

Plutarch tells the story of three Spartan women who are being sold as slaves. Their captors asked them what they had learned to do. The first replied, "how to manage a household well". The second said, "how to be loyal". The third's answer was, "how to be free". Is there a separate sphere of activities reserved for women, or should they freely and autonomously choose what they wish to do? It must be remembered that all three were slaves. It is reported that the third committed suicide.[1]

Finally, the political constituencies will be different. Human resource developers will appeal to bankers, humanitarians to NGOs, action groups, idealists. Although Keynes said of bankers, "Lifelong practices . . . make them the most romantic and least realistic of men", they are looking for returns for the investments in health.

Human development is defined as the enlargement of choices, the presentation of options. Happiness cannot be delivered. But opportunities for exercising one's choices can. Income is part of such enlargement, but only part. Health, education, self-respect, participation in the common life, cultural identity, are other important aspects. Nor is the presence of happiness an indication that these options exist. People can be happy in subjection.

Human development is development of the people, for the people and by the people: of the people means jobs and incomes; for the people means social services; and by the people means participation.

The choices of one group should not be enlarged at the expense of others. Equity means that the choices of one section must not mean reduced choices of another. Sustainability means that they should not be at the expense of the options of future generations. This sets limits to the amount of debt (international and domes-

1. MARTHA NUSSBAUM, 'Women's Lot', *New York Review of Books*, vol. 33 no. 1 January 30, 1986.

tic) that can be incurred now, to the damage to the physical environment (raw material exhaustion and pollution), and it covers political and administrative sustainability.

The *Human Development Reports* of 1990, 1991 and 1992 present a Human Development Index that has caught the public's eye, but has also been criticized. While analytically the weakest part of the *Reports*, it has drawn most of the attention. It is a composite index, consisting of income per head, life expectancy and literacy rates (plus years of schooling). Why try to catch a vector in a single number? ask the critics. If the three components are highly correlated with each other, a single one will do; if not, we want to know why, and separate them. Putting them together obscures the issue. In any case, what is included and what is excluded, as well as the weights attached to its components, are arbitrary.

In defence of the composite Human Development Index (HDI) it can be said, first, that it does catch the eye, and for simple presentation is better than a long list of separate indicators. But more important is that, with all its imperfections, it shows up the inadequacies of alternative measures such as the GNP. With all its weaknesses, it can be used as a kind of intellectual muscle therapy that cures us of intellectual cramps, such as an obsession with the income measure.

The most important point to make about any measure or index is that the concept of human development is, of course, much wider, deeper and richer than any single measure. (This is also true of other measures, like temperature.) It does not catch the many dimensions above a minimum condition.

Complaints have been voiced that the data underlying the social indicators, and therefore the HDI, are unreliable. The same critics then often add the complaint that they are also very scarce. The double complaint is reminiscent of a scene in a Woody Allen film. Two women return from a holiday in the Berkshire hills. A friend asks them, "what was it like?" One of the women replies, "Oh, the food was absolutely poisonous!" The other chirps in, "Yes, and the portions were so small!"

Looking at the record of human development over the last three decades, we see that development has succeeded in human terms. Since 1960 life expectancy has increased by 16 years, adult literacy by 40 per cent, nutritional levels by over 20 per cent, and child mortality rates have halved. Whatever may be the case about international income gaps, gaps in terms of human indicators have closed. While average income per head in the South is 6 per cent of that in the North, life expectancy is 80 per cent, literacy 66 per cent, and nutrition 85 per cent. So far so good.

It must, however, be remembered that the HDI is, like income per head, also an average. It therefore conceals discrepancies between rich and poor, men and women, urban and rural residents. It is always important to break up the HDI into these specific categories, such as what is the proportion of girls at school, what is their life expectancy?

But there are several reasons why the average HDI is a better indicator of human development than average income. First, income distribution is much more skewed than literacy and life expectancy, which is reflected in more weight to the very few very high incomes. Literacy has a maximum of 100 per cent; life expectancy in a life span of about 100 years, which, in spite of all the progress in medical knowledge has not been extended.

This means, second, that a high average tells us something about the distribution, though clearly not everything. Since the non-poor have access to public services before the poor, reductions in infant mortality, etc., are indications of improvements for the poor. Third, many would argue that any upward move in the HDI is an improvement, which cannot be said of any increase in income.[1]

Fourth, there is surely much less scope for relative deprivation in the social indicators than in income. This does not mean that choices do not have to be made, say, between extending the life of an old man by ten years, and that of ten young women by one year. But we do not envy in the same way the educational and health achievements of those who do better as we do their wealth and income.

Fifth, reducing international gaps in human indicators is both more important and more feasible than reducing international income gaps. Sixth, impact measures like the HDI distinguish between goods and anti-bads (like filters that reduce pollution),

1. A feminist might say that higher school enrolment for boys, without an equivalent increase in that of girls, only equips them to oppress and exploit women more effectively.

24

which only bring us back to zero. Unnecessary food requirement due to unwanted pregnancies, excess work or looking for work do not show up as benefits. And finally, human indicators register over- and mal-development as well as underdevelopment and deprivation. There are diseases of affluence and problems of over-eating, and over-spending, which show up in shorter life expectancy. But the chief advantage of the HDI is political: it focuses attention on important social sectors, policies, and achievements, which are not caught by the income measure.

Various refinements of the HDI are possible. One might argue that the geometric mean is preferable to the arithmetic mean, because the arithmetic mean implies a trade-off between its components, whereas if any one of them is zero the product is also zero. But there is a case for keeping the index simple, particularly since sensitivity analysis has shown that the ranking of countries is very robust with respect to changes in the assumptions, including changes in the weights attached to its components.

The main criticism, however, remains that the weighting is arbitrary.[1] Suggestions have been made to overcome this. We might, for example, use not annual income but income earned over the average life expectancy. Obviously, of two societies with the same decent, annual income per head, in one of which people live 20 years longer, this one is to be preferred. And the single figure for lifetime income makes sense. But the implication that length of life can be traded off for money (is a life of 60 years with $ 10,000 per year as good as a life of 20 years with an annual income of $ 30,000?) is not generally acceptable. If it were desired

1. Income is, of course, also highly arbitrary. This springs not only from the fact that it is determined by income and asset distribution, but also from the absence of a distinction between goods and anti-bads. Anti-bads should not be counted as net income, but as regrettable necessities. Bads can arise from three sources: enemies, nature and the economic system itself. Defence and police expenditure is an anti-bad arising from the first. Adequate heating or air-conditioning, housing, clothing and feeding arise from the second; and expenditures caused by advertisers, or by emulation of those who are better off, from the third. Like ransom or blackmail they can be regarded as the extraction of payments for the removal of a self-created nuisance. As a result of these adjustments, the national income can vary between zero and its currently registered amount. The problem is further complicated by the fact that some "artificially" created demands (e.g. through education) are valued very highly: the demand for beauty, goodness and truth, and the commodities in which these values are incorporated. Bads cannot be equated with artificial creation. Value judgments are inevitable.

to incorporate some reference to income distribution, the mode or the median would be a better measure than the mean, because it would disregard the few very high incomes. Unfortunately, these figures are not available.

I have said earlier that development studies have been re-unified, and much of what we have learned from the developing countries has been found to apply, with some modifications, to the industrial countries too. But using the HDI with its three components − income with a cap, life expectancy and literacy − we find that they are all bunched; that, having achieved 79 years' life expectancy and nearly 100 per cent literacy, there is not much to distinguish one country from another. Adding years of schooling to the literacy index does differentiate industrial countries somewhat. Removing the cap in income per head at the poverty line and replacing it by a log function above the poverty line enables us perhaps to draw better distinctions.

In order to examine the human condition in the advanced countries indicators outside the HDI can be used. Drugs, crime, homelessness are clear signs of social failure. Divorce rates are more dubious. Some might regard them as indicators of the breakdown of the social fabric, others as widening the range of choice. Opinions differ over whether they should be bracketed with cancer and AIDS as a curse of our times, or celebrated along with aspirin and anaesthetics as a welcome liberation from past miseries. Similarly for some forms of suicide. Yet, some of the human problems of industrial countries are the same as those in developing countries. One in eight children in the USA does not have enough food to eat.

How should freedom be treated in human development? Its importance can be seen from the fact that material basic needs can be perfectly satisfied in a zoo or in a well-run prison. Yet, economic analysts have so far tended to neglect it. It may be tempting to say that freedom and human rights are so important that they should be incorporated in a human development index. But there are also arguments against it.

First, it might be thought that freedom is so important that no amount of literacy or life expectancy should be able to compensate for its deprivation. Secondly, judging the amount of freedom available, unlike measuring life expectancy or literacy, can be quite subjective. Thirdly, situations with respect to freedom are highly volatile. A country can change overnight from a dictatorship to a democracy, while income, and even more education, are much more sticky. Fourthly, to guarantee freedom does not call for scarce resources, as the positive human rights do. (But opportunity costs may be involved. Not removing people from their land may mean forgoing a dam that would have raised agricultural output.) Finally, we should want to see how freedom is related to income, education and health, and we can do this only by separating them.

An attempt to relate freedom to development suggests two conclusions. First, while freedom is not a necessary condition for development, neither is autocratic government. Freedom is entirely consistent with development, even at quite low initial levels. The idea of "grub first, then morality" is not confirmed by evidence.

Second, whenever authoritarian or totalitarian regimes have pursued human development, sooner or later the call for freedom by the people became irresistible. In Latin America, in East Asia, in the Soviet Union and in Eastern Europe the evidence is clear. Even Hitler lasted only 12 years. This should not be a cause for complacency, but it is ground for hope.

It is sometimes said that developing countries cannot afford the resources required by human development. But military spending in the Third World has increased by $ 10-15 billion per year. It is now three times their expenditure on education and health. And within the education and health sectors much more is spent on curative, urban hospitals than on preventive rural health services, and on universities for middle-class students than on basic education. Public enterprises providing goods and services to the better off are subsidized. Corruption and capital flight are ubiquitous. Expensive prestige projects are carried out. while low priority is given to the social sectors, and within them to the basic services for the poor. Ultimately, it is not lack of resources, but the absence of political commitment, that is at the heart of human neglect.

In the next section I shall discuss the concept and measurement of poverty. This is not a purely academic exercise, but it has important practical implications for any attempt to reduce poverty.

27

7. Poverty: Concepts and Measurement[1]

Before we can answer questions about the fate of the poor in the past, and what we can do to reduce poverty, certain preliminary questions have to be asked, if not answered. These relate to the concept of poverty and its measurement. I shall not be concerned with the concept and measurement of inequality as such, only in so far as it bears on poverty.

Perhaps the first question is, how should we identify the poor? The common practice of using fractiles of income recipients – deciles or quintiles or quartiles – has its uses but also has serious defects.

First, these figures have often been applied to households rather than to persons, or adult-equivalents, and therefore make no allowance for the fact that some households are large, others small, some consist of children, others of older people.[2] There is considerable disparity in ranking incomes, including imputed incomes from home-produced goods and services (or expenditure, always including expenditure on self-produced goods) per household and incomes (or expenditure) per head. Large households tend to have low income per person but high income per household. However, ranking by household income approximates ranking by income per adult equivalent less badly than by income per person, because larger households tend to have a higher ratio of children to adults. Income per head is a much better measure of poverty than income per household. Michael Lipton notes that only under two circumstances might income per household be a better measure. First, if indivisible assets (a car or furniture) or other economies of scale in consumption or forms of joint consumption are important, dividing the flow of services by the number of family members would understate the level of wel-

---

1. I am indebted for helpful comments on this section to Joachim von Braun, Marty Chen, Rolph van der Hoeven, Michael Lipton, John Mellor, Erik Thorbecke and Andrew Weiss.

2. See MICHAEL LIPTON, *Demography and Poverty*, World Bank Staff Working Papers no. 623, Washington D.C., 1983, pp. 58-61 and G. DATTA and J. MEERMAN, *Household Income or Household Income per Capita in Welfare Comparisons*, World Bank Staff Working Paper no. 378, Washington D.C. 1980.

fare enjoyed by each. But this is not likely to be important in very poor families. Second, as we have seen, larger households tend to have a higher ratio of children to adults, and therefore their income approximates income per consumer unit more closely than income per person does.[1] Figures for the ideal measure, income per adult equivalent, are often not available. Nor is it possible to give precise weights to males and females at different ages for total requirements to attain a given level of welfare.

Second, looking a bit deeper than mere statistics, and moving from the measurement to the causes of poverty, we may identify the poor by their social and economic class, people who lack physical assets, or have assets of only low value – the landless workers, the proletariat, the small peasant who owns dry, un-irrigated, poor land; or by residence – the rural poor, the urban poor; or by their lack of human capital – people with low educational attainments, stuck in low-paying jobs without access to retraining; or by ethnic group – the tribes in India, the Muslims in Malaysia; or by the region in which they live, frequently the South, or the mountains, or areas distant from the capital city; or by the stage they have reached in the age cycle – young families with children or the old in some countries; or by the fact that they suffer from barriers to entry into jobs or capital markets, such as discrimination on grounds of race or sex; or by sex, family size and age (and sex) of the head of the family – households with many children and other dependants, single parent, female-headed families, widows (in India); or by the season of the year – poverty rising in the rainy season; or by the fact that they are temporarily or chronically handicapped, to which some of the just mentioned conditions provide clues. Poverty has many dimensions, some of which reinforce each other, and concentration on deciles, even when adjusted for adult-equivalents and therefore the size and composition of households, relative price

---

1. To correct for these two factors, household equivalent scales have been suggested. These give lower weights to additional household members (e.g. children) when dividing the value of household expenditure by household size. See ANGUS DEATON and JOHN MUELLBAUER, *Economics and Consumer Behaviour*, Cambridge: Cambridge University Press, 1980 and ANGUS DEATON, 'On Measuring Costs: with Application to Poor Countries', *Journal of Political Economy*, vol. 94, no. 4, 1986.

changes, post-tax incomes and social services provided free, may obscure some of these. We need supplementary information. Many of these conditions give strong hints, and some may give definite information, about whether poverty is likely to be permanent or temporary.

Third, knowing a household's or a person's share in total income does not tell us how long they have been in that fraction. Perhaps we need not be unduly worried if a student is poor (as long as poverty does not damage his health), if we know that he will be much better off later. But poor people's incomes tend to fluctuate from year to year, and from season to season within the year, depending on the weather and other hazards. These people will save in good years and dissave in bad ones. Consumption expenditure will, therefore, be a better measure of their poverty than income. (It has the additional practical advantage of being often more easily gathered than income data, which can be quite uncertain for owner-operated farms or firms, for which no books are kept and for which the concept of net profits is often vague.)

Knowing how long the poor have been in the poverty group also raises other questions. Two societies with the same income distribution by deciles enjoy very different levels of welfare, if in one the poor move rapidly up in the income scale, while some new entrants start poor, whereas in the other the poor and their children are condemned permanently to languish in poverty. Or compare two societies, in one of which incomes are determined each year by a series of lotteries, voluntarily entered by people who love gambling, and who become rich and poor in quick succession, while in the other the same unequal income distribution that would result from such a lottery is permanent. Or consider a society in which there is no inheritance and everybody saves exactly the same amount each year between ages 21 and 65. At any given moment, the index of inequality would be quite high, yet looking at lifetime's earnings this could be a highly egalitarian society.[1]

1. The example is taken from BRIAN BARRY, 'Claims of Common Citizenship', *The Times Literary Supplement*, vol. 47 no. 4, 20-26 January 1989, p. 52. The article is a review of HENRY PHELPS BROWN, *Egalitarianism and the Generation of Inequality*, Oxford: Clarendon Press, 1988, where a similar example is given.

Albert Hirschman has coined the expression "tunnel effect", in analogy to a lane of cars stuck in a tunnel. If the cars in one lane never move on, while the other lane passes them by, the people in the lane that are stuck become despondent. The despair and hopelessness bred of poverty is absent if there is hope that, though you are stuck for a while, there will soon be a chance to move on and perhaps even overtake the neighbouring lane. On the other hand, rapid mobility between income groups, other than through expected changing lifetime earnings, creates its own problems of insecurity, which a society in which status and related income are more permanent, is spared.

Over a person's life, there are normally periods of greater and less poverty. Young parents with small children, and old retired people are sometimes poorer than young parents without children, both of whom are working, or young, income-earning adults, still living with their parents but yet unmarried. Life-cycle poverty tends to be less severe than lifelong poverty because it can be partly alleviated by borrowing.[1] But life-cycle poverty is probably less important in developing countries than in industrialized ones, where the nuclear family is more pronounced, and where poverty is more the result of achievement than of ascribed status.[2]

At the same time strokes of misfortune do hit families in developing countries and may cause temporary poverty. Lipton cites Gaiha, who has found substantial mobility in and out of the two or three lowest deciles. Lipton suggests "that this mobility is due mainly, not to life-cycle factors, but to the fact that *different* households and villages, in any of two given years, are hit by (a high incidence of) environmental or personal misfortune".[3]

1. For a discussion and considerable evidence on this, see LIPTON, *Demography and Poverty*, pp. 54-57.

2. See MICHAEL LIPTON, 'Who Are the Poor? What Do They Do? What Should They Do?', Lecture to the Center for Advanced Studies in International Development, East Lansing, Mich., Michigan State University, March 13, 1988, pp, 16-18 and the references given there to Paul Schultz and R. Gaiha. Lipton distinguishes between disturbances causing temporary poverty that (a) are environmental or due to the family; (b) are predictable or irregular; (c) affect a few or entire communities.

3. *Loc. cit.* p. 17. ROBERT CHAMBERS writes movingly, "Among the physical factors which impoverish, accidents have been neglected, yet many of the poor are exposed to disabling accidents. Rural activities such as quarrying, mining, fishing, hunting, build-

For poor women, however, life-cycle poverty can be severe; especially for female heads of households without adult males to help (as a result of death, divorce, illness, absence or disability). Among the poorest of the poor are young widows and elderly individuals with no adult male to help manage the family enterprise or negotiate the tenancy, labour or credit problems.

Though poverty and vulnerability are often equated ("vulnerable groups" standing for the poor), Robert Chambers correctly distinguishes between them. "Poverty can be reduced by borrowing and investing; but such debt makes households more vulnerable".[1] There are trade-offs between poverty and vulnerability (or between security and income). Vulnerability is a function of external risks, shocks and stress, and of internal defencelessness.

Next, we may ask, is poverty absolute or relative? Poverty lines vary between climates, cultures and social and economic environments. The poverty line for the USA is at a substantially higher income than that for Bangladesh. The US Bureau of the Census publishes figures showing that 15 per cent of Americans live below the official poverty line. Clearly, these are much better off than the majority of Bangladeshis. Is there a component in poverty that has to be defined in relation to the mean (in which case poverty is inevitable, for there will always be some below the average), or to the bottom of the 80 per cent above the lowest 20 per cent, or to one-third of average national income per head, or to some other reference of what is regarded as a minimum decent standard in a society? Some authors regard all poverty as relative, but this is surely confusing inequality – an evil, but a different evil – with

---

ing, brick-making, ploughing, and herding, and urban activities – in factories, transport and construction – are often physically hazardous. The resulting accidents are rarely counted and little considered in the literature, yet again and again, individual case studies of destitute households reveal an accident as the event which impoverished – disabling an adult, especially a breadwinner. At a sudden blow, the body, the poor person's greatest and uninsured asset, is devalued or ruined. From being an asset, at one stroke it becomes a liability that has to be fed, clothed, housed, and treated. A livelihood is destroyed, and a household made permanently poorer", 'Editorial Introduction: Vulnerability, Coping and Policy', *IDS Bulletin,* vol. 20 no. 2, April 1989, p. 4. Misfortune can lead to permanent poverty.

1. CHAMBERS, *loc. cit.,* p. 1.

poverty. Everyone in a society can be equally starving, and we would not want to say that they are not poor.[1] Some measures of inequality give greater weight to income distributions that are unfavourable to the very poor, and thereby catch an element of what we mean by "relative poverty". Anthony Barnes Atkinson defines what he calls "the equally distributed equivalent income" of a given distribution of total income. It is that level of income per head which, if enjoyed by everybody, would make total welfare exactly equal to the total welfare generated by the actual income distribution. Atkinson's measure is 1 minus (the equally distributed income divided by the average actual income), and therefore varies between zero and one.[2]

Karl Marx wrote about the man who lived in a small cottage and was perfectly happy until a neighbour came along who constructed a palace.[3] Then the cottager began to feel deprived. Relative deprivation is deprivation that results from comparing our level of living with that of a reference group with higher incomes.[4]

It is, however, important to note that not all poverty resulting from rising average incomes is relative; *absolute* poverty can also result from higher average incomes. Amartya K. Sen analyses this by saying that poverty can be an absolute notion in the space of capabilities, though relative in that of commodities or charac-

1. The opposite is more difficult to establish. It might be thought that it is logically quite possible to have great inequality combined with the absence of absolute poverty. But, analytically, in such a society the relative component in poverty (or, as it is called in this context, in deprivation) will become more pronounced, and, empirically, it is not easy to think of many societies in which great inequality is combined with absence of absolute poverty. Perhaps Kuwait is the exception that tests the rule.

2. A. B. ATKINSON, *The Economy of Inequality*, Oxford: Clarendon Press, 1976.

3. KARL MARX, 'Wage Labour and Capital' in KARL MARX AND FREDERICK ENGELS, *Selected Works*, vol. 1, Moscow: Foreign Languages Publishing House, 1958.

4. Some forms of conspicuous consumption by the rich are enjoyed by those with lower incomes. The British royal family's stage coach and the gold-plated car of a couple called Sir Bernard and Lady Docker gave pleasure to readers of the mass journals. So must the pictures of the lifestyles of the rich and famous disporting themselves in *The New York Times'* "Evening Hours". The popularity of shows like *Falcon Crest* and *A Current Affair* on television indicate that people like to watch the rich living it up. Most Americans do not spend much time hating the very rich, and vicariously enjoy their riches. Whether the same is true of the parties by Mr Forbes and Mr and Mrs Steinberg is an open question.

teristics.[1] A number of different factors can account for this. Some of these are the result of goods and services either ceasing to be available or rising in price more than money incomes; others of changes in conventions and laws; others again of deeper psychological causes, such as shame at not being able to afford what has become socially necessary.

If the benefits from a primary education depend on watching certain television programmes at home, those who cannot afford a television set are absolutely worse off, when the average family in that society acquires a set.[2] The television set does not reflect a new need that arises as incomes rise, but satisfaction of the same need (to be educated) requires a higher income. The poor in California are absolutely deprived if they do not own a car, for public transport has deteriorated as a result of most people owning cars. The wide availability of refrigerators and freezers affects the structure of retailing and impoverishes those without these durable consumer goods.[3] Or, turning to low-income countries, as some groups get richer, land is diverted from producing grain to producing fodder crops or meat and dairy products, so that grain becomes more expensive, possibly raising poverty among the poor. In these cases the structure of supply is altered unfavourably to the poor. Or if an essential good is in inelastic supply, the growth of income of a particular group may raise its price so much that the poor are worse off.

In a richer society poor people may be forced to buy over-specified products to meet more essential needs: food that is processed, packaged, advertised, and correspondingly more expensive; drip-dry shirts, even though they may prefer to iron a cheaper, no longer available shirt themselves. It is as if one had to buy a Dior dress in order to keep warm. The disappearance of low-cost items as incomes rise is well reflected in Marie-Antoinette's admonition to the poor, when bread was short, "Let them eat cake!" (Rousseau had referred to it much earlier.)

1. AMARTYA K. SEN, 'Poor, Relatively Speaking', in his *Resources, Values and Development*, Oxford: Basil Blackwell, 1984, chap. 14.

2. T. C. COOPER, 'Poverty', unpublished note, 1971, quoted in SEN, *Resources, Values and Development*, p. 336.

3. *Ibid.*, p. 337.

Then there are changes in conventional standards and legal restrictions that accompany greater prosperity, which may be unfavourable to the poor. If you are a rural dweller, you can pitch up a tent that provides shelter against the elements. But if you live in New York City, you must not put up a tent in Madison Avenue. In the bush you can wear only a loin cloth, but if you work in London you have to wear a shirt, suit, tie and shoes, and perhaps carry a neatly rolled umbrella. Higher minimum standards of housing are imposed on you by the higher incomes of the city dwellers, or by restrictions on what structures you can put up.

Adam Smith wrote that customary standards also determine what is a necessity.[1] To have no shoes in England is to be deprived of a necessity, though this is not so for women in Scotland, and for either men or women in France. But the shame that the shoeless feel when appearing in public in a society in which wearing shoes is part of social custom is not relative; they are not more ashamed than others. It is an absolute deprivation.[2] Peter Townsend reports that it may be impossible to avoid shame in the nineteen eighties in London if one cannot give one's children treats.[3] These feelings might in turn derive from a sense of lack of participation in community life, or lack of self-respect.

To view shame in the face of others possessing more goods as an absolute form of poverty leads, however, to somewhat odd conclusions. As Robert H. Frank has noted, "we may be prepared to believe, on the one hand, that the millionaire bond trader Sherman McCoy and his wife in Tom Wolfe's novel *Bonfire of the Vanities*, really do *require* a chauffeur and limousine in order to transport themselves without shame to a dinner party just a few blocks from their apartment. On the other hand, few of us would feel comfortable calling them *impoverished* if they were suddenly deprived of their car and driver."[4]

1. ADAM SMITH, *An Inquiry into the Nature and Causes of the Wealth of Nations*, London: Everyman, Home University Library, 1776.

2. AMARTYA K. SEN, 'Poor, Relatively Speaking', chapter 14 in *Resources, Values and Development*, Oxford: Basil Blackwell, 1984.

3. Reported by GEOFFREY HAWTHORN in Introduction to AMARTYA SEN, *The Standard of Living*, Cambridge: Cambridge University Press, 1987, p. XI.

4. ROBERT H. FRANK, review of AMARTYA SEN, *The Standard of Living, Journal of Economic Literature*, vol. 27, no. 2, June 1989, p. 666.

This view of shame also leads to odd remedies. They may lie more in the realm of psychology than of economics. Educating people not to be ashamed when they do not have shoes (or linen shirts, another example of Adam Smith's) but proudly to display their different lifestyle, as the members of the German *Wandervogel* did before the Great War, or the hippies more recently, is one cure. Or it may become possible to reduce such forms of absolute poverty by taking the shoes or the linen shirts away from the better-off, or by a heavy tax on shoes and linen shirts.

In view of the fact that absolute poverty is partly a function of average living standards, it is clear that "absolute" does not mean fixed in time. The absolute level of poverty can rise, as incomes increase. The capability of appearing in public without shame, of participating in the life of the community or of maintaining self-respect will vary with the conventions, regulations, and material comforts of a society.

Fred Hirsch in his book *Social Limits to Growth*[1] analyses positional goods. The absolute enjoyment of an uncrowded beach depends on relatively superior knowledge, compared with that of others. Here again, it is absolute deprivation that is a function of a relative disadvantage. But it has always seemed to me that Hirsch drew excessively gloomy conclusions from the existence of positional goods. Many people enjoy crowded beaches. And not everyone wishes to become a Field Marshal. One of the happiest days in my life was when I was promoted from Private to Lance Corporal.

If, for the moment, we confine our attention to the head-count measure of poverty (we shall see in a moment that other dimensions are also important), the next question in assessing the fate of the poor is whether the absolute number of poor or the proportion of poor in the total population (the head-count ratio) has increased. With rapidly increasing populations, it may be thought that the concept relevant to judging the success of strategies in eliminating poverty should be the proportion of poor. It may also be asked, as discussed above, whether the members (and fam-

---

1. FRED HIRSCH, *Social Limits to Growth*, Cambridge, Mass.: Harvard University Press, 1978.

ilies) of the groups of poor people have largely remained the same or whether their composition has changed.

Next we must ask how we proceed from money income shares or income levels, on which we have plenty of data, but which are largely irrelevant, to real income shares or levels, which are more relevant to assessing inequality and poverty. Ideally, we should have an index for the minimum needs cost of living, allowing for price changes and consequential substitution between items in the basket. Together with other indicators, discussed below, we might then make estimates of what Seebohm Rowntree,[1] at the turn of the century, in his research on poverty in York, called primary and secondary poverty. Minimum needs bundles, stipulated by nutritionists or other outsiders, are seldom sensible and often not feasible. But if we cost actual bundles bought, the question arises whose cost of living should be used: that of the poorest, the poor, or those on the borderline? It has been argued that the poorest are always in poverty, those above the borderline almost never, and that it is the cost-of-living of those on the borderline that matters.

Primary poverty is defined as the inability to command enough income (or expenditure) to buy the bare necessities of life. This poverty line is usually constructed by estimating the cost of a minimum diet of essential food items and the fuel needed to prepare it. This can be done either in a rather mechanical way, by calculating the cost of a strictly minimum needs diet; or, it can be done better by allowing for the behaviour of actual consumers and observing how they spend their money on food. Having calculated the cost of an empirically observed, appropriate, minimum diet, and having discovered that non-food essential items such as clothing and lighting absorb about 20 per cent, these are added. This percentage has again been found empirically to be the irreducible minimum of income or expenditure spent on items other than food.[2]

---

1. B. SEEBOHM ROWNTREE, *Poverty: A Study of Town Life*, London: Macmillan, 1901.
2. See V. DANDEKAR and N. RATH, *Poverty in India*, Poona, 1971. The authors take data from the Indian National Sample Survey and record, for rural and urban consumers, the percentage distribution of expenditure on foodgrains and substitutes, other items of food, fuel and light, clothing, and others. They find that in 1960-61 more than 90 per

There is an inconsistency in this way of arriving at a poverty line. The minimum food requirements are derived normatively, by calculating how much the minimum food requirements would cost; while the non-food items are determined by observing how much people actually spend. In order to remove the inconsistency, we would have to assume that what people *actually* happen to spend is what they *need* to spend on non-food items, clearly an unrealistic assumption. It might well be that, if the non-food items were also determined normatively, the poverty line would be quite different, probably higher.[1] On the other hand, the poverty line does not comprise public services that are free, such as education and health services.

Since the needs of children are less than those of adults, (and since there are economies of scale in food expenditure in households) we should calculate the income (or consumption) per adult-equivalent. This would indicate the shortfall of income (or consumption) for a typical member of that group, e.g. a member of a household of a given age- and sex-composition to obtain the required amount of calories. We then count the number of people falling below this line, and find the ratio of these to the total population. This is the head-count ratio. But this ratio tells us neither how far below the poverty line the poor are, nor how poverty is distributed among them. Therefore, in addition the income-gap measure has been used. It measures the average income shortfall of all the poor as a proportion of the poverty line. But these two measures do not tell us how poverty is distributed among the poor. A. K. Sen has added a measure of the distribution of poverty among those below the line.[2] "One gets a measure of poverty P that depends on three parameters, viz., the head-count ratio H, the income-gap ratio I as a proportion of the pover-

cent of the expenditure of the poor was devoted to food and fuel for cooking. These are the ultra-poor.

1. The poverty line is established by multiplying the money required to buy the food basket by the reciprocal of the ratio of food expenditure to total expenditure. Since this ratio is higher, and the reciprocal therefore lower, for poor people than for the better off, if the latter ratio is chosen, the poverty line is raised.

2. AMARTYA K. SEN, 'Poverty: An Ordinal Approach to Measurement', *Econometrica*, vol. 44 no. 2, 1976.

ty line and the Gini coefficient G of the distribution of income among the poor:[1]

$$P = H[I + (1-I)G].\text{''}$$

A criticism of this measure of poverty is that the weights used for the shortfall from the poverty line depend on the rank order that a poor person occupies among all the poor. The severity of someone falling $ 1000 short of the poverty line depends on how many poor are ahead of him. "Imagine a parade in which everyone walks past in order of their income; what the rank order measures is how far you are from the person just at the poverty line." This introduces an element of relative deprivation (though within the poverty range) into a measure of absolute poverty.[2] Sen argues in defence of this that "the lower a

---

1: THEOREM 1 in *loc. cit.*

2. See A. B. ATKINSON, Original Sen, *New York Review of Books*, vol. XXIV, no. 16, October 22, 1987, p. 43. The Foster-Greer-Thorbecke class of poverty measures overcomes several limitations of Sen's measure. In particular, it is decomposable in the sense that total poverty of a group is a weighted average of the levels of poverty of the subgroups. See JAMES FOSTER, JOEL GREER, and ERIK THORBECKE 'A Class of Decomposable Poverty Measures' *Econometrica*, vol. 52 no. 3, May 1984, and JOEL GREER and ERIK THORBECKE, 'A Methodology for Measuring Food Poverty Applied to Kenya', *Journal of Development Economics*, vol. 24 no. 1, January 1986. The measure is

$$P = \frac{1}{n} \sum_{i=1}^{q} \left(\frac{gi}{z}\right)^a$$

where n is the total number of households, gi is the income shortfall of the ith household, z is the poverty line, and q is the number of poor households below the poverty line. This measure raises the proportionate shortfall from the poverty line to a power a, the magnitude of which reflects concern for this shortfall. When $a = 0$, reflecting no concern for the depth of the shortfall, the measure becomes the head-count ratio. When $a = 1$, reflecting uniform concern for the depth of poverty, the measure reduces to HI, the product of the head-count ratio and the income gap ratio. When a exceeds 1, the measure can be used to show any degree of heightened sensitivity to the poorest of the poor. For certain values of a, the poverty aversion parameter, it satisfies practically every desirable axiomatic property a poverty measure would be expected to satisfy in addition to being additively decomposable, a great advantage in any empirical application. It overcomes the rank ordering limitation since, for example, for $a = 2$, the poor are weighted according to the square of their shortfall. By raising the proportionate shortfall from the poverty line by a power x, the measure, therefore, shows heightened sensitivity to the poorest of the poor. It allows for aggregating poverty measures for different groups, for person is in the welfare scale, the greater his sense of poverty".[1]

Another possible criticism of measures such as Sen's and other similar scalar measures of poverty is that they are trying to catch too much in a single indicator, valid for all dimensions of poverty, for all countries, at all times. The ability to present a single figure has great attractions, but also costs. Some might prefer to disaggregate different dimensions or aspects of poverty and present them distinctly. Sen, normally the distinguished distinguisher,[2] becomes here a lumper.

Disaggregation could be done by a vector measure of poverty, such as the "Dissatisfaction of Basic Needs". People are asked about some aspects of basic needs: e.g. for education, the questions are about access to primary schools, level of education of the head of the household, dependency ratio, etc. For shelter, the questions may be about overcrowding, the quality of water, access to sanitary facilities, the precariousness of the residential structure, etc. Similar questions may be asked about food, health, clothing, fuel or transport. If the answer to *any one* of these questions shows an inadequate level, basic needs for that household are not satisfied and it is counted as poor. This multidimensional measure does not allow for substitution between different basic needs.

Secondary poverty Rowntree defined as a situation in which real incomes are adequate to buy the minimum needs basket, but for one reason or another (he identified drink, gambling and inefficient housekeeping) the poor do not spend the money on satisfying these needs. Primary poverty is in*suff*icient resources, secondary is in*eff*icient use of adequate resources. The distinction gained in sharpness when A. K. Sen analysed the standard of liv-

different food preferences, and for different prices. This measure has been extensively used in both theoretical and empirical applications. It has also been applied to measuring food poverty, based on typically consumed diets, in JOEL GREER and ERIK THORBECKE, 'Food Poverty Profile Applied to Kenyan Smallholders', *Economic Development and Cultural Change*, vol. 35, no. 1, October 1986.

1. MICHAEL LIPTON shows that the second derivatives of the Sen index have unacceptable properties. See 'A Problem in Poverty Measurement', Amsterdam: North-Holland, 1985, pp. 91-97. He proposes a simple measure for the ultra-poor, among whom income cannot be very unequal and $G=0$, and two separate measures for the moderately poor.

2. The phrase is John Toye's.

ing as "capabilities" and "functionings", which refer to the capacity to convert resources into well-being. Primary poverty refers to lack of resources, secondary to a flaw in the conversion mechanism.

In getting at primary poverty, money income has to be corrected for price changes. General consumer price indexes may not be relevant to determining the price changes of the goods bought by the poor. There are five distinct issues.

First, in developing countries, even more than in developed countries, different groups do not face the same prices for the same goods. The urban cost-of-living is higher than the rural, and costs vary from region to region. For this reason money income shares deflated by a general urban price index may overstate inequalities and rural poverty. Food in rural areas is between 5 and 15 per cent cheaper than in urban areas. Unfortunately, lower average rural incomes more than compensate for this effect and raise the incidence of poverty in rural areas.

Second, different groups consume different goods, and the same goods in different proportions. Prices do not change in the same proportion for all groups. Food forms a higher proportion of total expenditure for the poor (and within food, coarse grains), and if its price rises by more than average prices (and that of coarse grains more than those of other food items), poverty is underestimated by money income shares deflated by a general price index (or by a general food price index). The same problem arises for both cross-section and time series data.[1]

Third, as different prices change in different proportions, consumers will substitute cheaper food items for more expensive ones. Ideally, the new basket bought should be the basis for calculating changes in real income.

Fourth, we have already seen that with rising average standards certain items, especially important to the poor, may cease

1. In rural India cereal prices for different decile groups of the population moved unequally in the nineteen fifties and sixties. The average price of cereals has risen by more for the poor than the rich. This was due partly to higher price rises for coarser cereals, normally consumed by the poor, and partly to a shift to superior cereals in the consumption basket of the poor. See PRANAB K. BARDHAN, *Pattern of Income Distribution in India: A Review*, Calcutta: Statistical Publishing Society, 1974.

to be available and be replaced by more expensive items; and the same items may be subject to more sophisticated treatment through more packaging, a higher degree of processing, advertising, or types of "improvement" which raise their costs to the poor, especially the urban poor and subsistence farmers switching to cash crops and beginning to be dependent on market purchases.

Fifth, some goods and services are provided free to the poor, but they are rationed. If, for example, health services are provided without a monetary charge, but the queuing time has lengthened, this is equivalent to a rise in the price of these services. Such changes do not show up in price indexes.

In trying to measure poverty we may envisage the process as the removal of six veils. The removal of each veil gets us nearer the facts that we want to measure, but the outer veils are not therefore unnecessary. First, there is money income, which does not reveal anything about changes in the prices of the goods and services bought.

Second, there is real income, adjusted for changes in the general price level. Third, there is real income adjusted for the region-specific, and commodity-specific purchases of the poor, and for the non-availability of important items. Compared with the money and effort that have gone into calculating international purchasing power comparisons, rather little has gone into comparisons of purchasing power of different income groups. But even the measure of real income has certain defects. It ignores the welfare derived from leisure. Attempts to estimate the value of leisure run into problems about what value to attach to it.

The concept of real income does not always include non-marketed and non-priced subsistence income, such as that from crops grown and consumed within the household, or the services of housewives. Sometimes attempts are made to impute these. The concept fails to account for free social services and the benefits from pure public goods. And, if presented as an average for an income group (the nation, a province, a region, or the household), it fails to account for distribution. To some extent this deficiency can be overcome, as already remarked, for national figures by using not the mean, which is biased by the few very large incomes, but the median or the mode, though reliable figures on these are rarely available. Life expectancy can also be incorporated, as has been seen, by giving not average annual income, but average life-time income. Two societies, or two income groups, may enjoy the same average annual income, but in one people live, on the average, to age 50, in the other to age 75. While some of these distributional and social considerations can, therefore, in principle, be incorporated in average real income per head of the income group, or the socio-economic group, there are many important aspects that remain concealed.

Fourth, there are direct measures of physical inputs to meet basic needs, such as calories consumed, yards of cloth bought, cubic feet of house room occupied, hospital beds available, school enrolment, letters posted, etc. These are still instruments or means, but they penetrate behind the veil of money and identify "characteristics" of commodities and services. A measure of dietary energy intake relative to requirements (not easily determined) would be a good scalar measure of nutritional status, if supplemented by the type of impact indicator of basic needs discussed under the fifth heading, such as infant mortality, literacy and morbidity. "There is a strong case for using access to adequate food as the scalar indicator, at least for the presence of ultra-poverty. That is not because people, children or households 'live by bread alone'. It is because 'access to adequate sources of nutrition' turns out to be a very good, and in a sense self-weighting, *summary* of what most people mean by absence of ultra-poverty: health, shelter, education, even mobility, are all reflected in nutritional status, although not in a linear or otherwise simple way".[1]

This measure of adequate access to food is a particularly good indicator of ultra-poverty, of the standard of living of the poorest of the poor. They spend about 80 per cent of their income on food, and this proportion does not decline when their income rises, as it does for those above the ultra-poverty line. The Engel curve, viz., the declining proportion of income spent on food as income rises, (and the Bennett curve, viz., the declining proportion of food

---

1. LIPTON, *'Who Are the Poor?'*, p. 4.

consisting of starchy staples, such as cereals and roots) begins to register only above the range of ultra-poverty.[1]

Fifth, there are impact measures of health, mortality, literacy, morbidity, which register "capabilities" or "functionings".[2] Weight for age or height for age (in children) and weight for height (in adults) are anthropometric measures trying to get at one purpose of nutrition: the full, healthy development of the body. These measures look behind income and what it is spent on, at the inputs in relation to requirements, and the skills and abilities of converting goods and services into human functionings. One may have more money and more food than another, but be more undernourished because she has parasites in her stomach, or is pregnant or lactating, or has to work harder collecting water and wood, or lives in a colder climate, or has a higher metabolic rate, or a larger body. Or, having less education, she may marry earlier, produce more children, and thereby raise the food requirements of the household. The impact is, moreover, determined not only by income and the ability to convert what it buys into nutritional status, but also by social services, provided free of charge.

Not only are figures for average income (or expenditure) per head not very closely correlated to these human indicators, so that quite low-income countries perform well, while some high-income ones perform poorly, but the International Food Policy Research Institute in Washington, D.C., among others, has done a good deal of research on how specific groups of small farmers and landless labourers change their nutritional status as their incomes rise. In some cases nutritional status drops as households enter into commercial transactions and their incomes increase, while they produce less of the subsistence crops. On the other hand, on the whole different basic needs indicators are very highly correlated with one another, so that recording the composition of poverty is less important than its level.

---

1. MICHAEL LIPTON, *Poverty, Undernutrition and Hunger*, World Bank Staff Working Paper no. 597, 1983; '*Who Are the Poor?*'; and BHANOJI RAO, 'Measurement of Deprivation and Poverty Based on the Proportion Spent on Food', *World Development* vol. 9 no. 4, April 1981.

2. SEN, *The Standard of Living*.

The nexus between income (or expenditure) per head and nutritional status is stronger in some areas of the world, such as South and East Asia (but not parts of West Asia) and weaker in others, such as Africa. The precise reasons for this are a matter for research, but it is plausible to assume that factors such as education (particularly in health and hygiene), infrastructure, such as safe water and sewerage, and the distribution of power within the household, between men, women and children, are important components. Clearly, this is a very important question for policy, because the answer to the question of the nexus will determine whether opportunities to earn income or the provision of public social services should have priority.

Finally, as we have already seen, much of the information on income and consumption and their impact is based on the household as the unit of observation. Removal of the sixth veil would reveal the distribution of the benefits from basic necessities and services *within* the household and show the impact on specific individuals, adults and children, men and women, able-bodied and disabled. As has been argued elsewhere in this lecture, consumption per head is a better measure than consumption per household, where such figures are available. At least for Africa, there is no evidence that women or children are discriminated against inside the household. Amartya Sen has suggested that India could learn from Africa how to reduce the "gender-bias" against women, which produced "30 million missing Indian women", who would be living now, if African attitudes to women prevailed in India.[1]

If food is scarce, it is sensible to provide the chief breadwiner, who has to work harder, with an adequate diet, even if this is at the expense of other members in the family; otherwise everybody will lose. In many societies this will be a woman.

So far we have assumed that the numerator is income or physical quantities and the denominator of these indicators is the number of persons, so that we get measures of income, or of food "per head". But not all persons have the same requirements.

1. AMARTYA K. SEN in *The Balance Between Industry and Agriculture in Economic Development*. Vol I: *Basic Issues*. Edited by KENNETH J. ARROW; Basingstoke: Macmillan/IEA, 1988.

The correct indicator is "adult equivalent", so that we can allow for the fact that children need less food than adults. This is, of course, quite independent of the question of whether some members of the household get less in relation to their requirements.

As we have seen, these human impact indicators have some advantages over income or consumption indicators, in addition to the fact that they measure ends rather than means; but they are useful as complements rather than replacements. Specific human and social indicators make, for some purposes, better sense than average income. The reason is that income distribution can be highly skewed (there are no upper limits to income), while e.g. life expectancy or literacy have a definite maximum – say 100 years (or 78 years, as the highest recorded average life expectancy) or 100 per cent. But the incidence of these indicators between different groups (e.g. men and women or rich and poor, or urban and rural) can throw light on the distribution of well-being in a society. Ideally, we should have indicators of life expectancy, infant mortality and literacy that are adjusted for inequalities in their distribution.

Another advantage is that they measure over- as well as under-development. There are diseases of affluence, just as there are diseases of poverty. A third advantage is that it makes sense and is realistic to attempt to reduce gaps (between rich and poor, men and women, urban and rural dwellers) in life expectancy, literacy and infant mortality, while it makes less sense, and is often neither feasible nor desirable, to reduce gaps in income per head. A fourth advantage is that impact measures sift "goods" from items that should be counted as costs or "anti-bads". Food consumed to meet excess food requirements, resulting from unwanted pregnancies, or children that die, long walks to collect water or fuelwood, or in search of jobs, or between unconsolidated plots of land, show up not as increases in welfare, but as regrettable, though possibly avoidable, hardships. So do the higher housing and transport costs that urban dwellers incur, but that are counted as higher incomes, giving the false impression of higher levels of welfare.

It is, however, a drawback that there is no easy and clear way of aggregating these human indicators into a composite one, as we have seen when discussing the Human Development Index. GNP appears to have great attractions of precision by comparison. But, as Amartya Sen asks, "Why must we reject being vaguely right in favour of being precisely wrong?"[1]

An attempt to aggregate three human indicator into a single index is the Physical Quality of Life Index (PQLI).[2] It gives one-third weight each to life expectancy at year one, infant mortality and literacy. But it is not only arbitrary, it also aggregates where we should wish to disaggregate. We have already seen that, on the whole, different basic needs indicators are very highly correlated with each other, so that only one, say life expectancy, is needed and the PQLI is then unnecessary. But if in a society literacy indicators are good, while health is poor, we should want to know why, not blur the difference by a single index. The same criticism can, of course, be made of the GNP as a measure of welfare. When whisky, consumed by the rich, goes up, and milk, consumed by the poor, down, the GNP figure may register an increase. But such inadequacies of the GNP measure were precisely among the reasons why we had to complement it by physical and impact indicators. But with only three indicators, disaggregation is both easier and more illuminating than with the large number that go into the GNP. This is quite independent of the question as to whether prices – market prices or shadow prices – are a good set of weights with which to aggregate national income.

Moreover, the PQLI measures more the quantity of life, than its quality, although at low income levels illness often leads to death, so that longer lives tend to mean also healthier and more productive lives. But it does not include any measure of basic needs such as security, justice, freedom, human rights, etc. It would be possible to register a high PQLI in a zoo or even a well-run prison. And, although at low incomes illness often leads to death, the PQLI has no independent indicator of morbidity,

1. SEN, *The Standard of Living*.

2. MORRIS D. MORRIS, *Measuring the Condition of the World's Poor: The Physical Quality of Life Index*, London: Frank Cass, 1979.

absence of which is surely one of the most basic of needs.[1] Life can be nasty, brutish and long.

As already mentioned, the *Human Development Reports for* 1990 and 1991 of the United Nations Development Programme present a Human Development Index. It combines deprivation in life expectancy, literacy and minimum decent income, based on purchasing power comparisons. A minimum value and an adequate value are specified for each of the three indicators. These are the end-points of a scale from one to zero for each measure of deprivation. Placing a country at the appropriate point on each scale and averaging the three scales gives its average human deprivation index, which, when subtracted from one, gives the human development index. As in the PQLI, the weights are arbitrary.[2]

An alternative approach to that of looking for a single indicator is to use life expectancy as an integrating concept for human, social and demographic analysis. Sir Richard Stone and Dudley Seers have pioneered this system of accounts. The essence of this method is to express the lifetime chances of different groups with respect to schooling, unemployment, illness, marriage, migration, etc. We can then say how many years (or months), on the average, a group spends in pre-school, primary, secondary, tertiary education; at a technical college, at a university; how many regularly employed, how many unemployed, how many on holidays, how many in retirement, pensioned, unpensioned; how many in a particular town, region or country, and how many outside it; we can add to these the months spent in hospital, or sick at home, or on a psychiatrist's couch or in prison; how many in a first, second, nth marriage, how many single, divorced, widowed. By following a cohort through a sequence of such states we can estimate the probability of transition from one state to another, for which data are more readily available than for the length of stay

---

1. See Paul Streeten with Shahid Javed Burki, Mahbub ul Haq, Norman Hicks and Frances Stewart, *First Things First; Meeting Basic Human Needs in Developing Countries*, for the World Bank, Oxford: Oxford University Press, 1981, chapter 3 'The Search for a Suitable Yardstick', pp. 87-89, and Lipton, *Poverty, Undernutrition and Hunger*.

2. *Human Development Report 1990*, and *1991*, for the United Nations Development Programme, New York, Oxford: Oxford University Press.

in the state. Such lifetime profiles are useful supplements to income per head. Thus, for example, Dudley Seers' unfinished article[1] showed that a male born in Great Britain in 1971 could look forward to 68.9 years of life, during which 12.2 years would be spent in school, 41.3 years employed or self-employed, 2.7 unemployed. This profile could then be compared with profiles of those born in Brazil, Malaysia, Hong Kong, and with the profiles of different social classes, by sex, in Britain.

A serious shortcoming of all measures so far discussed is that they do not view poverty from the point of view of the poor, but apply external, professional standards to it. A quite different approach to measuring poverty is to ask people how miserable they perceive themselves to be. Such questionnaires can take different forms. For example, a sample of households may be asked not only what they consume but also what they consider an adequate level of consumption to be for different goods. Or people could be asked whether they think their income is too low, just adequate, or more than enough.[2]

Psychologists have not found a high correlation between such indices of satisfaction and some of the previously discussed measures of poverty. They have also found people at all income levels declare that about the same additional percentage of their actual income would be required to meet their needs and make them satisfied.

In re-surveying villages in Gujarat after 20 years N. S. Jodha found that the households whose real income per head had

---

1. DUDLEY SEERS, 'Active Life Profiles for Different Social Groups: a Contribution to Demographic Accounting, a Frame for Social Indicators and a Tool for Social and Economic Analysis', 1982, unpublished. See also his 'Life Expectancy as an Integrating Concept in Social and Demographic Analysis and Planning', *Review of Income and Wealth*, vol. 23, no. 3, September 1977; RICHARD STONE, *An Integrated System of Demographic, Manpower and Social Statistics*, Paris: UNESCO, 1970; *Towards a System of Social and Demographic Statistics*, United Nations Statistical Office, ser. F, no. 18, New York: 1975, and STREETEN *et. al.*, *First Things First*, chapter 3.

2. PETER TOWNSEND, in his *Poverty in the United Kingdom* (Harmondsworth: Penguin Books, 1979) asked a large number of questions, ranging from basic needs to styles of living and social interaction. The response scored zero if the reply corresponded to the social norm, and 1 if it was below it. The responses were then added up for each household and showed a strong negative correlation to income. Below a critical level of income, the deprivation score rose sharply.

declined by more than five per cent were, on the average, better off on 37 of their own 38 criteria of well-being. Besides income and consumption, they were concerned with independence, especially from patrons, mobility, security and self-respect.[1] This should serve as a warning against attempting to simplify measures of poverty into single indicators, especially those relying on income and consumption, and against relying solely on quantitative indicators. Any attempt to understand poverty must include the way in which poor people themselves perceive their situation.[2]

There are numerous non-material or not readily measured benefits, often more highly valued by poor people than material or measurable improvements. Among these are good working conditions, freedom to choose jobs and livelihoods, self-determination, security, self-respect, liberation from persecution, humiliation, oppression, violence and exploitation, the assertion of traditional cultural and religious values (often the only thing a poor person can assert), empowerment or access to power, recognition, status, adequate leisure time and satisfying forms of its use, a sense of purpose in life and work, the opportunity to join and participate actively in voluntary societies and social activities in a pluralistic civil society, with institutions that are layered between the individual and the central government. These are all important objectives, valued both in their own right and as means to satisfying and productive work. Many of these can be achieved in ways that do not increase the measured production of commodities, while a high and growing national income, even if properly distributed, can leave these basic needs unsatisfied. No policy maker can guarantee the achievement of all, or even a majority of these aspirations, but policies can create the

1. ROBERT CHAMBERS 'Editorial Introduction', p. 2. The reference is to N. S. JODHA, 'Social science research on rural change: some gaps (a footnote to debate on rural poverty)', in PRANAB BARDHAN, forthcoming, *Rural Economic Change in South Asia: Methodology of Measurement*. See also N. S. JODHA, 'Poverty Debate in India: A Minority View', *Economic and Political Weekly*, Special Number, November 1988. For a good discussion of non-measurable aspects of poverty, see ROBERT CHAMBERS, *Poverty in India: Concepts, Research and Reality*, Institute of Development Studies Discussion, Paper no. 241, Brighton, January 1988.

2. But a person may be miserably poor and not feel deprived. See below, p. 51.

opportunities for their fulfilment.[1] In assessing and measuring successes or failures in the pursuit of these objectives, it is important not to fall victim to the twin fallacies that only what can be counted counts, and that any figure, however unreliable, is better than none.[2]

A. K. Sen has argued that neither states of mind, the utilitarian measure, nor characteristics of commodities, the Gorman-Lancaster measure,[3] but human capabilities (potentials) and functionings (actuals) are at the heart of our poverty and welfare concerns. A person (particularly in some cultures a woman) may be miserably poor, but not feel deprived. There is a character in one of Anita Brookner's novels who is so modest that she does "not even presume to be unhappy".[4] Susan Minot in her novel *Folly* writes of a woman who "not only did . . . not think of making certain choices herself, she was completely unaware of having the desire to do so". In parts of India, women and girls report much less frequently than men and boys of being ill. Or the person may enjoy adequate food, but be too ill to absorb it or too uneducated to prepare it nutritiously or share it among fewer children. The ability, or capability, not only to keep alive, but also to be well nourished, healthy, educated, productive, fulfilled, these are the objectives of good policy, and incomes or the goods they buy are only one type of instrument to achieve them.[5]

It is important to bear these considerations in mind. None of them means that income and consumption are not important as indicators of poverty. Returning to income measures, we may ask next whether consumption or income is an appropriate measure

---

1. Keynes proposed the toast to the Royal Economic Society, "To economics and economists, who are not the trustees of civilization, but of the possibility of civilization." The same applies to their contribution to meeting basic needs.

2. The story is told that during the great Lisbon earthquake of 1755 a pedlar was selling anti-earthquake pills. Under the then equivalent of the Food and Drug Administration he was accused of fraud and hauled before the sheriff. His defence was, "What would you put in their place, your Honour?"

3. W. M. GORMAN, 'The Demand for Related Goods', *Journal Paper* J3129 Ames: Iowa Experimental Station, 1956; and K. J. LANCASTER, 'A New Approach to Consumer Theory', *Journal of Political Economy*, vol. 74 no. 2, 1966.

4. ANITA BROOKNER, *Latecomers,* New York: Pantheon Books, 1989.

5. SEN, *The Standard of Living* and *Resources, Values and Development.*

of poverty. Data for consumption and income are sometimes inconsistent. Consumption may be thought to be the appropriate welfare and impact measure. Income may have to be used to repay debt; or it may have to be saved for a time when consumption threatens to decline even lower; or it may be spent on an addiction. Two of Seebohm Rowntree's reasons for secondary poverty – drinking and gambling – can be regarded as addictions which we might want to deduct from income before arriving at resources available to meet basic needs. Today we would add drugs.

Then we may ask whether we should use cross-country or time series comparisons? Cross-country evidence is popular, but it tends to neglect policy options if it suggests inevitable sequences; time series data, on the other hand, (a) are unreliable, (b) are much more time-consuming, (c) do not lend themselves to generalizations, and (d) may also encourage undue determinism *if* general conclusions about policy are drawn from them. The twentieth century is different from the nineteenth, and its last decade may turn out to be different from earlier ones. The stock of knowledge has changed, and will change in the future, coexistence of countries at vastly different income levels changes the fate of any one country, and many other factors invalidate conclusions drawn from a more advanced country to a poorer one, whether in cross-country or time-series comparisons. Both cross-country and time series data sometimes lead to the tacit but unwarranted conclusion that all countries have to follow the same path as the now industrialized ones. None of this means, of course, that sensible and careful use of either set of data cannot be very illuminating. If a choice has to be made, it will depend on what it is we want to know. Time series show the evolution of certain states, while cross country comparisons can point to policy options. But the two sets should be regarded as complementing each other, particularly if good judgment and historical knowledge are added.

Policy issues will be discussed elsewhere. But there is one issue that is directly related to the concept and measurement of poverty; it is how to monitor success in poverty reduction resulting from the policies of aid donors. Ideally, donors would like to know changes in the number of poor people, in the severity of their poverty, in the length of time they are in poverty, in the changes in the impact on health, education, population growth, work performance, etc., and in the costs of the remedies.

Before suggesting measures that can serve the desire of donors to monitor poverty reduction, it is useful to remind ourselves that perceptions, and therefore indicators of poverty, may not be the same for donors as for recipients. We have seen that there are women so modest that they do not even presume to be unhappy or ill, as surveys in India have shown. The same may apply to low castes, to underclasses, or to other groups whose welfare is valued less in the society concerned than it is by the donors. This differential valuation may even be shared by these neglected or oppressed groups. The notion that each should count for one, and no one for more than one, is not universally accepted. Such differences may give rise to conflicts, to the resolution of which the institutional proposals below may make a contribution.

In the light of the foregoing discussion three measures are proposed for monitoring poverty by donors. First, income or expenditure or consumption per head or, better, per adult equivalent; per household figures should be used only if nothing else is available. Consumption has the drawback that it leaves out savings, and therefore potential future consumption, but is, at any rate for low-income people, preferable to income. Then a poverty line has to be defined, so that those below this line are counted to be in poverty. For the purpose of combining the dimensions of poverty as measured by income or consumption into a single figure, the Foster-Greer-Thorbecke index is probably for practical purposes the most useful. It combines the head count ratio, the proportionate shortfall of the average poor person below the poverty line, and a poverty aversion parameter that gives greater weights to the poorest of the poor.[1]

---

1. See FOSTER, GREER and THORBECKE, 'A Class of Decomposable Poverty Measures'. Additional advantages of this index are that it is decomposable by groups or regions, and that, by choosing the poverty aversion parameter = 0 it reduces to the head count ratio, by choosing it = 1, it shows the head count ratio combined with the average shortfall below the poverty line, and by choosing it larger than one, any degree of sensitivity to ultra-poverty can be introduced. See footnote 2, p. 39.

Second, calories per head or, better, per adult equivalent, in relation to calorie requirements, as laid down by some reliable organization, such as the World Health Organization. The needed data for this measure are fewer than for income or expenditure, but greater than for food consumption per head (allowing for different prices), which might be a substitute for calories. The data are also often more reliable. But they are inadequate by themselves, partly because the requirements standard is controversial, and partly because they do not account for important other dimensions of poverty than food. Third, the proportion of income or expenditure spent on food. A proportion higher than, say, 75 per cent indicates poverty, and an unchanging proportion with growing income, ultra-poverty. Since this ratio rises with family size, there is no need to adjust it for household size or other household characteristics.[1]

If these three indicators yield roughly the same number and groups of poor people, confidence in the estimate is justified. Unfortunately, it is likely that the three indicators will identify different groups of people as poor. If this turns out to be the case, greater scrutiny of the data and search for additional data is indicated. Among these would be anthropometric measures such as weight for age or height for age of children between birth and nine years, or weight for height, for countries or regions in which undernutrition and poverty are likely to be related. In other countries various other basic needs indicators may be in order, such as school attainment, literacy rates, floor area per head, land area per head, etc. Over longer periods it is in any case useful to supplement these measures by indicators of changes in life expectancy of the poverty groups or, if unavailable, of the population as a whole, and of changes in the ratios of men to women.

A crude but simple indicator for which data are normally available is the price of some staple food in relation to the money expenditure on consumption (or the money income) of poor people. There is clearly a trade-off between accuracy and costs of gath-

---

1. See PAUL GLEWWE and JACQUES VAN DER GAAG, *Confronting Poverty in Developing Countries*, Living Standards Measurement Study Working Paper no. 48, Washington, D.C.: World Bank, 1988, p. 8.

ering indicators. The cheapest indicators are likely to be the least accurate.

The question of monitoring, though it may appear to be a purely recording effort, does, however, raise policy issues. On the one hand, monitoring of poverty reduction and income distribution by donors is regarded by recipient countries as intrusive and perhaps even violating national sovereignty. On the other hand, donors believe that their responsibility to the taxpayer is to account for the use of aid funds and to ensure that poverty reduction is achieved, if this is the purpose of the aid. Donor institutions are distrusted by recipients, because they fear that extraneous criteria may enter into the process; and recipients' institutions are distrusted by donors, because they may wish to conceal unsuccessful performance. To resolve this conflict it is necessary to design institutions that are trusted by both sides, and monitor reliably and objectively.

In addition to having to gain the trust of both sides, and be responsive to their needs and demands, these institutions would have to fulfil the function of buffers between donors and recipients, would have to be sensitive to social and political conditions, and would have to have the expertise to judge the impact of programmes on poverty reduction. They should also be helpful in building up the indigenous capacity of poverty monitoring in developing countries.

One possible solution would be to adopt the method that the Organization of European Economic Cooperation practised under Marshall Aid. The USA generously withdrew from the monitoring process and encouraged European governments to monitor each other's performance. Analogously, groups of countries, such as those of East Africa, would get together, and one, say Uganda, would monitor the performance of another, say Kenya or Tanzania, and vice versa. Technical assistance would initially be needed to acquire or strengthen the professional capacity to do this.

Another solution would be to appoint a mutually agreed council of wise men and women, with a competent secretariat, who would be performing the monitoring, possibly again combined with technical assistance for the strengthening of indigenous capacity. A third solution would be to aim at the creation of a genuine global secretariat, with loyalties to the world community, socially and culturally sensitive, and at the same time technically competent. The secretariats of existing international organizations such as the World Bank have not quite reached that point, and are not perceived by recipients as being truly global. Reforms in recruitment, training, and promotion would be needed, and perhaps in the governance and location of these institutions. Decentralization to strong regional offices would be necessary. The staff would be in daily contact with the people they serve.

Whatever institutional solution might be adopted, there is virtue in introducing a degree of competition into the monitoring process, so that a variety of methods may be tested against each other. At the moment it is feared that the large international financial institutions exercise a monopoly of power and wisdom, and propagate at times prematurely crystallized orthodoxies. The proposed buffer procedures or buffer institutions should contribute to the building and strengthening of indigenous research and monitoring capacities of the recipient developing countries. For research on poverty and action against poverty tend to go together, as the investigations of Charles Booth and Seebohm Rowntree at the beginning of the century, and of Sidney and Beatrice Webb, of the World Bank and of the Specialized UN Development Agencies have shown.

Finally, it might be asked whether it is important to know the facts about poverty. We may say "Yes", because what we know, or think we know, enters into our theories, models and policies. Ill-informed or ignorant action can be ineffective or counter-productive. It can contribute to the aggravation of poverty. In the attempt to help one group we may hurt another, or even the one chosen. On the other hand, firm knowledge is very hard to gain. The fate of the English poor during the early Industrial Revolution is still an unsettled issue. Action cannot wait for the results of research, and proposals to study sometimes serve as excuses for inaction. We have to act on whatever inadequate knowledge we possess, as best we can.

APPENDIX

Hunger

1. Introduction

The need for food is perhaps the most basic of all human needs. People must eat, even if they drink unsafe water, are illiterate, and are not inoculated or vaccinated against diseases. Poor people spend between 70 and 80 per cent of their total income on food, and more than 50 per cent of any additional income above subsistence levels. The poorest of the poor continue to spend the same proportion on food as their pitiful incomes rise, until they reach the point when this proportion begins to decline. As their incomes rise further, they spend a smaller proportion on food, of that smaller proportion a smaller proportion on cereals, and of that smaller proportion a smaller proportion on the cheaper cereals. Lack of adequate food makes people not only hungry and less able to enjoy life, it also reduces their ability and, by causing apathy and in extreme cases lethargy, their willingness to work productively, and thereby to raise the means to combat their hunger. In addition, it makes them more susceptible to disease by reducing their immunity to infection and other environmental stresses. Prolonged malnutrition among babies and young children leads to reduced adult stature; severe malnutrition is associated with decreased brain size and cell number, as well as altered brain chemistry. Malnutrition of women during pregnancy results in low birth weight of their children, which is a particularly important cause of infant mortality. Children who suffer from severe malnutrition show lags in motor activity, hearing, speech, social and personal behaviour, problem-solving ability, eye-hand coordination and categorization behaviour, even after rehabilitation.

Hunger in this essay includes all conditions resulting from inadequate food intake. From acute starvation in a famine, to liability to illness and debility due to food deficits, to energy deficits leading to apathy that are not experienced as hunger, to undernutrition, malnutrition and the occasional pangs of hunger experienced by poor people, that do not have

57

harmful effects on life or work. Excluded from consideration is hunger of those who have the capacity to satisfy it but do not wish to do so because they are fasting for religious reasons, or are on hunger strike, or wish to conform to some model figure, or suffer from anorexia nervosa, etc. The distinction is interesting because it brings out the need to differentiate between capabilities, functionings, commodities, needs and utilities.[1] If we wanted to isolate achievements, the fasting monk and the protester on hunger strike would be included among the undernourished, and their freedom of choice to forgo the food would be registered under a separate indicator. A case can be made for either treatment.

Among the world's chronically hungry people are the ultrapoor, the landless and nearly landless labourers, young children of poor families, pregnant and lactating women, and the old. They live in Asia, on the Indian sub-Continent and in Indonesia and the Philippines, and in Sub-Saharan Africa. They constitute about 10-15 percent of households, containing 15-20 percent of the population and 17-25 percent of pre-school children in these countries. About a billion people consume less food than they would like, continue to spend this same proportion on food as their incomes rise, and hundreds of millions are handicapped by undernutrition.

According to a World Bank study there are 340 million people in the developing countries suffering from nutritional deprivation (inadequate calories to prevent stunted growth and serious health risk), which represents about 16 per cent of their populations. In low-income countries this proportion rises to 23 per cent. The same study suggests that 730 million people suffer from undernourishment by having "not enough calories for an active working life". This amounts to 34 per cent of the population of all developing countries and 51 per cent of the low-income countries. A study by Reutlinger and Alderman[2] estimates the number of undernourished at over 800 million people.

Hunger and malnutrition today are not mainly the result of a global shortage of food. So far, over the long run, Malthusian predictions of population increasing faster than food have not come true. Current world production of grain alone could provide everyone with more than 3,000 calories and 65 grams of protein daily. It has been estimated that 2 per cent of the world's grain output would be sufficient to elim-

1. See SEN, *Resources, Values and Development*; *The Standard of Living*; *Commodities and Capabilities*, Amsterdam: North Holland, 1985; and JEAN DRÈZE and AMARTYA SEN, *Hunger and Public Action*, Oxford: Clarendon Press, 1989.

2. SHLOMO REUTLINGER and H. ALDERMAN, 'The Prevalence of Calorie-Deficient Diets in Developing Countries,' *World Development*, vol. 8 no. 4, April 1980.

inate malnutrition among the world's 500 million malnourished. Between 1950 and 1984 real cereal prices - the amount of manufactured goods that could be bought with a ton of cereal - fell by over a third - i.e. by 1.3 per cent per year.

It is true that since 1984 world food production per head has fallen (between 1986 and 1988 by 14 percent) and is now (1989) back at where it was about two decades ago. The agricultural resource base has deteriorated, new technologies have not been forthcoming or not been applied at the same rate as before, and depressed farm prices have discouraged production. Population growth has continued to be high. So, at least at the moment of writing, problems of supply are once again in the foreground. And some observers argue that the rapid growth of grain production per head since 1973 was achieved by overploughing land and overpumping water, with the result that soils were eroded and water tables dropped - an unsustainable situation.

Malnutrition is not primarily a problem of an imbalance between calories and protein. Most surveys have found that if energy intake is adequate, protein needs are also satisfied, and if not, protein is burned up for energy requirements.

The problem is not only one of production, but also of distribution: it is not primarily physical food shortages, but social and political arrangements at the international level that are responsible for the unprecedented amount of hunger and malnutrition. It is the fact that hunger today is unnecessary that makes its continued existence so shocking. The productive capacity of the world is now capable of feeding all the mouths in existence, yet it fails to do so. The problem is partly one of the distribution between countries, regions and income groups, between sexes and within households. In general, it is the very poor, who spend most of their income on food, who suffer most from hunger and malnutrition. In many countries more than 40 per cent of the population suffer from calorie-deficient diets, and about 15 per cent show deficiencies of more than 400 calories per day. Within families it appears that children, and in some societies, such as North India and Bangladesh, women, particularly when pregnant or lactating, receive inadequate amounts of food. Calorie deficiencies vary by geographical area, season and year.

The production of cereals by developing countries grew between 1961 and 1980 at an annual rate of 2.9 per cent, while consumption grew at 3.2 per cent per year. As a result, cereal imports in the developing countries grew from about 15 million metric tons to 64 million tons. In the same period cereal production in the advanced countries

59

grew by 3.1 per cent per year but consumption by only 2.5 per cent. The difference was exported to the developing countries. Their share in world imports of cereals rose, as a result, from about 36 per cent to 43 per cent. Since the bulk of the increase in food production has occurred in the advanced countries, and since global redistribution through grants is ruled out for political reasons, developing countries must either earn more foreign exchange to buy the food, or grow substantially more food themselves. (Food availability in the developing countries increased from 208 kilograms per head in 1961 to 218 kilograms in 1976.) This is particularly true of Africa, until 1981 the only region in the world where food production has grown less rapidly than population. Since 1981 Latin America has also registered a drop in food production per head.

The other part of the solution is the generation of adequate incomes of the poor, including both production for their own consumption and cash to buy food in the market. For farmers this means security of tenure or ownership of land, a regular outlet for sales and a supply of credit. Extra food production is necessary to meet the additional demand created by population growth and higher incomes per head, and to prevent soaring food prices from cancelling the effects of higher purchasing power.

To achieve perfect nutritional standards is virtually impossible. A reasonable objective is to reduce the significant handicaps from nutritional deficiency. Many people in rich countries present medical problems from being overweight and obese, but no great social significance is attached to these ills. There may be as many as 7 million Americans suffering from malnutrition. In poor countries, people have adapted to mild cases of calorie deficiency by attaining a lower weight and height, by being less active, and, in the case of women, by ovulating less regularly.

Growth of incomes and of food production, important though they are, are not sufficient to eliminate hunger and malnutrition. Receiving more food does not necessarily meet the nutritional needs of poor people. It may simply meet the needs of the worms in their stomachs. Hunger and malnutrition is a problem of the pathology of the environment, and raising food intake by itself may not help. Cases have been recorded where it made things worse, because the extra food consumption of the earning members of families was matched by extra physical efforts, and the rest of the family got less. In other cases, extra income was spent not on food, and nutritional standards fell, as families moved out of the subsistence-oriented economy and became subject to the

influences of the market. It may be that it is not more food that is needed, but education, safe water, medical services, reduced work loads,
fewer unwanted pregnancies, shorter walks to or between work places,
counter-pressures to advertisements, or a land reform to permit people
to make better use of their higher incomes and of the additional food
supply. Food needs can sometimes be met more effectively by reducing
requirements rather than by raising availabilities.

Raising the real incomes of the poor so that they can buy more food
is clearly one important way of reducing hunger and improving nutrition. But this is a slow and cumbersome process and there are speedier
and more direct ways. Iodine deficiency, which can cause goiter, apathy, and proneness to other diseases, is easily remedied by iodizing salt.
More difficult to remedy are deficiencies in vitamin A, which can cause
blindness and death in children, and deficiencies in iron, which lead to
anaemia and reduced productive power. Protein-energy malnutrition,
which may cause irreversible brain damage in children and apathy in
adults, is the most difficult to remedy. Yet, it is the most serious problem in malnutrition, followed by deficiencies in iron and vitamin A.

Apart from the emergency of famine, nutrition policies for the chronically malnourished poor call for a long-term, sustained effort. Intervention can take the form of agricultural policy, supplementary feeding, food fortification programmes, food subsidies and rationing, and
complementary policies (such as employment creation) in non-food sectors. Particularly important are policies for foreign trade and the exchange rate, which determine how much the farmer gets for his crop.

The entitlement approach to hunger and malnutrition, pioneered by
A.K. Sen,[1] suggests that diversified employment and earning opportunities are as important as growing more food. It is true that this creates
risks, such as the decline in markets or the rise in the price of food, but
there are also risks in aiming at food self-sufficiency: harvests may fail
or the soil may deteriorate. The need to consider such options is particularly important for Africa, where food production has fallen behind
population increase. The best solution may be not to grow more food,
but to create diverse, remunerative export industries.

Since hunger is largely a problem of poverty, and since the poor
spend their money on different kinds of food from the rich, policies that
encourage greater production of poor people's food – such as cassava,

---

1. *Poverty and Famines: An Essay on Entitlement and Famines*, Oxford: Clarendon Press
and New York: Oxford University Press, 1981 and Drèze and Sen, *Hunger and Public
Action*.

corn, sorghum and millet – can help reduce hunger and malnutrition. Food marketing and storage programmes can reduce regional, seasonal, and annual shortfalls in supplies and increases in prices. Policies to encourage production of food for the poor should extend to all aspects of agricultural policy, including research into new varieties, extension programmes, credit and marketing.

Supplementary feeding may take place in schools, at work, or at clinics for pregnant or lactating women. With the receipt of extra institutional food, however, meals at home may be curtailed, so that the vulnerable groups do not get much additional food, and, at least in the case of schoolchildren, these programmes do not reach the groups particularly at risk, such as children below school age. Here again, the ease of intervention (because schools already exist and delivery is cheap) is inversely related to its importance. Food supplementation at the work place, if neither the food nor the extra energy is diverted to other activities, serves both a basic need and productivity.

Special foods and food fortification, as in the case of protein and vitamin fortification and salt iodization, have been successful up to a point, though they meet with both technical and political difficulties. General subsidies to food are very expensive, absorbing up to 20 per cent of budgetary expenditure in some countries, and selective programmes, such as food stamps, are difficult to administer. Programmes are easier and cheaper to administer if the subsidies are for food that is eaten only by the poor. Rich countries tend to tax poor urban food consumers in order to subsidize relatively better off farmers. Poor countries have tended, at least until recently, to tax (often indirectly and in a disguised form) poor farmers in order to subsidize food such as high-quality wheat and rice that is consumed by the better-off urban groups. But among the poorest are rural landless labourers and urban dwellers who have to buy food and are sometimes helped by these subsidies.

An efficient and equitable system of subsidies to poor consumers that does not penalize poor producers of food is expensive and both administratively and politically difficult. When agricultural prices are increased as an incentive to production, measures should be taken to prevent greater malnutrition among those poor who have to buy food. Some countries have successfully overcome these difficulties.

The eradication of hunger and malnutrition is not only a problem of making the land more fertile and women less fertile. Action is needed on other fronts. Safe water and the prevention of intestinal diseases would enable people to absorb the same amount of food more effectively. Less time spent on collecting firewood and water, or on walking between unconsolidated plots of land, would reduce the food required for women. So would a reduction in unwanted pregnancies or premature deaths of babies. Education can help people to avoid diseases, such as diarrhoea, thereby raising absorption of food, and it can help them spend their money more wisely on nutritious food and prepare food more economically and hygienically; they can learn to complement their diet with local food; educated women tend to marry later and have fewer children. The battle against early weaning and against the use of baby formula has hit the headlines, but the desire of women to cease breast feeding is often part of the general process of modernization and urbanization, and the desire to emulate the more advanced groups in the country.

Hunger and malnutrition are the result of a complex set of conditions, all stemming from poverty. But although most people suffering from calorie deficiencies are poor, not all poor people suffer from such deficiencies. Some quite high-income countries and groups of people suffer from considerable malnutrition, and some low-income countries have none. Amartya K. Sen has said that the danger today does not arise from Malthusian pessimism (the fear that food production does not rise with population), but from Malthusian optimism (the false belief that if we have solved the problem of food production, we have solved the problem of hunger).

The eradication of hunger is ultimately a question of the political power of the poor. It is sometimes said that free markets give everyone access to the labour force, and thereby to the opportunity to earn enough to meet all needs. But, as Partha Dasgupta has pointed out,[1] "at systematically low levels of nutrition-intake a person's capacity for work is affected adversely. There is thus a possible vicious circle here. Those who have not title to non-wage income are vulnerable in the market for labour, their sole means of generating income." Not until basic needs are met can the market mechanism be said to guarantee productive work.

While power structures and the alignment of interest groups are such that entitlements to adequate food supplies are denied to the poor, hunger will continue. In some conditions, the interest of the ruling group can be harnessed to alleviate poverty and hunger. Infectious

1. PARTHA DASGUPTA, 'Power and Control in the Good Polity', in *The Good Polity*, edited by ALAN HAMLIN and PHILIP PETTIT, Oxford: Basil Blackwell, 1989; see also PARTHA DESGUPTA and DEBRAJ RAY, 'Inequality as a Determinant of Malnutrition and Unemployement: Theory', *Economic Journal*, vol. 96, 1986 and 'Inequality as a Determinant of Malnutrition and Unemployement: Practice', *Economic Journal*, vol. 97, 1987.

diseases do not draw the line at class or income boundaries. The repeal of the Corn Laws in 1846 was in the interest of the industrial classes because it provided cheap food and low wages. A well-nourished, healthy and educated labour force is a more efficient labour force. But while such interests can be harnessed to hunger removal, in the last resort it is the access to political power of the poor themselves which alone can guarantee adequate food supplies to all. This does not mean that only one type of political system can guarantee hunger eradication. Historical evidence has shown that a wide variety of regimes have eliminated the worst types of hunger within a short period. But some types of regimes make this achievement impossible. Some form of participation of the poor in making the decisions that affect their life and work is helpful, though not a necessary condition. But ultimately, the problem of eradicating hunger is a political problem rather than a nutritional or economic one.

2. The Need for a Multi-Pronged Attack

To understand and combat hunger, malnutrition and undernutrition, we must abandon the notion that these are simply the result of an imbalance between food production and population. We have seen that hunger is the result of the pathology of the environment. Many factors determine this environment. They can be roughly divided into factors working on the supply of food and those working on the impact of available food on nutritional status. A principal objective of agricultural policies in developing countries is to raise the rate of growth of the production of food. A useful mnemotechnic device is to divide the factors on the supply side on which policies must work into six "Ins".

1. Incentives (or prices)
2. Inputs
3. Innovation (technology)
4. Information (diffusion of technologies through extension) services)
5. Infrastructure
6. Institutions (credit, marketing, land reform)

These six "Ins" or *In*struments provide a framework for understanding and eradicating hunger. Incentives are important for stimulating farmers to grow more food. It is the prices that farmers get for their crops in relation to the prices they have to pay for their inputs and their consumer goods that determine how much and what kinds of food crop are produced. But price incentives are not enough. Farmers must also have access to inputs: fertilizer, equipment, water, credit, etc. With limited land and labour, and a given technology, food supply runs into rapidly diminishing returns. We also need technologies to raise production with given resources: new high-yielding varieties, irrigation, etc. It is the role of innovation, of technical progress, which has for 200 years postponed the Malthusian limits. Technical progress has been largely institutionalized. Technological innovation is of no use unless the information is disseminated and accepted by farmers. We also need an appropriate infrastructure of roads, harbours, railways, storage facilities, etc., to get the crops to the markets and the inputs to the farmers. Without such a distributional network, incentives and innovations are frustrated. And we need social infrastructure – education, health and nutrition – to produce an efficient rural labour force. Finally, we need institutions, such as rural banks, efficient marketing institutions that buy, store, transport, ship and process the crops from producers to consumers and that bring the inputs to the farmers. To these we should add the need to change the composition of agricultural output in favour of the higher-value crops, as long as the risks attached to growing and selling these do not exceed the extra benefits. Some of these "Ins" are best provided by a market, others by action in the public sector. It is the complementary and supplementary actions of the private and public sectors that produce the results, e.g. the combination of correct pricing policies for food, with the provision of roads and vehicles and research.

Complex and difficult choices arise within each of the six "Ins". Consider infrastructure, normally at least partly provided at public expense. There are choices between physical, legal, human, social and producer-specific types of infrastructure to be made; choices between centralized and decentralized types of infrastructure, choices between infrastructure for small, deficit farmers and the landless versus large farmers, producers and consumers, choices between maintenance of existing and new projects, and choices between different methods of financing expenditure on infrastructure. The same is true for institutions and for information. Should, for example, extension workers concentrate on single lines of conveying information or should they combine several? All these activities compete for scarce resources with directly productive investment in food production.

Another set of choices arises in the phasing or sequencing of the six "Ins". Where infrastructure, institutions and innovation are already in place, it will suffice to emphasize price incentives. Alternatively, some of these "Ins" can be induced by others. Prices can stimulate innovation,[1] institutions and even public action on infrastructure. In other cases, action on one front can be a substitute for action on others. Heavy public subsidies to well-chosen inputs can be a substitute for higher prices of outputs. Phasing and sequencing are of the utmost importance, since most countries are too poor to do everything at once.

The six "Ins" refer mainly to the supply side of food for the eradication of hunger. As we have seen, measures are also needed for creating remunerative employment and incomes, for health and education, for reducing food requirements through eliminating unnecessary work (e.g. land consolidation to eliminate long walks between plots) and unwanted pregnancies, for population control and family planning, and for the distribution of food within households. Even with more than adequate food supplies and incomes, people starve either because parasites in their stomachs or because parasitic landlords-moneylenders, or, in some societies, because male heads of households deprive them of access to the nutritional benefits of food. The attack on hunger comprises reforms at the micro-micro level, what goes on within the family, at the micro- and meso-level, how macropolicies affect particular groups, at the macro-economic level, what happens to the exchange rate, and at the macro-macro or global level, what is the system of land distribution and money lending. It also involves changes in the power structure and at all intermediate levels, both private and public, and at the global level.

Food policy makers start from a fundamental dilemma. Should they keep food prices high in order to encourage production of food and raise the supply for all, including the poor in the long run, at the risk of hunger and starvation of poor food buyers in the short run? Or should they keep food prices low in order to ensure affordable food for poor buyers at the risk of aggravating food shortages in the future? The dilemma is aggravated by the fact that many food producers are also poor. There are two ways of resolving the dilemma. First, the policy makers may set high prices and then take specific measures such as rationing and subsidies to protect poor buyers. Or they may set low prices and compensate producers by subsidies to inputs or to their crops. The third horn of the dilemma is that the capacity to raise tax revenue or to administer rationing or fair price shops is very scarce in developing countries.

1. Yujiro Hayami and Vernon W. Ruttan, *Agricultural Development: An International Perspective*, Baltimore: John Hopkins University Press, 1971, 2nd revised edition, 1984.

Another dilemma is whether to "target" food subsidies on the most needy groups or cover a wider group, possibly the whole population. There are bound to be leakages either way. It is very difficult to implement a programme that covers *all* the poor, and *only* the poor. Wider coverage can become very costly, narrower coverage runs the danger of leaving out needy people. It also taxes scarce administrative capacity. It is better to err on the side of excess coverage, and recuperate some of the revenue through forms of taxes that do not hit the most vulnerable, at least directly, such as a tax on alcohol or cigarettes.[1]

The multi-pronged attack applies also to the agents. We think normally of government action through taxes, subsidies, employment programmes, feeding programmes, etc. But non-governmental organizations such as Oxfam and private agents also have important roles. For example, Amartya K. Sen[2] has shown the importance of a free press, both as an early warning system about impending famines and as a pressure group on governments to respond quickly and adequately to threats of famine.

3. Export Crops Versus Food for Domestic Consumption

There has been a good deal of discussion of the respective merits of export crops and food for domestic consumption. Some have argued that if the comparative advantage points to export crops, it is they that should be promoted and the foreign exchange earned be used for inputs into agriculture or industry, or even for food imports. On the other hand, there have been those who have argued that export crops impoverish the poor, deprive the people of food, and lower nutritional standards. It has also been argued that they are ecologically destructive.

A parallel debate has gone on over the respective merits of marketing more food, whether for the domestic market or for exports, against growing more food for consumption within the farm household that grows it. Some of the arguments that apply to the debate on exports versus food for domestic consumption also apply to the debate on more marketing versus more production for own consumption.

Clearly much depends on the institutional arrangements. If export crops are grown on large plantations, perhaps owned by foreigners,

---

1. For a fuller discussion, see the Fifth Lecture.

2. AMARTYA K. SEN, 'Development: Which Way Now?', *Economic Journal*, vol. 93, 1983, reprinted in *Resources, Values and Development*; DRÈZE and SEN, *Hunger and Public Action*.

which generate little employment, while food is grown by small farmers, the impact on income distribution will be different according to which type of crop is promoted. If the foreign exchange earned by export crops accrues to the government and it spends it on arms or office buildings, while the receipts from food would have gone to the poor peasants, again the distributional impact will be different.

The interesting fact, at least in Africa, is that there is little evidence that there is a necessary conflict between the two. Where land and labour are not scarce, the movements in export crops go in the same direction as the movements in the production of food for domestic consumption. There is also little evidence that nutritional standards have suffered as a result of the growth of export crops, though sugar in Kenya may be an exception. There are several reasons for this. First, certain services can be in joint supply and help both export crops and food. Among these are extension, marketing, and supplies of inputs. Similarly, equipment and fertilizer can be used to raise the production of both. It can also be the case that similar complementarities exist on the side of demand: the demand for food by the farmers who grow export crops creates a stable market for local food supplies and encourages their increase. For some export crops, such as cotton, a part of the export crop can be used as food, in the form of edible oil, or as feed in the form of cottonseed cake.

In spite of the positive relationship between export crops and food in some conditions, clearly conflicts can arise. Where there has been in the past unwarranted discrimination against food crops, there is a case for removing that discrimination. Colonial governments have tended to favour export crops by improving infrastructure, such as transport, marketing and distribution services, compared with facilities for domestic food consumption. Research activities and extension services also have been concentrated on export crops, particularly if linked to large firms with market power and capacity to process the crops and make profits by raising prices in the face of an inelastic demand. On the other hand, export crops have often borne higher taxes than food crops and are more easily controlled by governments, since they often grow in specialized regions, they have to pass through ports, the buyers are more concentrated, etc. But economists have a bias in favour of trade, whether international or intranational, and against locally consumed food. Such biases, where they exist, should be removed.

Some scholars have gone further and have criticized colonial governments for destroying the integrated farming-herding systems which, in precolonial times, protected the ecology while allowing substantial food production. In Africa, in precolonial days, farmers opened their fields in the dry season to pastoralists who brought their herds to graze on the harvested millet and sorghum stalks. The animals were fed through the grazing, they manured and fertilized the soil with their dung, and the cattle hooves broke up the earth around the plant stalks, allowing oxygenation of the soil. The herdsmen traded their milk for the farmers' grain, and people, animals and land were simultaneously maintained. The introduction of monocrop cash production (peanuts, cotton) by colonial governments destroyed this system. In addition, well digging concentrated animals round watering sites and their trampling turned them into small deserts. Post-colonial production further encouraged this erosion of land, and in the view of some contributed to the present famines. It is, however, not clear how the traditional system could have been maintained in the face of a rapidly growing population.

In some cases export crops face an inelastic world demand. Then production should be curtailed and total proceeds raised, unless current price rises reduce future demand, appropriately discounted, by more than present gains. Such reasoning underlies the attempts to design commodity aggreements for tea, cocoa, coffee, sugar, spices, etc. Much current research is devoted to raising further the productivity and production of such export crops, not always to the benefit of the growers. The difficulty here is that, in the absence of effective commodity agreements, the national efforts of small countries are not coordinated with those of the growers and exporters in other competing countries.

A shift to export crops sometimes reduces the role of women in societies in which they traditionally produce, prepare and distribute food. In spite of the higher family income earned, this can lead to a reduction in nutritional standards. Sometimes the men migrate to other areas and leave their families with less food. But few generalizations are possible. Sometimes women increase their labour in food crop production to compensate for the reduced labour of men, sometimes producing surplus output for sale, thus raising both their income and their independence. A case is reported from Cameroon where men took up cocoa, coffee and bananas, abandoning the food farms they had previously cultivated. Women took up the slack. But the women grew the food crops in an entirely different way from the men, using a system of cultivation which involved small, daily outputs of labour throughout the growing season, in contrast to the men who had cultivated a combination of crops, requiring occasional short peaks of concentrated labour.

The result was an increase in total output, of export crops and of food crops, where the additional food was grown by fewer people (only women) who used more labour-intensive techniques than the average labour intensity of men and women combined in the past.

The impact of changes to export crops on (a) expenditure patterns as a result of cash accruing to different members of the family, and in large, discontinuous lumps rather than as a steady flow, (b) distribution of food to different members of the family, and (c) the allocation of time and effort by women to different types of work, are important areas of study. On the other hand, a shift to export crops may raise employment opportunities and therefore offer more people access to food. Jute is produced more labour-intensively than rice. A shift from rice to jute in Bangladesh therefore creates more jobs and contributes to better nutrition.

A good deal depends on the distribution of land and the mode of agricultural production. If export crops benefit large plantations or commercial farms, whereas food is mainly produced by small farmers or their wives, a switch to export crops can aggravate inequality in access to resources, income earning power and land ownership. (Examples are sugar in Jamaica and cotton in El Salvador, but even in Africa the trade bias has favoured the large export-oriented farm and firm.) Export crops are often grown more efficiently in large farms, and the change-over can lead to an impoverishment of small farmers. In African countries, additional export earnings tend to increase the income of small farmers, and the extra foreign exchange contributes to the ability to break bottlenecks in transport and agricultural inputs, which are important for food production. This was certainly the case in Tanzania in the early eighties.

How much should be devoted to export crops is also determined by trends in the cost of international transport, which in turn is affected by oil prices. The lower these costs, the stronger the case for international trade. Expectations of higher future transport costs, other things remaining equal, would justify a move towards reduced dependence on foreign trade.

Foreign exchange is often one of the scarcest resources, while its increase can make fuller use of many domestic resources possible and contribute to greater food production, as well as to higher imports of food itself. It has already been mentioned that it is sometimes possible to increase the production of both export crops and food for domestic consumption, particularly if improved technologies are introduced. In some cases the opportunity costs of increasing exports are very small, and the choice does not arise. Land may be plentiful, and little labour and other inputs be required. Where domestic food production does decline, it is possible to encourage home gardens simultaneously with the expansion of export cash crops to ensure continuing adequate nutrition. A Kenyan Ministry of Health study of 1979 showed little evidence that five export crops (coffee, tea, cotton, pyrethrum and sugar cane) had been detrimental to nutritional status. We have seen that the only possible exception was sugar cane.

However, some qualifications are needed to the notion that resource allocation should be guided by comparative advantage, so that a comparative advantage in an export crop can buy more food from abroad than would be produced at home. The comparative advantage is not God-given but itself determined by the direction of research, and research has been heavily biased in favour of export crops and the staple grains, to the neglect of "inferior" food such as millet, sorghum and cassava. With the growing importance of human capital, the direction of comparative advantage can be quite strongly influenced by research, extension services, education, and other forms of investment in human beings. It is no longer only or even mainly "endowments" that determine specialization in international trade, but conscious policy decisions.

Recently, there have been some successes in research on these "inferior" food crops. In Zimbabwe hybrid varieties of maize, in the Sudan high-yielding, drought-resistant strains of sorghum, and in Nigeria a disease-resistant variety of cassava with three times the yield of native strains, have been developed. But a complete elimination of the bias in favour of export crops, combined with the provision of credit and delivery systems would change the comparative advantage and convey benefits to poor people. There is also some evidence that poor people are more likely to produce the things they themselves consume, and to consume the things they produce. There are several reasons for this. First, when households switch from semi-subsistence cropping for their own needs to monocropping for export, their incomes may rise but their nutritional status drop. Second, monocropping for export may raise the risk of crop failure, even though the average returns are higher. Third, export crops often take a long time to mature, and the outcome may turn out to be less profitable than expected. Fourth, there is a distributional consideration in favour of growing food. There are two dangers in simply raising the productivity of the poor by switching to export crops.

First, there may not be adequate demand for the things they produce, or export taxes may be levied, or marketing margins may be high; and, second, the price of food, on which they will want to spend

71

a large part of their income, may rise sharply, particularly if the change involves shortages of food in local markets. These two dangers are more likely to be avoided if the poor can meet their own needs in somewhat more self-sufficient units than would be indicated by a strict application of the theory of exchange and comparative advantage. This applies to families and households, to villages, to nations and to groups of poor nations. There are distributional advantages in this mutual meeting of basic needs which have to be set against the conventional claims of the aggregate gains from trade, which may be greater but less well distributed, more uncertain, or longer delayed.

In some countries such as Zambia, Mali and Tanzania, a dilemma arises. The above arguments for encouraging smallholder production of food for local consumption are strong. At the same time, foreign exchange scarcities constitute a bottleneck to expansion because they reduce the availability of consumer goods, fuel, transport equipment and fertilizer. If productivity in food production is to be raised, growth of inputs is necessary, and this frequently depends on importing these inputs. Productivity growth depends crucially on moving towards machinery, fertilizer and pesticides which often have to be imported and cost foreign exchange. Imports have been scaled down to the minimum, so that, without extra aid, an increase in exports is the only solution. Local food production and consumption cannot be raised without raising exports, but exports can be raised only by curtailing food for local consumption. Non-project, untied foreign aid combined with the right policies can transform this vicious circle into a virtuous one.

Generalizations, such as export crops are grown on large farms, food crops on small; export crops are grown as monocrops, food crops in diversified farming enterprises; or use more or less female labour, are quite impossible to justify, though they are often made. Some progress has been made by combining output, sales and methods of production in different ways. The best guideline is to avoid dogmatism on this issue and to promote policies that raise and stabilize the incomes of poor people, whether through exports or food for domestic consumption or both, and to make sure that they have access to the food.

To sum up the controversy: the passionate opponents of export crops, the value productivity of which is often higher than that of food production, have, on the whole, not provided good reasons for their attack, but there is a kernel of truth in their criticism of the advocates of comparative advantage as a guide to foreign trade. This can be summed up under the following headings.

1. Comparative advantage can change, particularly as a result of

changes in the direction of research and human capital formation.

2. The institutional arrangements as to who benefits from foreign sales (government through export taxes, parastatals, foreign firms, plantations, large commercial farmers) and from domestic production of food (small farmers) make an important difference.

3. Local production and local markets of food can be harmed or destroyed by foreign trade. In spite of higher earnings to the country, local food prices may rise or certain foodstuffs may cease to be available. But local self-sufficiency in food, like national self-sufficiency, may also harm the poor.

4. Higher incomes to the growers do not always mean that nutritional standards of all members of their families are improved.

5. Export crops sometimes carry higher risks in production, the costs of foreign transport, and foreign demand.

6. The distribution of benefits (and power) between men and women, and between government and private agents, may be different.

7. Foreign trade contributes to a change in tastes which can both make the country more vulnerable and reduce nutritional standards.

8. Monocropping for export can be ecologically harmful.

9. In many situations experience has shown that food and export production are not alternatives but complementary.

4. Distribution of Food Within the Family

In the past, it tended to be assumed that if the head of a household earns enough income to feed all members of his family, they will be adequately fed. More recently, the distribution of food within the family was more closely examined. The results are still controversial. According to some, women and children, especially girls below 4 years old, are discriminated against in favour of adult men and boys. According to others, such discrimination is greatly exaggerated. Where children and women receive less food than adult men, this can be partly explained in terms of their lower requirements, their working less or their lower productivity. It is generally agreed that in some cultures, such as Bangladesh and Northern India, girls below 4 are suffering from food discrimination. Of course, there are disproportionately many small children in poor families, and they are among the most vulnerable groups. It may also be that poor families have to concentrate on feeding the member most likely to bring in earnings, and that is often the male adult. In Africa, female children are favoured compared with males. In many cultures it is the women who dispose the food; they control grain stores and deplete them to feed themselves and their families. It is not likely that they will be entirely subservient to the selfish demands of their husbands.

If poor families suffer from hunger and undernutrition, it is not always best to raise their income, however desirable this may be on other grounds, if we are concerned with raising the nutritional status of their children. The GOBI package designed and propagated by UNICEF – growth charts, oral rehydration, breast feeding and inoculation – may be a more effective and quicker way to improve children's nutrition, where they had been suffering from diarrhoea.

Seasonal fluctuations in food consumption increase the damage both by making the shortfalls worse for the very poor, and by increasing their number compared with a count taken on an average day. The range of benign adaptation for any given individual is likely to be exceeded, and more individuals will drop into the group of severely undernourished. In Gambia, for example, women's weight declined between pre-harvest and post-harvest seasons by 5 kilograms, and food intake per day was 60 calories lower. In Bangladesh the difference in calorie consumption per kg dropped from 62 to 50. Some of these variations may be planned. The variations may correspond to variations in required work or to the high cost and wastage of storing food. Temporarily raising body weight may be the best way to overcome these difficulties. As we have seen, there may also be a range of benign adaptation. But for very poor people the shortfalls indicate serious stress, particularly since the periods of low intake coincide with increases in diseases and infections and higher prices of food bought.

5. Engel's and Bennett's Laws

There are several regularities in food consumption, which have been formulated in "laws". Engel's law states that the proportion of a family's budget devoted to food declines as the family's income rises. Although it is sometimes derived from the proposition that the capacity of the stomach is limited, it should be noted that it is expenditure, not amount of food eaten, that Engel's law applies to. Calories consumed level off well before expenditure. The law does not apply to very poor families, whose expenditure rises proportionately or even more than proportionately, as their incomes increase. It is between 80 and 85 per cent of their total outlay. The poverty line has at times been defined as

74

that level of income at which the proportion of expenditure on food begins to decline. It is among members of the group below this poverty line that the risk of nutritional damage is greatest.

Bennett's law states that the ratio of starchy staple foods consumed declines as incomes rise. Starchy staples, comprising mainly grain and root crops, are the cheapest form of food. As incomes rise, families diversify their consumption into dearer calories. The quality of food, measured by prices paid for it, rises with income. When income is calculated for the purpose of testing these laws, addictive expenditures (e.g. on cigarettes) and interest on loans may have to be deducted before determining available income, for they do not represent discretionary components of income. While Engel's law refers to expenditure on food, relative to income, Bennett's law refers to sources of food calories relative to income. A third law says that the average quality of food calories, measured by prices, rises with incomes.

Until recently the number of undernourished people was greatly overestimated as 40-60 per cent of the population in low-income countries such as India or Nigeria. The true figure is nearer 10-15 per cent. The reasons for past overestimates are many, but largely an overestimate of required calories, neglect of the ability of people to adapt, within a range, to lower food intake without damage, and various statistical reasons relating to differences in climate, work load, and age- and sex-structure. Food requirements depend not only on climate, work, age, size and sex, but also vary both between individuals and for any given individual for different times. People can also adapt, within a range, whose width is controversial, and for a time, to lower food intake without damage. This does not mean that there are not many more deprived people than undernourished people. The 40-60 per cent may well lack many of the ingredients that make human life worth living (adequate shelter, schooling, health services, productive assets, access to power) and they may suffer from time to time from hunger and deprivation. But they are not chronically undernourished, and they require different projects and policies. The poor need more and better schooling, safe water, better health care, more productive assets and more power. But food deficiency is not their main problem. Giving them more food may simply leave them poor and fat. It is, however, the main problem for the ultrapoor whose principal need is higher nutritional status. These ultrapoor spend, as we have seen, 80-85 per cent of their income on food, and this ratio does not fall as their income rises. They also consume very cheap, especially cereal calories, whereas less-poor people spend large portions of increases in incomes on tastier and dearer calories.

Weight for height (in adults), height for age and weight for age (in children) are measures of undernutrition. Extreme shortfalls can lead to impaired physical development, leading to stunting, threatening mental development and even survival. But to feed more to children suffering from only moderate shortfalls may only lead to obesity. Other measures, such as better schooling, safer water or better health care deserve higher priority. Provided weight for height is adequate, low height for age probably has few disadvantages for adolescents and adults.

It might at first be thought that if people have enough income to buy adequate amounts of food for all members of the family, hunger is absent. But adequate income is not enough. For any given level of income there are wide variations in nutritional standards achieved. First, average income for a country may conceal wide differences in the distribution, and countries like Libya or South Africa, with quite high incomes, include many people below the poverty line. Second, the relative price of food may be different between countries and income groups. Even though total income is adequate for one country or one income group, higher prices of food, even though compensated by lower prices of other goods, put these groups at nutritional risk. Third, for the same income level, the amount and quality of social services, particularly health and education, provided free, will vary between countries, so that for the same income level and income distribution, different performances will be registered. Fourth, there are gaps between income received and available for expenditure which are due to constraining obligations such as rent, interest payments, and perhaps some forms of addiction such as smoking. Fifth, food needs will vary according to the size, age, and sex composition and the amount of work of members of the household. Sixth, even for the same age, sex, climate and activity food needs vary for different individuals and for the same individual at different times.

6. International Trade in Food

In the twenty-five years between 1960 and 1985 international trade in food increased both absolutely and as a ratio of total food supplies. In 1960 world imports of food were about 8 per cent of production, in 1985 12 percent. Food imports by developing countries doubled in terms of calories per head in the 1970s and then increased very little in the 80s. By the mid-1980s imports provided about 15 per cent of their total food calories. This growing dependence gave rise to serious problems. Commercial food imports cost foreign exchange. Some developing countries were faced with serious debt service problems. At the same time the prices of their export commodities had fallen to all time lows. Not only had domestic agriculture been discouraged by subsidized food imports, but tastes had been changed in the direction of wheat (of which imports by developing countries rose two and a half times in the 1970s), away from the commodities that could be produced in the developing countries economically.

As we have seen, by and large, the advanced and richer countries have taxed the majority of relatively less well off urban consumers to subsidize the better off minority of food growing farmers. In the poor, developing countries, the majority of the relatively poorer rural population, including the food growing farmers, have been exploited to subsidize the minority of better off urban communities. As a result, the world has produced large food surpluses in the advanced countries. Some of these have been used for food aid, others for commercial sales to socialist and developing countries.

But these policies have not been the only cause of the growing food exports from the developed to the developing countries. There are more fundamental forces at work. In the advanced countries, higher incomes are not spent on food. The growth of agricultural output due to research combined with the difficulty of redeploying resources from agriculture to other sectors, leads to a tendency to overproduce and export. In the developing countries, on the other hand, a large proportion of higher incomes is spent on food. Paradoxically, in those developing countries where domestic food production is growing fastest, the demand for imported food also grows rapidly. This is so because of the multiplier effects of agricultural growth on incomes and the demand for food, the autonomous growth of demand in other sectors, as well as the need to import feedstuffs for cattle. Demand for food and feed rises even more rapidly than the domestic supply of food. It is therefore the middle-income developing countries, in which food production has grown rapidly, which have been the booming markets for the food surpluses of the advanced countries.

7. Food Aid

International food aid can play a useful part in alleviating hunger in low-income countries, although its beneficial role has been disputed. Most obviously in cases of disaster, whether natural or man-made, it can provide emergency relief. Its role as a more permanent instrument of policy is more controversial, particularly because it can reduce incentives to grow food domestically, and therefore aggravate the longer-term problems of hunger.

There are at least seven criticisms that have been made of food aid, other than emergency famine relief. First, it reduces the pressure on recipient countries to carry out policy reforms, especially with respect to producer incentives and nutritional objectives. Second, it tends to depress domestic farm prices, to discourage domestic agricultural production and to reduce the spread of production-increasing agricultural technology. Third, it is unreliable, because it depends on donors' surpluses. When needs are greatest, i.e. when prices are high, it tends to dry up. Thus, in the plentiful year 1970 annual food aid exceeded 12.5 million tons, whereas in the food crisis of 1973-4, when the price of wheat rose by 50 per cent, annual shipments fell to below 6 million tons. Not only the amount and timing but also the country distribution serves the political, economic and military interests of donor countries. Thus in 1982 and 1983 Egypt received 18 per cent of the food aid distributed by the Food Aid Convention. Moreover, since donors make their allocations in terms of money, higher prices buy a smaller amount of grain. Fourth, if administered through state agencies, it is said to reinforce state hegemony over people and does not reach the poor. Fifth, it promotes an undesirable shift in consumption patterns away from staples and towards wheat and wheat flour. Sixth, it disrupts international commercial channels. Seventh, it leads to unfair burden sharing between donors, if the price of food contributions is overvalued.

The principal objection, that it discourages domestic agriculture by depressing prices, can be met by using the counterpart funds from the sale of the food aid at market-clearing prices to make deficiency payments to the farmers who would otherwise be injured, so that supply prices are restored to the level at which they would be without the food aid. (Even food distributed free, say in schools, frees budgetary revenue if the government would otherwise have paid for it.) In this way the amount by which expenditure on food aid reduces demand for domestic food is channelled back to the farmers and incentives are fully restored. The reason why this obvious solution has not been adopted more frequently is the budgetary/political constraint. Financially straitened governments normally find other uses for the collected revenue of greater importance and cannot, or do not wish to, collect additional revenue. The argument that counterpart funds should be used for deficiency payments to farmers applies also to subsidized food imports, or to those admitted at an overvalued exchange rate.

Food aid can also be used to finance additional food consumed by construction workers on infrastructure projects for agriculture. Or food aid can be linked with other forms of agricultural assistance to avoid neglect of agriculture. Or additionality of demand can be ensured by distributing the food or its money equivalent to the poorest households who could otherwise not afford it. But the importance of the charge has been greatly reduced, if not entirely eliminated, by the fact that many developing countries have become substantial food importers. (Only in low-income African countries is food aid increasing as a proportion of food imports.) In such a situation the traditional roles of food aid and financial aid are reversed. Food aid, in so far as it replaces commercial purchases, becomes fully convertible foreign exchange, whereas financial aid often remains tied to procurement, commodities or projects. It has, however, been argued that the free foreign exchange made available to governments presents an obstacle to fundamental reforms, such as devaluation of the exchange rate, or investment and reforms in agriculture, which would raise food production. This is not, however, an argument against food aid, but against all forms of intergovernmental aid. Such aid can be used either to support or to delay reforms.

Food aid can be used either as balance of payments support or as budgetary support. The two extreme cases are, first, where the food aid is wholly additional to commercial purchases and is sold by the government in open markets at market clearing prices, yielding government revenue in the form of counterpart funds of the maximum amount; or second, where the food aid wholly replaces commercial imports and the foreign exchange saved is used to buy other imports, or more food, or to repay debt.

Historically, there are many instances of food aid that did not harm domestic food production. Forty per cent of Marshall Aid consisted of food aid, yet European food production flourished, excessively. Similarly, South Korea, Israel and India received large amounts of food aid, without apparent long-term harm to their agriculture.

The charge of disruption of commercial sales is greatly reduced by the shrinking and now small role of food aid in total world food trade. If food aid wholly replaces commercial sales by the donor (the government pays the farmers what they otherwise would have earned) no disrupting effects on sales by other countries are suffered. Ensuring additionality, e.g. by linking it with job creation for poor people who spend a large portion of their income on food, also reduces the damage to commercial sales.

Additionality of supply is also important in order to meet the charge

79

that advanced countries that are commercial food importers are faced with higher prices than if, in the absence of food aid, the food had to be sold through commercial channels, lowering prices. The valuation of the food aid has to be done in such a manner as to ensure fair burden sharing between food surplus donor countries and food importing donor countries.

Another charge against food aid is that tastes depend, to some extent, on relative prices and food availabilities (and are not given exogenously, as is often assumed in economic analysis). A prolonged policy of finer grain imports changes tastes away from domestically produced foodstuffs and, it is alleged, increases dependency on foreign supplies. The situation has been described as analogous to drug addiction, countries becoming "hooked" on grain. It should, however, be remembered that these changes in tastes have many causes, connected with development and urbanization, with commercial import policies, with the growing value of time as incomes grow, and reduced time available to women to prepare food as they join the labour force, and that food aid is only one, possibly small, contributory cause.

The volume of food aid has been greatly reduced in the last 20 years. Food aid has, however, increased since 1975. In the sixties it had been as high as 16-17 million tonnes in some years. In 1973-4 the cereal tonnage had fallen to 5.5 million tonnes. In 1976-7 it was 9 million tonnes and in 1984-5 had risen to 10.4 million tonnes. The 1985-6 figure is higher because of emergency aid to Sub-Saharan Africa. There has been an increasing proportion of non-cereal food aid, not covered by these figures, especially EEC aid in dairy products. The aid component in food aid has also increased and more has gone to the poorest countries. Africa has benefited at the expense of Asia, and within south Asia Bangladesh at the expense of India, and project and emergency aid have replaced bilateral programme aid.

At the same time, so-called subsistence crops such as sorghum, millet, yams, cassava and bananas could be traded in local and even national markets, if they were not discriminated against. Low prices of subsidized grain, the import of which is encouraged by overvalued exchange rates, or which is supplied by food aid, discourage the production of these "poor man's crops" for the market. Although devaluation would encourage the production of export crops, the demand for the subsistence crops would also rise and would constitute an incentive to produce more. The precise amount would depend on the elasticities of substitution in supply and demand. Relatively little research is done on these crops, although there are some exceptions, such as sorghum in

Maharashtra and the Sudan, and maize in Zimbabwe. The International Institute for Tropical Agriculture in Ibadan (Nigeria), which is part of the system set up by the Consultative Group for International Agricultural Research, specializes in research on roots and tubers. But more could be done for these crops, especially millet and sorghum. Even where research on food crops has been successful, African countries lack the indigenous research capacity to adopt and adapt the results of this research, so that much expenditure on research has low yields.

To give greater encouragement to research on subsistence crops would have the advantage that they can be grown on marginal land, do not require a sophisticated technology or complex skills, are ecologically benign, and have frequently great nutritional value. They can also be used to supplement the preferred cereals when these are in short supply, through additions to wheat flour or maize meal. But even if research in this area were to yield good returns there are limits to what can be expected. These crops, particularly roots and tubers, are bulky and expensive to transport. Storing and processing them is costly and often capital-intensive.

The various criticisms that have been advanced against food aid have led to the recommendation of better alternatives. Among these is a financial insurance scheme. Countries would then be able to buy food in commercial markets, and not be dependent on the political vagaries of donors. Unfortunately, such insurance schemes have not been very successful in the developing world, largely for the well-known reasons of adverse selection and moral hazard. The International Monetary Fund's Compensatory Financing Facility was extended in 1981 to apply to cereal imports. The criticism of unreliability of supplies can also be met by multi-year commitments of grain at flexible delivery. These can be bilateral or by groups of donor countries.

Food aid, properly designed and administered, is only one way in which the international community can help poor people in poor countries to be better fed. But its success depends on the ability to match the motivation and mobilization of food surpluses from advanced countries to the food needs of developing countries. A more sensible approach would be for the international community to support efforts by developing countries to eradicate hunger. Many domestic measures aiming at this entail difficulties. A land reform, giving land to the tiller, may cause a temporary drop in food production. A tax reform may lead to capital flight. Redistribution of income through employment generation may lead to inflation, balance of payments difficulties, strikes and

81

capital flight. If the international community is serious in wishing to eradicate world hunger, it should provide resources to the reforming governments to tide them over such temporary crises and difficulties. They would be like the present Structural Adjustment Loans of the World Bank; only they would be Radical or Reformist Adjustment Loans.

8. The Limits of Food Supply

We have seen that for a long time, people have expressed concern that population growth will outrun food supply and force people to starve. In fact so far food has increased more rapidly than population. In the last quarter-century, 1,800 million additional people were born into this world. Agriculture has responded to this by producing enough food and better quality food for these extra people. While certain regions, such as Africa, and certain groups, have faced shortages, global quantities and qualities have not fallen short. Fears in the early 1970s of chronic global food shortages have proved wrong.

This does not mean that we can be complacent about food supplies. There are limits to raising food production. Environmental threats arise from the package of fertilizer, irrigation, pesticides and mechanization. Water is becoming a very scarce resource. The chemical effects of fertilizers can be hazardous. Pesticides also threaten human health. Forest clearance, slash-and-burn agriculture and cropping on hillsides in arid zones have led to soil erosion throughout South America, Africa and South Asia. Desertification may be spreading. There are ways of avoiding or at least reducing these threats, without reducing food production. For example, chemical pesticides can be replaced by natural pest predators and resistant crop strains. Terracing, intercropping and agroforestry can reduce soil erosion. Economies in the use of water can be achieved by raising the efficiency of irrigation systems. Pressures on available land can be relieved by more intensive cultivation. But this can lead to erosion, water shortages and fertilizer and pesticide runoff. Erosion can be reduced by no-till farming, but this implies greater reliance on herbicides. Pest control can lead to resistant species. The high yielding varieties make greater claims on water, fertilizer and pesticides and reduce the genetic diversities of the wild varieties.

Sustainable food production calls for soil conservation and erosion control; more organic rather than artificial fertilizer and recycling of plant and animal wastes; conservation of water resources; more efficient irrigation, re-use of water and crops of less water demand; promotion of diversity of biological strains in agriculture and symbiotic relationships between cultivated and wild biota.

Many of these ecologically sound policies coincide with policies for greater equality. Ecologically sound techniques are particularly appropriate for small farmers. A land reform redistributing land to small farmers would also generate the demand for food crops.

SECOND LECTURE
Global Institutions for an Interdependent World

1. Dominance: The Condition for an International Order? – 2. Utopia: The Global Solution. – 3. Improving International Institutions. – 4. The Need for Institutional Innovation. – 5. Desirable and Feasible? – 6. Orwellian Blocks – 7. Coordination among Oligarchs. – 8. Global Balkanization. – 9. Conclusion.

1. Dominance: The Condition for an International Order?

In this lecture I shall talk briefly about the past, then survey the present and finally glimpse into the future.

What functions do we expect to be characteristic of a working international order that is concerned with developing underdeveloped regions, in the context of a growing world economy, and with an equitable distribution of the gains from growth? I think we can name at least three or four.

First, it is helpful, if not essential, that there should be a centre that generates balance of payments surpluses, an excess of exports over imports, for the benefit of the developing regions.

Second, there should be financial institutions that convert these surpluses into long-term loans or equity investments on acceptable terms. This requires banks, corporations and aid agencies. In addition to the need to convert an excess of exports over imports into long-term financial instruments, certain additional financial functions are useful to support these loans and investments. For example, the foreign lending should be counter-cyclical, so that when the centre contracts the periphery can expand and contribute to the stabilization of the system. It is also helpful if the centre acts as lender of last resort and as the provider of the means of payment for international transactions.

Third, there must be the industrial and technological capacity to produce the capital goods or intermediate products required for industrialization, on which the loans are spent, and which contribute to the trade surplus. This capacity will be, at least in the early stages of the development process of the periphery, mainly in the centre, from which the surpluses and the loans originate.

Fourth, and here I hesitate because the exercise of this function is controversial, it seems helpful if the previous three functions are supported by a strong military power that enforces contracts and keeps the peace.

Between the Napoleonic wars and 1914 these functions were carried out by Great Britain under the Pax Britannica. The surpluses were generated by Britain; the financial institutions were established in the City of London; the "dark satanic mills" of the North of England manufactured the industrial products, and the British navy ruled the waves. Critics have said that, when benign dominance was replaced by predatory dominance around 1910, the British navy waived the rules. The management of the gold standard after 1910 placed the burden of deflationary adjustment on other countries. But, though this was an order dominated by Britain and run in the interest of Britain, it contributed to the development of large areas in North and South America, South Africa, Australia and New Zealand.

There was not much of an order between the two world wars. Britain had become unable, and the USA was still unwilling to assume the leadership functions. When agricultural prices fell, the USA imposed the Smoot-Hawley tariff in 1930. The USA did not function as lender of last resort (discounting in a financial crisis), and did not keep markets open in periods of glut for the purchase of distress goods. There was no counter-cyclical lending; on the contrary, a boom at home caused an increase in foreign lending, and in a depression the USA reduced both lending and imports. The result of the absence of the coordination, or carrying out, of the four functions was the depression and the war.

For twenty-five years after the Second World War, and largely as a result of it, the United States assumed these functions under the Pax Americana. Large balance of payments surpluses were generated by the United States, which led for a time to the fear of a chronic dollar shortage. But the USA opened its market, and the Marshall Plan, reconstruction aid, and long-term direct investment by multinationals soon converted the dollar shortage into a dollar glut, and made Keynes's prediction of America becoming a high-cost, high-living economy come true. Jean-Jacques Servan Schreiber's book *The American Challenge* (1968) even predicted that the power of USA multinational corporations constituted a long-term threat to Europe. The USA trade surplus fell from 4.5 per cent of her GNP in 1947 to 0.5 per cent in 1950.

The mighty dollar replaced sterling and New York became an important financial centre. Its financial institutions soon matched and overtook those of the City of London. The United States became, for a while, the industrial workshop of the world. America held a nuclear umbrella over Europe and Japan, and used its military power to enforce the peace as it saw it. As in the case of Britain half a century earlier, in the 1960s benign dominance turned into predatory dominance. The USA began to exploit the foreign acceptance of its reserve currency to extract goods and services from abroad. During the inflationary period of the Vietnam war America offered, in return for large purchases of goods from the rest of the world, depreciating short-term assets in the form of dollar balances in American banks.

After 1970 the power of the USA declined and we witnessed what Bhagwati calls the diminishing giant syndrome. The share of US GNP in the world's fell from about 40-45 per cent in the 1940s to 16-17 per cent in 1988. Its competitiveness in both old and new industries, and its economic growth rate declined. The large twin deficits, in the budget and the balance of payments, are symptoms of this decline. In 1970 imports were 4.1 per cent of America's GNP; in 1980 9.1 per cent; and in 1989 18.1 per cent. Other symptoms are the decline in research and development, the failure of primary and secondary education (3,000 students drop out of high school every day), the falling production of scientists and engineers, and the low savings and investment ratios. The physical infrastructure is crumbling and the social infrastructure is neglected. Field Marshal Lord Roberts (1832-1914), no "lefty", said "Social Reform is a preliminary to any thorough system of National Defence". Casino capitalism has replaced managerial capitalism.

There are some who dispute the thesis of the decline of American power in the world economy. Sam Huntington[1] and Joseph

1. SAMUEL P. HUNTINGTON, 'The U.S. – Decline or Renewal?', *Foreign Affairs*, vol. 67, Winter 1988-9.

Nye[1] write of renewal, of a return to a more long-term, pre-war trend. Seizaburo Sato writes, echoing Henry Luce, "The 20th century was the American century. The 21st century will be the American century."

Americans react constructively to crises. Pearl Harbor, the second World War, Sputnik, the Arab oil embargo, ended periods of complacency. Winston Churchill said, "In the end Americans will always do the right thing, after exhausting all other alternatives".

America is losing confidence just when others seek to accept it as leader and imitate it. The Chinese protesting students held up the Statue of Liberty (with a Phrygian cap and renamed goddess of reason) as their symbol. But the evidence of reduced assumption of the leadership role as well as of reduced world power is too strong.

Since 1970 there has been a lack of coordination of the four functions sketched out above. The world has become fragmented, schizophrenic. The USA went off gold in 1971, 40 years after Britain had done the same in 1931. The current account surpluses were generated, first, by the capital surplus countries of a few oil exporting desert sheikhdoms and, in the 1980s, by Japan and Germany. Germany's has disappeared since reunification, but Japan's is growing again.

The financial institutions proliferated, not only throughout Europe, East Asia and Japan, Hong Kong, Singapore and Bahrein, but also in the Cayman Islands, the Bahamas, Luxembourg, the Channel Islands, Ireland and other tax and regulation havens. Anyone with $ 3,700 can buy a licence to operate a bank in the Caribbean island Monserrat.

The industrial capacity has shifted to Germany, Japan, and the newly industrializing countries; but these new economic giants are military pygmies, while the military giants, the USA and until recently the USSR, are weakened in their economic power partly by their large military expenditure. One does not have to subscribe to the thesis of Paul Kennedy's book *The Rise and Fall of*

---

1. JOSEPH NYE, 'No, the U.S. Isn't in Decline', *New York Times,* October 7, 1990.

the Great Powers [1] that economic supremacy translates into military power, overstretch and supersession by the next comer, to see that America was weakened by its large military expenditure. Of course, other factors than defence spending contributed to the economic decline, such as growing rigidities, distributional coalitions, and over-consumption. But the overstretched defence budget was one of the factors, and the resulting unfavourable trade balance led to the desire for reduced military commitment in Europe, Asia and the Pacific. [2]

What future scenarios are likely? I shall try to sketch out four possible developments of the world economy. But before doing this, let me rule out certain possibilities. In the seventies there was some talk about a Pax Arabica, with the Arab OPEC countries taking over the functions of the dominant economy. Even if the price of oil were to rise again, this scenario has never been a likely one. More plausible is a future Pax Japonica or Nipponica. Some observers have compared the present situation of Japan and the USA with that of the USA and the UK between the wars: as Britain then, so the USA now is unable, and as the USA then so Japan now is unwilling to assume the leadership role. It is not inconceivable that the Japanese, with their immense adaptive power, will eventually become the dominant economy. But at present they lack some important ingredients for this role. They have no large domestic market for manufactured goods; their imports are not labour-intensive raw materials, they have no military power, they are not internationally minded and there is, at least at present, no global appeal or prestige in the Japanese ideology,

---

1. PAUL KENNEDY, *The Rise and Fall of the Great Powers: Economic Change and Military Conflict, 1500-2000*, New York: Random House and Unwin Hyman, 1988.

2. There is, in general, no clear correlation between the proportion of GNP spent on defence and economic performance. Britain was spending 5.7 per cent in 1937, against 28.2 per cent for Japan, 36.4 per cent for the USSR and 23.5 per cent for Germany. Yet, Britain's economy was one of the weakest. In 1985 South Korea spent a higher proportion than any NATO country except the USA and Greece. Sweden, a successful economy, spent about as much as most NATO countries (3 per cent). Singapore and Taiwan, highly successful economies, spent even more than South Korea (6.8 per cent), while the economically weak countries of Eastern Europe spend far less. See PHILIP TOWLE, 'Last Days of the American Empire', *London Review of Books*, 19 May 1988, p. 8.

message or lifestyle. They are still ideologically outside the dominant Judaeo-Graeco-Roman culture. While Gunnar Myrdal, looking at the American Negro problem, said in a passage cited by the Supreme Court "separate must mean unequal", the Japanese say "for Japan to be equal requires Japan to be separate. If not, it could only be inferior; a colony of the West."

Russia is probably ruled out for some time as a candidate for the dominant economy. One hears murmurings about a future Pax Sinoica, with the Chinese taking over, or a Pax Europa, but these do not look like strong probabilities on present evidence. I shall briefly discuss four possible developments: a Utopian global scenario, a block scenario, an oligarchic scenario, and the possibility of global Balkanization.

2. Utopia: The Global Solution

The fragmentation of the four functions of an international order contributes to the current confusion, but it also holds the opportunity for a much better solution. Our present interdependent, pluralistic, multi-polar world is less stable, and more in need of promotion of peace, prosperity, and global leadership than past orders, but no single power is both able and willing to assume these functions. This presents us for the first time in history with the opportunity to create a world order based not on dominance and dependence, but on equality, pluralism and cooperation. But this would call for the exercise of our creative institutional imagination and sacrifices of national sovereignty.

We are suffering from a lag of institutions behind technology. The revolutions in the technologies of transport, travel, communications and information have unified and shrunk the globe,[1] but our organization into nation states dates back to the Peace of Westphalia in 1648, and to the 19th-century unifications of Germany and Italy. When the nation states were founded, the city states and the feudalism that preceded them had become too

---

1. This does not mean that people have necessarily benefited from this technological globalization. Economic and technical progress translates at the global level even less than at the national level automatically into human well-being.

small for the scale of operations required by the Industrial Revolution. The political institution therefore was adapted to the new industrial technology, to the roads, railways and canals. The nation state was then a progressive institution. But I am not a technological determinist. The adaptation of institutions to technology is not an inevitable process. The Middle Ages had, for example, lost the Roman technology about roads, baths, aqueducts and amphitheatres, and these were allowed to fall into disrepair. But now the nation state, with its insistence on full sovereignty, has become, at least in certain respects, an obstacle to further progress. It has landed us in several Prisoners' Dilemma situations: each nation acts in its own perceived rational self-interest, and the result is that every country is worse off. It pays each nation to pursue this mutually destructive course, whether others do likewise or not. To overcome such destructive outcomes calls for a high degree of trust, moral motivation (even if, as in the case of the Prisoners' Dilemma, it is honour among thieves), co-operation or compulsion.

I shall not discuss the desirability or the feasibility of a world government. If it ever were to come about, it would probably be the result of a trend we are already beginning to observe. What I have in mind are technically clearly defined areas of international cooperation, or delegation upwards to a global body. The Universal Postal Union, established in 1875, may serve as a model.

Common interests and conflicts are running nowadays across national boundaries. The European farmers are in conflict with the European industrialists and the public and outside competitive producers, who have to pay for the Common Agricultural Policy. The advanced countries' textile manufacturers are aligned in the Multifibre Arrangement against Third World textile exporters and consumers in their own countries. The nation state has shown itself to be an inappropriate level at which such issues can be resolved.

Clearly, Prisoners' Dilemma outcomes move the world economy away from a more to a less efficient allocation of resources. There exist, therefore, potential gains, by moving back to more efficient allocations. According to Coase's theorem, in the absence of transaction costs and with full information, a legal framework and well-defined property rights, it pays each state to reach agreements with other states to avoid, by compensation payments, this damage and make all better off than they would have been in the outcome of the Prisoners' Dilemma.[1] For example, the USA emits acid rain to Canada. If the damage is greater than the benefits to the USA, Canada could offer compensation to the USA for relinquishing the emission of sulphur dioxide, the chief component in acid rain, and still be better off than it would be in accepting the acid rain; or, if the benefits are greater than the damage, the USA can offer compensation to Canada for accepting the acid rain and still be better off than it would have been, had it been prevented from inflicting the damage. But as we all know to our regret, we are far away from outcomes according to Coase's theorem, although we are not always at the other end of the spectrum, the Prisoners' Dilemma. Coase's theorem remains useful, in spite of its unrealistic assumptions, in drawing our attention to the fact that there are unexploited mutual profit opportunities when Prisoners' Dilemma situations arise. I obviously do not wish to say that compensation always, or even often, ought to be paid. The losers, such as the English landlords after the repeal of the Corn Laws in 1846, may not deserve to be compensated; or, even if they do deserve it, the administrative costs and the losses from imposing taxes to finance the compensation may be so large as to make the compensation uneconomic. But the fact that it *could* be paid draws our attention to potential unexploited gains.

Add to the Prisoners' Dilemma the free-rider problem, according to which each country relies on others to bear the costs of arrangements that benefit everybody. As a result, public goods, such as peace, an open trading system, including freedom of the seas, standards of weights and measures, well defined property rights, international stability, a working monetary system, or conservation of the global environment, are undersupplied, while public bads, such as wars, pollution, and poverty are oversup-

1. I am indebted to Michael Lipton's analysis of the relation between Prisoners' Dilemma and Coase's theorem in a different context in 'The Prisoners' Dilemma and Coase's Theorem: A Case for Democracy in Less Developed Countries?' in *Economy and Democracy*, edited by R. C. O. Matthews, New York: St. Martin's Press, 1985, pp. 49-109.

plied. The situation has been described in parables and similes such as the tragedy of the commons, social traps, the isolation paradox, etc.

Under the present system there are gains to uncoordinated action. It pays any one country to put up protectionist barriers, whether others do so or not; to build up its arms promises security to any one country, whether others do so or not; any one country can to its advantage pollute the common air and the oceans, whether others do so or not. It pays any one country to attract capital from abroad by tax incentives, whether others do so or not, thereby eroding the tax basis. These ultimately self-damaging and possibly self-destructive actions can be avoided, in the absence of self-restraint, only either by a dominant world power imposing the restraints, or by cooperation or by delegation of some decisions to a transnational authority, with the power to enforce restraint.

The ranking of preferences with respect to, say, contributing to a common good by each country is the following:

1. My country does not contribute while others do. (Free rider, defection of one.)
2. My country contributes together with others. (Cooperation.)
3. No country contributes. (Prisoners' Dilemma outcome.)
4. My country contributes while no other country does. (Sucker.)

Behaviour by each according to 1, or the fear of 4, leads to outcome 3. Although 2 is preferred to 3, we end up with 3, unless either rewards and penalties, or autonomous cooperative motivations lead to 2. Incentives and expectations must be such as to rule out outcomes 4 and 1, so that if I (or you) contribute, I (or you) will not end up a sucker. In the absence of such motivations, the result is that such public goods as peace, monetary stability, absence of inflation, expansion of output and employment, an open world economy, environmental protection, debt relief, raw material conservation, poverty reduction and world development will be undersupplied.

It has been shown that iterative games of the Prisoners' Dilemma type lead to non-destructive outcomes.[1] The partners learn

---

1. ROBERT M. AXELROD, *The Evolution of Cooperation*, New York: Basic Books, 1984.

and adopt mutually beneficial strategies. I have already said that we find ourselves in between the two extremes of Prisoners' Dilemmas and Coase's outcomes. For several reasons it is harder to reach cooperative agreements in international transactions than in others, in which mutual trust and a sense of duty play stronger parts. There are now many states, and large numbers make agreements more difficult. We do not have a world government that could enforce agreements. Change is rapid, which undermines the basis of stability on which agreements are based. The absence of a hegemonic power also removes the sanctions against breaking the agreement. And all these factors prevent the trust from being built up, which is an essential precondition for international agreements.

Examples of Prisoners' Dilemmas on the global scale are ubiquitous. Above all there is the arms race, which, though we have so far avoided a major nuclear war, has contributed to hundreds of minor wars, mostly in the Third World; then there is competitive protectionism, through which each country casts its unemployment onto others; competitive exchange rate movements, by which unemployment or inflation are exported; investment wars in which countries forgo taxation to attract a limited amount of investment; research and development wars and the resulting technological nightmares; the denial of debt relief by banks and of guarantees by governments; environmental pollution; competitive interest rate increases; the depletion of ocean reserves and the destruction of species (more than half of all living species may disappear within our lifetime) are only some of the areas in which these battles are now being fought.

To avoid these traps, coordination and enforcement of policies are needed. But coordination means that each country has to do things it does not want to do. The USA has to balance its budget in order to lower world interest rates; Germany has to grow faster, but does not want to suck in guest workers from Turkey and Yugoslavia; many say Japan should import more, but it does not want to hurt its domestic industries. And so on.

Even Mrs Thatcher, that archpriestess of free markets and state minimalism, in a speech to the United Nations in New York on 8 November 1989, has come to recognize that in order to avoid

94

global warming and coastal flooding, countries that emit carbon dioxide and other gases that trap heat in the atmosphere would have to act together, that restrictions would have to be obligatory, and their application would have to be carefully monitored. Any one country acting by itself would be at a competitive disadvantage by having to incur the higher costs of protecting the environment.[1]

The challenge is to replace the past international orders based on dominance and dependence, or disorders that showed fragmentation and lack of coordination, by a new pluralistic order built on equality.

3. Improving International Institutions

From the point of view of human development, the principle of one state one vote in the UN General Assembly (though its resolutions have only recommendatory power) cannot be justified. Respect for persons applies to equality of status enjoyed by individuals within a nation, but not to corporate entities such as states. In the United Nations context, however, it could be said that the voting rights in the Assembly compensate for the gross economic inequality manifested in international trade and the military inequality recognized in the great powers' permanent membership and veto power on the Security Council, which can reach decisions with binding force. It should also be remembered that the large and growing majority of the world's people live in the developing countries. A further justification for voting by states lies in the overriding importance of avoiding war. And the state is the institution with a monopoly of force. Yet, considerations of law and order in international relations have to be tempered by those of social justice. In civilized relations, including international relations, bargaining and negotiations do not occur in a space of pure power politics, but always appeal, openly or tacitly, to mutually accepted or acceptable values and norms.

---

1. *The New York Times*, 9 November 1989, p. A 17.

The United Nations and its many organizations have not yet adjusted to the post-cold war era. They have been subjected to many criticisms, and numerous proposals have been made for their reform. Many have put the blame on institutional inadequacies. It is true that badly designed institutions can be formidable obstacles to reform. But even the best institutions cannot work if they are not supported by political power. In the final analysis the past defects of the United Nations agencies were not the result of institutional inadequacies, overlaps here and gaps there, of low-level representation at important meetings, of lack of coordination, or of managerial flaws, but of lack of commitment by member governments. There were successes: the crisis in Africa, in Cambodia and in San Salvador called forth the best in the UN. In the prevention of natural disasters, in the eradication of contagious diseases and in limiting damage to the environment the UN agencies have been quite successful. Some argue that the United Nations have been more successful in the social and economic fields than in peace-keeping, others see it the other way round.

State sovereignty, which still dominates the world order, has become inadequate and indeed dangerous. In the area of peace-keeping, the unrealistic distinction between external aggression and internal oppression must be abandoned. The predominant threat to stability is conflict within countries and not between them. There is an urgent need to strengthen international human rights law. Many of the most destabilizing troubles come from within states – either because of ethnic strife or repressive measures by governments. Conditions that lead to tyranny at home sooner or later are likely to spill over into search for enemies abroad. Consider the Soviet's invasion of Hungary and Czechoslovakia, the South Africans in Angola and Mozambique, and Iraq in Kuwait. An ounce of prevention is better than a ton of punishment. And prevention of aggression is an important task for the UN.

Urgent new claims in international coordination have been added to old ones, in the context of shrinking public expenditures. The East European countries' claims are less than those of, say, India, on grounds of poverty, and less than those of, say,

Thailand, on grounds of good performance. But if the ground is the promise to move to a more peaceful world order, their claims are strong. Ideally, resources from the industrial countries to Eastern Europe and the Soviet Union should be additional to those going to the Third World. If there is going to be a peace dividend, this could be the source of additionality, but its existence, or its use for this purpose, is controversial. Competing claims for the countries of sub-Saharan Africa and for the industrial countries themselves are being made.

4. The Need for Institutional Innovation

There are international institutions that work well. They never hit the headlines. They carry out their alloted tasks in a quietly effective manner. The Universal Postal Union, founded in 1875, whose task it is to perfect postal services and to promote international collaboration, the International Telecommunication Union, the World Meteorological Association, the International Civil Aviation Organization and the World Intellectual Property Organization, have clearly and narrowly defined technical mandates, are non-politicized, and implement their tasks competently. Their success is due largely to their covering technical issues.

International coordination has also worked well in areas where the advantages are great and visible: the wide, though not universal, adoption of the metric system, the adoption of Greenwich Mean Time in 1884, on which the world's time system is based, and the establishment of an international regime for containing contagious diseases.

Other international institutions have worked less well, among them the United Nations Conference on Trade and Development (UNCTAD) and the United Nations Educational, Scientific and Cultural Organization (UNESCO). Their mandates were broad, overlapping with those of other organizations, perceptions about the future, about objectives, and about which policies had which results differed, and the debates in their councils brought in extraneous political controversies. It is from these negative experiences that some have drawn the conclusion that international cooperation is unnecessary and undesirable.

International coordination or cooperation can take different forms.[1] There can be full harmonization of policies, such as the adoption of common standards, for example the metric system. Or it can mean joint expenditures for a common purpose, such as on international air traffic control. Or it may involve submitting to agreed rules. Or it can amount to the continual exchange of information, such as that on illegal capital flight or on matters of public health. Or, as in the case of macroeconomic coordination, it can involve joint decision-making on monetary, fiscal, trade and exchange rate policy.

Let me now give a few illustrations of the kind of institutional innovation at the global or transnational level I have in mind, that would avoid Prisoners' Dilemma outcomes. These would realign modern technology and political institutions and avoid the negative-sum games to which Prisoners' Dilemma situations give rise.

When I propose institutional innovation here, I am not thinking of legions of international bureaucrats or gleaming, glass-plated headquarter buildings and pools of high-paid consultants with more secretaries and manicured receptionists. My concern is for procedures, rules, norms, implying changes in behaviour, forums for negotiation or exploration. Many of these can be adopted by existing organizations. Nor is necessarily more coordination of functions involved. Some of these innovations can take a regional form, others should be global.

a. Mobilizing Surpluses: An International Investment Trust

Imagine that Marshall Plan aid to Europe had been given as commercial loans instead of grants, and that repayments by European surplus countries like Germany had to take the form of recycling the debt service to developing countries. Everybody

---

1. See RICHARD N. COOPER, 'Panel Discussion: The Prospects for International Policy Coordination', *International Economic Policy Coordination*, edited by WILLIAM H. BUITER and RICHARD C. MARSTON, Cambridge: Cambridge University Press, 1985, pp. 369-370.

would be better off. Germany would not be exhorted to expand its economy, the USA would run a much smaller current account deficit, and the developing countries would have access to capital. Or imagine that the OPEC surpluses of the 1970s and early 80s had been recycled through an international trust. Comparing the World Bank's lending with that of commercial banks, interest rates would have been lower, selection of countries and projects more careful, inflation and counter-inflationary monetary restrictions would have been reduced, and world growth would have been higher.

First then, there is a need for a new institution that would mobilize the current account surpluses of Japan (and any other persistent surplus country) to developing countries in need of capital. This recalls Keynes's proposal for a Clearing Union, which had precisely this role.

The Japanese are now inclined to invest the bulk of their excess savings in the most capital-rich country, the USA, thereby sustaining its twin deficits in the budget and the current account. It is generally agreed that the USA will have to reduce its large budget deficit and its current account deficit. What, then, would be the fate of the Japanese surplus? If the United States were to reduce its twin deficits without a corresponding expansion anywhere else, Japan's exports and growth would decline. This would give a powerful deflationary impact to the world economy, a world economy which already is suffering from high unemployment.

The current conventional wisdom is to exhort the Japanese to consume and invest more at home. But this seems quite wrongheaded. In a world starved of capital one should be immensely grateful to any country that is prepared to generate excess savings for the rest of the world. To request a country, ready to produce and save more than it absorbs at home, to step up its consumption borders on the immoral.

My proposal is to establish an International Investment Trust that would issue bonds (and perhaps other financial assets) to central banks and private agents, that are multilaterally guaranteed against devaluation and perhaps indexed against inflation.

Unless the reduction in the US current account deficit is accompanied by increased loan demand elsewhere (or by domestic
expansion in Japan and Germany), the world economy is threatened with growing deflation and unprecedented unemployment.
Recycling to creditworthy developing countries through the proposed International Investment Trust is a sensible alternative.
The rate of return on assets acquired from the Trust by lenders
would be lower than that on US Treasury bonds, but it would be
safer (threatened by neither inflation nor devaluation), and this
should make it attractive to the surplus country lenders. The
loans would be on commercial terms, to the newly industrializing countries.

Can existing institutions, such as the World Bank or the regional development banks undertake this task? In principle they
could, and this would be better than global deflation. But some
competition in lending procedures, an invitation to experiment
with alternative lending styles, and some limits to the size and
monopoly power of lending by any one institution is clearly
desirable.

It is not proposed that the whole of the Japanese current account surplus should be mobilized in this way. Japan has a
deficiency in housing. It has been said that the Japanese live in
rabbit hutches. The share of residential building in total repro-
ducible fixed assets is only 25 per cent in Japan, compared with
35 per cent in the United States. Many Japanese spend four hours
a day commuting. Infrastructure and especially the modernization of coastal ports for domestic freight transport are other candidates for investment funds. More land set aside for urban parks
may be desirable. But the whole Japanese surplus could be used
domestically only at the cost of diminishing returns on investment
or increases in consumption of already affluent people, and a
lowering of the Japanese growth rate. With it would go a lowering of the growth rate in other parts of the world. We should
be grateful for a nation that combines the work ethic with
the saving ethic, and makes capital available to the rest of the
world.

The table below shows rough orders of magnitude in the
world's current account balances.

Deficits	$ billions	Surpluses	$ billions
United States	-60	Japan	+100
		Holland	+10
Other industrial countries	-90	Switzerland	+10
Developing countries	-30	Germany	+10
		Errors & omissions	+50
Total	-180	Total	+180

It may be asked whether the Japanese surpluses will last. Some have argued that they are the temporary result of over-adjustment to the oil price rises in the 1970s and that, with falling oil prices, they will automatically disappear. Others claim that they arise from adversarial trade policies. Others again see the reason for the high savings rate and the low consumption rate in Japanese culture. The Japanese savings rate has been running at 27 per cent of GNP, and some economists have maintained that this high propensity to save is "structural", that it is deeply embedded in Japanese tradition and culture. When interest rates were lowered in 1986 savings did indeed fall. But in 1989, when interest rates were raised against inflation, domestic spending and imports dropped again.

Others have argued that the high savings rate is the result of the Japanese age distribution. In the long term, the aging Japanese population will probably reduce the savings ratio. On a life-cycle theory of savings, the young save in order to live on their savings in their old age. Japan has had a higher proportion of young workers to both old people and dependent children than other OECD countries. If this interpretation is right, the savings rate will decline over the next 15 years. But when this will be is uncertain, and meanwhile the surplus is likely to remain, although the areas with which it is incurred will be changing.

Even if the Japanese surpluses were not to continue, while some countries have deficits, others must have surpluses, and it is on these that the International Investment Trust would draw. With reduced defence expenditure in the OECD countries, an excess of savings over domestic absorption (consumption plus investment) is likely to arise, and the Fund can offer its bonds to the individuals and institutions whose savings will become available.

If the Japanese were to divert the whole surplus to domestic use, by raising either their consumption or their domestic investment, they would have to accept a lower growth rate and higher unemployment. The global economy would also suffer from deflation. If, on the other hand, the surplus were likely to continue, a source of foreign investment other than the United States would have to be found. This would provide a major opportunity for a reform that would be in everybody's interest: the OECD countries (including the United States and Japan), the developing countries, and the global economy would all benefit.

A recycling of these surpluses to the developing countries, on commercial terms, by a multilaterally guaranteed International Investment Trust would have the following advantages: the surplus countries would find safer returns for their foreign investment, not subject to devaluation and inflation; the OECD countries would find a larger market for their exports of capital goods and other products to the Third World; the developing countries would find a new source of capital on acceptable terms for their development needs; and as a result the global economy would resume higher employment and growth.

The purpose of the proposal is to bring together, to mutual benefit, three now grossly underutilized pools of resources: the current account surpluses of the excess savers, in search of safe returns; the underutilized industrial capacity and skilled unemployed of the OECD countries, on whose exports some of the recycled loans will be spent; and the vast idle or underemployed unskilled and semi-skilled manpower of the South, hungry for capital. And all this in the service of a growing world economy.

Some have argued that Japan should give directly more aid to low-income countries. In fact, Japan has increased its contribution to the World Bank and the International Monetary Fund and has expanded its bilateral aid programme. But although Japan should give more aid, the reason is not its current account surpluses, but rather its high income. By the same criterion, the USA, Canada, the UK, and Australia, all deficit countries, should also give more aid. Japan's surpluses are a reason for it to undertake more long-term foreign investment and lending on commercial terms. If a surplus were a good reason for giving more aid, deficit countries would soon plead that their deficits are a reason for giving less. But that would be comparable to the rich man who found himself with temporary liquidity problems, and then cut first his contribution to Oxfam. The criterion for giving aid is income per head, as is reflected in the accepted measure of overseas development assistance as a percentage of GDP; for lending commercially or for investing abroad, it is the size of the current account surplus.

An important difference between the type of intermediation of the OPEC surpluses in the 1970s and that of the Japanese and German surpluses in the 80s is that the former consisted largely of government loans, the latter are from private lenders. Japanese and German private banks can mediate in the bank lending, and in portfolio and equity investment of some of the private savings. Japanese private direct investment can also make a contribution. But, although the Japanese banking system has been quite remarkably adaptive and has developed the capacity to channel international loans, financial innovation may be required, because a multilateral institution is better suited for providing the guarantees and for accomplishing at least part of the task. The World Bank and its affiliates, the International Finance Corporation and the International Development Association, also may not be able to accomplish the whole task, though they could contribute to a solution. It is for consideration how multilateral these new institutions should be, how much of a government guarantee is needed, and whether the loans should be guaranteed against currency depreciation and indexed against inflation.

An imaginative additional step that goes beyond the mobilization of the surpluses would be to graft an interest-rate-subsidy scheme onto the mobilization mechanism, for the benefit of low-income countries. Contributions to this window should not be made according to the size of the surplus on current account, but instead according to income per head, preferably in a progressive fashion, so that the contribution as a percentage of national income would rise with rising incomes per head. The cost-effectiveness of such aid would be quite high, because a small interest subsidy would make it possible for large investment funds to be recycled to poor countries. Moreover, conditions of good macro-economic policies could be attached to the concessional loans, so that their efficient use is further enhanced. Some of these could be on-lent to domestic borrowers by a development finance corporation, if it were thought that this would improve incentives for economic use.

Some observers advocate that the surpluses should be used to refinance and relieve debt, mainly that owed by Latin American countries. But the result of such proposals would be to aid the banks in the industrial countries rather than to foster productive investment in poor countries. It might amount to rewarding greedy lenders and profligate borrowers. However desirable it might be to deal with old debt in such a way as to restore credit-worthiness in Latin America and to resume world growth (and I shall discuss this later), the fact remains that there are large areas of the world, such as South Asia, which have been careful to avoid a debt problem, at least until recently, have prudently husband-ed their resources, and could make excellent use of the scarce funds provided by the Investment Trust.

Another objection that has been raised to proposals for mobi-lizing the surpluses is that as long as the US budgetary deficits continue, the reduction or elimination of the Japanese surpluses will exert pressure on world capital markets, which might have adverse repercussions on Latin American debtors. The reply to this objection is that the US deficits are, in any case, unsustain-able and that mobilizing surpluses for the developing countries would raise their demand for US exports and contribute to the reduction or elimination of the US current account deficit. This is surely a better way of stimulating the world economy than ei-ther the present exhortations to Japan to buy more from the USA or, in the absence of expansion abroad, further contraction in the USA. In addition, monetary expansion in Japan and Europe might rekindle inflation, while continuing US deficits would threaten the fairly open world trading system. The recycling of the surpluses to the Third World, whether by the World Bank or by a new International Investment Trust, offers a solution that yields safer returns to the surplus countries; a reduction in the deficit without restriction of the domestic economy to the United States; much-needed resources to the developing countries; and a non-inflationary expansion for the world economy.

b. Towards a World Central Bank

The present international monetary system or non-system, a mixture of fixed and fluctuating exchange rates, is not satisfactory. Firms find themselves suddenly facing much stiffer competition as a result of a movement in the exchange rate. Long-term investment in productive capacity is therefore discouraged. Claims for protection of various kinds are made against what is seen as unfair competition. The location of investment is determined not only by long-term cost considerations but also by the movement of exchange rates. Some of this will be through take-overs and buy-outs, and competition will be reduced.

The use of the dollar as an international reserve asset is subject to well-known difficulties. The generation of dollars by the USA is not guided by the international need for liquidity in the light of price stability, full employment and growth. The Special Drawing Rights (SDRs) have so far not fulfilled the need for an international liquid asset. It is therefore desirable to consider the need for a single world currency and a global central bank.

Bankers are not the most popular species of men. And it is not obvious that we should hand over our fate to a new group of global central bankers. John Kenneth Galbraith wrote, "The sense of responsibility in the financial community as a whole is not small. It is nearly nil."[1] John Maynard Keynes, once listening to an astonished complaint about the stupidity of a banker, replied, "Remember, they only compete with one other." And in *Essays in Persuasion* he wrote, "Banks and bankers are by nature blind. They have not seen what was coming . . . Lifelong practices . . . make them the most romantic and least realistic of men . . . if [the bankers] are saved, it will be, I expect, in their own despite".[2] On

1. J. K. GALBRAITH, *The Great Crash 1929*, Harmondsworth Penguin Books, 1961, p. 20.
2. JOHN MAYNARD KEYNES, *Essays in Persuasion*, London: Macmillan, 1931, pp. 176, 178.

receiving Keynes's second draft of his proposals for an International Currency Union, D. H. Robertson wrote to him on 27 November 1941: "I sat up last night reading your revised 'proposals' with great excitement, − and a growing hope that the spirit of Burke and Adam Smith is on earth again to prevent the affairs of a great empire from being settled by the little minds of a gang of bank-clerks who have tasted blood (yes, I know this is unfair!)."

In spite of this bad press, bankers, particularly central bankers, fulfil an important function. Long-term capital-intensive investments are needed for economic growth and development. Fluctuating exchange rates discourage this form of investment, because it cannot be known which will turn out to be profitable. In the past the stability of the currency of the dominant economy has played the role of an international standard and store of value, in addition to having been a means for the settlement of debts. The attempt to move towards a world currency with the creation of Special Drawing Rights has been so far not altogether successful. But if we wish to move in the direction of a pluralistic, democratic world order, a world currency will have to be an important part of it. After the last war, Maynard Keynes proposed the creation of bancor, the name he gave for a world currency.[1]

There has been progress towards the establishment of a European central bank, which will be associated with the role of the European Currency Unit. It could evolve as one of several regional reserve currencies. The European central bank would then be one of these regional central banks whose activities would be coordinated by a global central bank. The global central bank, being the lender of last resort, would also have to exercise regulatory and supervisory functions in order to avoid moral haz-

---

1. Everywhere we read about the emergence of a single global capital market. According to TAMIM BAYOUMI this is not so. (*Saving-Investment Correlations* IMF Working Paper 89/66, Washington D.C., August 1989.) He found that for the period 1965-1986 for most countries savings rates are about equal to investment rates, suggesting the absence of an internationally integrated capital market. This could be the result of government counteracting greater private divergencies. For 1880-1913 there are much wider divergences between domestic savings rates and investment rates. It could be that exchange rate volatility has replaced controls as a barrier to international integration in the later period. On the other hand, the surprising result could be due to the way that savings are calculated.

ard problems. It would probably also be necessary to introduce some coordination of budgetary policies, so that any one country cannot run large budget deficits, going too much out of line with others, and draw capital to itself.

Long-term capital-intensive investments are needed for economic growth and development. Fluctuating exchange rates discourage this form of investment, by creating or exacerbating uncertainty about future profitability. In the past the stability of the currency of the dominant economy has played the role of an international standard and store of value. The dollar is still the most important of these currencies, although the Japanese yen and the Deutsche Mark are increasingly used. The attempt to move towards a world currency with the creation of Special Drawing Rights has been so far not altogether successful. They have not replaced the major world currencies as instruments of international settlements. If we wish to move in the direction of a pluralistic, democratic world order, a world currency will have to be an important part of it. It would provide the basis for stability and reduced uncertainty that freedom of movement requires. But it could initially be a combination of SDRs and the major trading currencies.

The IMF is the primary candidate for an embryonic global central bank. Some critics have charged the IMF with excessive emphasis on expenditure-reducing, and not enough on expenditure-switching policies. Others have charged it with an excessive concern with specific means (devaluation, monetary and fiscal austerity) rather than with results (improvements in the balance of payments). Both of these criticisms lead to the complaint that IMF conditionality has led to excessive reductions in demand, and excessive underutilization of resources, including, above all, excessive unemployment. Pressures on surplus countries to expand demand would also help fuller employment of resources. Ideally, however, the surpluses should be used for long-term investments in capital-hungry developing countries.

The International Monetary Fund is, of course, not a global central bank. Such an institution would have to be given the power to conduct open market operations to regulate the world currency for transactions purposes, to prevent panic runs on deposits, and to maintain the stability of the financial system. Even a small possibility of a financial breakdown should lead to our making provisions against it.

In the event of a run on the banks, the central bank is the lender of last resort, providing the public, at a price, with the liquid resources it wishes to hold. It has become a commonplace to say that, with 24-hour rapid communications, international financial markets have become fully integrated, so that a run on the banks in any one country can bring down the whole international financial system. As things are now, the monetary authorities (the Treasuries and central banks) have responded to this globalization by coordinating their efforts to regulate and supervise financial transactions. The IMF and the Bank of International Settlements in Basle have supported these international arrangements, though somewhat half-heartedly.

Above all, there is therefore a need for an international lender of last resort.[1] Repeated swings between euphoria and despair among national bankers – with despair leading to serious collapses of enterprises – led Bagehot 120 years ago to identify the function of a national lender of last resort as crucial for the Bank of England. His arguments were soon accepted. Just as the Bank of England has performed this function in times of crisis, so it also took on the function of limiting, by suggestions rather than by direct order, excess lending in good times. Such a stabilizing function is now desperately needed at the global level, as the enormous swings in bank sentiment, and with it cross-border lending, clearly show. The lender of last resort has to exercise restraint in good times, as well as provide insurance in bad. The purpose would be not only to assist in a crisis, but to avoid the occurrence of crises. The problem of moral hazard – that banks, knowing they would have access to funds, overlend or lend imprudently – can be avoided by asking them for good collateral and charging a penal interest rate, or by leaving them in doubt as to whether funds will be available to them. In the case of sovereign debt the "good collateral" could consist of the acquisition by the international lender of last resort of the banks' claims at a discount.[2]

1. I am indebted to Michael Lipton for suggestions for this sub-section.
2. MICHAEL LIPTON and STEPHANY GRIFFITH-JONES, *International Lenders of Last*

The IMF and the central banks of the major trading countries would, as a first step, form a coordinating committee to manage world liquidity.[1] As the role of the IMF in providing world liquidity increases, its regulatory function would have to grow with it. The role of the SDRs, or whatever international liquid asset is decided upon, would grow as a substitution account is established. Member countries would deposit foreign exchange into it and receive SDR-denominated certificates in exchange.

Cooperation between countries to avoid unemployment, inflation, and protection is necessary if mutually destructive outcomes are to be avoided. It is usually the poor who bear the brunt of such outcomes. Specifically, joint policies on lowering interest rates are necessary. Investment in all industrial countries is low and productivity growth is declining. No one country can afford to reduce its rate, for fear of losing capital. Cooperation to lower interest rates and raise investment is neded.

An extension of the powers of the IMF, in line with Keynes's proposals at Bretton Woods, in the direction of a global central bank would contribute to stability and growth in the world economy. Whether countries are ready to coordinate their fiscal and monetary policies, and to permit the freer movement of goods, capital and labour that would be called for by a global central bank, and, to go one step further (as recommended by Keynes), by a single world currency, is, to say the least, an open question. Countries respecting democratic civil rights pride themselves on an independent judiciary (but not necessarily accompanied by an independent central bank). Should not the same principle be applied to a global monetary authority, independent of national political control?

c. An International Debt Facility

At the heart of the recalcitrance of the debt problem lies the conflict of interest over who shoulders the costs of continuing debt

Resort: Are Changes Required?, Midland Bank Occasional Paper in International Trade and Finance, March 1984.

1. ANDREW W. MULLINEUX, 'Do We Need a World Central Bank?', *Royal Bank of Scotland Review*, no. 160, December 1988.

service or of debt relief: the banks, the industrial countries' tax-payers, or the developing countries. If the banks, is it the managers, the shareholders or the depositors? If the taxpayers, is it the rich or the poor? If the developing countries, is it the urban or the rural people, the rich or the poor?

Much has been written about the international debt. Four main methods of debt reduction have been proposed.[1] Each involves reducing the present value of the discounted flow of all future receipts due to the creditor. The first is debt-equity swaps, or the conversion of fixed-interest debt into equity, a claim to a share in the profits. The lending bank sells its loan at market value for local currency in the debtor country, and uses the receipts to buy equity capital. No additional foreign exchange is required from the debtor, but the inflationary impact of the deal should be reduced. This is a form a debt reduction, though not necessarily of debt relief, since it does not necessarily reduce the present value of the payments due, though of course it may.[2]

The second method is cash buy-backs, in which the debtor country uses its foreign exchange to buy back loans at market value. The discount will be greater than under the previous method. The foreign exchange needed for this transaction may come from the World Bank or the International Monetary Fund. Here again, the impact on the debtor country is inflationary.

In the third method, or collateralization, old debts are exchanged for new debts, but either at lower face value or at lower interest rates. The debtor may, for example, issue long-term "exit" bonds. Against the new debt the debtor provides collateral. Here again, the World Bank or the IMF may help.

The fourth method is guarantees, proposed in the Brady Plan of 1989. Here the World Bank or the IMF guarantee the new debt. It has been suggested that a special trust fund be set up to meet these guarantees under the auspices of the international financial institutions.

The proposal of international debt relief (or debt reduction), conditional on policy reform, combined with government guar-

1. Stephen Browne, *Foreign Aid in Practice,* London: Pinter, 1990, pp. 152-153.
2. The distinction is due to Max Corden, 'The Theory of Debt Relief: Sorting out Some Issues', *Journal of Development Studies,* vol. 27, no. 3 April 1991, p. 137.

antees of the reduced debt, is perhaps different from some of the other proposals, because it applies to the present situation, from which it would be hoped that a lesson would be learned, and that it would not be repeated. On the other hand, since the possibility of repetition cannot be excluded, some global equivalent of a bankruptcy facility might well constitute a permanent feature of the global landscape.

On the assumption that some part of the outstanding international debt will have to be written off and partial relief will have to be granted to the borrowers, two questions arise that call for a coordinated, global solution. Both involve the free-rider problem, and therefore require concerted action.

One would expect that normally a reduction of the contractual value of a debt (debt relief) would reduce the actual repayments received by the creditor. In some situations, however, debt relief can lead to *larger* debt service payments than would be made in the absence of the relief, as well as more obviously to gains for the debtor. This would be so if it led to increased domestic investment, more productive work, and greater current sacrifices in the debtor countries, both because more resources would become available and because the incentive to invest and work would be improved. Higher investment would lead to higher growth, and the additional resources in turn to a larger amount of debt service payments. The means would become available, and the incentive to make current sacrifices for the sake of larger production later, both of which would be absent or much less if it were expected that a higher proportion of (or all) resources would have to be devoted to debt service.

But although all banks would benefit from such a general debt relief, because growth and exports could be resumed by debtor countries, each bank has an incentive to let others make the concessions. Relief by only one or only some means that the remainder of the payments goes to pay interest to those not having made the concessions, and thus frustrates the purpose of the exercise. Each bank has an interest in not giving relief, whether others give relief or not. At present, banks already sell their claims at discounted values to other institutions, including to some debtor countries; but this is no help to the debtors, unless the debt reduction is passed on to the debtor country. The buying back by the debtor country at lower value tends to be inflationary, since it involves a large current liability. But the free market does not solve the problem of this passing on of debt relief to the debtor, because of the logic of collective action and the free-rider problem. Concerted action by all to forgo part of the claims by all lenders is necessary in order to reap these gains. This would be one of the functions of the International Debt Facility. The possibility that debt service payments would actually be larger is, of course, not essential to the working of the operation.

Second, after part of the debt has been forgiven, multilateral guarantees are needed for the remaining debt. In this lies the attraction to the creditors to forgive part of the debt. Here again, concerted action by the USA and other creditor governments, the Fund, the Bank and the debtor governments is needed. Only then can normal lending be resumed. Neither the market nor the uncoordinated actions of governments can bring about this solution of the debt problem. It is in the interest of any one government *not* to guarantee, whether others guarantee or not. But it is in the interest of the major lending countries' governments to jointly guarantee the debt. This coordination would be another function of the International Debt Facility.

An additional function of the Facility would be to buy the debts from the banks at a discount and then to forgive the debtors part of the debt. This may benefit the banks, because the market price of their debt may rise. The outcome will depend on whether the facility has prior claims on interest and repayments to other creditors, and on how large the holdings of the facility are. The proposal takes different forms, but in essence it amounts to a debt reduction. The functions could be fulfilled by existing international institutions such as the World Bank and the International Monetary Fund.

d. Commodity Price Stabilization

The failure on the part of the developing countries and UNC-TAD to reach agreement on a working scheme of commodity price stabilization is due partly to absence of political agreement,

and partly to the weak analytical basis on which it was presented. The case had been based largely on micro-economic arguments about stabilizing or raising producers' or consumers' incomes, or improving incentives. In my view a much stronger case
can be made on macroeconomic grounds. Lord Kaldor,[1] Ravi
Kanbur[2] and others have shown that different pricing methods
for primary and manufactured products, combined with the fact
that primary products are imported inputs into manufactured
goods, lead to alternations of inflation and unemployment with
fluctuating and depressed incomes in the exporting countries.
Commodity price stabilization schemes can contribute to reduced inflation and unemployment in advanced importing countries, and to income stabilization and enhancement in developing
exporting countries. This nexus depends, however, on the continuing link between raw materials and manufactures. Peter
Drucker has expressed doubts about this.[3] He has argued that recent advances in technology have weakened or even broken that
link, as well as those between employment and production and
between finance and trade. But the volatility of commodity prices
with the swings in manufacturing activity suggests that the link
still exists.

Primary commodities (minerals and agricultural raw materials) are inputs into the manufactured products of the industrial
countries. Rises of commodity prices lead to inflation in industrial countries, because manufactured goods are priced on a mark-
up basis. When inflation is fought with monetary and fiscal contraction, unemployment rises. In the exporting developing
countries, the incomes of poor exporters fall. The instability also
discourages investment in these commodities. When the primary
objective is to fight inflation, low commodity prices are welcomed

1. NICHOLAS KALDOR, 'The Role of Commodity Prices in Economic Recovery',
World Development, vol. 15 no. 5, May 1987.

2. S. M. RAVI KANBUR, 'How to Analyse Commodity Price Stabilisation: A Review
Article', *Oxford Economic Papers*, vol. 36 no. 3, November 1984, pp. 336-358, and S.M.
RAVI KANBUR and DAVID VINES, 'North-South Interaction and Commodity Control',
Centre for Economic Policy Research Discussion Paper Series no. 8, 1984; published
later in *Oxford Economic Papers*.

3. PETER F. DRUCKER, 'The Changed World Economy', *Foreign Affairs*, Spring 1986,
pp. 768-791.

by industrial countries. But the burden is shifted to the poor producers, and aggravated by illiberal trade and migration policies of the depressed industrial countries. Depressed prices and low investment then lead to the next violent price increase, and the cycle is completed. The instability has been made worse by the tendency of the international financial institutions to advise each exporting country separately to devalue, to export more of its main commodity, and to diversify into others, irrespective of the fact that this has led to global surpluses and falling prices of all commodities.

What is needed is a revival of Keynes's proposal for the International Trade Organization. By stabilizing commodity prices both inflation and unemployment in the industrial countries are reduced. Incomes in the developing countries are stabilized and raised, by encouraging investment. And the world economy can expand at a stable rate. "Back to the future of Bretton Woods" would not be a bad slogan for the 1990s.

e. Global Energy Policy

Nobody can call the events since 1973 in the area of global energy satisfactory, from the point of view of either exporters or importers of oil. We have suffered from wild zig-zag movements of oil prices, leading to periods of conservation, high cost exploitation and exploration of alternatives, followed by periods of waste, closing down of high-cost wells and cessation of conservation. Not only are the wrong signals and incentives given in the energy sector, but the high oil prices lead to inflation, which, if countered by monetary contraction, is followed by deflation, unemployment and underutilized capacity, and deprives industry further of incentives and means to spend on conservation and the exploration of new sources and alternatives.

A more sensible course would be for selling and buying countries to agree on a future price of oil in, say 20 years' time. This might require a gradual, agreed increase by, say, 2 per cent per year. Investment would be stabilized, based on stable predictions. Inflationary and deflationary impulses and unemployment would be reduced, and the exploration of alternatives would be encouraged, while the resources for this would be made available.[1]

f. An Industrial Investment Board

At present the world economy lurches between excess capacity and scarcity in the products of industries, the plant of which takes a long time to construct and, once constructed, lasts a long time. Steel, fertilizer and ship building are examples. It is not, as the cobweb theorem assumes, that businessmen learn from recent experience, without learning that their learning process is wrong. The problem is that, in the absence of coordination, there is nothing to learn. If A's investment depends on B's (or the absence of B's), and B's on A's, the outcome is in its nature indeterminate. It is not that the market fails, but that there are no relevant market signals or incentives or allocation mechanisms to communicate, unless decisions are coordinated.

At a minimum an exchange of information about intentions for investment plans, on the pattern of the British National Economic Development Offices, would help to introduce greater stability. A further step would be to coordinate the planning of investment decisions, although this must not be permitted to degenerate into cartel-type market-sharing arrangements. An institution such as a board for fixed investment in durable plant with long gestation periods would provide the forum to discuss such matters.

g. Global Taxation

The absence of a system of global taxation is an important incentive for capital flight, which in turn constitutes one of the major damages suffered by developing countries from their coexistence with industrial countries. It implies either that investment and

1. On the problems of commodity agreements, the temptations to operate outside the agreements, and therefore without them, and how to overcome these difficulties, see PAUL STREETEN, 'Dynamics of the New Poor Power', in *A World Divided: The Less Developed Countries in the World Economy*, edited by G. K. HELLEINER, Cambridge: Cambridge University Press 1975; expanded version in *Resources Policy,* June 1976.

growth are lower than had the capital been retained, or that more money has to be borrowed from abroad, with the higher debt burden this involves.

One step towards a global system of taxation would be to sign treaties to secure an exchange of information between the losing and the haven countries that would permit the collection of taxes on foreign investment income. This would presuppose the adoption of taxation by residence, as well as by origin, so that income by all residents is taxed, wherever it arises, and all income arising in the country is taxed, wherever the subject resides. It would also assume that tax laws are implemented and no evasion occurs. Double taxation agreements would prevent the same income being taxed twice. This would permit the collection of taxes due on foreign investment income. In 1989 several OECD countries ratified a Multilateral Information Sharing Agreement, negotiations on which started in 1980, on the exchange of information of data on capital flight. The Draft Convention on Mutual Assistance in Tax Matters has been confined to industrial countries, but should be opened to developing countries. Of course, tax evasion has been only one of the motives for capital flight. Corrupt receipts of money, differential interest rates, exchange controls, bad macroeconomic policies, risks of expropriation, are among others.

Revenue-sharing has been proposed by Carlos Diaz-Alejandro, who suggested that the United States should hand over the money collected from a withholding tax on interest on deposits of Latin Americans to the Inter-American Development Bank.[1] The USA has already accepted this principle for the proceeds of assets seized from narcotics trade from nationals of countries with which the USA has concluded Mutual Legal Assistance Treaties. These proceeds are shared between the USA and the relevant country. It constitutes a useful precedent.[2]

In addition to reducing capital flight, global taxation would

1. CARLOS DIAZ-ALEJANDRO, 'Latin American Debt: I Don't Think We Are in Kansas Anymore', *Brookings Papers on Economic Activity*, no. 2, 1984.

2. JOHN WILLIAMSON and DONALD R. LESSARD, *Capital Flight: The Problem and Policy Responses*, Washington D.C.: Institute for International Economics, Policy Analyses in International Economics, November 1987.

provide a pool of resources for global use. In the current climate of retreat from global commitments, the proposal of a global progressive income tax will appear even more Utopian than some of the others. Nevertheless, it is worth exploring how such a scheme might work. The main principle of global taxation would be to move towards a system of automatic collection of revenue, but not automatic disbursements. Disbursements would remain conditional not only on obvious factors such as size of population and level of poverty, but also on performance in economic policy, human development, human rights, and similar areas. Conditionality should be replaced by a dialogue between the tax authority and the recipient country, which would be part of a global compact.

The present target of 0.7 per cent of GNP would be replaced by a progressive levy. The ratio of national income taxed for each country would be progressive with income per head. There would be a low exemption limit, and another limit entitling countries to receive grants.

If a progressive international income tax, levied progressively according to average income per head on total national income, is regarded as too radical, there are other bases for taxation which may be found more acceptable. Such bases for global revenue would be oil, the arms trade, international tourism, licence fees on patents and copyrights, or a tax on all international trade, or capital movements. Ideal taxes would be those imposed on carbon dioxide and sulphur emissions or pollution of the oceans.

h. A Global Competition Policy

In the USA the Webb Pomerane Act encourages firms to band together in monopolistic action against foreigners, while the Sherman Anti-Trust Act forbids similar action in the domestic market. It is true that not many companies are registered under this Act, partly because they do not wish to reveal their proprietary knowledge, as would be required, and partly because domestic anti-trust prosecution has greatly declined. But the asymmetry in treating monopolistic exploitation of citizens and that of foreigners, especially weaker foreigners, is glaring. A global order based on fairness, equality and human solidarity would apply the same principles to international transactions as are applied to domestic ones. A global monopolies and restrictive practices commission may be required to examine the scope of competition, restrictive practices and similar problems.

i. Monitoring Buffer Institutions for Aid

In the section on poverty I discussed several ways in which accountability to the taxpayers of donor countries can be combined with respect for national sovereignty. Mutual monitoring by developing countries themselves, a council of wise men and women who are trusted by both sides and a move towards a genuinely global secretariat with loyalties to the world community were examples of how the aid dialogue can be removed from acrimony.

j. A Technological Agency

Technology, in addition to bringing undreamt of blessings, can also bring nightmares. The impact of information technology on employment and income distribution, the electronic nightmare as painted so vividly in Kurt Vonnegut's *Player Piano,* the Frankenstein nightmare arising from biotechnological experiments, the nightmare of the terrorist atom bomb in the suitcase, and the less discussed problems that arise from conflicts between democratic accountability and highly technical decisions, from missile systems to exchange rates, the research and development wars embarked upon from three powerful collective sentiments: collective greed, fear, and pride, call for international action.[1]

k. A Global Health Agency

Health also has become globalized. AIDS is the most discussed problem. The impact of environmental degradation and decay,

---

1. I am indebted to Ronald Dore for discussion of these ideas.

such as global warming, ozone depletion, toxic and radioactive waste disposal, deteriorating water and air quality, deforestation and desertification, on health are also much discussed. There are important shifts in immigration patterns, increasingly from the Third World. It is no longer possible to draw a sharp distinction between domestic and international health. National self-interest requires international cooperation or global measures. Japan has become the leader in the funding of international health.

l. International Migration

The pressures for international migration, for economic, political and environmental reasons, are growing. In Europe and the USA political sentiment against immigrants is rising, and will increase further if unemployment increases.

The fact that the world is divided into sovereign states, and that there is no world government, has important implications for all members of the human race. Some of these are detrimental to human development. They are due partly to natural and historical conditions and endowments, and partly to erected barriers against equalizing tendencies. International action is needed to resolve these contradictions.

m. A Global Environmental Protection Agency

Just as in an uncoordinated world each country has an incentive to pour its problem of unemployment, metaphorically, into the yards of others, so does it, literally, cast its muck into the neighbouring gardens or into the oceans, the atmosphere or the land which are the global commons. Acid rain that kills forests, the emission of chlorofluorocarbons that destroy the ozone layer, the global warming resulting from the burning of fossil fuels, overfishing in common waters, are examples of global abuse that can be stopped only by global agreements that limit national sovereignty in order to achieve national objectives.

The domestic environmental problems of rich countries are often in conflict with poverty reduction in developing countries, while the domestic environmental problems of poor countries both arise from, and contribute to, poverty. But the global environmental problems are shared by the whole of humanity and call for global solutions. The issues are sufficiently important to warrant a special appendix to this Lecture.

5. Desirable and Feasible?

Two types of objection can be made to these proposals: one on grounds of desirability, the other on grounds of feasibility. First, it may be said that creative institutions are not designed on a drawing board, but are the spontaneous responses to challenging situations. Designed institutions, such as the League of Nations, the World Economic Conference of 1933, the International Trade Charter, the Special Drawing Rights, all failed, while the multinational corporation, the Eurocurrency market, the globalization of the 24-hour capital market and the swap arrangements between central banks, none of which sprang from grand designs, are considerable successes. The Bretton Woods institutions are the exception, but they were born after a world war and the complete breakdown of a previous order.

My reply would be that these spontaneous institutions themselves need designed institutions to regulate them. The current debt crisis is a direct result of the unregulated recycling of OPEC surpluses by greedy lenders to profligate borrowers. Had something like the proposed International Investment Trust been in place in the seventies, we would have been spared many of the present pains. So much in reply to the charge that the proposals are undesirable.

A different criticism is that, though desirable, they are not feasible; they are utterly unrealistic and Utopian. There are five replies to such a criticism, in defence of Utopian proposals. First, Utopian thinking can be useful as a framework for thinking, in the same way that physicists assume for some purposes a vacuum. The assumption plainly would not be useful for the design of parachutes, but can serve other purposes well. Similarly, when thinking of tomorrow's problems, Utopianism is not helpful. But for strategic purposes it is essential. Second, the Utopian vision gives a sense of direction, which can get lost in approaches that are preoccupied with the feasible. In a world that is regarded as the best of all feasible worlds, everything becomes a necessary constraint and all vision is lost. Third, excessive concern with the feasible tends to reinforce the status quo. In negotiations, it strengthens the hand of those opposed to reform. Fourth, it is sometimes the case that the conjuncture of circumstances changes quite suddenly and dramatically, and that the constellation of forces, unexpectedly, turns out to be favourable to even radical innovation. Unless we are prepared with a carefully worked out, detailed plan, that yesterday may have appeared utterly Utopian, reforms will lose out by default. Nobody would have expected only a few years ago the dramatic changes in Central and East Europe, the Soviet Union, China and South Africa. Although the subsequent fate of the Special Drawing Rights was disappointing, when they were established the creation and acceptability of an international liquid asset came as a surprise to many. Fifth, the Utopian reformers themselves can constitute a pressure group, countervailing the self-interested pressures of the obstructionist groups. Ideas thought to be Utopian have become realistic at moments in history when large numbers of people support them, and those in power have to yield to their demands. The demand for ending slavery is a historical example. It is for these five reasons that Utopians should not be discouraged from formulating their proposals, unencumbered by the inhibitions and obstacles of political constraints, in the same detail that the defenders of the status quo devote to its elaborations, from thinking the unthinkable.

6. Orwellian Blocks

In spite of my plea for the Utopian exercise of the institutional imagination, for the practice of informed fantasy, I would be the first to agree that the likelihood of any of these steps towards a global order, based on pluralism and equality, being implemented is minuscule. I therefore turn now to a more probable scenario, the formation of blocks. The most recent precedent is that of the inter-war period. There was the Ottawa Agreement of 1932 and the Sterling Area or, as it was then called, the Sterling Block. There was the French Union; and the USA with the Monroe doctrine. The fragmentation of the world into blocks gave scope for the ruthless rather than the strong. Trade between blocks had been minimized. The exclusion of the Japanese from South and Southeast Asia by the British, French and Dutch was a major cause of Japanese aggression. The exclusion of Germany from the Western blocks contributed to the Second World War.

The multilateral system that had been built in the quarter century after the war has been undermined by the formation of the Group of Five, Group of Seven, and the Summits. What we may see emerging is something that resembles Orwell's picture in *1984*: Oceania, Eurasia and Eastasia. Lester Thurow has recently pronounced in Davos, in a Swiss valley next to the valley in which Nietzsche pronounced God as dead, that "GATT" is dead, and that multilateralism will be replaced by blocks. But it is well known that GATT has nine lives, and it may echo, according to Jagdish Bhagwati, the British imperial cry, "the king is dead; long live the king!"

The liberal world order that the USA had advocated after the war had never been accepted by Europe and Japan. Germany yielded to open her market in return for American troops and defence against the Soviet Union. In the eighties the USA itself retreated from liberal trade. And the USA, Japan, Germany, France and Britain retreated from multilateral institutions.

If this trend is continued, we might see the formation of three blocks. Europe with her ex-colonies in Africa will become 'Fortress Europe'. The USA, Canada, Mexico, the Caribbean Basin and parts of Central and South America will form a second block. Japan and the Pacific Rim, with the four Asian tigers, and possibly ASEAN (Indonesia, Philippines, Malaysia, Singapore, Thailand) would form an East Asian block. (But it must be remembered that Japan's largest market is now the USA, taking 39 per cent of its exports, and that South Korea and Taiwan are more integrated with the USA than with Japan.)

At the same time, Japan's trade with the whole of Asia is larger than its trade with North America. Other tentacles of members of these blocks will reach out to outsiders, such as some Caribbean countries to Britain, ex-French colonies to France, Europe to Central and East Europe, etc. and these will weaken the block formation.

It is not clear that there is uniform support for such block formation. Singapore and Malaysia, for example, are keen to preserve a multilateral, open trading system and to maintain a strong American presence, and are suspicious of a yen block. Japan's attempt at regional block formation could be the reaction to fears that there might be a retreat from GATT-led free trade, and that it might be excluded from its two main export markets, the USA and Europe.

There are, however, good reasons for an East Asian block. Apart from the growth of trade among these nations, Japan has become a bigger market for Asian manufactures, rather than an exclusive importer of primary products. In addition, the yen is playing a more important role in international capital markets and other countries' foreign exchange reserves. Japanese interest rates are low, and its savings abundant. Finally, Japanese foreign investment in the region has increased. The East and South-East Asian economies are becoming vertically integrated, producing components for one another.

Much would depend on what form these blocks would take; whether, for example, Europe will be an open, outward-looking community, part of a global order, or a highly regulated, bureaucratic block. François Perroux's *L'Europe sans rivages*[1] contains a global, cosmopolitan vision (though not one of laissez-faire or even free trade), which must be contrasted with that of an enlarged, exclusive, inward-looking super-state. If Perroux's vision is realized, blocks can be envisaged as a step towards an integrated, global system. Since a global system cannot be achieved at once, regionalism may point the way to it.

In the longer run, there will be competition in manufactured exports from Mexico, China and India. Mexico will be incorporated in the US-Canada block; China perhaps go with Japan.

This solution need not be as horrifying as Orwell painted it. It

---

1. FRANÇOIS PERROUX, *L'Europe sans rivages*, Paris: PUF 1954.

is a second-best compared with the multilateral, pluralist solution, but can produce a well-working system. We have succeeded in avoiding major wars for quite a long period. The block system would permit styles of living to be maintained within each block. The Europeans would not have to give up their long holidays, generous social welfare system, workers' participation in management, and minimum wages, or to accept the low rates of return on investment of the Japanese, more interested in long-term presence, and maximizing market shares than in short-term profits. There would be problems of origin, for excluding Japanese producers may mean excluding American products, if they were made by the Japanese in America. The trade between the blocks would be managed through market-sharing and cartel agreements.

A faster rate of growth within each block fostered by homogeneous attitudes and institutions, could lead to more trade between the blocks, even though the ratio of trade to GNP is lower for any given level of income, than in a more open, though more slowly growing, world economy. What some regard as stumbling blocks could become building blocks.

But there are drawbacks to such a system. First, its exclusivity, like that in the inter-war period, may encourage aggression. Second, some areas might be left out. This is matter of concern, even if it were not to lead to aggression. It is not clear what would be the role of South Asia. India is a potentially important country in the global economy, but there is no clear role for it in this scenario. What would be the role of Russia and the Commonwealth of Independent States? There might be an alignment of Europe with them.

While the pluralistic section was devoted to a normative discussion, this section's concern is more positive. But there are interesting normative questions arising from the block scenario. Apart from the question of the nature of the blocks and their policies, there is the question of the optimum number and optimum size of the blocks. Are three blocks, *ceteris paribus*, better than two? The literature on optimum currency areas is only part of this subject.

7. Coordination among Oligarchs

A third scenario is presented by the USA, Japan, and Germany, (or with the addition of Britain, France, Italy and Canada) together deciding to rule the world. Fiscal and monetary coordination between the three, plus any additionally coopted powers, would be required. This is not easy to achieve.

There are authors who oppose coordination between governments and advocate competition. But competition in the market place and even reduced government intervention in trade policy call for international cooperation – cooperation to refrain from intervening. Free trade is not the same as laissez-faire. It has to be enforced, just as anti-monopoly legislation has to be enforced. Moreover, nations and their governments are not like individuals or companies competing atomistically in markets. They are concerned with objectives other than economic ones, and react to one another's actions. The silliness of attempting to follow national policies without regard to others is illustrated by a remark, attributed (possibly apocryphally) to a distinguished American economic adviser to Presidents, "Let others worry about their exchange rates, and we'll worry about ours!"

At the same time, it is important to remember that coordination of policies can be ineffective (because similar policies can be substituted for those agreed upon) or, worse, harmful. This is the case if the coordination is based on false analysis or wrong predictions (or if there is disagreement on say, the question as to whether the deficit affects the interest rate); or if the coordination gives rise to countervailing private power, say of trade unions pushing up wages; or if the coordination removes constraints on bad, politically convenient policies, such as inflation; or if it diverts attention from domestic reforms in the expectation that others will act (e.g. US expectation that Germany and Japan will expand sufficiently to make its reduction of the deficits unnecessary).

Coordination does work, though often only in response to a crisis. After the stock market crash on Monday 19 October 1987 every country expanded and the feared depression did not occur.

The oligarchic solution has the drawback that the interests of non-participants are only incidentally served. Stephen Marris has proposed a response to oligarchy: the creation of a Group of Non-Five. It would include all members of the IMF and GATT who are not members of the Group of Five. Its objective is to restore multilateralism in trade, payments, development, etc. This Group would lobby for representation on the Group of Five and its Summits. But the ultimate aim would be to make itself redundant.

8. Global Balkanization

We are witnessing a surge of ethnic and national sentiments. The fragmentation, Balkanization or Lebanonization of the world into small nation states has been progressing rapidly in the ex-Soviet Union, in Eastern Europe, Yugoslavia, Iraq, and India. There are 5,000 peoples in the world and only 183 members of the United Nations. Like the above-mentioned Group of Non-Five, there is a possible need to create an organization of non-state nations, such as the Kurds, Armenians, Basques, Scots, Welsh, Cornish, Québécois, Cree Indians, Catalans, South Tyroleans, Tibetans, Australian aboriginals, and the Palestinians. Some have already achieved statehood, such as the Lithuanians, Latvians, Estonians, Slovenes, and Croats. The non-state nations now have the Unrepresented Nations and Peoples Organization (UNPO). Their Charter was signed on 11 February 1991 in The Hague. The conditions for membership are the renunciation of terrorism and the acknowledgement by a majority of citizens. A world in which states proliferate is not going to be a very safe one.

9. Conclusion

The problem is how to adjust to a world in which the power of the dominant economy, the USA, has declined, without its being replaced by a single or a small group of new dominant leaders. My call for new, global institutions must not be misunderstood as a call for more international bureaucracies. They, alas, have often been not an instrument of, but an obstacle to, international reform. At the same time, the questions of recruitment, training, and promotion of a genuinely global civil service, with loyalties to the world community, sensitive to social and political issues but not the victims of political pressures, technically expert, but aware of the limits of these techniques, should be high on our agenda. But when I speak of institutions I have in mind rules, procedures, norms, valuations, frameworks for enforcement, as well as organizations, what some call "regimes", which, I would hope, would replace the past regimes of dominance and dependence by one of pluralism and equality.

APPENDIX

Institutions for "Sustainable" Development

1. Introduction. – 2. Threats to the Environment of Developing Countries. – 3. Economic Growth Versus Environment. – 4. Human, Sustainable Development: Policy Issues. – 5. Global Institutions for Suitable Development.

1. Introduction

I now want to turn to one type of institutional reform that has occupied centre stage in recent discussions: institutions concerned with preserving our physical environment.

Sustainable development, in the words of the report of Gro Harlem Brundtland, chairman of the World Commission on Environment and Development, is "development that meets the needs of the present without compromising the ability of future generations to meet their own needs".[1] This definition is sufficiently vague to cover many contingencies. J. R. Hicks wrote similarly half a century ago, but thinking only of one generation, that "the purpose of income calculation in practical affairs is to give people an indication of the amount which they can consume without impoverishing themselves".[2] Even this definition is elusive, because the maximum amount of consumption that an individual can expect to maintain while keeping the initial level of wealth intact depends on his expectations of future prices and interest rates.[3]

Sustainable development has come to mean much more than maintaining intact the physical and human capital that produces an income stream (or increasing it in line with population growth, technological developments, intertemporal preferences, etc.). Maintenance, replacement and growth of capital assets, both physical and human, is certain-

---

1. *Our Common Future,* Report of the World Commission on Environment and Development, Oxford: Oxford University Press, 1987.

2. JOHN R. HICKS, *Value and Capital,* 2nd edition, Oxford: Oxford University Press, 1946, p. 172.

3. Whether the current high levels of real interest rates lead to premature raw material exhaustion, or whether they allegedly choke off investment sufficiently to avoid this, is an important subject for sustainable development. It is, however, not explored in this paper. Higher investment, stimulated by lower interest rates, need not, of course, be raw material consuming or polluting but can consist of raw-material-saving technology, scrubbers and other pollution-reducing devices. It follows that the recent unprecedentedly high interest rates are unambiguously bad for the environment. I have argued elsewhere that there is no case for a positive pure time discount rate. See PAUL STREETEN, 'What do we Owe the Future?' *Resources Policy,* March 1986.

ly one aspect of sustainability. Physical wear and tear, technical obsolescence, and the depreciation of human capital have to be taken into account.

A second aspect, to which much attention has been paid recently, is maintaining the physical environmental conditions for the constituents of well-being. Unless the environmental resources serving as inputs are valued in themselves, it is the results, not the means, that must be sustained. This implies avoiding polluting the water, air, and land on which our lives and our work depend, and avoiding the exhaustion of renewable resources that are essential for production, unless adequate replacement by other forms of capital is provided. (It may imply increasing these environmental resources, again depending on population growth, technology, preferences, etc.)

Related to this is a third aspect of sustainability, which is resilience. The system must be able to adjust to shocks and crises, to be sufficiently flexible and diverse, with respect to resources (including biological diversity) and practices (including approaches to knowledge), to maintain itself in the face of an uncertain future.

A fourth aspect is avoiding burdening future generations with internal and external debts. Although to anybody burdened with a debt liability there corresponds an equivalent asset holder, this does not mean that the net debt burden is zero. Tax liabilities, and the ability to enjoy interest receipts, have important effects on incentives to work, save, and risk, in addition to the distributional impact.

A fifth aspect of sustainable development is fiscal, administrative and political sustainability. A policy must be credible and acceptable to the citizens, so that there is sufficient consent to carry it out. Fear of popular protest in the form of mass demonstrations or riots can frustrate reforms. In order to be sustainable politically, the course of opposition and resistance has to be traced and measures to overcome it have to be designed. The administrative apparatus must be capable of carrying it out on a continuing basis, and revenue must be available to meet the needs of public expenditure. International peace and domestic security are important dimensions of political sustainability.

A sixth aspect is the ability to hand over projects to citizens of the developing country, for their own management, so that foreign experts can withdraw without jeopardizing their success. This implies training local counterparts and helping to create local technological, managerial and administrative capacity.

Sustainability is therefore a multi-dimensional problem. It implies responsible behaviour towards future generations, despite the fact that they have no vote and cannot put direct pressures on policy makers. The main concern of this paper is the second and third aspects, environmental sustainability.

"Sustainability", by itself, is however not a clearly defined term. First, there is the problem, already mentioned, whether one should be concerned with sustaining the constituents of well-being or its determinants, whether with the means or the ends. Clearly, what ought to matter are the constituents, the health, welfare and prosperity of the people, and not so many tons of minerals, so many trees, or so many animal species. Yet, some of the writings on the subject confuse the two. If in the process of curing ovarian cancer the Pacific yew trees (or even the spotted owl) had to be reduced in number, in order to produce the drug taxol, people's health must be given priority over trees. Of course, some would want to attach end-values to many of the constituents, in so far as they are part of "nature". This view might be called ethical environmentalism in contrast with prudential environmentalism. Economists do not question such human preference.

Then there is the question as to sustainability at what level, or at what rate of growth or decline? There is nothing sacrosanct about the existing stock of resources. Population in Western Europe is stationary or may decline, but Kenya's population will be three times today's in 2025, and world population will be more than 8 billion people, compared with 5.5 billion today. Sustaining income per head for mankind may imply increasing the stock of resources. On the other hand, substitution possibilities in response to relative price changes and technical innovation imply the ability to run some down. Population growth, technological innovations, and intertemporal preferences will determine whether the stock should be increased, kept constant or reduced, and at what rates, or whether its composition should be changed. But, as *The Economist* has put it, "sustainable development is still useful. Like many important ideas, it is better than nothing for as long as there is nothing better."[1]

2. Threats to the Environment of Developing Countries

The principal threats to the physical environment of the developing countries can be grouped under the following headings.

1. Continuing rapid rates of population growth
2. Accelerating rates of urbanization

1. *The Economist,* September 16 1989, p. 77.

3. Atomic energy: accidents, waste disposal, sabotage

4. Damage done by persistent pesticides and other dangers to the food chain

5. Damage done by industrial trace materials and toxic waste disposal

6. Destruction of forests and soils, plant and animal life

7. Silting and salination

8. Global and regional transnational concerns about warming, the ozone layer, acid rain, ocean pollution, etc.

It will be seen that this list overlaps, but is not identical, with a similar list that could be drawn up for advanced industrial countries. Whereas poverty is the main cause of environmental degradation in poor countries, it is opulence in the rich countries. Poverty and population pressure[1] drive people to the cultivation of ever more marginal land. This erodes the soil and depletes shallow water resources, causing growing poverty as crop yields fall and women spend more time collecting firewood and fetching water. It is estimated that 14 million people in the developing countries have become environmental refugees, driven from their homes by environmental degradation. The poor are both the cause and the victims of environmental degradation.

The rapid rates of population growth are the consequence of the introduction of modern death rates, resulting from modern death control, into societies with little cheap and effective birth control, and hence with traditional birth rates. At low income levels children are wanted because firewood and water have to be collected and many household chores have to be done. Old people need sons to look after them. Even young parents need many helpers. There is a vicious circle between the desire for large families, which leads to environmental damage, and the need for more hands to overcome the damage.

The so-called demographic transition from one equilibrium, in which both death rates and birth rates are high, to another, in which both are low, is both difficult and slow. The implications of this demo-

---

1. Rober Chambers has drawn my attention to the accumulating evidence that in some, and possibly in many, environments more people can be a condition for less degradation and more sustainable agriculture. For example in Nepal increased erosion in areas near the forest margins have been found to be not the result of increases in population and in cultivated areas but of depopulation and the collapse of terraces which can no longer be maintained for lack of people. In the Kakamega District in Kenya, it has been found through aerial transects and ground truthing that the density of trees varies with the density of population and with the smallness of landholdings. He cites many sources from different parts of the world.

graphic transition have been discussed at length, and all that is needed here is to note that it involves heavy environmental pressures in the poorest societies. Population growth in the developing countries is about five times as great as it is in the advanced countries in the second half of this century. The world's population has doubled since 1950. The share of people living in the advanced countries has fallen from 35 per cent in 1950 to about 20 per cent today, and continues to fall. The 80 per cent in the developing countries account for less than 20 per cent of the world's consumption. If present trends continue, world population will not stabilize until a size of 10 or 11 billion is reached. About 40 per cent of the population in the developing countries is less than 15 years old, compared with 30 per cent in the developed countries. The high dependency ratio implied by such an age distribution puts a heavy burden on the working population, on social services such as education, on the government budget, and on the ability to mobilize resources for development.

It is anticipated that between now and the year 2000 one billion people will be added to the populations of cities, more than the total number in cities now. The fastest growing cities are in the developing countries, where the ability to cope with the strains of urbanization is weakest. Here again, the literature is large and it must suffice to mention the high costs of urban services and the threats to the environment from pollution of air and water, congestion, noise and disease transmission.

The dangers from atomic energy, on which many developing countries are embarking, stem from the threat of the proliferation of nuclear weapon capability, reactor failures, the difficulties of disposing of radioactive waste, the possibility of diverting plutonium by terrorist groups, and the uncertainty about radiological standards. Less widely discussed but perhaps at least equally serious is the potential threat to civil liberties that arises from the need to protect societies against terrorists and saboteurs. The need for armed guards and possibly private armies to guard nuclear power stations can bode ill for human freedom. While all these problems also exist in advanced countries, the level of technical competence for dealing with them is lower in developing countries. Some of these dangers have implications that reach beyond national boundaries. They call for international coordination or transnational, global institutions, to be discussed more fully below.

The attraction of using cheap and effective chemical pesticides in agriculture in countries where the pressure to grow more food is very strong is clear, but the long-term adverse effects can be immense.

The urgent advances of industrialization will tend to spread trace materials of industrial origin: mercury, cadmium, polychlorinated biphenyls and other substances can have poisoning effects on people. Paper that is chlorine bleached contains dioxin and other organochlorines, which, in sufficiently large doses, are hazardous substances. Lavatory paper, tampons, tissues, milk cartons, coffee filters and disposal diapers contain it.[1] Firms from advanced countries have used developing countries as the dumping ground for their toxic waste.

The destruction of tropical forests as a result of the need for fuel (or for foreign exchange from the export of wood), with the associated adverse effects on soils, is now well documented, though the effects on climate and the global atmosphere, and on the alleged mass extinctions of plant and animal species, are more controversial. Dams have caused silting and irrigation canals have led to salination, destroying the fertility of the land.

A concern for environmental protection for developing countries is often met with hostility. It is felt that the industrialized countries have achieved high levels of living and now wish to prevent or slow down the same process of industrialization in the developing countries, for the sake of preserving values that are mainly the concern of the rich. Sceptics of environmental protection can also say that preserving the environment has many of the ingredients beloved of women's magazines – animals, a strong medical interest, and a readily identifiable villain. It is a cause that appears to appeal to the most advanced sociologists and to those who detest change in any form, to old women of both sexes and to the revolting young of unidentifiable sex, to the silent majority and the screaming minority, to the young swingers and to the old danglers. The majority of respondents in a recent Louis Harris poll in the USA rated a clean environment more important than a satisfactory sex life.[2] No wonder, then, that some spokesmen for the developing countries have said to those from the developed countries: "you have enriched yourselves by rapacious exhaustion of scarce raw materials and polluting the environment, and now you want to stop the world and want us to get off. We shall worry about the environment when we have become as rich as you."

Such reactions, perhaps less common today than a few years ago, are entirely understandable. It is generally true that the benefits of

1. Recently there has been a reassessment of dioxin. It is now regarded as only a moderate threat to human beings. It appears far less risky, for example, than asbestos, radon, nickel, coke, chromates or smoking.

2. *The Atlantic Monthly,* October 1990, p. 46.

133

additional production and incomes are greater, the lower the income per head, and the harm done by pollution is less, the lower the level of industrialization, urbanization, and production. For this reason, it would be absurd to impose uniform environmental standards everywhere, irrespective of the level of development. But it is often cheaper to design processes that are low in destructive material discharges than to try later to modify these wastes and damages, once they have been generated. There is no reason why developing countries should not learn from the mistakes of the now advanced countries and avoid courses of action that they would later regret. It has been found that the additional costs attributable to environmental and health safeguards in non-environmental projects have ranged from zero to 3 per cent of total project costs. Costs are lower the earlier the protective measures are added to the project design. Increasingly, these protective measures are being incorporated in the basic design of projects, such as emission controls for industrial plants. Prevention is much cheaper and more effective than cure. Sound watershed management, for example, which protects reservoirs from siltation and floods, costs much less than rehabilitation of a deforested, eroded watershed.

It remains true that the rich countries' consumption of energy is profligate. They enjoy spacious houses with high heating and cooling costs, and sprawling cities with roads clogged by two or three cars per family. The advanced countries produce about half of the 6 billion metric tons of greenhouse gases emitted each year, with only one fifth of the world's population. Energy consumption in the developing countries is expected to grow at a rate of 5 per cent a year, from 2,000 million tons of oil equivalent (mte) today to over 3,000 by the end of the century. All countries will have to raise their energy efficiency and develop new and renewable sources of energy.

The UK rate of population growth, for example, is 0.2 per cent per year, with a population of 58 million, while that of Bangladesh is 2.4 per cent per year with a population of 117 million. This means an extra 116,000 people in Britain, and 2.8 million in Bangladesh, or 24 times as many. But each person in Britain consumes energy equivalent of 40 barrels of oil per year, or 4.6 million barrels for the 116,000 newcomers. Each Bangadeshi consumes only one barrel of oil-equivalent energy per year, or 2.8 million barrels for the annual new arrivals. The implications for the greenhouse effect for Bangladesh are that it may lose one fifth of its territory to the rise in the sea level.[1]

1. Letter by Mr NORMAN MYERS in *The Times*, 7 August 1991.

3. Economic Growth Versus Environment?

The problem of "growth versus the environment" is wrongly posed. Growth is simply the intertemporal dimension of any strategy. Production, consumption, poverty reduction, income redistribution, employment, environmental protection, must each have a time profile, and this may give rise to inter-temporal trade-offs. Economic growth is a side-effect, not the aim, of a rational economic policy. It could be that sustainable development calls for *more*, not less growth. It certainly calls for *differently composed* growth from the one we witness in many countries now. For, although zero growth is not an option, unless sustainable development is consciously pursued, zero or negative growth could well be the result.

With technology given, four options should, theoretically, be considered. First, we may abstain from producing as much as we otherwise would, in order to reduce pollution and raw material exhaustion, which are closely linked to the pattern of production. We opt for fewer goods, in order to be saddled with fewer bads. Second, we devote resources that would have produced goods to produce products that combat pollution: more anti-bads. Whether this implies stepping up the rate of growth of national product, slowing it down, or changing its composition, depends on conventions of national income accounting. Much that is now counted as part of net national income should be deducted as intermediate production, as anti-bads, required to combat the bads produced in the course of generating the NNP. There is something to be said for the foundation of a Society for the Promotion of Anti-Bads.

Third, we may step up the production of goods, notwithstanding the fact that they aggravate pollution, to a degree that compensates for the growth of pollution: more goods to make up for the growth of bads. Finally, we may produce different products, with different characteristics. These are not as attractive as those that would have been produced without regard to pollution, but with the compensating merit that they carry with them less pollution: goods that are not quite so "good", but that generate also fewer "bads". Cars may travel more slowly, but are also less polluting. Compared with these four options zero growth, sometimes advocated, would be not only a blunt, but also an ineffective instrument for achieving a sustainable environment. The only way to sustain literally the resource base is to cease production and consumption altogether. This would mean, sooner or later, zero people.

In practice, it is normally much cheaper and more effective to take preventive action before the creation of bads than to compensate for their generation or to produce instruments to combat them. Just as it is easier to build distributional objectives into the growth process, or protection of the poor into the adjustment process *ab initio,* so it is more effective to build environmental objectives from the beginning into the direction and composition of growth.

In addition, there is much evidence that some previously polluting agents can be used profitably and harmlessly, so that no trade-off arises. It points to the existence of unexplored and unexploited profit opportunities, which can be seized as a result of environmental regulation. Effluents, previously discharged into rivers, have turned out to have commercial uses. When unexplored and unexploited profit opportunities are discovered, bads can be transformed into goods. This may require some expenditure on technical research. In other cases, cheap substitutes can be used to replace damaging substances. Du Pont, the world's largest producer of chlorofluorocarbons (CFCs), had discovered some equally cheap substitutes, which made the provisions of the Montreal Protocol of 1987 (signed by 57 countries), for the protection of the ozone layer (which protects us from certain types of cancer), acceptable. International Business Machines Corporation, America's largest source of CFC-113 emissions, had reduced its emissions in May 1991 by 95 per cent from the 1987 level. In the Ottawa Agreement of 1988 some industrial countries bound themselves to reduce the volume of CFC emissions by the end of the century to half the 1986 level.

The leading electronics companies have moved more rapidly than expected to phase out the use of industrial cleansers that damage the ozone layer. CFCs are used, in addition to air conditioners, refrigerators and foam insulation, to clean circuit boards and sensitive electronic components. Now cheaper, more effective and less damaging alternatives have been discovered, including warm, soapy water.[1] Some companies have developed circuit boards that need no cleaning at all.

Solvents used in the manufacture of pressure-sensitive tape were replaced with solventless raw materials, reducing 1,100 tonnes of solvent emissions and saving $ 1.5 million in one factory alone. On another tape-making line, an inert condensation type solvent recovery system recycles about 2,500,000 lb of solvent previously emitted in the atmosphere at an annual saving of $ 750,000 in solvent, production and energy costs. Modification of a plant boiler to burn high-hydrocarbon exhaust from a maker saved a million dollars in add-on pollution control

1. *The New York Times,* 15 May 1991. D 11.

and is likely to recover $ 270,000 of energy annually. Ammonium sulphite produced in reactors during the formulation of iron oxide, previously discharged through a waste water treatment plant into a river, is now concentrated in a vapour compression evaporator and sold as liquid fertilizer worth about $ 271,000 a year; savings in pollution control equipment totalled $ 1 million Examples could be multiplied.[1]

Environmentalists claim that these discoveries have important implications for other environmental concerns, including the reduction of the use of fossil fuels, which contribute to global warming, the elimination of CFCs from aerosol cans, and the formulation of cleaner petrols.

Professor Michael Porter of the Harvard Business School has shown that environmental regulations are entirely consistent with maintaining international competitiveness. In his book *The Competitive Advantage of Nations,* he found that countries with the most rigorous requirements often lead in exports of the affected products. The reason for this paradoxical conclusion is that regulations force companies to redesign their technology, to innovate, and to find new uses for waste products. The result in the medium to long term is often lower costs and improved product quality. Processes are adopted that lower the use of scarce or toxic resources and that recycle profitably previously wasted by-products.

Three types of questions have to be investigated: first, the relationship between differently composed rates of population growth and of income per head, and the discharge of harmful substances; second, the relation between these substances and the physical environment; and third, the impact of these changes in the physical environment on the health and well-being of human beings. The first is technical, the second physical, the third biological and physiological.[2] Having answered these three sets of factual questions, the problem becomes one of evaluating any remaining conflicts between higher incomes and environmental degradation and sharing fairly any sacrifices, either of the environment or of income, between the partners. Such fair sharing will involve compensation of poorer countries by richer ones for accepting measures of environmental protection that are either more costly or reduce the rate of growth. This can be done, for example, by issuing permits for emissions in excess of their needs to low-income countries, which they could sell to the high-income countries, who will want to use

1. *The Times,* 15 October 1984, Science Report by TONY SAMSTAG, 'Pollution prevention pays handsomely'.

2. See ROBERT DORFMAN, 'Protecting the Global Environment: An Immodest Proposal', *World Development,* vol. 19 no. 1, January 1991.

more permits than they have been initially allocated. A system of monitoring both the state of the environment, and individual countries' performance and discharges, will be needed, as well as mechanisms for penalizing offenders. The United Nations Environmental Programme (UNEP) now has a Global Environmental Monitoring System (GEMS), although it is grossly underfinanced.

There is now firm evidence available to answer the first question, viz. the relation between income and certain types of pollution. The main conclusion is that urban SO_2 concentrations, and urban suspended particulate matter levels are *lower* per cubic metre in high-income cities than in low-income cities. It is also evident that these concentrations have been falling in high-income and middle-income cities between 1980 and 1989.

4. Human, Sustainable Development: Policy Issues

There is some overlap with, but there are also important differences between, the environmental problems of poor and rich countries. Poverty has been one of the most important enemies of sustainable environment, and environmental degradation has reinforced poverty. As has already been said, the poor are both the cause and the principal victims of environmental degradation. To be freed from this vicious circle not only sustains the environment, but is above all beneficial for the human beings who live in it. The fundamental concern of the development effort is not with enlarging the choices of trees, but of humans. Deforestation and soil erosion as a result of the growing need for fuel wood; the spread of schistosomiasis or bilharzia from stagnant water reservoirs; the spread of onchocerciasis or river blindness from running mountain streams; these are the environmental problems of poor rural people, caused by them and imposing suffering on them. The eradication of poverty will also remove these environmental threats, and their removal will contribute to the reduction of poverty.

The first lesson is that late industrial starters can learn from the mistakes of earlier starters. It is possible to avoid in the beginning the creation of the environmental damage that the advanced industrial countries have inflicted upon themselves, and the wasteful uses of energy that the Western style of industrialization has involved. Heavy dependence on oil supplies and being hooked on the motor car, can be avoided by more energy conservation and greater use of indigenous sources of energy. These would also contribute to greater self-reliance.

A second set of policy questions relates to the international location of dirty processes. Just as differences in factor endowments guide the allocation of resources according to comparative advantage, so differences in pollution costs should in principle guide international specialization of industry. The costs of pollution will tend to be lower in many developing countries and the benefits to be derived from industrial production higher, because incomes are lower. For both these reasons, a shift of polluting activities from the industrial countries to the developing countries can be envisaged. The rule might be summed up by saying, what some find grubby, others find groovy.

A distinction should be drawn between *local*, *regional* and *global* pollution. *Global* pollution includes the spread of persistent pesticide residues that can be carried far beyond national frontiers; acid rain that ruins forests; the burning of fossil fuels, and the release of carbon dioxide, methane, nitrous oxides and chlorofluorocarbons (CFCs) into the atmosphere that may lead to the greenhouse effect and global warming; (although some say it will usher in a new ice age); deforestation, especially in the tropical rain forests, which may upset the ecological balance and deplete genetic resources; the pollution of the oceans through oil spillage or dumping from ships; the pollution of air streams by jets; the destruction of the ozone layer through chlorofluorocarbons, which causes skin cancer, cataracts and other health problems; ultraviolet radiation that may lower the harvest of soybeans, the world's leading protein crop; and there are other induced changes in the global climate; chemical wastes that seep downwards to poison ground water and upwards to destroy the atmosphere's delicate balance; and so on.

Regional pollution arises from the geophysical linkages between several countries, such as river pollution, desertification and regional air pollution. Deforestation in the Himalayas causes flooding in Bangladesh. DDT is banned in the USA, yet it is found in the mud of Lake Siskiwit near Lake Superior, carried by the wind. Acid rain, sulphur dioxide emitted from US coal-fired power plants, is carried to Canadian forests.

Local pollution is confined within national boundaries, such as the eutrophication of a lake from fertilizer or sewage discharge. Local environmental problems are also presented by traffic congestion in cities, pollution of beaches and along coastlines, and suburban sprawl. It would be legitimate for a country to restrict activities and products that would affect it and that result from another country's activities, but such restrictions must not be used as a pretext for protectionism by the industrial countries, where the pollution is purely local and remains confined to the area of production in the developing country. Taxes imposed by industrial countries on their pollution-intensive activities can be used by them as an excuse to exclude imports from countries that can conduct these activities at lower social costs without harm to the importing country. The "sweated environment" argument for protection is as fallacious as the "sweated labour" argument. The international free trade unions are misguided (or act in the interest of rich country trade unions) in advocating a clause in GATT that would insist on the same environmental standards for all countries, so as not to give an "unfair" advantage to poor countries.

A third set of policy questions relates to the return to the use of some natural products that had been hit by the invention of synthetics, but in the production of which the costs of pollution had not been allowed for. Pyrethrum against DDT is one example; natural fibres against synthetic fibres, another. Some of these natural products have the advantage not only of being free from pollution, but also of being produced (efficiently) labour-intensively (often with female labour) and contributing to rural development, and therefore to employment and reduced rural-urban migration.

A fourth set of questions concerns the actions developing countries should take in the face of growing scarcity of non-renewable natural resources. Many of these have not been priced according to their scarcity, taking into account a proper social discount rate and risk premium. A correct pricing policy would provide incentives for more economical use of these products, for switching to products that use less of these materials or none, for a search for new sources of these materials, and for the development of substitutes. Meanwhile the higher revenue earned by the material-exporting developing countries should be used for diversification and development, while developing countries dependent on their imports but without corresponding high-priced exports should be insured against damage from higher prices.

Economists have a bias in favour of using prices to reduce pollution and raw material exhaustion. Non-economists object to using taxes to discourage damaging activities and to granting "licences to pollute" and licences to despoil. The differences rest upon attaching different moral evaluations to different things. People value the opportunity to express *disapproval*, which would not be reflected in a fine balance of benefits and costs. Licences are normally not given for activities that should be stamped as illegitimate. (But licences are given in the USA to carry guns.) Putting a price tag on a highly valued item demeans it. The opponents of price policies may also think that the motive makes a difference, whereas taxes are indifferent to motives.[1]

But it is not enough to estimate the possibility of exhaustion and to attach a price to these materials, allowing for time and uncertainty; what is also needed is coordinated action between the developing countries in which these non-renewable materials are to be found. Incentives, both rewards and penalties, are required to secure joint action, and agreement on rules about how increases in revenue derived from joint scarcity pricing should be shared and used for development. In particular, ways should be found to mitigate or prevent harm being done to developing countries that depend on the imports of these materials.

A fifth set of questions concerns the role of transnational companies for environmental policy. In the new international division of labour, which would be guided by differential pollution costs in different countries, the location of certain "dirty" processes in developing countries could be one of the functions of the transnational corporation. This could be done either by the firm locating certain "dirty" processes within its vertically integrated system of operations in a developing country where the social costs of pollution are lower and the benefits from industrialization higher, or by transferring the whole integrated operation to such a country. The argument would be analogous to that of locating unskilled or semi-skilled labour-intensive processes and products in developing countries. One important advantage is that the transnational corporation, if it is from an industrial country, will act as a pressure group to ensure access for the products to the markets of the developed countries, which might otherwise put up protectionist barriers under the pretext of environmental protection.

5. Global Institutions for Sustainable Development

The problems of the local environment, mainly of concern to the developing countries, are different from those of the global, the principal

---

1. See WILLIAM J. BAUMOL's review of STEVEN KELMAN's book *What Price Incentives? Economists and the Environment, Journal of Economic Literature*, vol. 20 December 1982, pp. 1105-1106. Baumol replies to the possible view of economists that these ways of thinking are irrational: "But, as Kelman asks, is it irrational to distinguish between manslaughter and murder? After all, the victim is equally dead in both cases! He cites Justice Holmes' telling aphorism 'even a dog distinguishes between being stumbled over and being kicked'". He adds, "In a profession committed to a position that we should not tell people what they *ought* to want, and that the utility functions, which we usually accept as given data, are what should enter the social maximand, it ill behooves us to reject such beliefs out of hand".

concern of the industrial countries. Common property rights to a local pond or grazing area are often respected, and behaviour has evolved that prevents their destruction. Not so for the global commons. Our present interdependent, pluralistic, multi-polar world is less stable, and more in need of the promotion of peace, prosperity, conservation and global leadership than past orders, in which a single dominant power has assumed these responsibilities. As I have said above, no single power is both able and willing to assume these functions today.

As we have observed, just as in an uncoordinated world each country has an incentive to pour its problem of unemployment, metaphorically, into the yards of others, so does it, literally, cast its muck into the neighbouring fields or into the oceans, the lakes, the atmosphere, the land, or the food chains which are the global commons. Acid rain that kills forests, the emission of chlorofluorocarbons that destroy the ozone layer, the global warming resulting from the burning of fossil fuels, overfishing in common waters, are examples of global abuse that can be stopped only by global agreements that limit national sovereignty.

The domestic environmental problems of rich countries are often in conflict with poverty reduction in developing countries, while the domestic environmental problems of poor countries both arise from, and contribute to, poverty. But the global environmental problems are shared by the whole of humanity and call for global solutions, although they have a lower priority in the developing countries. Financial contributions from the industrial countries are therefore essential.

The solution to mutually destructive actions pursued by each country separately is the establishment of a global environmental protection agency, with powers of enforcement. Each country, by sacrificing some of its national sovereignty, gains more in the pursuit of its national interests than it would have done, had it continued to act independently.

Such an agency would require substantial finance and powers. A tiny step in this direction was taken in November 1990 when 25 industrial and developing countries agreed to establish a Global Environment Facility (GEF), which will be run jointly by the World Bank, the United Nations Development Programme (UNDP), and the United Nations Environment Programme (UNEP). Starting out with an initial commitment of about $ 1.5 billion, the GEF became operational in 1991.

Initially modest resources will be devoted to providing help in financing programmes and projects that affect the global environment in low-income developing countries. Experimental pilot projects will, it is hoped, provide contributions to the deliberations of the June 1992 UN Conference on the Environment and Development in Rio de Janeiro.

Four areas have been selected for the operations of the Facility.

a. Protecting the ozone layer. the GEF's work will be coordinated with the implementation of the Montreal Protocol to phase out the use of CFCs, halons, and other harmful gases.

b. Limiting greenhouse gas emissions. The emission of carbon dioxide, CFCs, and methane will be limited, the adoption of cleaner technologies and fuels will be encouraged, as well as reforestation and forestry conservation.

c. Protecting biodiversity. The diversity of species contributes to materials for medicines and industrial products, genetic resources for food production, and the regulation of climatic and rainfall patterns.

d. Protecting global water resources. The Facility will support programmes that encourage planning against oil spills; to abate water pollution, to prevent and clean up toxic waste pollution along major rivers and to conserve water bodies.

Developing countries with GNP per head of less than $ 4,000 will be eligible for GEF funding for investment projects and supporting services.

The initial steps towards a Global Environmental Protection Agency should be on very specific issues, such as the Montreal Protocol or the International Whaling Commission. A sharp and narrow focus in the early stages will prevent endless discussion, frustration and acrimony. But it needs broadening and reforming in several respects. First, its mandate should be enlarged so that concerns such as desertification, acid rain, water scarcity, land-based pollution and urban degradation are also covered. The relationships between global, regional, national and local problems should be recognized. Second, there should be wider participation from the developing countries in the Facility's management. And third, the funding has to be enlarged. Contributions could be partly voluntary and partly derived from new forms of international taxation.

THIRD LECTURE

The Judo Trick:
The Role of Direct Private Foreign Investment
in Developing Countries

1. Introduction. – 2. A New Form of Partnership. – 3. The Judo Trick or Crowding In: The Role of Microenterprises. – 4. Foreign Investment and Macroeconomic Policies. – 5. Regional Integration. – 6. Export Processing Zones. – 7. Government Intervention and Performance Requirements. – 8. Transnational Corporations and Basic Needs.

1. Introduction

Direct private foreign investment has been fairly concentrated on the middle-income developing countries. Under 30 middle-income countries account for over 90 per cent of total direct private foreign investment, and within this group Brazil and Mexico, joined more recently by Singapore and Malaysia, dominate the figures. Over 60 per cent went to these four countries. But the small flow of investment (of the order of 5 per cent of total OECD flows) to the poorest countries does not necessarily reflect its importance. First, even these small flows may be quantitatively important in relation to the economy of a particular poor country. Second, even quite a small amount can be more important than the quantity indicates if it contributes a missing component, breaks a bottleneck, or has spread effects on the rest of the economy in technology generation, employment creation, or foreign exchange earnings. Since it cannot be expected that the total quantity of investment to the low-income countries will increase by much very quickly, or that host governments can do much to influence it, it is all the more important to concentrate on measures that get the maximum multiplier effects from whatever small investment there is. One proposal of this kind is discussed in the section on the judo trick. Other forms of new institutions are discussed below. An invitation to explore such approaches is the main theme of this lecture.

145

Much has been written about the role of private foreign investment and the multinational corporation in development, both in its creative role as a package combining capital, management, marketing and technology, and as a harbinger of exploitation. Without wishing to defend or attack either the proposition that the Ford Motor Company is the nearest thing to the Ford Foundation, or, on the other hand, that the transnational company is, if not the devil incarnate, the devil incorporated, some useful guidelines for private foreign investment in the least developed countries can be laid down.

Before doing this, it may be useful to remember that there are two different approaches to direct private foreign investment: the analysis in terms of financial flows, and that in terms of industrial organization. The former is the older approach, but has become important again as a result of the debt crisis and the search for finance. But it should be remembered that (a) the financial contribution is bound to remain small and (b) although it has the virtue of sharing in losses as well as profits, one would expect the net returns on the average and in the long run to be higher, and the foreign exchange burdens to be heavier, than those on fixed interest borrowing.

The second approach is the more modern one, and it is based on the integration of the theory of international investment with that of industrial organization. The emphasis in this paper will be on this approach and on institutional innovations, partly for the reason that the interest in finance arising from the debt crisis is relatively unimportant for the poorest countries, and partly because the quantitative importance of this form of financial flow is bound to remain small. The principal guidelines are the following.

First, it is clear that private foreign investment, to be successful, calls for complementary and supplementary action in the public sector. Roads, railways, ports, airports; education and research; nutrition and health services for farmers and factory workers are preconditions for productive and remunerative private investment. Few private investment projects can flourish if there are no schools or no clinics. And the physical and social infrastructure is normally provided by the public sector. This applies also to the schemes proposed in this lecture.

Second, the foreign firm should not replace or drive out but should encourage the growth of domestic enterprises. More of this will be said below in the section on how to make the foreign firm complementary to the informal sector enterprise.

Third, institutional innovation and hybrids can often combine the virtues of different types of traditional institutions. An important area of policy is the imaginative exploration of new legal and business institutions which combine the considerable merits of the transnational corporation with the maximum beneficial impact on development objectives. This area comprises joint ventures, i.e. joint both between private and public capital and between domestic and foreign capital, which go further than window dressing by giving the developing host country access to information and decision-making, and various provisions for divestment and gradual, agreed transfer from foreign ownership and management to the host country. Thus, countries wishing to curb the power of large foreign groups in their manufacturing sector may find investment reduced. This may make it advisable to institute a "joint sector" in which public capital is combined with private national management with or without an equity stake, or public capital is combined with private international capital. Another possibility would be a management contract with a transnational firm.

Thought and action in this area have suffered from a poverty of the institutional imagination. It has lagged behind the advance of the scientific and technological imagination, and the global vision of transnational firms. Discussions have turned on the ideological dispute between private and public enterprise. Yet the real issues have little to do with the locus of ownership. The large, privately owned companies are run on lines not very dissimilar to those of public sector institutions. The challenge is to design mixed or hybrid companies that simultaneously harness private energy and initiative, yet are accountable to the public and carry out a social mandate. The British Commonwealth Corporation can serve as a model. In Britain it is claimed as a wonderful example of private enterprise by the Conservatives, because it is run by a board consisting of businessmen and bankers, without interference by any government department, and has to cover its costs without subsidy, and it acclaimed by the Labour Party as a model of socialism, because it is in the public sector and draws some of its funds from the British Exchequer.

Equally arid has been the dispute over the virtues and vices of private foreign investment. Some developing countries dislike private profits, some dislike foreigners, and foreigners earning private profits can be an explosive mixture. But here again, the task should be to identify the positive contributions of foreign firms and the social costs they impose on the country, and to explore how the former can be increased, and the latter reduced. A proposal of one type of arrangement in which there is a gradual transfer to national (or regional) ownership and management is discussed below. There is a need for a legal and institutional framework in which social objectives that are not normally part of the private firm's objectives can be achieved, while giving the firm an opportunity to earn profits by contributing efficient management, marketing and technology.

The quantitative contribution of private foreign investment and transnational firms in the poorest developing countries, outside mining and plantations where these have not been nationalized, is probably bound to remain small. But its qualitative role as a centre round which to cluster small domestic enterprises, and as a potential mobilizer of domestic enterprises remains to be explored. Some suggestions will be made below.

There has been by now a good deal of experience in the growth of lending to very small and poor businesses. The Grameen Bank in Bangladesh has been one of the first, but the experience has been replicated in many other countries. One important lesson is that even without collateral, poor people tend to repay loans, particularly if peer group pressure exists. Another is that, combined with some training in accounting, book-keeping and management, these loans have multiplier effects that create jobs for other poor people. They break the grip of the usurious moneylender and enable people to start businesses who could not have done so without these loans. There is a potential role here for foreign banks.

2. A New Form of Partnership

The transnational corporation clearly has an important part to play in assisting the progress of the developing countries. Hostility to it by host governments has been greatly reduced and been replaced by an eager welcome, and understanding on both sides has grown. Transnational corporations and host country officials have gathered experience, the number of transnational corporations and with it competition among them has increased, and the desperate need for foreign exchange resulting from the debt crisis, the fact that payments are linked to the ability to pay, together with growing reluctance by the banks to expose themselves further, have made developing countries more welcoming. At the same time a number of obstacles still stand in the way of greater participation of transnational corporations in the development process. New institutions and new procedures are needed to overcome these remaining obstacles.

These obstacles are partly practical, arising from the difficulties of operating in countries with shortages of skilled manpower and basic utilities, and partly political. The latter include the sometimes still ambivalent attitudes of the governments of developing countries and the resulting political risks faced by the companies. The reluctance to welcome whole-heartedly transnational companies, though much less than it used to be, has itself a number of causes. First, there is the fear, whether justified or not, that they may exploit their market power and deprive the country of valuable resources in general, and, through remittance of profits abroad, aggravate balance of payments difficulties.

Second, there is the fear that the enterprise will form a foreign enclave, whose activities will not benefit and may harm the rest of the society. Third, political fears of foreign domination or interference may add fuel to economic fears of exploitation. The debt crisis has greatly reduced these fears, and many developing countries are now eager to welcome transnational corporations. But areas of friction remain.

The remaining suspicion is fed, on the one hand, by disasters, such as that at the plant of the Union Carbide Corporation in

149

Bhopal, or the "Nestlé kills babies" scandal, and, on the other, by domestic industries, such as the computer firms in Mexico, who try to keep out foreign competitors. The behaviour of the United Fruit Company in bribing a high official in Central America to break a banana cartel (ending in the dramatic suicide of Eli Black), of ITT in trying to prevent the election of Allende in Chile, and, once elected, to depose him, and of Lockheed (not a transnational corporation) in bribing Prince Bernhard of The Netherlands to buy its aeroplanes, may not be typical of all transnational companies. But it still colours popular and populist attitudes in developing countries. On the other hand, like the role of the oil companies in the overthrow of the Iranian Prime Minister Mossadegh in 1953, these incidents have probably already been forgotten in the light of the positive benefits the companies are expected to bestow.

The scandals mentioned above, just as the shining models of some of the agricultural projects of Booker McConnell or Shell, or of the appropriate technology project plant of Philips, Eindhoven, in Holland, raise the difficult question of attribution. Are the blessings or the curses to be attributed to the transnational corporation, or to exceptional circumstances, or to individuals or to the policies of the local governments? What an analysis ought to bring out are the characteristics peculiar to *all* transnationals, or to all in a typical sub-set of transnationals (e.g. in manufacturing, or in manufacturing for export), and *only* to transnationals, or to those in the sub-set, so that the benefits cannot be reaped by other means. This will not be attempted here.

It is well known that foreign enterprise has the capacity to bestow great benefit on the economy of the host country. It can combine the provision of capital, of a team of skilled people and access to foreign markets; it can transmit rapidly the latest products and technology to the host country; it can encourage the growth of a number of ancillary domestic enterprises; it can create jobs and earn foreign exchange; it can contribute to tax revenue; and it can reduce the economy's dependence on imports and increase its capacity to export.

The international community could help by investigating ways in which the fears of both host governments and private firms can be allayed and the advantages maximized. Such assistance may not be necessary in middle-income countries, where the promise of profits is a sufficient incentive. But the low-income countries, by themselves, may not offer adequate attractions, apart from mining and plantations, which are nowadays often in public hands.

The proposal is to devise a form of joint enterprise through which finance, skilled manpower and training are provided in a way which is acceptable to the host governments and which carries sufficient profit to be attractive to the foreign firms.

One way of achieving this would be for a private foreign firm to establish a joint enterprise with a local government or government agency, such as a local development corporation, or a local private company. The foreign firm should put up not more than 49 per cent of the capital, but enough to benefit when the enterprise succeeds, and of course suffer if it fails. It should have a substantial minority interest, while the local government has the dominant interest.

Such a holding would often be sufficient to secure a decisive role in management. But it might be possible to arrange in special circumstances that, in the initial phase, the foreign investor should hold a higher percentage of the equity, as long as the arrangement for eventual transfer to local ownership is clearly stated. The foreign firm might also provide some of the money on a fixed interest basis or in the form of preference shares.

The equity interest of the foreign firm would be bought out by the local government at the end of a suitable pre-arranged period. This period could be ten years, with provision each year after say seven years to extend for a further five years up to say fifteen years, or longer in the case of e.g. plantation enterprises. Various other forms of 'rolling' continuation could be devised, such as a possible extension of another five years, etc. Alternatively, the period could be longer, but there could be options at fixed points when either the local government could buy out or the firm sell out.

Managerial and technical staff would initially be provided almost exclusively by the foreign firm, perhaps under a management contract, but with the obligation to train local replacements within the specified period before buy-out. This is where the poorest countries suffer from the acutest scarcities, and where a direct stake (as contrasted with advice through technical assistance) can be most helpful. The rate of replacement by local managerial staff could not be specified contractually, but the local government would be able to use its representation on the board to ensure that it went forward at a satisfactory pace.

Housing and community services should be provided by the local government or an appropriate local statutory body set up for the purpose. In view of the relatively short period of ownership participation, the foreign firm's capital should be concentrated on productive activities.

The scheme would operate through a tripartite agreement between the parent government of the firm, the local host government, and the private foreign firm concerned. The parent government and the local government would provide a guarantee against expropriation. The parent government (or the World Bank) might also provide aid funds in appropriate cases to enable the local government to finance its participation or, either directly or through one of the international financial institutions, to help finance housing or community services required for the project.

Procedures for assessing an appropriate value at the time of buy-out would have to be agreed upon in advance, as well as procedures for arbitration should disputes arise.

What are the advantages of the proposal? Most of the advantages of private foreign enterprise are preserved. The foreign firm brings into the host country capital, together with technology, market access and a team, possibly with local experience, and the overhead facilities and international experience which the firm can provide are thus made available. At the same time the fears which local governments or public opinion may feel are removed. The opportunity for exploiting indefinitely a monopoly or oligopoly no longer exists. The fear of foreign ownership and domination is removed.

The transnational company, on the other hand, acquires a guarantee against expropriation, combined with the incentive to enjoy a share in the profits. Clearly, it would still carry some of the commercial risks of failure, but political risks would be eliminated. The buy-out arrangement after an agreed period releases capital and know-how. These very scarce resources can thus be used on a revolving basis for initiating and pioneering new ventures and are freed from maintaining a going concern, which can more easily be transferred to local shoulders. The "spread effects" of enterprise on the rest of the economy are thus increased.

Where at present political risks are high, foreign firms require a high rate of return as compensation. But it is these high rates that induce host countries to expropriate, when they find that "companies are taking out more than they put in". With the elimination of these risks, required returns will drop, and the fears leading to expropriation will have been removed.

With political risks high, there is a dilemma for the foreign firm. If it remits its profits abroad it is, as we have seen, charged with "taking out more than it put in", and it constitutes a burden on the balance of payments. This burden can be avoided only if its contribution to the production of tradable goods is sufficiently large. Otherwise, in order not to be such a burden, the rate of growth of foreign investment in the country (from ploughing back profits) has to exceed the rate of return on foreign capital plus depreciation. Assume this to be only 15 per cent per year. (The yield on American manufacturing investments in the developing countries outside Latin America has been nearer 20 per cent.) It is extremely unlikely that the total capital stock in the country grows at this rate. National income is not likely to grow at a rate faster than 5 per cent and, with a constant capital-output ratio, the stock of capital will not grow faster than 5 per cent. But unless it does, the foreign firm will have to buy out an increasing proportion of the host country's capital assets. This is particularly serious if, as in many African countries, initially little locally owned capital exists. No country can tolerate such growing alienation of its assets. Even if it did, the process would inevitably come to an end when all capital is owned by foreigners. The proposed scheme is a way out of the dilemma. By lowering the required rate, it removes both the fear of a large and growing foreign exchange drain and the fear of an alienation of the capital stock. It is in this respect like multilateral disarmament. By reducing the stock of weapons, the reasons for having weapons are removed.

The proposed scheme would be particularly suitable for large-scale agricultural enterprises and for countries with a small entrepreneurial and managerial class, like those of Africa. If new enterprises were successfully established, existing ones might also be converted into this type. Regimes committed to replacing foreign by domestic economic activity might, instead of expropriation, be persuaded to work for the transformation of foreign-owned enterprises into the new type of joint venture.

If such a scheme were to be accepted by the parent governments, it would be desirable to present it as a form of transfer which combines adaptability to different circumstances with sufficient concreteness to have an appeal. It would need to be announced with a good deal of publicity, after careful preparation and consultation with selected host governments and transnational corporations.

3. The Judo Trick or Crowding In: The Role of Micro-Enterprises[1]

The recent emphasis on the role of private enterprise and free markets has been useful. It has been partly a healthy reaction against excessive early faith in the power of governments to direct the economy, to manage businesses, and to correct market failures. But unregulated markets can be both inefficient and cruel. Joan Robinson once said that the Invisible Hand can work by strangulation.

It is important to concentrate the activities of the government on areas in which private efforts are absent or more inadequate than those of the government. Government activity often is complementary to private enterprise and efficient markets. The aim should be to avoid crowding out, and to achieve "crowding in".

1. An earlier version of this lecture is contained in a volume honouring Hugh Stretton. It is *Markets, Morals and Public Policy*, edited by LIONEL ORCHARD and ROBERT DARE, Sydney: The Federation Press, 1989, pp. 77-103. I am grateful to Marty Chen, Kenneth Chomitz and Peter Mayer for helpful comments. I am also indebted to stimulating conversations with RONALD DORE and his books *Flexible Rigidities, Industrial Policy and Structural Adjusment in the Japanese Economy 1970–80*, Stanford, Calif.: Stanford University Press, 1986, and *Taking Japan Seriously: A Confucian Perspective on Leading Economic Issues*, Stanford, Calif.: Stanford University Press, 1987, especially chapter 9.

Government intervention should provide the conditions in which markets and enterprise can flourish. As I shall argue in my next lecture, market-orientation and state minimalism, far from going together, are incompatible. A well-designed policy calls for interventions to maintain competition and avoid restrictive practices, monopolies and cartels, to conduct good macroeconomic policy, to provide physical and social infrastructure, and some research efforts. It may also require new types of institutions about which more later. Governments should also take care of the victims of the competitive struggle, both for humanitarian and for efficiency reasons. The informal sector can play an important part in providing a safety net. But the policy of looking after the victims of the competitive struggle by encouraging the informal sector to provide a safety net (it should not be a safety hammock) can be carried out beyond this point and can make a substantial contribution to production and productivity growth.

The informal sector has been much discussed. It comprises four quite distinct groups. First, there are the self-employed, sometimes working with unpaid members of their families. They are a heterogeneous group, ranging from shoeshine boys, street vendors, rubbish collectors, petty thieves, prostitutes, drug traffickers, smugglers, and self-appointed tourist guides and bag carriers to jobbing gardeners, and small-scale producers such as blacksmiths, carpenters, sandal makers, lamp makers, bricklayers, bus and taxi drivers, seamstresses, repairmen, cobblers, bakers, shopkeepers, auto mechanics, and builders who sometimes earn more than workers in the formal sector. Some formal sector workers use their savings to set up such enterprises for themselves in the informal sector.

Second, there are the casual workers, hired on a day-to-day basis in the docks, in construction, transport, and services. If the criterion for being in the informal sector is the method of hiring, then some workers hired casually by quite large firms should be counted as being in the informal sector.

Third, there are workers employed on a regular basis by small-scale, labour-intensive, not bureaucratically controlled firms outside the formal sector. Fourth, there are the "outworkers", working in their homes under the putting-out system.

Another distinction is that between three quite different kinds of informal sector firm. First, there are the productive, entrepreneurial, often rapidly growing firms. They often graduate to middle-sized, and occasionally to large, firms. Second, there are the viable family firms, neither dynamic nor lame ducks, who stand midway between the first and the third category. Third, there are the absorbers of the lame ducks thrown out of the formal sector, or incapable of entering it: small family firms of infirm, old or otherwise unemployable people. An elderly, infirm couple who live above their small grocery store, but are not bound by the laws about closing hours, might be entirely unemployable elsewhere. If their receipts exceed their costs, they earn a small producer's rent. They constitute the safety nets for personal incapacities and the disasters that befall people, and the shifts in demand or technology that occur in the formal sector. The second type has been swollen in recent years by declining aggregate growth rates and austerity programmes that have thrown people out of employment in the formal sector. The activities of these firms are anti-cyclical, swelling with a decline in aggregate demand, and declining with its growth. At the same time, the crisis also provides opportunities for some firms who belong in the first category, although if they are linked, say through subcontracting, to the formal sector, their behaviour will be procyclical. Nevertheless, they benefit from fluctuations, for they will receive excess orders in booms, when the large firms run into capacity limits, and in slumps, when these firms wish to convert fixed into variable costs by hiving off employees and transforming them into subcontractors.

Informal sector firms,[1] in the right setting, thrive on certain advantages over large-scale, formal sector firms. These advantages may be:

1. locational, when raw materials are dispersed and the enterprise processes them, or when markets are local and transport costs high;

2. relating to the process of production or the product, when

---

1. The term "informal sector" is used here interchangeably with small-scale, or micro-enterprise sector.

the work requires simple assembly or other activities that are best carried out by hand or with simple tools;

3. relating to the market, when operating on a small scale for a local market has lower costs than larger-scale, more distant operation, or when the service has to be rendered where the customer is;

4. relating to adaptability and responsiveness to changing demand or technology, because of the absence of high fixed costs.

In the informal sector employment is largely supply-driven, absorbing fairly easily additional entrants (although there are also barriers to entry into some informal sector enterprises, particularly the need for some capital, and employment is offered by small businessmen *demanding* labour), whereas in the formal sector employment is largely demand-driven (although in the public sector there is a *supply*-driven component). There is also the work of women, until recently invisible in some cultures, who perform hard work without being counted as members of the labour force because their product is often not sold for cash.

According to the ILO. *Kenya Report*[1] informal sector activities are

"a way of doing things, characterized by

a. ease of entry;

b. reliance on indigenous resources;

c. family ownership of enterprises;

d. small scale operations;

e. labour-intensive and adapted technology;

f. skills acquired outside the formal educational sytem;

g. unregulated and competitive markets."

1. International Labour Office, *Employment, Incomes and Equality: A Strategy for Increasing Productive Employment in Kenya*, Geneva: International Labour Office, 1972, p. 6. Among other definitions of the informal sector are the following: self-employment; unpaid family workers, domestic servants and those self-employed who are not professionals and technicians; workers in small-scale units of production, sometimes including domestic servants and casual workers; sometimes also low-wage employees of "modern" firms; unprotected, unregulated economic activities; illegal, clandestine and unregistered activities; "traditional" sector; "subsistence" sector; "marginalized mass"; very small economic units or micro-businesses; an abnormally swollen, overdistended tertiary sector of minimal productivity; a sector in which wage rates equal marginal productivity. For sources of these and other definitions, see MICHAEL HOPKINS, 'Comments on Professor S. Kannappan' in *Fighting Urban Unemployment in Developing Countries*, edited by BERNARD SALOMÉ, Paris: Development Centre of the OECD, 1989, pp. 69-73.

It is easy to dismiss the informal sector as a useless concept.[1] It is equally easy to romanticize it and to think of it as a potential of high productivity, of competitive capitalism, harassed and discriminated against by mercantilistic, predatory and interfering bureaucrats. A few years ago, the mayor of New York was trying to drive street vendors off the streets of Manhattan.

The informal sector certainly is a very heterogeneous collection of people and activities. There are some whose marginal productivity is zero or negative, because their activities only take away from the sales of others, or because they only create nuisances and then extract payment for their removal. Beggars, petty thieves, small vendors, pushers of unwanted services, are manifestations of disguised unemployment. Even genuinely productive firms often break the law and evade taxes. Many informal sector employers exploit their workers at least as much as formal sector employers. There is no point in glamorizing them, or in overstating their contribution to production.

Another way in which the informal sector has been misleadingly romanticized is by holding it up as a splendid example of entrepreneurial competition and free enterprise capitalism. The informal sector has its peculiar modes of behaviour and formalities. As the studies of Hernando de Soto (one of the leading proponents of this form of activity) and of Judith Tendler have shown, relations between firms in the informal sector are sometimes characterized by a striking degree of cooperation.[2] They share inputs when these are in scarce supply; when one firm has a large contract and its neighbour does not, it shares the contract with the other firm by subcontracting or hiring its owner as a temporary worker; there is work-sharing not only between firms, but also

1. For a well reasoned criticism of the concept see LISA PEATTIE, 'An Idea in Good Currency and How it Grew: The Informal Sector', *World Development*, vol. 15 no. 7, July 1987. Although the critique by Peattie is well argued, I do not think it necessarily leads to the abandonment of the concept. The exploration of the specific linkages, some positive, others negative, between firms and policies that she asks for can surely be done within the conceptual framework suggested by the "informal sector".

2. See HERNANDO DE SOTO, *The Other Path; The Invisible Revolution in the Third World*, New York: Harper & Row, 1989 and JUDITH TENDLER, The Remarkable Convergence of Fashion on Small Enterprise and the Informal Sector: What Are the Implications for Policy? mimeo 1987.

when the demand for labour is reduced. Not much attention has been paid to this fact, partly because it contradicts the idealized individualistic picture of firms in active competition.[1]

While, on the one hand, the informal sector should not be glamorized, there are, on the other hand, actually or potentially highly productive small enterprises, some of whose owners earn more than some workers in the formal sector. They tend to use more labour per unit of capital and per unit of output, and often use it intensively, remuneratively, and highly efficiently.[2]

In Peru some informal sector firms absorb those who wish to, but cannot enter the formal sector. In Argentina, on the other hand, people with secure but ill-paid jobs in the formal sector opt to earn extra income and gain additional mobility in the informal sector.

Some people who work in the informal sector also work in the formal sector. Sometimes members of the same family are engaged in both. Some characteristics of the informal sector can be found in the formal sector, such as casual hiring of labour. Some firms are informal with respect to some of their activities (not paying certain taxes, working without some licences, casually hiring some of their workers), and formal with respect to others. We have seen that some informal sector incomes are higher than some formal sector earnings. It is impossible to count and record the informal sector, because, by its nature, no official records exist.[3] But in spite of these obstacles to a clear and neat definition, the concept meets a real need and I shall not abandon it.

1. See JUDITH TENDLER, *loc. cit.*

2. Some caution is necessary. Obviously, not all small-scale, informal sector enterprises are efficient, or economize even in the use of capital. The working capital requirements of small enterprises are often higher than those of larger ones. And even the lower capital/labour ratio can be bought at the cost of a higher capital/output ratio. But the proposed scheme should ensure that such waste is minimized. For evidence of the efficiency of small-scale industries (overlapping with the informal sector, though not identical), see *Small Scale Industries in Developing Countries: Empirical Evidence and Policy Implications*, by CARL LIEDHOLM and DONALD MEAD, International Development Paper no. 9, East Lansing, Mich.: Department of Agricultural Economics, Michigan State University, 1987.

3. Since less interventionist governments will tend to include in their national accounts activities that more interventionist governments do not count, because they are illegal, it is easy to overstate the growth performance of countries that have followed the World Bank's advice to rely more on markets. World Bank reports have not always paid attention to this distortion of growth figures in comparing good and poor performers.

There are those who believe that the informal sector is entirely the creature of mistaken government policies. "Get the prices right, deregulate, decentralize, liberalize and privatize, and the informal sector will disappear." The evidence does not show, however, that modern technology, even with the most "realistic" equilibrium prices for labour, capital and foreign exchange, can absorb the numbers of workers who will be seeking jobs at wages that can support them.

There are four reasons for paying attention to the informal sector. They arise from the triple needs to increase production, employment (recognition and self-respect), and incomes, and the need to avoid political rebellion.

First, the informal sector represents a potentially large reserve of productivity and earning power. Although not all informal sector activities contribute potentially to productivity and earnings, some do.

Second, the labour force in the low-income countries is likely to grow rapidly in the next 15 years and neither agriculture nor the industrial formal sector is capable of absorbing even a fraction of these additions, to say nothing of the large number of already unemployed or underemployed. Workers seeking remunerative employment are likely to grow at a rate of 2-3 per cent per year in many developing countries. The labour surplus economies of Java and Bangladesh represent the future for Asia, where at this time there are still relatively few landless workers seeking jobs in the towns. The situation is further aggravated by the low world growth rates. The combination of population growth, urbanization and recession has swelled the informal sector, which presents the only hope for jobs.[1]

---

1. This approach has been critized as excessively Eurocentric. The critics say, the notion of a "labour force" comprising all able-bodied men and women between, say 15 and 60, is not applicable to many developing countries. The problem is not to find jobs, but to redefine "work". The "idleness" of the women in purdah, the gossips in the cafés, the begging priests and monks, the small-scale rentiers, the useless pedlars, the idle bureaucrats, should, according to Clifford Geertz, not be suppressed and these people should not be encouraged to "work", but the notions of "idleness" and "work" should be redefined, so that these "underemployed" are kept "outside the work force but inside society". (CLIFFORD GEERTZ, 'Myrdal's Mythology', *Encounter*, July 1969.) The evidence does not seem to have confirmed that this is the preference of the workless, whenever

A third reason is that, although the informal sector should not be equated with the poor (we have seen that some members of the informal sector earn more than some in the formal sector and many poor are outside the informal sector), it is in the informal sector where many poor people are to be found. By harnessing its potential for generating incomes (and self-respect), not only is efficient growth promoted but also poverty is reduced. If its productivity and remunerativeness can be raised without depriving the high-productivity sector of resources, and hence not only of more production but also of the opportunity of future employment, there is no conflict between efficiency and equity.

A fourth reason is that prolonged unemployment leads to alienation and a sense of worthlessness, and can be a source of rebellious instead of productive activity. Governments in power have a particular interest in not upsetting the existing order and peace, and using the informal sector as a vote bank.

Normally one would wish the informal sector neither to be subsidized at the expense of the high-productivity formal sector firms, nor to be squeezed out by privileged formal sector firms. The task then is to make these informal sector enterprises complementary to the larger-scale, formal sector firms, including foreign multinational corporations. Now they are often competitive, and, aided by the government, the large firms often drive out the small ones. Both Mao's declared strategy of walking on two legs and the success of the Japanese in combining a modern and a small-scale industrial sector illustrate the possibility of successfully combining the two sectors. The East Asian success stories illustrate how the marketing of manufactured exports can be undertaken by foreign firms. In Singapore, it was transnational corporations that marketed the output of wholly or majority-owned local subsidiaries. In other countries it was the importers in the advanced countries, retail and department stores, wholesalers or trading companies that performed these functions. The Koreans used foreign buyers in the early stages of development not only to sell their goods but also to acquire

opportunities to earn arise. It would, however, be worth exploring whether activities in the informal sector that do not show high economic returns may not be valuable by some other standards.

knowledge about styles, designs, and technologies. The current trend towards modular manufacturing, according to which some quite small firms produce components for assembly in large firms, also encourages the growth of informal sector firms. All these are illustrations of ways of using the power of the large firms, the Goliaths, in their self-interest, for the benefit of the poor, the little Davids, rather as a judo fighter uses the power of his opponent for his purposes. Let us call this the judo trick, partly because it uses the leverage of an initially antagonistic force with multiplied effect, and partly because it uses the force of what is usually regarded as a powerful, strong opponent for the benefit of the weak.

One model for such a symbiosis in agriculture has been pioneered by the already mentioned Commonwealth Development Corporation, first in the Kulai oil palm project in Malaysia and then in the Kenya Tea Development Authority. A modern nucleus estate does the management, the processing, the exporting, the marketing, and provides the extension services and the credit for a group of smallholders clustered round the estate. The activities best carried out on a large scale, with modern techniques, are done by the nucleus estate, while the growing of the crop is done by newly settled smallholders. This type of project has proved highly successful, although it is rather management-intensive and the calls on skilled professional management and extension services would have to be reduced if it were to be replicated on a large scale in labour surplus economies, such as those of South Asia. Another model is the National Dairy Development Board in India. The production of milk, largely by women, remains traditional and informal, while processing, credit and marketing follow modern, formal sector lines.

A similar model has been followed by private foreign agro-businesses. It has been called the "core-satellite" model, or contract farming or smallholder outgrower scheme.[1] Companies like

1. DAVID J. GLOVER, 'Contract Farming and Smallholder Outgrower Schemes in Less Developed Countries', *World Development*, vol. 12 nos. 11-12, November-December 1984, and 'Increasing the Benefits to Smallholders from Contract Farming: Problems for Farmers' Organizations and Policy Makers,' *World Development*, vol. 15 no. 4, April 1987. Also ARTHUR GOLDSMITH, 'The Private Sector and Rural Development: Can Agribusiness Help the Small Farmer?,' *World Development*, vol. 13 nos. 10-11 October-

Heinz, Del Monté, United Brands, Nestlé and Shell, provide marketing, equipment, technical assistance, credit, fertilizer, and other inputs, as well as ancillary services, and smallholders grow fruit and vegetables. In order to balance bargaining power in drawing up contracts, the smallholders have to be organized. Then they can use their power both directly and indirectly on the government to give them political support. The high fixed costs of processing plant make it important for the company to secure an even and certain flow of inputs, which is ensured by the contract. It is preferable to either open market purchases or a plantation with hired labour, though contract farming is sometimes supplemented by these other forms. The smallholders, in turn, acquire an assured market, credit and inputs at low costs. I do not advocate the replication of these schemes, for too little research has been done on the precise division of gains and conditions for the optimum smallholder benefit, but these are worth exploring.

This type of institutional arrangement can combine some of the advantages of plantation farming, such as quality control, coordination of interdependent stages of production and marketing, with those of smallholder production, such as autonomy, keener incentives and income generation for poor people. But the possibility of abuse of its monopsonistic power by the private company against the smallholders makes it necessary to have either smallholder organizations with countervailing power or public regulation.

No similar type of arrangement exists as yet in manufacturing. One can easily imagine a large, modern manufacturing plant round which are clustered informal, small, enterprises doing repairs, manufacturing components and spare parts, and providing ancillary services such as transport, handling, cleaning, packaging, catering, etc. The nearest thing to such an arrangement is the system of modular manufacturing. It has, for example, replaced or perhaps complemented the assembly line as a method of manufacturing cars. It involves designing and assembling an entire motor car as a series of sub-assemblies, or modules. Suppliers of these

November 1985, and the Special Issue on Contract Farming and Smallholder Outgrower Schemes in Eastern and Southern Africa of the *East Africa Economic Review*, Economics Department, University of Nairobi, August 1989.

components (e.g. dashboards, sunroofs or doors), with their lower labour costs, could concentrate on the nuts and bolts, leaving to the large firms styling, packaging, marketing and distribution.

Such a project, to make use of informal sector enterprises, would require changes in government policies. The first step would be to stop repressive regulation, harassment and discrimination against the informal sector; to stop, for example demolishing informal sector houses, subject, of course, to some urban planning for open spaces. In Peru a Union of Formals and Informals has been formed to reduce government regulations and bureaucratic meddling.[1] It is an interesting example of a reformist alliance, in which formal sector enterprises make common cause with informal ones, sharing with them their experience and uniting in exercising political pressure. The next step would be to adopt policies and to create institutions with respect to the provision of credit, information and imported inputs (e.g. tariff remission for the informal sector). As to credit, innovative steps are needed for small loans and new types of collateral, such as inventories, or an unlicensed bus, or plots of land in shanty towns. Another option is the mobilization of peer pressure, as in the Grameen Bank in Bangladesh. A third step would be to remove legislation that gives the formal sector special advantages in buying from or selling to the informal sector.

1. See 'Peruvians Combating Red Tape' by ALAN RIDING, *The New York Times*, July 24 1988, p. 3. This article cites Hernando de Soto, head of the Institute for Liberty and Democracy in Lima, that 60 per cent of Peru's work force operates outside the formal economy and accounts for 38 per cent of its gross domestic product; 95 per cent of public transport in Lima is in the hands of informal operators, 98 per cent of new homes, most of them in shantytowns, are built without permits, and 80 cent of clothing, and 60 per cent of furniture are produced by the informal sector. According to the same source it takes 289 days to register a new company, so most people do not bother. Since this article appeared, HERNANDO DE SOTO's book *The Other Path* has been published. It contains an impassioned introduction by Mario Vargas Llosa. There de Soto estimates that in Peru the informal sector makes up 48 per cent of the total labour force. Its members work 61 per cent of all man-hours and create 38 per cent of the GDP. They have set up 274 markets in Lima; they run 93 per cent of the buses; and they have built 42 per cent of the houses. See also 'An Interview with Hernando de Soto', *Health and Development* vol. 1 no. 1, March-April 1989. There are, however critics of de Soto's enthusiasm. My friend Jaime Mezzera, with the International Labour Organization (PREALC) in Santiago, estimates the informal sector's contribution in any Latin American country at no more than 15 per cent.

The implications of this proposal for policy are quite radical. For example, the common prescription is to lower real wages in order to raise employment. But in this model, a rise in real wages may increase employment and incomes in the informal sector. The production of spare parts, repairs, and ancillary activities, such as cleaning, transport, packaging, are carried out inside the firms in the organized sector while wages are low. When they are raised, these activities become worth contracting out to small informal sector firms not subject to minimum wage legislation. These firms carry out these activities in a more labour-intensive way, and benefit from the new contracts. Even if the workers previously engaged on these activities inside the formal sector firms were to be dismissed (rather than redeployed), and were to add pressure on incomes in the informal sector, the savings in capital and profits may be enough to produce higher incomes as well as more jobs for the subcontractors. This would be the case, for example, if the self-employed small entrepreneur works harder than the same man as paid foreman or manager. A similar effect is produced by legislating for a shorter working week, to which the informal sector firms are not bound. Higher taxes, avoided or evaded by these enterprises, work in the same direction.[1]

It is true that, for such efficient and income-raising subcontracting to occur, the initial in-house production by the formal firms may have been sub-optimal. For, it may be argued, if it pays to subcontract at the higher wage, it would have done so also at the lower wage. In this case stubbornness, inertia or ignorance stood in the way, and the rise in the wage wakes up the businessman. But there may have been non-pecuniary offsetting advantages in in-house production, which are more than offset when costs rise. These may be the result of transport, communication or transaction costs, or high training costs with greater probability that the trained subcontractor may leave than the in-house worker.

Other linkages between formal and informal sector firms

1. See FRANCES STEWART and JOHN WEEKS : 'Raising Wages in the Controlled Sector', *Journal of Development Studies*, vol. 16 no. 1, October 1979. Ronald Dore has suggested that the same effect can be achieved by the Japanese practice of high average wages with lifetime employment and a retirement age at 50. The worker then sets himself up in a small subcontracting business, and makes use of his connection with the large firm, which regards him as loyal and reliable.

affecting competing and complementary inputs and products should be carefully traced.[1] If high growth rates in the formal sector are not to be impeded, it is important not to deprive it of scarce factors, such as capital, management or wage goods, for the benefit of low productivity activities. This implies that the capital and organizational capacity should be recruited from within the informal sector. At the same time, it is also important that the expansion of the formal sector should not raise the prices of goods necessary for production in the informal sector. This appears to have happened in Colombia, where a housing project for the rich was intended to generate incomes for workers. But the resulting price increase in concrete and steel led to price rises in sheet metal and cardboard, jeopardizing the building efforts of the poor.[2]

A second illustration is to be found in a modern version of the 18th-century putting-out system. Subcontracting by large firms to small, sometimes informal sector firms or cottage industries is quite common in the developing world. But there is still much scope for importing houses in advanced countries or retail chains independent of developed country producer interests to apply the putting-out system to informal sector firms in developing countries. The large firm provides the materials, the designs, the credit and the marketing, while the informal sector firm produces the clothes, the sport equipment, the electronic components, the cloth and woodwork for handicrafts, or the crops. The British retail chain Marks and Spencer have employed this modern putting-out system not only in England but also in some developing countries.

There opens up another use for the judo trick. The political

1. SANJAYA LALL distinguishes between the following linkages: establishment, locational, informational, technical, financial, raw material procurement, managerial, pricing, other distributional, and diversification. 'A Study of Multinational and Local Firm Linkages in India', in her *Multinationals, Technology and Exports*, London: Macmillan, 1985, pp. 269-270.

2. See LISA PEATTIE, *loc. cit.*, p. 858. The terms of trade between the informal and formal sectors are an important determinant of the division of gains. The "reserve army of unemployed" will tend to keep incomes and prices of informal firms low, while productivity growth in formal firms will tend to be passed on in higher wages, rather than lower prices. In addition, there may be unequal bargaining power. An "unequal exchange" may result.

power of these retail chains, such as Atlantic and Pacific Stores or Safeways, can be used to counteract the pressures for protection by the producer lobbies in the industrial countries. Their interest in low-cost, labour-intensive imports coincides with those of the poor producers in the developing countries. If institutional safeguards are adopted to prevent exploitation and sweated labour, firms such as Marks and Spencer can do more for the poor of the world than Marx and Engels.

In addition to new institutions, policies will have to be revised. Thus, many economists have opposed minimum wage legislation on the ground that it prevents higher employment. But, as we have seen, if a higher wage level or a shorter working week, applied only to organized sector firms, forces them to contract out to the informal sector activities previously carried out inside these firms, this can be a gain in employment and earnings. For these activities are likely to be carried out in a more labour-intensive way in the informal sector than they were inside the large firms. One characteristic of the distinction is the flexibility of incomes in the informal sector compared with rigidity downwards in the formal sector. Therefore its absorptive capacity of labour is higher and policies that make it worth while to give more business to the small firms are to be welcomed.

The measures needed to implement such a policy can be summarized under the following headings:

1. First, a more favourable economic environment for the informal sector should be created. At present, macroeconomic policies tend to discriminate against it. For example, investment incentives confine tax concessions to formal sector firms. Overvaluation of the exchange rate combined with import restrictions and undervaluation of the interest rate handicap the access to inputs and credit of informal firms.

2. Second, it is necessary to design new institutions of the kind indicated above. The access of the poor to assets should be improved. In agriculture this policy has worked. It is more difficult to apply it in urban industry. Steps are being taken to provide these small entrepreneurs with credit. The Grameen Bank in Bangladesh has found many imitators in other countries. The Inter-American Development Bank wants to establish itself as the

bank for Latin America's informal sector. The International Fund for Agricultural Development has successfully lent to businesses without collateral. Pressures for repayment can be exercised by peer groups, and by making small loans for short periods. Loans should be primarily for working capital. Judgment of the borrower's reliability can replace conventional collateral requirements.

3. Third, returns to these enterprises must be raised. It is not enough, as is often said, to raise their productivity, for productivity gains can be passed on in the form of lower prices to often better off buyers in the formal sector. It is the earning power, the remunerativeness of the enterprise, that matters.

4. Fourth, employment opportunities must be improved. Even though the informal sector is often defined as supply-driven, there are obstacles to entry and to employment, which can be reduced.

5. Fifth, the demand for their production should be raised. Since poor people tend to buy the goods produced by the poor people in the informal sector, policies that generate incomes for poor people will also raise the demand for their products.[1]

6. Sixth, access to education, training and health services must be improved, both as an end in itself and in order to raise the productivity of the poor. Technical training and instruction in simple managerial techniques, such as accounting and book keeping, marketing and technical know-how are important. The identification and provision of missing components, such as market information, infrastructure or technical know-how can yield great benefits at little cost.

7. Seventh, transfer payments out of public funds are also required to provide a safety net, not only for the unemployables, the disabled, the sick, the old, but also to tide people over periods of no earnings, of failure of their enterprises or temporary inability to work.

Another way of categorizing the necessary public sector measures to make the symbiosis between multinational corporations

1. See LIEDHOLM and MEAD, *op. cit.* and RADHA SINHA, PETER PEARSON, GOPAL KADEKODI and MARY GREGORY, *Income Distribution, Growth and Basic Needs in India*, London: Croom Helm, 1979.

or large domestic firms and the informal sector successful can be summarized with a mnemotechnic device. It is the seven "Ins" or Instruments previously discussed for agriculture:

1. Incentives: prices of both inputs and outputs must be right.

2. Inputs: both imported and domestic inputs, including credit, must be available.

3. Institutions: access to marketing institutions and credit institutions and a non-corrupt, efficient administrative apparatus must exist.

4. Innovation: the right small-scale technology, appropriate for small enterprises often does not exist and research and search should be provided to create and find, and adapt it.

5. Information: a knowledge bank for technology should provide means of spreading the results of research and search among the firms. Also instruction in management, book-keeping, simple cost-accounting and recording should be provided.

6. Infrastructure: roads, communications, harbours, and utilities must be available if the output of the informal sector is to be sold in national and international markets.

7. Independence: permit and encourage self-reliance and freedom from excessive regulation and harassment.

In the manner described above, the informal sector can be made complementary to the formal with respect to access to markets, inputs, information and technology, the small-scale firms to large-scale firms, domestic to foreign firms, public to private firms, and non-governmental organizations to governments. The putting-out system of foreign retailers or importing houses is an example of the symbiosis between foreign large and domestic small enterprises. Similarly, private voluntary organizations engaged in helping informal sector projects should find ways of co-operating with government departments and multinational corporations, which are often in a better position to finance and replicate successful projects.

Our knowledge of the informal sector in most developing countries is still rudimentary. What we need is both time series and cross-country studies of informal sector activities to show at what income levels, with what policies, which activities, actually or potentially, contribute to employment, productivity, earning power, production, and growth.

It has been emphasized that the encouragement of complementarities should not be done at the expense of the growth of the high-productivity, modern sector. On the contrary, the small units should contribute to raising the productivity of the large ones. According to S. P. Kashyap, handicaps for large firms and biases in policy against them are largely responsible for the growth of small-scale enterprises in India.[1] Nor should there be any form of exploitation, such as child labour, inhuman working conditions, sweated labour, or monopsonistic depression of the prices at which outputs are bought. Fears have been expressed that the informal sector enterprises have been reduced to a state of "peonage" by their formal sector principals.[2] Nor should there be monopolistic overpricing of the intermediate products supplied by the formal sector as inputs to the informal enterprises. Such overpricing could be the result of import restrictions or other barriers to entry. In Sierra Leone the large-scale flour mill, which supplies flour to small-scale bakers, is protected by an exclusive import licence, and therefore can sell its flour at prices over twice those of potential imports.[3] The policies must be designed to mobilize the energies of the small-scale firms, and to make use of their lower costs, more labour-intensive techniques, greater employment creation, and wider dispersion of technology, without, on the one hand, sacrificing efficiency and innovation, and, on the other, depriving the informal sector, by underpricing outputs or overpricing inputs, of adequate rewards and humane working conditions.

Encouragement for the view that the informal sector, or at any rate the sector containing small-scale firms, can be the dynamic sector of the future comes from an unexpected source: the

1. S. P. KASHYAP, 'Growth of Small-Size Enterprises in India: Its Nature and Content', *World Development*, vol. 16 no. 6, June 1988.

2. SANJAYA LALL, *op. cit.*, p. 270. Lall, however, concludes from his case study that "on the whole, their benefits from being linked outweigh their costs", p. 288.

3. ENYINNA CHUTA and CARL LIEDHOLM, *Employment and Growth in Small-Scale Industry*, London: Macmillan, 1985, p. 144.

literature on Flexible Specialization, mainly applied to trends in the advanced, industrial countries.[1] The move from standardized, large-scale mass production to small-scale, flexible firms is the result of changes in demand and supply. On the demand side, the mass consumer has been replaced by a more sophisticated type with higher purchasing power and more differentiated tastes. On the side of supply, the technology for energy and information has encouraged decentralization of production and smaller size of firms. "Mass production is the manufacture of standard products with specialized resources . . . ; flexible specialization is the production of specialized products with general resources . . . "[2]

In Mexico a large number of small, decentralized workshops (*maquilas*) and household units are subcontractors for the large firms. The uncertainties of the 1980s have encouraged the rise of these units which produce specialized products with a broadly skilled and weakly specialized labour force. The division of labour resembles the Japanese *kanban* where many small suppliers and subcontractors are clustered round a large firm. Similar patterns are to be found in Northern Italy (the so-called "Third Italy") and other parts of Europe, with their regional clusters of small, cooperating, flexible firms.[3] As demand and technology changes, skills and products can be easily switched and adapted to the new situation. The shoe industries around Novo Hamburgo in Brazil and Leòn in Mexico are organized on this basis and have encouraged the growth of rural industries.

1. See JUDITH TENDLER, *op. cit.*, and CHARLES F. SABEL, *Changing Models of Economic Efficiency and their Implications for Industrialization in the Third World*, Department of City and Regional Planning, Cambridge, Mass.: MIT, 1987 and in *Development, Democracy, and the Art of Trespassing, Essays in Honor of Albert O. Hirschman,* edited by ALEJANDRO FOXLEY, MICHAEL S. MCPHERSON, and GUILLERMO O'DONNELL, Notre Dame, Ind.: University of Notre Dame Press, 1986, pp. 27-55.

2. *Ibid*, p. 40. The *marxisant* terms are "Fordism" and "post-Fordism", not, of course named after the Ford Foundation but after Henry Ford and his famous remark that the American public could have their model T any colour they liked as long as it was black. The term was coined by Antonio Gramsci to describe a phase in the history of capitalism.

3. Recent evidence shows, however, that some of these firms in the Third Italy have gone bankrupt, others have been taken over by large firms. It seems that they have a tendency to merge into the first and second Italy.

As Judith Tendler has pointed out, there has been a role reversal, and in this literature the formal sector firms, interpreted as the traditional, large-scale, fixed-cost, mass-production firms, are seen as "sick", whereas the flexible, small firms are capable of responding dynamically to changing demand and technology. Not only have they taken over the leadership, but they are also more humane and responsible in their work relations. There is also a new form of cooperation between the small firms, and the old confrontation between labour and capital is replaced by one between the managers, owners and workers in the small, subcontracting firms, on the one hand, and the large buyers of their output on the other. In addition, supportive local institutions evolve that provide information, technical know-how and training. All this holds out great productive and social promise for the informal sector, especially if supported by the right social policies.[1]

4. Foreign Investment and Macroeconomic Policies

It is fashionable to extol "outward-looking" trade and industrialization policies as good for growth, employment, poverty reduction, and income distribution and to condemn "inward-looking" ones. In the same vein, it is generally held that transnational corporations and private foreign investment that are attracted by a "realistic" exchange rate, a docile and cheap labour force,

1. The idea of flexible specialization can be carried from the domain of production into administration and culture. A sluggish centralized bureaucracy corresponds to Detroit's assembly line. The new problems of government, deteriorating public schools, soaring health costs, shrinking tax revenues, persistent welfare demands, call for different forms of government: more decentralized, some privatization and contracting out of certain services, more delegation to schools. The home, with computer, fax machine, copier and telephone, replaces the large factory; the video the large cinema; the stereo the large opera house. In architecture, Fordism took the form of mass and geometry, LeCorbusierism and towerblocks, while post-Fordism rejects public and corporate architecture, and stands for smallness, individualism, privacy, choice. Informality may win across the board. The main thesis of the judo trick, however, is not to subscribe to this view, but to say that Fordism and post-Fordism can be simultaneous and complementary. Assembly line factories can franchise and subcontract, and can house their workers in individually designed houses. Theme parks for the masses can compete with home entertainment and soon with "virtual reality".

and good export prospects contribute more to the host country than those attracted by highly protected domestic markets and overvalued exchange rates combined with import restrictions, high wages and underpriced capital.

It is, however, not clear how helpful this kind of distinction is. First, if we look at the process historically, most successful outward-looking policies were preceded by a phase of inward-looking protection. Industries that have grown up under protection, producing for the home market, then became exporters. Volkswagen Brazil is only one of many examples of a foreign investment that originally catered for the domestic market and later became one of the most successful exporters. Zimbabwe presents an illustration of a country that laid the foundations for successful exports during an enforced inward-looking phase. Brazil laid the foundations of its good performance in the inter-war period, when depression and the war had cut it off from world trade. All now-industrial countries initially protected their manufacturing industries. The simple division into outward- and inward-orientation is ahistorical.

Second, much industrialization takes the form of replacing imported inputs into the production of exports by domestic inputs. This applies also to foreign investments. Is this to be classified as inward-looking, because it substitutes domestic inputs for imports, or as outward-looking because it increases the value added in exports? Of course, those who define "outward-looking" as neutrality between import substitution and exports, and as using free market prices as signals and incentives, have a ready answer. But this is a somewhat biased definition and some authors have defined "outward-looking" in a more symmetrical way, as biased towards exports.

There are other problems with this simple distinction of trade and industrialization policies. One is that the dichotomy may not exhaust all directions in which the policy may look. A discriminating policy may look at the expanding markets of the newly industrialized countries or the countries of Eastern Europe and the Commonwealth of Independent States rather than at the outside world at large, just as the newly industrializing countries in the nineteenth century that followed England did not look primarily

173

at England for their markets, but at one another, at Germany, the USA and Latin America.

Then there is the well known problem of aggregation: can all developing countries emulate the model of the East Asian exporters? If all developing countries matched Taiwan's proportion of the labour force or of GDP devoted to exports, the need to absorb this vastly larger volume of exports would run into difficulties. Formally, of course, it is true that the extra revenue earned by these exports would be spent on extra imports. The phasing of trade liberalization would be different for different countries, and not all exports would be dumped simultaneously. The commodity composition and the export/GDP ratios would be different for different countries and at different times. Many developing countries would continue to export primary products. Since labour-rich, resource-poor developing countries, as the Asian tigers were initially, are likely to have a larger proportion of their labour force in exports than are resource-rich, labour-poor countries like Brazil and Argentina, the impact on world markets would not be concentrated. Some exports would be directed to other developing countries whose vested interests are less strong in clamouring for protection. And, as a result of trade liberalization, counter-protectionist pressure groups in the developed countries, such as agriculture in the USA, would gain in strength.

In spite of these mitigating circumstances, there are bound to be severe adjustment problems in the importing countries. If growth rates in the industrial countries are sluggish and unemployment is high, protectionist barriers are likely to go up, or the terms of trade are likely to deteriorate for manufactures exporters.[1]

It is often claimed that "outward-looking" policies make labour-intensive exports profitable, and that this is good for employment and income distribution. But there is no reason why some forms of import substitution should not be carried out in a labour-intensive way. If a country undervalues its exchange rate,

1. See PAUL STREETEN, 'Comment' in *Hard Bargaining Ahead: U.S. Trade Policy and Developing Countries*, edited by ERNEST H. PREEG, New Brunswick: Transaction Books, Third World Policy Perspectives, no. 4 Overseas Development Council, 1985, pp. 58-60.

it makes imports more expensive and encourages exports. Undervaluation of the exchange rate looks outwards with respect to exports, just as overvaluation looks outwards with respect to imports. Private foreign investors may take these signals as given and adapt to them, or they may wish to influence and shape them, by exercising pressures on governments, either for protection or for tax concessions or for subsidies.

Although the recommendations based on the distinction between outward- and inward-looking are too simple as a guide to policy, it is true that foreign investments that are attracted by the low costs of available inputs, such as cheap and docile labour, a stable political climate, a well managed economy, and perhaps some subsidies to infrastructure, such as trading estates, or a subsidy to power, or export zones, or remissions of tariffs on imported inputs, are preferable to investments that are attracted by highly protected domestic markets. This is particularly true of small countries, which have no large market to offer. In Singapore, which provides an attractive export base, foreign private direct investment is over 10 per cent of gross domestic product. The horror stories of negative value added (or value subtracted), documented for highly protected import substitution (such as the Philippine car industry), can, of course, in principle also be found in export industries. Just as it is possible to combine high private profits to foreign firms with large social losses by excessive protection of the domestic market, so it is possible to over-subsidize and undertax export production, and combine private profitability with negative value added. But in practice it may be politically more difficult to give very large support in the transparent form of subsidies to inputs than in the more hidden form of import restrictions that protect the markets for outputs.

An empirical study by Blomstrom, Kravis and Lipsey shows that transnational corporations can make an important and increasing contribution to manufactured exports of developing countries.[1] According to this study the share of US, Japanese and

1. MAGNUS BLOMSTROM, IRVING B. KRAVIS and ROBERT E. LIPSEY, *Multinational Firms and Manufactured Exports from Developing Countries*, NBER Working Paper no. 2493, Cambridge, Mass.: National Bureau of Economic Research, January 1988.

Swedish transnational firms in manufactured exports of developing countries has increased from the sixties or seventies to the present. But the lesson for the low-income countries has to be qualified in that these firms were mainly in technologically oriented industries, and in the newly industrializing countries (NICs). Even in the NICs, in less technologically oriented industries, such as food, textiles and clothing, exports of locally owned firms were growing faster than those of transnationals.

5. Regional Integration and Foreign Investment

Regional cooperation among developing countries is much talked about but little has been achieved. The reason for this is disputes over the location of industry and therefore the division of the benefits. The most advanced country in the region, with its superior infrastructure, skills and institutions, will tend to attract the new investments and the poorer countries will be deprived. If, on the other hand, provisions are made for compensation payments to the poorer members, the richer object to having to make these sacrifices. One solution to this problem is the founding of a new form of joint venture between a foreign company and the member governments of a union. The company would locate itself and produce according to commercial criteria, where costs are lowest. Its shares would be held partly by member countries of the union. If desired, it would be possible to allocate more shares to the lowest income members. In this way the company would combine low-cost, efficient location and operation, not subject to political horse-trading, with a sharing of the profits between member countries that would compensate the poorest members for their disadvantages.

6. Export Processing Zones

In view of the low incomes and small size of the domestic market in most low-income countries (the exceptions are India and China), the best hope of attracting foreign investment in manufacturing is in export processing zones. One of the assets poor countries have to offer is a cheap labour force. If the labour force is disciplined, ready to learn and well motivated, it can attract foreign investors interested in producing components or engaging in processes that are labour-intensive. Export zones have been set up in many countries for this purpose. And, at first sight, their existence seems to vindicate the doctrine of comparative advantage, according to which countries with a plentiful supply of labour should concentrate on the production and export of labour-intensive goods. Mauritius has had outstanding success in attracting foreign investment. Its manufactured exports are now worth more than twice those of sugar, its dominant export in the past. Its economy has been growing at 5-7 per cent a year for four years. There are, however, dangers to host countries in this type of investment.

It is foreign capital, know-how, enterprise, management and marketing that are highly mobile internationally, and that are combined with the plentiful, but internationally much less mobile, domestic, unskilled or semi-skilled labour. One set of factors (enterprise, management, knowledge and capital) are in relatively *inelastic* supply *in total*, but easily moved around the world in response to small differentials. They are therefore in *highly elastic* supply *to any particular country*. The other factor, labour, is in *highly elastic* supply domestically, but *immobile* across frontiers. The situation is equivalent to one in which plentiful unskilled and semi-skilled labour itself, rather than the product of labour, is exported. The surplus of the product of labour over the wage, resulting from the cooperation of other factors, in less elastic supply, accrues to foreigners. The differential international and internal elasticities of supply in response to differential rewards and the difference in monopoly rents entering the rewards of these factors have important implications for the international distribution of gains from investment.

Since the firms operate in oligopolistic and oligopsonistic markets, cost advantages are not necessarily passed on to consumers in lower prices or to workers in higher wages, and the profits then accrue to the parent firms. The operation of this type of international specialization depends upon the continuation of

177

substantial wage differentials (hence trade unions must be weak in the host country so that low wage costs are maintained), continuing access to the markets of the parent companies (hence stronger political pressure from importing interests than from domestic producers displaced by the low-cost components and processes, including trade unions in the rich importing countries) and continuing permission by host countries to operate with minimum taxes, tariffs and bureaucratic regulation.

The packaged or complete nature of the contribution of the transnational enterprise, usually claimed as its characteristic blessing, is then the cause of the unequal international division of gains. If the package broke, or leaked, some of the rents and monopoly rewards would spill over into the host country. But if it is secured tightly, only the least scarce and weakest factor in the host country derives an income from the operations of the transnational firm, unless bargaining power is used to extract a share of these other incomes.

It appears to be the secret of the (South) Korean success story that the Koreans drew knowledge from inputs and equipment suppliers and from foreign buyers, and developed their own technical capacity through reverse engineering. Export processing zones contributed only 4 per cent to the total manufactured exports of Korea. The Koreans unbundled the package, tolerated majority foreign ownership only in export and high technology firms, and did not waste money on the rents in the foreign investment bundle. Technology transfer took the form of transferring knowledge from foreign brains to domestic ones.

It is sometimes said that the workers in the firms in export zones acquire skills which will later benefit the host country. But often these workers are young women who do not stay in the labour force when they get married. Moreover, the skills are often quite simple ones, such as using fingers nimbly for sewing or assembling parts for carburettors.

The situation is aggravated if there is technical progress of the kind that knocks out the advantage in labour-intensive production of the host country. The electronics revolution makes it possible to robotize whole textile factories and to relocate to the parent country. Other processes and products than the automated ones will still be left to which the labour force could be switched. But such switching has its costs. Skills acquired are wasted, workers have to be retrained, and the bargaining power of the host country and its labour force is further reduced.

The bargaining power of the host country and of its plentiful factor – semi-skilled labour – in such a situation is likely to be weak and the question is whether such a division of gains between parent firm and host country, between the foreign investment "package" and domestic labour, remains acceptable. The gains to the host country are confined to the wages of those employed if the alternative is unemployment. The fact that these earnings are in foreign exchange may put them at a premium, if the country suffers from a foreign exchange shortage. There may, in addition, be linkages, but these can be positive or negative.

A possibly more hopeful note can be struck if we remember that the electronics revolution economizes not only in labour, but also in supervisory and managerial talent. Since this is scarcer in developing than in advanced countries, the developing countries' comparative advantage in some of these lines may be reestablished. It would no longer be employment creating, but would still earn foreign exchange and tax revenue which could be used for job creation through public works or productive, labour-intensive investment. A number of research projects are devoted to finding out what the locational implications of recent technical progress are, but the empirical evidence is not yet in. While the type of foreign investment discussed has attractions for some countries faced with labour surpluses or foreign exchange shortages and poorly endowed with natural resources, the potential gains have to be weighed against the social costs and social risks, including a form of dependence and dualistic development of a new kind, different from that of the colonial mines and plantations, but similar in its distributional impact.[1]

---

1. There is a secondary problem. Assume the host country were able to provide some of the technicians or managers provided by the transnational corporation. It would then have to reward them with incomes not too much out of line with those received by the rich foreigners, or they would emigrate. Local replacement would make an egalitarian incomes policy more difficult or impossible. This threat to social objectives may be worse than the actual brain drain of professional manpower.

What are the lessons for policy? The most obvious conclusion is that developing host countries should share in the monopoly rents by appropriate tax policies. But this requires *joint* action of countries with similar attractions for the foreign firm in order to reduce the elasticity of supply with which any one country would be faced if it acted in isolation. Such joint action is difficult to achieve. The more successful the agreement on not giving tax concessions promises to be, the more attractive it is for any one country to break away, or to make the concessions outside the agreement. And the fear of someone breaking away is a deterrent for others to reach, or, once reached, to adhere to the agreement.

Thought should be given to how to introduce sanctions and penalties that would prevent such defections. The European Economic Community and the Association of South East Asian Nations have provisions against concessions above an agreed level. The situation may, however, be asymmetrical, if increasing tax concessions were not to attract additional investment, because they would be followed by other countries. The situation would then be like the kinked oligopoly demand curve. Both raising concessions and reducing them would reduce foreign investment.

Apart from sharing in the gains through tax collection, the host country can impose various conditions on the company. One would be to undertake the retraining should it decide to relocate elsewhere, or more generally to provide training outside its own work force for a flexible labour force. Another would be various ways of making the foreign factors complementary rather than competitive to indigenous factors. Some of these possibilities were discussed above: joint ventures, local participation in board membership, training requirements, etc. Others are discussed below. The aim would be to use the foreign investment as an instrument for the mobilization and improvement of local resources. The question is whether without protection of markets, without tax concessions, and without heavy subsidies to inputs, such conditions remain within the bargaining range that satisfies the objectives of both the foreign firm and the host country. Outside this range, more or less foreign investment has to be weighed against the still largely unexplored costs and benefits of this investment.

7. Government Intervention and Performance Requirements[1]

The generally prevailing view is that specific incentives to attract private foreign investments and transnational corporations, or to direct it into specific sectors or projects or locations, such as tax concessions, are not very effective. The reason for this may be that they tend to be small and that the investor does not regard them as permanent. Instability is regarded as a deterrent. On the other hand, the expectation that incentives may be provided in the future (e.g. restrictions on imports and on new foreign investment) could work as an incentive to invest now. Another reason for the apparent unimportance of specific incentives is that many similarly situated countries offer them. If only one country were to withdraw them while the others maintained theirs, it might well lose a good deal of investment.[2]

Probably more important than specific incentives, which are small and unstable, is the general investment climate, which is influenced by government policies, although not those directed specifically at the investment. Government attitudes to transnational corporations, macroeconomic policies with respect to a realistic exchange rate, a fairly uniform and not too high tariff structure, and low wages play an important part. Reliable infrastructure, good administration, political stability and absence of arbitrary and rapid changes in regulations are usually cited as more important than the regulations themselves.

At the same time it should be remembered that there are justifications for departures from such a uniform and open system. There is the well known terms of trade argument for tariff protection when a country has monopoly power. This is stronger for poor countries, for which the redistributional effect of such monopolistic action can be justified in the absence of adequate direct income

---

1. For a full list of host country incentives and disincentives to foreign investment, see Table 1 in STEPHEN GUISINGER, 'Host-Country Policies to Attract and Control Foreign Investment', in *Investing in Development: New Roles for Private Capital?*, THEODORE H. MORAN and contributors, Overseas Development Council, New Brunswick and Oxford: Transaction Books, 1986.

2. *Ibid.*

transfers; there are learning effects and infant industry encouragement, both to import substitutes and to exports; and there are
justifications for import restrictions combined with restrictions on
domestic production of certain types of consumer goods, the demand for which is heavily influenced by advertising, or by other
people's consumption, or by habit, or by ignorance or false beliefs.

In contrast to incentives, developing countries impose performance requirements on foreign firms. These may relate to raising
exports or lowering imports, offsetting import content of inputs
by export earnings,[1] use of local materials, employment, participation in management and ownership, local research and development, transfer of technology, training, etc.[2] They may, if effective, offset the incentive effects of the concessions. Alternatively,
if they are well designed and reduce monopoly rents, they may
only amount to a shift of benefits to the host country, without
affecting the amount of foreign investment.

Some countries use general principles that apply to all foreign
applicants, others use discretion for particular cases. The World
Bank found an inverse relationship between market size and universal (as opposed to discretionary) performance criteria.

Learning by doing is often cited as an argument for protecting
or, better, subsidizing the learning activity, in an infant industry.
The subsidy is justified only if the benefits from the learning
process do not accrue to the firm but are passed on to others in
lower prices (or if capital markets do not function). The argument
applies, in principle, as much to import-substituting as to export-
promoting investments. Indeed, it also applies to subsidizing foreign firms located abroad, if their learning process yields lower-
priced imports into the subsidizing country in the future.

8. Transnational Corporations and Basic Needs

So far the emphasis has been mainly on the supply side: how can
foreign investment contribute to making poor people more pro-

---

1. See the discussion of inward- and outward-looking foreign investment above.
2. For a discussion of such requirements, see PAUL STREETEN, *Development Perspectives*,
London: Macmillan, 1981, p. 283.

ductive? In this section we turn to the demand or need side and ask what contribution transnational firms can make to meeting basic needs. It is in the nature of the transnational corporation that it possesses a monopolistic advantage over its potential local rivals, for otherwise international investment would not occur. The local firms would have the advantage of familiarity with the surroundings. This advantage may take various forms, but one common form in consumer goods is the creation of goodwill through advertising and marketing techniques, as in branded foodstuffs. Another form is the incorporation of research and development expenditure, as in pharmaceuticals. A third form is large-scale production and the economies of scale with the restriction on rival entry that this entails. These monopolistic advantages enable the firm to reap monopoly profits until the advantage is eroded by competition, when the firm has to renew its attempt to reestablish the advantage. The sophistication of the products, and the complexity of the technology determined by the product design, are therefore not only a response to the high incomes and high savings in the mass markets of the developed countries, in which the transnationals are at home, but they are of the very essence of the transnational. Very simple consumer or producer goods cannot normally be protected through patents, trademarks, trade secrets or other forms of exclusion, and are readily imitated. Even when they can be so protected, the appropriation of profits does not last long. Unless they are much cheaper to produce on a mass scale (as is the case with buses, trucks or mopeds), the transnational has no special advantage in producing them. It is true that transnationals do produce and sell apparently simple basic needs products like bicycles, sewing machines, margarine, soap and washing powder. But these are hardly ever for the poorest segments of the population. Small-scale domestic firms, if given access to capital, other inputs, and markets, are often able to compete successfully and cater for the lower-income markets.

The provision of an adequate diet and health services is an essential part of meeting basic needs. But the branded, advertised, packaged and marketed food products and soft drinks of the transnationals do not appear to be capable of making a substantial contribution here. Alan Berg concludes a careful survey of transnationals and nutrition by saying that, in spite of the substantial time and energy devoted by governments to involving big business,

> there is little to show in the way of nutrition improvement. Nor are the prospects bright for reaching a significant portion of the needy with proprietary foods marketed in the conventional manner . . . the major impediment is the inability to reconcile the demand for corporate profit with a product low enough in cost to reach the needy in large numbers.[1]

In so far as "appropriate" products of a simple, not over-specified, kind, using local materials and local unskilled or semiskilled labour, have not been invented, so that there are gaps in the product range, there is clearly need for more R&D. But for the reasons given, the transnational does not have the incentive to devote its R&D expenditure to this purpose. For, having spent possibly substantial sums on an innovation, rapid imitation by small-scale firms would soon erode its profits and it would not be able to recoup its research expenditure. It is the very fact that the social benefits derived from such innovations exceed the private, appropriable returns, and that markets in developing countries are more competitive, that leads to the minuscule research that is done on appropriate basic needs products. An example would be a cheap, serviceable, say $ 50 refrigerator. The argument points to alternative methods of financing R&D.

Similar considerations apply to simple producer goods, such as hand tools (e.g. a spade for barefoot diggers) and power-driven equipment, both for small farmers and for small industrial and service enterprises. The appropriate technology may be missing or, though in existence, may be unknown in the country. But again, it is hard to see why the transnational company should have an incentive to spend its funds on developing such products. There are, however, exceptions. There is more scope in supplying capital goods required as inputs into the public provision of basic services (road building equipment, equipment for geologi-

---

1. ALAN BERG, *The Nutrition Factor*, Washington D.C.: Brookings Institution, 1973, p. 158.

cal surveys, such as remote sensing, medical equipment, drugs).
Not all goods appropriate for meeting the basic needs of poor people are simple and easily produced. Village education may use
television sets with programmes beamed from satellites.

The conclusion is analogous to those in earlier sections. The
role of transnational corporations and private foreign investment
has to be fitted into the host country's development strategy. This
can be done without sacrificing or even blunting the main objective of transnationals, which is to make a profit.

APPENDIX

Gains and Losses from Trade in Services

1. Gains and Losses to Countries from Trade in Services. – 2. Cost and Benefits Within Countries.

1. Gains and Losses to Countries from Trade in Services

Generalizations, particularly in economics, are always dangerous. Empirical work usually destroys even the most imaginative, subtle and ingenious generalization. On the other hand, to say that each case is unique and that no general lessons can ever be learned from any specific event in space and time is to abandon thinking and analysis. The intermediate position is found in typologies and taxonomies. What might serve in analysing country-specific gains and losses from trade in services is a typology by type of country and type of service. It would be helpful for a policy maker to look at a matrix, showing on one side characteristics of countries, on the other characteristics of services, and then to say: since my country is relatively small, has an income per head of $ x$, is surrounded by the sea, and has a service sector absorbing y per cent of the labour force, my policy towards a service in which the user has to be near the provider, in which competition is strong, and which is closely linked to commodity production and trade, should be such and such. Being away from libraries and other forms of documentation, I shall have to rely on generalizations which may well be abandoned or qualified in a more detailed examination.

A naive approach to the subject would argue that countries that advocate free trade in services have, on balance, to gain, while countries that oppose it have, on balance, to lose. But this is not necessarily true. Countries frequently wrongly perceive and analyse their gains and losses from policies they advocate. This is particularly true of developing countries.

The principal advocate of free trade in services has been the USA.[1] What are US gains? Clearly, the advocacy has applied largely to certain kinds of services, above all banking and insurance, and not to others, which would imply large-scale immigration of people from devel-

---

1. This essay is greatly indebted to JAGDISH BHAGWATI's 'International Trade in Services and its Relevance for Economic Development', Xth Annual Lecture of the Geneva Association, Oxford: Pergamon Press, 1985, and to DEEPAK NAYYAR's *International Trade in Services*, Exim Bank Annual Lecture, 1986.

oping countries. Some services involve movement of the user to the provider (haircuts in India, or Niagara honeymoons cannot be exported); others movement of the provider to the user (construction of buildings or roads). Still others do not require movement by anybody: information is passed along a wire, television can be beamed from a satellite. It may not be sensible to fly chartered planeloads of Americans to India to have their hair cut, but it is perfectly sensible to invite Indian construction companies, or consulting services, or doctors, or Mexican dentists to come to the United States and service consumers there. A truly general freeing of trade in services would give free access of nationals from developing countries to the users in the advanced countries. Such a step (as also the close link between some services and international capital flows) would mean encroaching on the time-honoured distinction between free trade in goods and permitted restrictions on the flow of factors of production. The distinction between factor mobility and trade becomes blurred.

A consistent policy of free trade in goods and services would remove all restrictions on migration of people who can provide services, at least on temporary immigration while the service is provided. At the moment the USA is advocating free trade in services which involve either locating Americans abroad or rendering services "along a wire", while not wishing to accept the services of Korean construction crews or Indian doctors in the USA.

There are three possible sets of gains for the USA. First, there is the gain from political support of powerful lobbies that would benefit from free trade, though these are not national gains. But politicians, according to one theory of the state, trade policies for votes, and if yielding to these pressure groups promises political support, this is a powerful motive for adopting them. The US multinational banks are such a pressure group and yielding to their demands constitutes the first type of gain to the US government, a political gain, though not necessarily a gain to the nation as a whole.

Ascending in the coverage of interests, there is a second set of reasons, which apply to the national interest of the USA. It can be argued that the US comparative advantage in services has increased, and that to exclude these leads to an unfair division of the gains from trade. But it must be noted that the services that are entering international trade are only a small part of the general expansion of the service sector in the US economy. It is true that some of these services are provided by government monopolies or by regulated private enterprises, so that comparative advantage is not always apparent or easy to determine, as it would be in competitive enterprises. But the fact that the USA has in general achieved substantial cost reductions in services connected with electronics and the transmission of information cannot be doubted. If, the USA says, it keeps American markets open to foreign goods but foreign markets remain closed to American services, this leads to a biased international division of labour, in which the USA loses. It will, of course, be argued that other countries' trade restrictions do not affect the benefits to any given country from liberalizing its trade. Adam Smith compared other countries' restrictions to rocks in your harbour, which are no reason for throwing in additional rocks. But in the present atmosphere of "reciprocity", the bargaining power over closing markets to goods, even though it would hurt the protecting country, can be used to achieve liberalization in services in other, importing countries.

At the third and highest level, free trade in services is thought to benefit the USA, and not only the USA but the world community as a whole. Since Ricardo economists have advocated free trade as beneficial to all participants. But as we know from the theory of the second-best, partial free trade can be worse than severer trade restrictions. Trade diversion may be stronger than trade creation. Only the elimination of *all* barriers to trade can, on certain assumptions, be shown to be in everybody's interest. Quite apart from arguments derived from the theory of the second-best, America believes in a liberal world trading order. Under the postwar Pax Americana it has upheld the principle of liberal trade in institutions such as the GATT, the IMF and the World Bank, and has provided the public or collective good of this type of trade regime. With the decline of American hegemony, with slower economic growth and with the large and persistent deficit in the US balance of payments, commitment by the USA to a liberal trading order has declined. But the USA still believes in the rule of law in international trade and opposes discretionary controls. At this level, free trade in services is not only good for America, but good for all participants.

In advocating this stance the USA does not stand alone. Other advanced, shall we say post-industrial or service countries, such as Great Britain and Switzerland, have joined the US call. Even some developing countries, such as Hong Kong and Singapore, which stand to gain from offshore banking operations, consent. At one time it was thought - mainly by the late Nicholas Kaldor - that productivity growth in services is slower than in manufacturing, and a growth strategy suggested discriminating against them. But this view is no longer popular and countries like Britain and Switzerland have made common cause with the USA.

Why then do the developing countries, led by India and Brazil, but also Argentina, Nigeria, Cuba, Eygpt, Nicaragua, Peru and Tanzania, fear that they would lose from liberalized trade in services? There are six arguments explaining the fear. The first argument is the reverse of the second argument of the USA. If comparative advantage in services has shifted to the post-industrial, advanced countries, to the service economies, it is feared that the developing countries would lose, either relatively or absolutely. This assumes, of course, that productivity improvements are not passed on in lower import prices or, if they are, that this prevents the growth of infant service industries in the developing countries.

A second fear is that negotiating about services will divert attention from keeping trade in goods open (or liberalizing it where it is now restricted), and thereby harm the developing countries in an area in which their comparative advantage is greatest. A particular form of this fear is the anticipation that concessions on services will be traded for relaxations of violations of the GATT spirit in such areas as the Multifibre Arrangement.

The third fear derives from various extensions of the infant industry argument. Although the developed countries have now a comparative advantage in services, the developing countries may acquire it in the future.

In fact, proficiency in the provision of services is not an exclusive feature of more advanced countries. Avianca, Colombia's national airline, is the second oldest in the world (after KLM). Banco do Brasil was for many years among the most profitable banks in the world. Reuters is now owned by Mexico. India's software industry is highly respected. Singapore Telecom is an innovative leader and Palapa, Indonesia's satellite communication system, is extremely modern. Korean and Taiwanese construction firms are world leaders. And the Philippines are becoming a force in animation of cartoons, architectural design and drafting.

Comparative advantage in services depends upon (a) the existence of certain types of infrastructure, subject to decreasing costs, (b) certain skills and aptitudes which can be learned by doing and whose initial learning phase can represent large fixed costs, (c) certain attitudes which may call for a cultural transformation. Moreover, services often require lumpy investments, with long gestation periods, and yield externalities and economies of scale. The initial comparative disadvantage is not God-given, and can be reduced and eliminated, but this process takes time. Meanwhile, protection may be justified.

189

This line of argument is reinforced if it is remembered that the developed countries protected heavily the same service industries in which they have now gained superiority. Even the most unsordid act in history, Marshall Aid, was combined with such protectionist measures. Half of US food and equipment to Europe had to be carried in American vessels, to the chagrin of maritime powers like Norway.

The infant industry argument as such is not, of course, a first-best argument for protection. If future gains compensate for current losses, including an appropriate interest rate, it constitutes a case for borrowing, possibly from the government if private markets are imperfect. But if the future benefits accrue to others than the investing firm, so that there are externalities, either a subsidy, or, if there are fiscal constraints, protection, is indicated. Under this heading one might also include restrictions intended to offset restrictive business practices by the foreign service provider. But this applies just as much to trade in goods as in services.

A fourth argument relates to the division of gains from trade. Transnational corporations are heavily engaged in trade in services: the large multinational banks, insurance companies and other financial institutions.[1] It is well known that intra-firm trade is not guided by the same considerations as arm's length trade, and the transfer pricing practised by multinationals can give rise to too small a share of the profits accruing to developing countries.

A fifth argument concerns the balance of payments. The developing countries now have a large and growing negative balance on service trade and they may fear that freeing this trade would put an additional burden on their balances of payments.

A sixth set of arguments relates to political, strategic or cultural factors. Some services, such as tourism or advertising, can be excessively intrusive, encourage the wrong attitudes in the local population, and disturb indigenous cultures. Others may be closely linked to areas of national sensitivity, such as the mass media, and be ruled out for foreigners. Others again may be regarded as part of the infrastructure and affect national security, such as telecommunications, shipping or banking. It is important, though not easy, to distinguish between barriers to trade and methods to preserve national cultures, security and autonomy. But even on narrowly economic grounds there is reason for caution. Some services, such as

1. Frederick F. CLAIREMONTE and John H. CAVANAGH, 'Transnational Corporations and Services: The Final Frontier', in *Trade and Development*, in *Trade and Development*, UNCTAD Review, no. 5, Geneva: United Nations, 1984.

financial services, give rise to movements of capital (and others, as we have seen, to movements of people). If a country wishes to maintain control of its capital outflow, free trade in financial services makes this more difficult. Past theory and practice have drawn a sharp distinction between the flow of goods and of factors of production.

There are two possible types of gains to the developing countries from freer trade in services. First, they may benefit from cheaper and more efficient imports of services provided by the richer countries. Cheaper banking and insurance services may help the production and export of developing countries, just as cheaper imports of steel reduce the costs of producing goods using steel. Secondly, they themselves may have a comparative advantage in certain services.

The first type of argument does not weigh heavily with mercantilistic-minded politicians, who see imports as a loss and exports as a gain. It can also be countered with the infant service argument, although there may be better methods than protection to encourage an infant service.

The advanced countries both dominate the trade in services, and have a large export surplus in services. Deepak Nayyar argues that this implies that they have a substantial interest in the liberalization of international trade in services.[1] As we have seen, it is true that their preponderance and their large export surplus suggest that they have a comparative advantage in services, and can benefit by selling even more when trade is liberalized. But there are arguments on the other side. The elasticity of demand for the services of a small newcomer is much higher than that for large established firms. If a developing country can establish a cost advantage in a market now occupied by large firms, its prospects are good. This applies to volume of sales. As to the terms of trade, again developing countries can benefit from the expansion of exports of services by advanced countries. If economies of scale prevail, or if prices have to be reduced for larger sales, the terms of trade of the developing countries will tend to improve.

The second argument has both economic and political appeal. Some developing countries such as South Korea have shown great competitiveness in construction. And there are others. Developing countries have acquired comparative advantage in communication software, punching data onto cards, conveying information of all sorts along a wire, in tourism, shipping, etc. In order to reap these advantages, it is important to insist in the negotiations that not only services in which the

---

1. NAYYAR, *op cit*.

advanced countries have superiority, but also those in which the developing countries are superior should be included. Domestic service by Central American maids, medical services by Indian doctors, and construction services by Korean crews would have to be freed, as well as American banking and insurance.

I want to end with two considerations that would justify some hesitation by developing countries to accept free trade in services. They have nothing to do with infant industry arguments, balance of payment losses, restrictive business practices, national sovereignty, cultural autonomy, externalities, infra-structure or "commanding heights", but I have not come across them in the literature.

The first consideration springs from a specific characteristic of services. Services are not storable. There are exceptions - software messages stored on a recording machine - but, by and large, they cannot be stored. They have to be consumed at the same time as they are being produced. They have been defined as those fruits of economic activity that you cannot drop on your toe. This gives added power to the provider of the service, if there are no adequate alternatives, and if the service is important. Electricity workers and railway workers have greater bargaining power than coal miners, because coal can be stocked and used while miners are on strike, whereas electricity and transport cannot. The bargaining power of the providers of services is greater than that of the producer of storable goods. Whether this is important in international trade, say in the case of trade embargoes or sanctions, remains to be seen. If a country became dependent on another country's essential service, say of shipping, this could lead to greater dependence than, say, imports of grain. In this sense, the growing international trade in services would reinforce a tendency already at work in the international economy, viz. growing *inter-dependence*. By this is meant not only the growth of benefits from international relations, but also the growth of possible damage, should these relations be disrupted. A strategy that is risk-averse might forgo some of the benefits of exchange and provide the service domestically at higher costs for the sake of avoiding the risk of damage, should trade be terminated. This constitutes an argument against free trade in services not usually presented.

The second consideration is concerned with equality. The international division of gains from free trade in services may be unequal, and, moreover, may make national policies for greater equality or an incomes policy more difficult. Consider a model in which two types of services have to be combined, one of which is highly skilled, the other unskilled. Let us take air transport. The providers of the skilled service, pilots, are in relatively scarce total supply, but highly mobile between countries in response to financial incentives. On a clear day, an airline pilot can see the world. The unskilled factor, ground personnel, is in highly elastic local supply, but immobile between countries. The result will be that pilots will earn large rents while ground personnel will get the bare minimum wage. Any country, even a very poor country, wishing to have an airline will have to pay its pilots the high international salaries or it will lose them. A policy to make incomes more equal domestically will be impossible. Both international and domestic inequalities will tend to increase. Other examples are transnational advertising, hotel chains, tourist enclaves, etc. The cause of the problem is differential elasticities of supply of types of services that have to be combined. These can cause more serious problems to developing countries than the direct effects of the brain drain, the loss to foreign countries of trained professional manpower.

2. Cost and Benefits Within Countries

More important than the impact of free trade in services on different countries – the subject of this Appendix – is its impact on individuals, families and groups of people within countries. It would be possible, for example, for service trade liberalization to benefit rich countries, but mainly rich people within these countries, and to harm poor countries, while benefiting poor people within these countries. In the bad old days when it was assumed that government could do no wrong, a benefit to a country was readily converted into a benefit to serving people through taxes, subsidies and social services. But according the current views, governments can do no right, and it is therefore important to trace costs and benefits to specific groups. I do not know of any work along these lines. Since much of the service trade is conducted by large transnational corporations, it may be presumed that a large share of the benefits would accrue, at least in the first round, to the capital and management of these corporations. If informal sector enterprises were included in the liberalized trade, some sections of the poor would benefit. An analysis could be conducted in terms of the relative labour and capital use of traded services versus non-traded goods and services. If the traded services were more labour-intensive than non-traded goods and services, liberalization would raise not only wages in these services, but in all sectors, and would benefit the wage earning groups. If the opposite were true, the reverse conclusions would follow.

FOURTH LECTURE

Markets and States: Against Minimalism and Dichotomy[1]

1. Introduction

If we call the doctrine that the "correct" prices and markets have an important role to play in allocating resources efficiently and equitably, in promoting choices, in enlarging freedom, and in decentralizing power, *Pricism*, and the doctrine that efficiency, equity and liberty call for minimum state intervention *State Minimalism*[2] (or laissez-faire), the currently prevailing view is that the two go together: get the government off our backs and let there be markets! The thesis of this lecture is the opposite: that for the proper working of markets strong, and in many cases expanded, state intervention (of the right kind, in the right areas) is necessary. It is possible to favour a strong state, with a limited agenda. It would confine itself to ensuring that individuals, and the social groups in which they associate, can pursue their own purposes with a minimum of frustration. This is not the thesis of this lecture. It argues for a strong state, with an expanded agenda, though a different one, differently implemented, from that which the state has commonly adopted in many developing countries.

---

1. An early version of this lecture but without some important sections and arguments, appeared in Louis Putterman and Dietrich Rueschemeyer, eds., *State and Market in Development; Synergy or Rivalry?*, Boulder & London: Lynne Rienner, 1992. This version also appeared in a special issue of *World Development*, vol. 21 no. 8, August 1993, pp. 1281-1298, edited by Laurence Whitehead.

2. The terms are due to Michael Lipton.

The expression "getting prices right" has undergone a curious transformation. In the 1960s it was intended to point to the calculation of correct shadow or accounting prices in the face of "distorted" market or actual prices. Because market prices reflected all sorts of "distortions",[1] including those caused by the existing and, from an ethical point of view, arbitrary income and asset distribution, it was the task of government to intervene and allocate resources according to the "right" shadow prices. The purpose of government intervention was to correct the distortions caused by the free play of market forces. More recently the recommendation has been reversed. It now is that developing countries should get rid of state interventions in order to permit market prices to reflect the correct opportunity costs and benefits. Distortions are now regarded as caused mainly (or only) by governments.

Gunnar Myrdal (1898-1987) has made a substantial contribution to the analysis of these problems. Some relevant aspects of his work are discussed in the next section.

A subsidiary thesis of this paper is that many distinctions, important for an understanding of the role of markets and the state, have been blurred in the neoclassical resurgence. Various theories of the state and their bearing on the relation between government and markets will be discussed, and a realistic one will be proposed. The need for a fuller discussion of managing the transition from the wrong to the right type of state intervention, and for a

---

1. The widely used notion of price "distortions" is not as clear as it may seem. Distortion is the deviation of the actual from some natural, proper, legitimate, norm. But there is no reason to believe that prices determined in free markets under laissez-faire reflect such a norm. Any one of an infinite number of income distributions would produce a different set of relative prices. Free market prices also reflect monopoly power, and do not reflect externalities in consumption (such as my wearing a tie only because you wear one) or in production (such as pollution). In conditions of widespread unemployment and underemployment wage rates do not reflect the opportunity cost of labour. In an economy already "distorted", an additional distortion may move it towards an improvement. For reasons such as these, the notion that government interventions "distort" an otherwise correct set of signals and incentives is highly misleading. In the presence of such "private distortions", the addition of "public distortions" can be a beneficial corrective. The flawed agenda of the governments in many developing countries is well summed up in the 1662 Prayer Book: "We have left undone those things which we ought to have done; And we have done those things which we ought not to have done. And there is no health in us."

normative political economy, to complement the positive theory, will be put forward. Finally, donor conditionality insisting on liberalization, deregulation, decentralization and privatization will be discussed.

2. Gunnar Myrdal's Contribution

The free, competitive market is a public good. My participation does not detract from yours, indeed it encourages yours. Like other public goods, it calls for public or collective action to maintain it. When I worked with the Myrdal team on *Asian Drama*,[1] in the sixties, we emphasized the need to use pricing policy rather than direct controls long before the current fashion for getting prices right had swept the profession of economics. We thought it important for the government to organize markets so that they work efficiently, but we did not confuse price *policy*, measures to encourage competition and the creation of previously absent markets, with the unrestrained play of market forces. *Getting* the right prices is open to two different interpretations. In the words of Michael Lipton, *setting* prices right is quite different from *letting* prices come right from state inaction. Contemporary discussions frequently also confuse the question, how large should be the state in relation to total economic activity, with the quite different questions, what policy instruments should the state employ and how should they be used?

In *Asian Drama* Myrdal criticized the kinds of government he called the "soft state". This critique has sometimes been misunderstood. It is plain that "softness" in Myrdal's sense is quite compatible with a high degree of coercion, violence and cruelty. The Tamils in Sri Lanka, the Indians in Burma, the Chinese in Indonesia, the Hindus in Pakistan, the Moslems in India, the Biharis in Bangladesh – to take six states he calls "soft" – would not claim excessively soft treatment. "Soft states" also go in for military violence, both internal and external. Their "softness" lies in

---

1. GUNNAR MYRDAL, *Asian Drama: An Inquiry into the Poverty of Nations,* Harmondsworth: Pelican Books, 1968.

their unwillingness to coerce people in order to implement declared policy goals such as collecting taxes, punishing evaders, (it
is mainly in industrial countries that people are sent to jail for not
paying taxes), implementing a land reform, and to resist the hard
powers of caste, land ownership, and cultural barriers. This lack
of social discipline is not the result of gentleness or weakness but
reflects the power structure and a gap between real and professed
intentions.

Although Myrdal is often regarded (and nowadays castigated)
as an advocate of central planning and heavy state controls of the
economy, a reading of *Asian Drama* shows that he thought the Indian economy was over-regulated and ill-regulated, and that the
number of discretionary measures should be greatly reduced.
The book expounds what has since become the conventional wisdom of using prices and non-discretionary measures as policy instruments for the allocation of resources. This means including
direct and indirect taxes and subsidies in the armoury of policy instruments (as well as public services) rather than direct quantitative controls, but it does not mean surrendering to the free play of
market forces if they reflect a highly unequal power, asset and income distribution. If these were given free reign, the process of
circular and cumulative causation would ensure that those who
already have gain most, and the have-nots would be deprived of
what little they have.

Myrdal was not only prescient, and more discriminating and
subtle than today's writers, in advocating the use of prices, but in
an early article anticipated the public choice theory of political
behaviour, including the role of pressure groups and deadweight
losses arising from what came to be known as rent-seeking activities.[1] He advocated the institutional approach for the analysis of
problems in the social sciences.[2] By this he did not mean an objection to abstractions and to rigorous theorizing or a turn to
purely historical or purely empirical work. He meant the need to

1. 'The Trend Towards Economic Planning'. *Manchester School of Economic and Social
Studies,* no. 19, 1951, pp. 1-42.
2. He was awarded the Nobel Prize in economics (together with Friedrich von
Hayek) in 1974 and the Veblen-Commons award, bestowed by the Association for Evo-
lutionary Economics, in 1975.

bring to bear all relevant knowledge and techniques on the analysis of a problem: economics, demography (of which he had an unduly high opinion), statistics, politics, sociology, anthropology, psychology, philosophy, history. He used to say that in an interdependent social system there are no economic, political, or social problems; there are only problems. The narrow focus on economic formulations serves, according to Myrdal, the interests of those who oppose reform. The neglect of some relevant areas of knowledge he called "opportunistic ignorance". The need for this multi-disciplinary approach has been vindicated by the current concern with the environment and "sustainable" development and the role of women, and the rising interest in cultural factors in development.

Myrdal applied his method also to the analysis of inflation, combined with widespread unemployment in the industrial countries of the North in the 1970s and 1980s, and either coined or was one of the first to use the term "stagflation". (He also invented the useful term "underclass".) He attributed the situation to the organization of producers as pressure groups, and to the dispersion and comparative weakness of consumers, to the tax system which encourages speculative expenditures, to the structure of markets and to the oligopolistic methods of administrative pricing. He condemned inflation as a socially highly divisive force.

The approach favoured by Myrdal is one neither of Soviet authority and force exercised for central state planning, nor of capitalist laissez-faire, but of a third way: that of combining the use of prices for economic and social purposes, with a direct attack on attitudes and institutions (and on overcoming obstacles and inhibitions). Prices are to be used as the instruments of reform, including the promotion of greater responsiveness of agents to prices. This approach has a greater affinity to that of those nineteenth century socialists who were dismissed by Marx as Utopian, who mapped out in detail what institutional and attitudinal reforms were necessary to improve society. Myrdal rejected both Marxism and neoclassical economics: the former because it believed that institutions (the super-structure) would be adaptable to the economic conditions (the base), the latter because it assumed institutions already fully adapted. Being neither adapted nor automatically adaptable, they have to be designed and planned. The difficulty, which Myrdal clearly saw, is that any instrument, even if used with the intention to reform, within a given power structure, tends to serve the powerful and to reestablish the old equilibrium. Even well-intentioned allocations, rationing, licensing and controls often reinforce monopoly and big business. The Indian economist Raj Krishna used to call them "first-round socialism". In resolving this conflict Myrdal relied on the possibility of self-reform that arises from the tensions between preferred and proclaimed beliefs and actions, as well as the empowerment of the poor.

Myrdal was preoccupied in many of his works with the conflict between ideals and reality, and with the question how, if the two conflict, one of them must give way. Much of conventional economic theory is a rationalization whose purpose it is to conceal this conflict. But it is bound to reassert itself sooner or later. When this happens, either the ideals will be scaled down to conform to the reality, or the reality will be shaped by the ideals.

3. How to Make Markets People-Friendly

The World Bank has promulgated the need for market-friendly government interventions.[1] But free markets are neutral institutions, which can work for good or ill. Whatever may be said for their efficiency, they are not tender-hearted towards their victims. The question (asked in the spirit of "putting people first") should be on what conditions markets are people-friendly. Certain conditions have to be met to make markets work efficiently, and to make them work for the benefit of people.

There are several ways in which government intervention can contribute to a more efficient functioning of markets. Not only should government provide a legal framework and maintain law and order, including the enforcement of contracts, property

---

1. *World Development Report 1991: The Challenge of Development,* Oxford: Oxford University Press, 1991.

rights, etc. and pursue the correct macroeconomic policies with respect to exchange rates, interest rates, wage rates and trade policy in order to ensure high levels of employment without inflation, and economic growth. It must also encourage competition by anti-monopoly and anti-restrictive practices legislation or by setting up competitive enterprises in the public sector, or by trade liberalization, or take over natural monopolies. There is nothing in the nature of free markets that either establishes or maintains competition. On the contrary, free markets make for conspiracies against the public, as Adam Smith knew. Yet, the virtue of markets depends on the existence of competition.

In addition to safeguarding competition, the government can intervene in the processes of price formation, production and finance in ways that make markets work better for all. It can encourage the introduction of private markets for insurance. The government can make banks buy private insurance. The biggest risk-takers would then pay the highest premiums. It can tax activities it wishes to discourage, e.g. pollution (by issuing tradable permits to pollute below certain levels) or traffic congestion or certain types of short-term stock exchange speculation (putting a high capital gains tax on assets held for less than three months), or the consumption of cigarettes or drugs or petrol, and subsidize those activities it wishes to encourage, e.g. the use of public transport, or education and health. It can intervene in preventing the growth of extreme regional inequalities and in town planning.

Government has a special role in promoting the development of human resources. By agricultural extension services it can improve the skills of farmers. By providing unemployment assistance and retraining facilities it can help workers to accept more readily new labour-saving technologies. By providing information and conducting research it can help to reduce monopolistic practices. By investing in physical infrastructure (such as irrigation to raise agricultural price elasticities, rural feeder roads to bring products to markets, harbours and communications), it can provide the conditions for price incentives (such as devaluation) to work, and stimulate private investment. It has been widely documented that by raising profitability, public investment can "crowd in" private investment. By assisting in the design and strengthening of institutions (for land reform, information, credit, or marketing), it can contribute to the effectiveness of price policy. And so on. Some of these activities will be accepted by even quite extreme marketeers. The two questions are, whether a shift from present, often very inefficient, state activities to these efficient ones can be achieved by a minimalist state, and what the functions of the state should be after the transition, once markets are working.

Perhaps the area of largest controversy is the state's involvement in the area of social services and its fiscal implications, and in changing the income distribution brought about by free markets. The problem here is not one of the failure of markets, but of their successes, responding to the signals of unequal income and asset distributions. The neo-liberals' view is that in any government's war on poverty, it is poverty that always wins. If we are concerned only with the need for government action to strengthen both the allocative and the creative functions of markets, such involvement would have to be justified not on grounds of social justice or human needs, but on grounds of human capital formation, of reducing barriers to income earning opportunities, and of promoting social stability.

Progressive taxes and social services are often said to be limited by fiscal constraints. The limits are not, however, lack of resources. Military expenditures (often large in very poor countries), the large losses of public enterprises, and reallocation within the social sectors from low priority towards high priority areas (primary and secondary education and preventive rural health services in low-income countries) can provide ample resources. The constraints are neither technical nor economic but political.

It is important to distinguish between public and private production, provision, and finance. Various combinations of private and public can be applied to these notions. Education or health services can be privately provided and publicly financed, through vouchers for private schools or hospitals, or subsidies. Charging for the cost of publicly provided services (like university education) means public provision and private finance. The production of some of the components of the service can be subcontracted by the government to a private producer. The optimum combination of producing, providing and financing depends on the particular circumstances of each case.

The proposition that pricism and state minimalism are incompatible is open to two interpretations. According to the strong interpretation, liberal markets require authoritarian regimes that prevent trade unions from pushing up wages, jeopardizing exports and foreign investment, and causing inflation, and special interest groups from grasping rents. "A courageous, ruthless and perhaps undemocratic government is required to ride roughshod over these newly created special interest groups" writes Deepak Lal.[1] This interpretation points to the East Asian economies (and perhaps Pinochet's Chile), cited as the great success stories. But it is questionable whether these regimes are truly liberal in the economic sphere. Their dirigisme is to some extent, and with important exceptions, market-oriented or market-friendly. But if there is evidence of an invisible hand, it is surely guided by a strong visible arm.

According to the milder, and more realistic interpretation, democracies and free markets can go together, although the ruthless efficiency of markets will then be tampered by the compassion of social provisions, as exemplified by the Scandinavian countries.[2] The current debate about the effects of the welfare state on incentives to work and save, on the swollen welfare bureaucracy and on inflation is, of course, provoked by this experience. But for the present purpose the focus is not on the state's welfare provisions but on its interventions in the areas of anti-monopoly legislation, research and development, information, marketing, physical and social infrastructure, and human resource development, all of which are conditions for the efficient functioning of markets.

---

1. DEEPAK LAL, *The Poverty of Development Economics,* Cambridge, Mass.: Harvard University Press, 1985, p. 33. See also ROBERT WADE, *Governing the Market,* Princeton, N.J.: Princeton University Press, 1990. Lance Taylor distinguishes between the four possible combinations of weak/strong states and competitive/cartellized or rigged markets. The weak state combined with competitive markets is James Buchanan's heaven. The strong state combined with atomistic markets is Deepak Lal's heaven. The weak state combined with monopolistic markets is Mancur Olson's hell. And the strong state combined with monopolistic markets is Douglass North's hell.

2. Contrasted with Lance Taylor's heavens and hells, this might be considered earth, or the real world.

The state minimalists are prone to argue asymmetrically. They have said, correctly, that market failure is not automatically an argument for state intervention, for this may produce even worse results. But they forget that government or bureaucratic or state failure is not necessarily an argument for private markets, at least not until much more empirical evidence is produced that the outcomes of government action in a particular case are necessarily worse than those of markets.

Shapiro and Taylor have pointed to a peculiar asymmetry in these models, "whereby individuals coalesce to force a political redistribution, but do not do the same in the market place. The political arena is depicted full of lobbyists and cartel builders, while the economy is presented as being more or less subject to competition".[1]

A related asymmetry is that rent-seeking has been indicted almost exclusively as resulting from public action.[2] It is, however, equally common in the private sector. Private allocation of contracts to subcontractors gives rise to rents in exactly the same way as import quotas. Adam Smith recognized businessmen's "conspiracy against the public" and "contrivance to raise prices", and landlords' and others' love "to reap where they never sowed". We would expect these observations by the father of market economics to encourage us to design strategies of state intervention to counteract these private rent-seeking activities. Instead, we are served today with two ideas: first, that rent-seeking is an entirely political phenomenon, and second, that the only way to reduce rent-seeking is to limit government. Both are wrong, or at least unproven without considerably more empirical evidence.[3]

---

1. HELEN SHAPIRO and LANCE TAYLOR, 'The State and Industrial Strategy', *World Development*, vol. 18 no. 6, June 1990, p. 867. There are some exceptions, such as Deepak Lal quoted above and Mancur Olson. Another asymmetry has been identified by Shapiro and Taylor. While it is pointed out that bureaucrats have no special talent for running an economy, they are called upon to do so in the authoritarian state that dismantles the controls.

2. See ANNE O. KRUEGER, 'The Political Economy of the Rent-Seeking Society', *American Economic Review*, vol. 64, June 1974.

3. For additional criticisms of the theory of rent-seeking see the section on neoclassical political economy below.

Private and public action often have to go together. Prices have their impact on demand and supply only if complementary action is taken by the government. A factory may depend on a road, which is normally constructed by the government. Increases in agricultural output in response to higher prices may depend on irrigation or research into new varieties. The ability to make use of high profit opportunities may depend on the availability of information about inputs and markets, provided by the government. When the IMF recommended Tanzania to devalue the shilling, no attention was paid to the fact that the transport system had broken down and, however attractive the prices for farmers, their produce could not have been transported to the ports. In South Africa, the "black" taxi trade is often upheld as a splendid example of the spirit of free enterprise. And so it is, if we accept the absence of an efficient and safe public transport system for the blacks. But with roads full of potholes and without public safety regulations, the accident rate is one of the highest in the world.

In Europe there is now talk of deregulating trucking (or lorry-driving). Now lorries are prohibited from picking up return loads and often have to return empty. After 1992 this regulation may be dropped. Two opposite tendencies will be at work. On the one hand, truck traffic may be reduced, because a given amount of traffic can be carried out by fewer journeys. On the other hand, the lower costs will make it pay to increase road transport. If the net outcome were to lead to more road traffic, safety and the health of the drivers would suffer. There would be more road congestion, and reduced loads and higher losses for the underutilized railways.[1]

One example of the complementarity or symbiosis between public and private sectors is the "crowding-in" effect (in contrast to the normally assumed crowding-out effect, resulting from higher interest rates), according to which public investment, often in infrastructure, stimulates private investment. Various authors have estimated these crowding-in coefficients to lie between

1. See WOLFGANG STREECK, 'The Social Dimensions of the European Community', a paper prepared for the 1989 meeting of the Andrew Shonfield Association, Florence, 14-15 September 1989, footnote 27 on p. 51.

one and two.[1] The fact of crowding-in is now well established. The task of government is to raise the productivity of the investment in both the public and the private sector. There are many other non-price, non-market measures, such as research, information, or the establishment of appropriate institutions, which the government must take in order to make the incentives of prices bite.

Some might say that, while the combination of price and non-price measures is best, to get prices right by itself is at least a step in the right direction. This is, however, not so. I have shown elsewhere that the right prices by themselves, without the complementary public sector action, can be ineffective or counterproductive.[2]

Japan and South Korea are often cited as examples of successful private-public sector cooperation. It is sometimes said that the relation is supportive, not antagonistic. But looking more deeply into the nature of successful state interventions, we note that the state in Japan and South Korea, as Jagdish Bhagwati put it, issues prescriptions rather than proscriptions.[3] They intervene by encouraging and promoting selected activities, not by prohibiting and restricting. Of course, to be able to get credit for only one type of investment, implies being prevented from doing another. Or to be prohibited from importing a good encourages domestic production. The distinction is not as clearcut as it may seem.[4] The skill of these policies does not lie so much in the disputed art of "picking winners" as in creating winners. Korean ship-building was created without the existence of the requisite skills or raw materials, and today competes

1. Mario Blejer and Mohsin Khan, 'Government Policy and Private Investment in Developing Countries', *IMF Staff Papers,* vol. 31, 1984; Sukhamoy Chakravarti, *Development Planning: The Indian Experience,* Oxford: Clarendon Press, 1987; Guillermo Ortiz and Carlos Noriega, *Investment and Growth in Latin America,* Washington, D.C.: International Monetary Fund, 1988; Robert Barro, *A Cross-Country Study of Growth, Saving and Government,* NBER Working Paper no. 2885, Cambridge, Mass.: National Bureau of Economic Research, 1989.

2. Paul Streeten, *What Price Food?,* London: Macmillan, 1987 and Cornell University Press, 1987.

3. Jagdish Bhagwati, *Protectionism,* Cambridge, Mass.: MIT Press, 1988, p. 98.

4. Again, Gunnar Myrdal anticipated the emphasis on encouragement or what he called "positive controls". The term is unfortunate, for controls suggest prevention.

successfully with the previously preeminent Swedish industry. Modern comparative advantage can be created by good government policies.

Japan uses government intervention to promote industrial productivity, by export incentives, barriers to protect the domestic market, low-cost credit to selected investments, and policies that favour business and education. In addition, there are numerous more covert policies to favour companies that move into government-approved types of production, such as commercial intelligence services, nationalistic patent policies, etc. The government practises an art despised and condemned by most US economists, who are minimalists, viz. industrial policy.

The South Korean public sector Pohang Iron and Steel Company (Posco) is one of the most efficient enterprises in the world (in spite of the complete absence of iron ore and coal in Korea), while the Steel Authority of India is a testimony to bureaucratic inefficiency. The Korean firm has financial autonomy, seeks to make profits, has clear objectives, has operating independence and is open to potential competition from domestic rivals and imports. It is not burdened with multiple social objectives and the incentive structure encourages it to export. The Indian Authority accepts losses, has confusing and multiple objectives, its finances overlap with the budget, it is subject to close political scrutiny and interference, its prices are politicized, and it is protected from competition through tariffs, import licensing and legal restrictions on domestic entry.

The East Asian success stories, moreover, illustrate that the same type of intervention, such as subsidized interest rates, that in Latin America have impeded growth, has been used by these governments to accelerate growth. The role of corruption and its control also contributes to explaining differential performance.[1] It is now generally acknowledged that "getting prices right" has not been the principal, and certainty not a sufficient, recipe for the success of East Asian countries, although their government interventions have been "market-friendly", and the markets have been "people-friendly".

1. See MYRDAL, *op. cit.*, vol. II, part 4 chapter 20 and ROBERT KLITGAARD, *Controlling Corruption*, Berkeley: University of California Press, 1988.

Differences in the institutional arrangements of the relations between managers of public enterprises and the public authority are also important. Managers are given sufficient autonomy to get on with their jobs, while remaining accountable to the public. With all the current talk about incorporating political variables in economic analysis, and endogenizing political change, there is remarkably little work done on how specific political and economic institutions function.

In Europe too, new forms of cooperation between local authorities, central government and firms have been evolving. In the Third Italy and in Baden-Württemberg in Germany methods of production called by some flexible specialization and by others diversified quality production have successfully combined markets, firms, local government and central government regulation.

There are different types of capitalism. One type, the Japanese and German, is characterized by close coordination between different firms, between firms and banks, between government and business, and between employers and workers; the other exhibits little coordination and conducts its relations at arm's length between firms, has no involvement of banks in the management of firms, and operates on the basis of hiring and firing within firms. One commits its resources to long-term goals, the other is more concerned with short-run financial flexibility. One emphasizes "flexible specialization" and product innovation, the other pre-set machinery whose performance does not depend on the skill of the workers, who are tightly controlled financially.[1]

Economists are trained in the study of the operation of economic forces within political, social and moral constraints.[2] This approach has to be supplemented (and in some cases replaced) by the study of the operation and manipulation of political, social and psychological forces within economic limits. More fundamentally, the distinction between economic and non-economic variables may not be tenable if the aim is to understand society.

1. See MICHEL ALBERT, *Capitalism against Capitalism*, London: Whurr, 1993.

2. A recent book, edited by JOHN DUNN, whose contributors are mainly political scientists and historians, is entitled *The Economic Limits to Modern Politics* Cambridge: Cambridge University Press, 1990. But this is not quite the companion volume needed to the political limits to modern economics.

4. The Civil Society

States and markets do not exhaust the players in this game. Frequently, although they need each other, they also weaken and undermine each other. States damage markets by regulations, licensing, and bureaucratic red tape. Markets tend to corrupt governments. Therefore there is a need for the civil society. It can contribute to more constructive relationships between the two.

Private voluntary organizations have come to play an increasing role, next to governments and profit-seeking companies. They comprise the most diverse organizations: religious, political, professional, educational, and cooperative organizations; pressure groups, interest groups and lobbies; institutions that are project-oriented, give technical assistance, provide disaster-relief, or are concerned with disaster-prevention, etc. Although they often claim to work without or even against governments, their contributions can sometimes best be mobilized by working jointly with governments.

The most successful NGOs in the Third World, such as the Self-Employed Women's Organization based in Ahmedabad, India, or the Grameen Bank or BRAC of Bangladesh, depend for their continuing and expanding (though not for their initial) operations on access to, and support and replication by, governments. Of course, in some situations their function is to criticize and exhort governments; or to fill gaps in government activities; or to do things at lower costs, with better results, and with more popular participation than governments. In other situations, when they promote their selfish interests, irrespective of the wider interests of the community, or when they reflect the dominant power of particular groups, government may be justified in trimming their influence.

The relationship between NGOs and governments can be understood as one of cooperative conflict[1] (or creative tensions), in which the challenge of the voluntary agencies and their innovative activities can improve both government services and the

1. See footnote 2, p. 228.

working of markets, and help to resolve tensions between them.

In some situations the state plays a passive role, only responding to the pressures of interest groups. The outcomes will then be determined by the power of these groups, which in turn depends on their size, age, motivation, and enforcement mechanisms. In other cases the state is more active, imposing regulations and restrictions that can give rise to competitive rent-seeking by private interest groups. In yet other situations, the private groups and the state work together for common objectives.

Functions are divided between the state and civil society. The institutions of civil society – churches, trade unions, interest groups, action groups, the media and many others – are often quite undemocratic, in spite of their rhetoric. There is then a need for the empowerment of weak and neglected groups within them: women, the unemployed, ethnic minorities. There can be undesirable concentration not only of economic and political, but also of social power.[1]

Though there is in the early stages of development a need to strengthen both states and markets, in fact they often tend to weaken and undermine each other. It is the institutions of the civil society that can intervene and inhibit such weakening and undermining.[2] Interactions between the state, markets and civil society are complex. Both too weak and too strong a state can discourage the growth of civil society. And too strong private organizations can undermine the power of the state, as in Sri Lanka or in Lebanon, or in the ex-Soviet Union, or in Yugoslavia, and lead to the dissolution of society.

---

1. Usually participation and democratization are discussed only in the political domain. But the other three sectors, the private sector, the civil society and the familial society also need democratization. While the world has found unworkable and has rejected the centralized process of decision-making in centrally planned economies, the same process governs relations between management and labour within capitalist and socialist firms. The same is true of the churches and the trade unions, and inside some families. We know that people do not give their best under regimentation.

2. MICHAEL LIPTON, 'The State-Market Dilemma, Civil Society, and Structural Adjustment', *The Round Table*, no. 317, 1991.

5. The Loss of Some Distinctions

Some important distinctions, drawn in the 1950s and earlier, have been swamped by the neoclassical resurgence. There is the already mentioned distinction between price policy, in which prices (including indirect taxes and subsidies) are used as instruments of policy, and laissez-faire, the free play of market forces without intervention to maintain competition,[1] to supply an infrastructure, information and research, to provide the formation of human capital, and to look after the victims of the competitive struggle.

There is the distinction between markets and the private sector. Privatization of a public enterprise without the managerial and technical personnel, without competition, and without the provision of infrastructure and information can only raise false expectations, while markets can exist where public enterprises compete with each other or with private ones, as Renault in France has done so successfully or the previously mentioned Pohang Steel Company in South Korea, or public enterprises in Singapore.

There is the important distinction between motivations in the private and in the public sector. Of course, self-seeking occurs in the public sector as it does in the private. What is so absurd is to maintain that this is the only motivation to be found there. Each of us behaves differently in different settings: as buyers and sellers in markets; as citizens voting in elections; as supporters or critics of government policies; as moral agents when our conscience is aroused. Sometimes we exercise the option of exit, at others of voice. To level these distinctions down to a uniform selfishness, and to equate rational with selfish behaviour is not helpful to understanding or policy-making.

Even behaviour in the market has been grossly oversimplified. Rational behaviour has been equated with selfish behaviour. All that it is necessary to assume for economic man to produce stable equilibrium outcomes is rationality in the sense of constancy and consistency of behaviour. Selfishness can manifest itself in impul-

---

1. It is odd how frequently even highly sophisticated writers confuse free trade with laissez-faire. Free trade has to be enforced by government intervention, both for governments and for firms.

siveness, inconsistency, inconstancy and irrationality. On the other hand, the perfect model of the rational person is the disinterested trustee, who administers funds completely unselfishly on behalf of others.

Finally, there is the distinction between centralized and decentralized government decision-making. Some of the criticisms made of a central bureaucracy do not apply to decentralized authorities (though others do apply). Decentralization can enhance participation, especially of small entrepreneurs and farmers, be more responsive to needs, gather more information, be more transparent and accountable, and improve the quality of government activities. They can also raise more resources, because the benefits are more visible. On the other hand, decentralized control can reinforce local power elites which are less responsive to the needs of the poor than central groups. Decentralization can also aggravate inter-regional disparities. The task is to design a structure of decision-making that combines the informational and motivational merits of decentralization and participation with central control.

6. Against Dichotomy: The Unimportance of the Private-Public Distinction

Going one step further, it can be doubted whether the very distinction between private and public ownership or management is relevant. Much of the discussion is conducted in binary terms: central planning versus free markets (which is not the same as private versus public ownership). Sometimes a spectrum between these two poles is considered, but the ideological values attached vary with the position on this spectrum. E.g., Soviet-type planning is bad; therefore the nearer we are to free markets the better. But an intermediate position between the two ends of the spectrum may be preferable to either. It is also possible to add dimensions to the linear spectrum that render the value choices more complex: the degree of democratic accountability, freedom versus compulsion, centralized versus decentralized decision-making, the degree of involvement of voluntary organizations. A regime combining certain features of intervention with others of a free market may then avoid the failures of the two poles and be preferable to either extreme.

Hybrid institutions that encourage initiative and enterprise, and are subject to covering their costs, but are at the same time accountable to the public, can harness the best of both sectors. The British Commonwealth Development Corporation, for example, is run autonomously on commercial lines, in the sense that it has to cover its costs (and to that extent is subjected to market discipline) and that its board consists of bankers and industrialists. It draws its funds mainly from the Exchequer (Treasury), and its objective is to maximize development, not profits. It does not only lend funds, withdrawing once a project is completed and participation becomes most important, like all other development agencies, but also manages firms and projects. In this respect it is unique. At the same time it trains local counterparts and hands over control, management and ownership as soon as the local people are ready, freeing its capital for new ventures.

There is also the large third sector briefly discussed above, neither private nor public, consisting of non-governmental, non-profit organizations, that draws on the voluntary energies of its members. Churches, colleges, universities, Oxfam, Bread for the World, orchestras, hospitals, museums, the Red Cross, Friends of the Earth, Amnesty International, charities, cooperatives, the Grameen Bank, neighbourhood organizations, local action committees, and many others draw on people's voluntary efforts and contribute often highly efficiently not only to the gross national product but to a flourishing civil society, essential for a democracy. Some libertarians (such as Mrs Thatcher) were eager to destroy this civil society, while reformers in societies in which it has been destroyed (such as Mr Gorbachev) had tried to build it up. But here again, as in the case of the complementarity of private and public activities, the strength of the civil society and of NGOs in particular often lies not in opposing the public sector, but in co-operating with it, whether for finance, or for replication of successful ventures, or for support in opposing exploitative local power elites. In other circumstances, for example when faced with a predatory state, their function is to combat it.

When I taught at the Oxford Business Summer School many years ago I came across a truly self-made tycoon. His parents had been immigrants from Central Europe. He had started penniless and had amassed a fortune, some of which he donated to the Oxford Centre for Management Studies. In the common room after his talk he told us that the important distinction in business is that between what he called "the institutions" and "private enterprise". By "the institutions" he meant the large firms, whether privately owned and managed or in the public sector. In these, ownership is divorced from control and management, and is anonymous. "Private enterprise" stood for the small firm, owned and run by the head of a family and a few employees. The principles of running a large private sector company and a public enterprise are very similar. The spirit of truly free enterprise is best exemplified in the small enterprises. To bracket these with the large corporations under the heading "private enterprise" can be very misleading.

7. Theories of the State

We now have a menu of theories of the state to choose from. According to the one I was taught when an undergraduate, an idealistic, competent and well-informed government, like Platonic guardians, or perhaps more like Fabian bureaucrats, reigns above the interest conflicts and promotes the common good. It is implicit in the writings of A. C. Pigou, Abba Lerner, Jan Tinbergen and James Meade. According to this old romantic theory the government can do no wrong.

The opposite theory, represented by the new classical Chicago economists, neoclassical political economists and the public choice school (better named the self-interest school), holds that the government can do no right. Citizens, politicians, bureaucrats and states use the authority of government to distort economic transactions for their benefit. Citizens use political influence and pressures to get access to benefits allocated by government; politicians use government resources to increase their hold on power; public officials trade access to government benefits for personal reward; and states use their power to get access to the property of citizens.[1] The result is an inefficient and inequitable allocation of resources, general impoverishment and reduced freedom.

A narrow interpretation of selfish political man (and woman), pursuing ruthlessly his/her interests, can lead to mutual impoverishment. According to one version the predatory officials and bureaucrats or politicians promote actively their selfish quest for money or power, according to another they respond passively to powerful pressure groups so as to stay in power. "The model of government motivations" has been simplified "into a single-track form, supplying the public sector with a brain transplant straight out of the marketplace".[2] Any intervention by this "predatory state" with the "magic of the market place" is bound to make matters worse. Government action is not the solution (as it is in the first theory), it is the problem – "invisible feet [of rent-seeking] stomping on invisible hands".[3] As has been said above, while according to the Platonic theory the government intervenes in order to correct "distortions", according to the public choice theory all distortions are due to government interventions. But according to both these apparently opposite views the state is an optimizing agency. According to the Platonic view it optimizes the welfare of the people as a whole, according to the public choice view that of special interest groups: those on whose support the politicians rely, the bureaucrats, the army, the politicians themselves. The Platonic view is normative (or naive); the public choice view crudely cynical.[4]

1. MERILEE S. GRINDLE and JOHN W. THOMAS, *Public Choices and Policy Change; The Political Economy of Reform in Developing Countries*, Baltimore: Johns Hopkins University Press, 1991.

2. JOHN P. LEWIS, 'Government and National Economic Development', in FRANCIS X. SUTTON, ed., *A World to Make: Development in Perspective*, New Brunswick and London: Transaction Publishers, 1990, p. 77. It should be noted that even in the market place individuals do not always behave selfishly.

3. DAVID COLANDER (ed.) *Neoclassical Political Economy*, Cambridge Mass.: Ballinger, 1985.

4. In advocating maximum delegation to markets as morally neutral systems of co-ordination, the self-interest school also ignores the fact, pointed out by many authors, that markets presuppose generalized moral norms, and particularly trust. See, for example, KENNETH ARROW, 'Political and Economic Evaluation of Social Effects and Externalities', in M. INTRILIGATOR, ed. *Frontiers of Quantitative Economics*, Amsterdam:

Even if it were true that politicians, bureaucrats and interest groups pursue always only their self-interest, this is open to different interpretations; some of these may be in conflict with one another and with the interests of others, others may be in harmony. There may, for instance, be a conflict between smaller present and larger future gains; or between "hot", impulsive and "cool", deliberated interests; or between concentrated smaller and more widely dispersed larger gains; or between certain smaller and uncertain larger gains; or, perhaps as important as interest conflicts between groups, the conflict between perceived smaller and actual but non-perceived larger gains.

A third theory, propounded by Anthony Downs and applicable only to democracies, holds that politicians maximize their own welfare by selling policies for votes.[1] Since not many (though a growing number of) developing countries are democracies, this theory would not have wide application among them, even if it applied to democracies.

Then there are social contract theorists, from Hobbes, Locke, and Rousseau to John Rawls and Mancur Olson. They say that citizens surrender some of their rights or liberties in return for protection against aggression, provision of collective goods, benefits from externalities, and other services from the state.[2] A limited sacrifice of individual autonomy – by increasing the prospects of avoiding related ills such as Prisoners' Dilemmas, the

North-Holland, 1971, and *Information and Economic Behavior,* Stockholm: Federation of Swedish Industries, 1973; JEAN-PHILIPPE PLATTEAU, 'The Free Market is not Readily Transferable: Reflections on the Links Between Market, Social Relations, and Moral Norms', Paper prepared for the 25th Jubilee of the Institute of Development Studies, Brighton, 1991, Cahiers de la faculté des sciences économiques et sociales, facultés universitaires Notre-Dame de la Paix, Namur, Belgium, November 1991. See also MICHAEL S. MACPHERSON, 'Limits on Self-Seeking; the Role of Morality in Economic Life', chapter 5 in COLANDER (ed.), *op. cit.,* pp. 71-85 and DANIEL HAUSMAN and MICHAEL S. MCPHERSON, 'Taking Ethics Seriously: Economics and Contemporary Moral Philosophy', *Journal of Economic Literature,* vol. 31, pp. 621-731.

1. ANTHONY DOWNS, *An Economic Theory of Democracy,* New York: Harper & Row, 1957.

2. Some countries, like Italy, give the impression that their citizens have entered with their governments into an *anti*-social contract: we shall not pay taxes, and in return we do not expect any public services.

isolation paradox, the free rider (and, worse, the sucker) outcome, and the tragedy of the commons – gives each citizen greater freedom and more benefits. The undersupply of public goods and the oversupply of public bads can be avoided by some enforced action by the central government.

Marxist theory says that the government is the executive committee of the ruling class and always serves the economic interest of that class. But this is open to different interpretations. Some Marxists regard the state as acting in the interest of international, metropolitan capital, extracting surpluses from the periphery for the benefit of the centre. This is the view of neo-Marxist[1] dependency theorists and was Marx's view of the relation of Ireland to England. Others regard the state as acting in the interest of an indigenous capitalist class, sometimes against the interest of the capitalists at the centre. According to both these views the state acts in the interest of a ruling class. A more sophisticated version of this theory holds that it is the function of the state to reconcile differences of interest within the ruling class, so as to maintain its power and the capitalist mode of production. According to this version it is possible for the government to impose measures in the interest of the exploited workers and small peasants, in spite of the loss of profit that this involves, if these measures save the system from revolt or revolution. It can also be that higher wages or a land redistribution, while reducing the profits of particular groups, raise total savings and/or lower capital-output ratios so as to increase the volume of the total surplus, though not the ratio of surplus to GNP. Others again regard the state as the agent of a "state class" or a bureaucracy.

Palaeo-Marxists like Bill Warren[2] hold that peripheral capitalism is a progressive, revolutionary force, making for productivity growth and economic progress. They make Dudley Seers's remark about the convergence of "Marxism and other neoclassical

1. As so often, the prefix "neo" is a euphemism for old hat.
2. See BILL WARREN, 'The Postwar Economic Experience of the Third World' in *Toward a New Strategy for Development, A Rothko Chapel Colloquium*, New York and Oxford: Pergamon Press, 1979. Marx himself, of course, originated this view in his writings on India.

doctrines" comprehensible.[1] And it is ironical that both neoclassical political economy and Marxism, two largely hostile and non-communicating groups, conclude that thinking and research about government policy for poverty reduction or income redistribution are futile. According to both, the predatory state inevitably acts in its own interest and that of powerful pressure groups; there is no place for disinterested, benign, altruistic government policies; only the forces of the free market are capable of advancing the good of society.

It is worth remembering, in the debate over market versus state, that real states fall under neither extreme. Dogmatism here leads to error even more than usual. A more commonsensical view, borne out by overwhelming evidence, holds that many governments are neither monolithic nor impervious to pressures for rational and altruistic policies. Moreover, if there is scope for a positive-sum game (as there is bound to be in the reversal of rent-seeking movements away from the Pareto frontier), and if the government can hold on long enough to tax the sum, the possibility of rational policies is opened up, even on the narrow assumption about predatoriness of the public choice school.

The structure of government decision-making consists of many departments, ministries, and agencies, and many layers from central government via provinces (or states in a federation) to village or town councils.[2] Power in some countries is divided between the legislature, the judiciary and the executive. Each of these pulls in a different direction. The obstacle to "correct" policy-making is neither solely stupidity nor solely cupidity, neither just ignorance nor simply political constraints or monolithic selfishness. On occasion, governments, like charitable foundations, universities or voluntary associations, do act disinterestedly and in the public interest, particularly, but not only, if there are pressure groups behind them. It is the existence of these pres-

1. See DUDLEY SEERS, 'Introduction: The Congruence of Marxism and Other Neoclassical Doctrines' in *Ibid.*, pp. 1-17.

2. See MICHAEL LIPTON, 'Agriculture, Rural People, the State and the Surplus in Some Asian Countries: Thoughts on Some Implications of Three Recent Approaches in Social Science', *World Development,* vol. 17 no. 10, October 1989.

sure groups with some power or influence that constitutes the "trustees for the poor", and the "guardians of rationality".[1] Count Oxenstierna may not have had the whole explanation, but knavery has no monopoly either.[2]

At the same time, there are areas in which a better analysis and a clearer sense of direction would help, just as there are areas where it is fairly clear what should be done, but vested interests, whether those of the policy-makers or of pressure groups on whose support they depend, prevent it from happening. Governments sometimes create rents and encourage rent-seeking; at other times they destroy rents and reduce wasteful competition in their pursuit. The private sector also creates and seeks rents. Some government officials act sometimes in their selfish interest; the same ones and others are, or want to be seen as, at other times, moral agents, acting in the common interest. Some pressure groups, individual or collective, domestic or foreign, are motivated by reason, solidarity, and morality.

According to this commonsense theory, for which there is overwhelming evidence, the state does not optimize anything, neither public welfare nor self-interest. It compromises, attempts to resolve conflicts, manages bargaining between groups, and occasionally leads. Gunnar Myrdal's notion of the South Asian "soft state", in which declared policies are not implemented or not enforced, fits into this picture. But so does that of the East Asian hard state, which pursues successfully both growth and equity.

1. See GERALD M. MEIER, *Emerging from Poverty, The Economics that Really Matters*, Oxford: Oxford University Press, 1979, p. 4. "The guardian of rationality" is Kenneth Arrow's phrase for the economist; "trustees for the poor" is Gerald Meier's. See KENNETH ARROW, *The Limits of Organization*, New York: W. W. Norton, 1974, p. 16. Without these two groups there is no Archimedean point from which any political economy that endogenizes politicians can lift itself out of full determinism and make room for the possibility of reform. If we accept determinism, we have no choice.

2. THOMAS BALOGH dedicated his book *The Dollar Crisis* to Lord Lindsay of Birker, the Master of Balliol College, Oxford: "who never quite could convince me that Oxenstierna had the whole explanation..." Count Oxenstierna had written to his son in 1648 "An nescis, mi fili, quantilla prudentia regitur orbis?" ("Dost thou not know, my son, with how little wisdom the world is governed?") Balogh, disagreeing with Lindsay, believed that it was knavery more than foolishness that was responsible for the world's troubles.

8. An Alternative Window

Some of the neoclassical theories regard the private sector as the source of wealth creation and the public sector as the domain of authority, exercised either benevolently or as a wasteful drain on resources. The distinguishing features of the state, according to this view, are that its membership is *universal*, and that it has powers of *compulsion* not given to other organizations.[1] According to some adherents of this view, many governments in developing countries have usurped the sphere of production, which should be left to the private sector. The remedy lies in the state withdrawing from this area, and confining itself to the protection of its citizens against external and domestic threats.

But it is equally possible to look at the same situation in a different way, with a different division of responsibilities. We may regard each sector, or better each sphere of responsibility, as creating different forms of wealth, and exercising different forms of authority and compulsion. According to this view, the private sector creates forms of wealth that can be sold for profit, the public sector those that, while also useful, cannot, because powerful externalities and inappropriabilities exist. Public goods are goods characterized by non-rivalrous consumption, so that one person's use does not detract from another's, and occasionally, though not always, non-excludability from the benefits whose costs are incurred by some. The classic example, given by John Stuart Mill, is a lighthouse (though its construction can, of course, be subcontracted to private firms, and though it benefits not all sailors but only ships in the region). Armed protection, monetary and employment stability, an efficient market, the administration of justice, mass education are other examples of public goods, or rather services. Certain types of infrastructure, such as underuti-

1. See JOSEPH E. STIGLITZ *et al.*, *The Economic Role of the State*, Oxford: Basil Blackwell, 1989, p. 21. Max Weber's classical definition of the state is that of a territorially defined organization "that successfully upholds a claim to the monopoly of the legitimate use of physical force in the enforcement of its orders". MAX WEBER, *The Theory of Social and Economic Organization*, A. M. HENDERSON and TALCOTT PARSONS, trs., New York: The Free Press, 1947, p. 154.

lized roads, bridges and subways, or harbours, dams and irrigation, are non-rivalrous but not non-excludable, for the provider can charge tolls or fees and exclude non-payers. But this means excluding some people, the benefits to whom would exceed the costs of supplying them. When price discrimination is impossible, the alternative is for the government to provide these goods and services free, and finance them by taxation.

Not all public goods should be produced, provided or financed by the central government. Some can be supplied by local government, or by cooperatives, clubs or other interested private parties, such as a group of farmers who jointly provide common control over common grazing rights. Others, like a common currency, some observers would take away from government control and put under the control of an independent central bank. Some need no institution or organization, like a common language, or trust, loyalty and truth-telling in transactions. But given the two characteristics of public goods of non-rivalry in consumption and, normally, non-excludability in charging for their use, the government (central and local) is one of the institutions (among others) that is particularly fit to produce, provide or finance some of these goods and services, particularly if no other institution can or will do so.

On the other hand, there are other reasons for public sector production than the public nature of goods. They include natural monopolies, if their regulation is less efficient, and merit goods, to which a high value is attached by the community, but which cannot be afforded by those who need them.[1] Or goods and services, such as the arts or museums or theatres, which are regarded as important, but would not exist if they had to rely wholly on private finance.[2] (There are also merit bads, or demerit goods, such as

---

1. I am indebted to Michael Lipton for clarifying the distinction between the private and public sector on the one hand, and private and public goods on the other. But he must not be held responsible for what I say here, for I suspect there is still disagreement between us.

2. Arts subsidies are often an elitist form of public spending. The most popular art forms (rock music, jazz, cinema, disco dancing, pantomime, country and western, visiting old houses and reading books) are the least subsidized. Most of those attending plays, ballet, concerts and galleries – the most subsidized – are relatively well off.

dangerous drugs, tobacco, alcohol and weapons, whose production or sale the government may wish to restrict or prohibit.)

Production is thus not confined to the private sector. Production of different things can and should therefore occur in both the
public and the private sector. And the same is true of authority.
The private sector exercises authority through work discipline
(and hiring and firing, giving and withholding payments), the
public sector through the army and the police. And the authority of the state depends on widespread voluntary acceptance by
the citizens. A worker can, of course, leave the firm and go to another, but citizens in many countries can also leave and move to
another country. States are also constrained by both super-
national bodies, like the European Community, and sub-national bodies, like provinces and municipalities.

The question as to whether the private and the public sector
use their authority for the benefit of the public or wastefully or
predatorily or exploitatively remains to be answered. Such shifts
between the two perceptions about the role of the private and the
public sector give, however, rise to very different evaluations.[1]
They reflect different ideologies, different ways of organizing,
filing, and evaluating the same observations. The role of profit, of
moral and aesthetic considerations, and of the use of force, will
appear quite different according to which of these two perceptions one accepts.

9. Rhetoric and Practice

The academic and political rhetoric about the virtues of the
market and the vices of the state is far removed from the actual
behaviour of libertarian governments that profess to follow this
rhetoric. While both the Reagan and the Thatcher administra-
tions decried the role of the state, the role of public expenditure
relative to GNP increased under both leaders. In 1990 the public sector in the USA spent 43 per cent of the national income.

---

1. See ROBERT L. HEILBRONER, 'The Murky Economists', *New York Review of Books*,
vol. 33 no. 7, 24 April 1986.

It was 40 per cent in 1980 and 38 per cent in 1970. This represents an increase of over 13 per cent over 20 years. It was the result of growing expenditure on defence, on state security and on social security, on research and development and, above all, on growing interest payments on the rising public debt in an economy without a sense of direction. These expenditures, and particularly those on research, reflect three powerful collective sentiments to which libertarians succumb just as much as interventionists: collective fear (defence and, more recently, environmental protection), collective greed (the desire to be competitive in international trade that leads to subsidies such as those to Sematech, the Pentagon-aided corporation consortium for improving the manufacture of semiconductors) and collective pride (the desire for international prestige reflected in the award of Nobel Prizes).

There are two important areas in this debate. One is concerned with the problems of the transition from excessively interventionist to more market-oriented and people-friendly policies; the other is normative political economy.

10. Problems of the Transition

Much of the literature is concerned with how much state intervention, what kind and by what means, but much less with the important question as to how to manage the transition (1) from excessive to reduced state intervention, (2) from interventions in the wrong areas to those in previously neglected important ones, and (3) from one form (say reliance on quantitative controls) to another (reliance on prices as instruments of policy). This is a problem with which many countries are faced today, not only in Eastern Europe and Russia, and for whose solution guidelines are needed. If, for example, reducing public sector employment is implemented by not replacing people who leave, the best will leave and only the deadwood remain. If salaries in the public sector are kept too low, demoralization and added temptation to corruption and the search for additional outside jobs are created. What Robert Klitgaard calls incentive myopia[1] can be more damaging than an overstaffed public sector. If staff are just sacked without the provision of alternative jobs, unemployment and poverty are created, or the burden of maintaining them is thrown on others. The examples of Sri Lanka and China have shown that liberalization that raises output and average incomes has been combined with rising infant mortality rates and falling life expectancy. It may be that demobilization, the change from a war to a peace-time economy, has lessons to teach. In many respects the experience of the British economy in both mobilization for the war and demobilization after it, has been wrongly transferred to developing countries. But some aspects of it may be relevant. *More* transitional intervention may be needed in order to reduce, or, more important, change the form of, past intervention.

11. Neoclassical Political Economy

I have already mentioned the two basic ideas of neoclassical political economy: that rent-seeking is an exclusively political phenomenon (and does not occur in the private sector),[2] and that the only way to reduce rent-seeking is to limit government action. There are several criticisms that can be made of this position.

First, as already pointed out by Adam Smith, rent-seeking is just as common in the private sector and government action may then be necessary to reduce or eliminate it. Anti-monopoly and anti-cartel legislation, import liberalization, and the creation of competing public enterprises are examples.

Second, as Jagdish Bhagwati has shown, in a situation where there are already many rent-seeking activities going on, the cre-

---

1. ROBERT KLITGAARD, 'Incentive Myopia', *World Development,* vol. 17, no. 4, April 1989.

2. Michael Lipton has pointed out that this belief depends on the view that private firms operate in "contestable markets", in which rents are constrained or eliminated by *potential* entry. Lipton's reply, with which I agree, is that this proposition is itself highly contestable (monopolies do exist), and that it applies to the public sector also, often indirectly. Private producers cannot compete directly with issuing an import licence, but they can substitute other goods for the import, which amounts to contestability.

ation of additional rent-seeking opportunities by government intervention can be productive.[1] The alternative use of these resources might be even more damaging. It is an application of the Theory of the Second Best. The creation of new rents can reduce or altogether destroy existing rents and existing competitive rent-seeking activities, in both the public and private sectors.

Third, as Michael Lipton has argued, it is odd that the objection is not to the creation of rents (and thereby to reducing the share available for wages and profits, and with it the creation of incentives to generate surpluses), but to the creation of rents in forms that give rise to competitive rent-seeking. Efforts and resources are diverted from productive to non-productive activities, e.g. to acquiring an import licence. Had the import licence been handed to the brother of the bureaucrat, or had it been sold corruptly to a merchant, and had no competition for it occurred, there would have been no social cost according to this theory. The theory does not seem to envisage any social gains (compared with the nepotistic or corrupt awards) from the fact that the rents are competed for rather than monopolized. In fact, the social costs of rent-seeking seem to arise only from competition for them, whereas corruption and nepotism appear to involve none!

Fourth, the theory assumes that all resources diverted to rent-seeking from productive activities, if rent-seeking were to end, could be returned to these activities.[2] It is quite obscure what these resources, released from lobbying and log-rolling are, how they can be transferred to productive activities, what the costs of transfer might be, and how their productivity might be affected by the transfer. Mrinal Datta-Chaudhuri has argued that "[p]erhaps more important than the resource cost of rent-seeking are the effects of the policy environment on the perception of economic agents. In such an environment, producers tend to become obsessed with the short run gains associated with cornering the licenses at the cost of the long run benefits connected with

1. See JAGDISH BHAGWATI, 'Directly Unproductive Profit-Seeking Activities', *Journal of Political Economy*, vol. 90 no. 5, October 1982.
2. See LIPTON, 'Agriculture, Rural People, State and Surplus'.

technological and managerial improvements".[1] But are the same people capable of pursuing these alternative activities?

Fifth, Michael Lipton again points out that the theory ignores the likelihood of rent-avoiding transactions (black or parallel markets, smuggling, and other illegal activities, abbreviated by Lipton to RATS) as a response to rent-seeking opportunities. Such substitution is normally assumed in neoclassical economics, but appears to be excluded here. According to neoclassical political economy invisible feet trample on the beautiful work of the invisible hand. But smuggling is one way in which the invisible hand can defeat, or at least reduce, the destructive efforts of rent-creating and rent-competition-creating invisible feet. Of course, illegal markets are wasteful compared with open and free trade. But they may be regarded as less wasteful than distorted, regulated and restricted markets without these subterranean outlets.

The case for state minimalism is, of course, not based solely on rent-seeking. It is widely believed that in most developing countries the public sector and public expenditure are "over-extended", hampering economic growth. The evidence does not confirm this. A recent econometric study, based on more than one hundred time-series and cross-country regressions, shows that government size and public expenditure are *positively* associated with economic growth, especially for developing countries.[2] Obviously, there is enormous scope for more efficient reallocation and restructuring of public expenditure, in particular (1) to make it complementary to private expenditure, (2) to reallocate it from low to high-priority areas, and (3) to fill gaps left by private activity. But there is no evidence that the state is over-extended.

---

1. MRINAL DATTA-CHAUDHURI, 'Market Failure and Government Failure', *Journal of Economic Perspectives*, vol. 4 no. 3, Summer 1990, p. 30.

2. RATI RAM, 'Government Size and Economic Growth: A New Framework and Some Evidence from Cross-Section and Time-Series Data', *American Economic Review*, vol. 76, no. 1, March 1986. See also CHRISTOPHER COLCLOUGH, 'Are African Governments as Unproductive as the Accelerated Development Report Implies?', *IDS Bulletin*, vol. 14, no. 1, January 1983, 'Structuralism versus Neo-Liberalism: an Introduction', chapter 1 of *States or Markets? Neo-Liberalism and the Development Policy Debate;* edited by C. COLCLOUGH and J. MANOR, Oxford: Clarendon Press, 1992.

12. Normative Political Economy

Much of the recent criticism of governments and states by the state minimalists, the neoclassical political economists, the theorists of rent-seeking and of directly unproductive profit-seeking activities, and of public choice, has been concerned with explaining why and how inefficiency, inequity and deprivation of freedom arose; with the *positive* political economy, partly of government failures, and, more importantly, of government successes in pursuing its selfish interests at the expense of the public. They have been useful in explaining bad policies and the absence of reforms, and have thrown light on regimes such as those of Amin, the Duvaliers, Marcos, Somoza, Trujillo and Mobutu. It has been truly said that in many developing countries the Invisible Hand is nowhere to be seen.

But in explaining the evils of predatory governments, and by advocating free markets, they have once again reasoned the state away, and reestablished the division between economics and politics. The task of integrating the two would consist in showing how the government, and pressures on it, can be used for the objectives of development. This would also help to explain the successes of development, from Japan to South Korea, Botswana and Costa Rica.

On the other hand, there are examples of political regimes that represent and promote the interests of the poor. In Malaysia, political power lies with the poorer Malays, while economic power lies with the Chinese and Indian communities. As a result, Malaysia has implemented policies that benefited the poor Malay community. In Zimbabwe, after power had shifted from a white to a black government, numerous measures were taken that favoured human and social objectives. For example, the share of primary education in total educational expenditure rose from 32 per cent in 1980 to 58 per cent in 1984 and real expenditure per head on primary education doubled.[1] In Malaysia and Zimbabwe influence does not go with affluence.

1. GIOVANNI ANDREA CORNIA, RICHARD JOLLY, FRANCES STEWART, *Adjustment with a Human Face*, eds. Oxford: Clarendon Press, 1987, pp. 292-3.

Much less interest has been shown in this *normative* aspect of the subject. James Buchanan, one of the founders of the public choice school, has, indeed, written on the processes by which efficiency is achieved, on voluntary contracts, institutions, decision-rules and constitution-making as guides to reform.[1] But there has been little interest in how to build up political pressures against the pressures for the destructive policies so well analysed by him and his disciples.

Frequently authors from different schools attribute poor policies to "lack of political will". But it is futile (or tautological) to say that the political will is lacking. It is an expression that should be banned from political discourse. One does not have to be a behaviourist to think that behaviour is the manifestation of will. If the will to action is lacking, there is no point in asking for the will to have the will to action. This only leads either to an infinite regress or to the charge of hypocrisy. It is a case of *ignotum per ignotius*. Political will itself should be subjected to analysis, and, for purposes of action, to pressures and to mobilization. It is more fruitful to think of how to create a political base for efficiency, equity and liberty; how to build up pressure groups, how to mobilize the poor, how to shape reformist alliances, how to recruit coalitions for progress, how to strike bargains, achieve compromises, forge compacts, resolve conflicts, or permit their tolerance, how to use persuasion, when to offer compensation to losers when total gains exceed total losses, etc. Amartya Sen has used the expression "cooperative conflict" for the relations within a family.[2] Similar relations exist both within the state and between it and pressure groups.

It might be thought that if such a normative theory had to be built on pure self-interest, no research would be needed, for peo-

1. James M. Buchanan, *Economics: Between Predictive Science and Moral Philosophy*, compiled by Robert D. Tollison and Viktor Vanberg. College Station: Texas A & M University Press, 1987, and *Liberty, Market and State: Political Economy in the 1980s*. New York: New York University Press, Brighton: Wheatsheaf, 1986. See also Agnar Sandmo, 'Buchanan on Political Economy: A Review Article', *Journal of Economic Literature*, vol. 28, no. 1, March 1990.

2. Amartya K. Sen, 'Gender and Cooperative Conflicts', Working Paper no. 18, Helsinki: Wider, 1987, and published in I. Tinker, ed., *Persistent Inequalities*, New York: Oxford University Press, forthcoming.

ple are very good in discovering and pursuing their interest. But we know from parables such as those of the Prisoners' Dilemma, the isolation paradox, the tragedy of the commons, social traps, and the free rider, that the pursuit of self-interest in society can be mutually destructive, and that there are ways of cooperation, apparent sacrifice and coercion that advance it. Moreover, there is no need to stick to the assumption of self-interested bureaucrats and politicians. Mobilizing the guardians for the poor and the trustees of rationality to put pressure on governments can produce good results even if governments are correctly analysed by the public choice school. Governments can also themselves initiate reforms either in their enlightened self-interest or from motives of public interest.

In analysing the sources of pressures on governments for reform directed at improving the lot of poor people, for example, six areas are further explored in the next lecture:

1. Common or shared interests between rich and poor.

2. Mutual interests and bargains between rich and poor, including the payment of compensation.

3. Interest conflicts within the ruling groups that can result in benefits for the poor.

4. Empowerment of the poor and participatory forms of organization.

5. Organization of distinct "trustees for the poor" and "guardians of rationality".

6. International pressures and support.

13. Donor Conditionality, Pricism and State Minimalism

Structural adjustment loans have been given by the World Bank on the condition that recipients *liberalize, decentralize, privatize* and *deregulate*. Pricism and market-orientation have been combined with state minimalism, both in domestic and in foreign policies. The change from exclusive project lending to programme lending with its macropolicy conditionality is the result of projects having gone sour because of the wrong macroeconomic policies. The policy conditionality was further supported by the belief that

it would support like-minded domestic political coalitions in recipient countries.

Apart from the (superficial) double paradox that foreign
donors are in a better position to know what is in the country's
best interest, and that the country does not have to pay a fee for
accepting this good advice, but gets rewarded with extra funds,
there are five problems with this type of conditionality.[1]

First, adjustment aid to mostly Latin American and Southeast
Asian debtor countries is aid not to the countries but to the banks
in the USA and other advanced countries, if the creditors are private banks and the alternative is default. This, of course, may
have contributed to the conversion of the multilateral banks and
a Republican US administration to programme lending.

Second, policies, like projects, are substitutable and avoidable.
The donor imposes a condition, which is met, but other policies
circumvent the intended result of the condition. This is the
macroeconomic equivalent of fungibility, which was regarded as
an objection to project aid. In both cases the donor's intentions
are frustrated. For example, the donor imposes as a condition devaluation, but subsequent inflation renders it nugatory. This happened in several African countries.

Third, donors' embrace of political groups advocating "correct" policies can be the kiss of death. An example was the pressure for devaluation on India in 1966.[2] It may be wiser to refrain
from seeking such allies and to encourage correct policies by
quietly signalling approval through the unconditional support of
good governments.

Fourth, in view of our ignorance of the impact of these condi-

---

1. On several reasons why this conflict may arise, see PAUL STREETEN, 'Structural
Adjustment: A Survey of Issues and Options', in *World Development*, vol. 15, no. 12, De-
cember 1987, 'A Survey of the Issues and Options', in *Structural Adjustment and Agriculture
in Theory and Practice in Africa and Latin America*, edited by SIMON COMMANDER, Overseas
Development Institute, London: Heinemann, 1989, and 'Program versus Project Aid:
A Role Reversal', *Methodus*, Bulletin of the International Network for Economic
Method, December 1989, pp. 14-15.

2. India *did*, of course, devalue, but the domestic groups that supported devaluation
lost credibility. There are examples illustrating the opposite, such as Belaunde and the
Alliance for Progress in the 1960s. Belaunde escaped political opposition to land reform,
which he advocated, by blaming the Americans, who made essential aid conditional on
it. The Peruvian congress acceded eventually.

tions, both in the transition period and ultimately, the premature crystallization of flawed orthodoxies should be avoided. The neoclassical doctrines are not scientific truths, and the ability of governments to implement them, even if they were such truths, and even if the governments were willing, is often in doubt.

Fifth, our confidence in the ability of the developing countries to implement the required macroeconomic policy reforms has declined.

In the light of this, at least as much attention as to macroeconomic policies should be paid in the aid dialogue to project design and implementation, to institution- and capacity-building, and to narrowly defined human rights.

14. Concluding Remarks

The theoretical case for free, unregulated markets depends on many conditions, which rarely exist in reality. Adam Smith is often cited as the authority for advocating laissez-faire and state minimalism. "Shakespeare did not say it, but it is true that some men are born small, some achieve smallness, and some have smallness thrust upon them. Adam Smith, the father of modern economics, has had to cope with a good deal of such thrusting".[1] Adam Smith defended particular liberties, not liberty in general, and he objected to particular government interventions (especially in foreign trade), not to government intervention in general. One person's "freedom from" and "freedom to" implies restrictions on other people's freedom.

Adam Smith thought that the state should undertake three main tasks: defending its citizens from the "violence and invasion of other independent societies"; protecting every member of society from the "injustice or oppression of every other member of it"; and "erecting and maintaining certain public works and public institutions, which it can never be in the interest of any

---

1. AMARTYA K. SEN, 'Adam Smith's Prudence', in *Theory and Reality in Development; Essays in Honour of Paul Streeten,* edited by SANJAYA LALL and FRANCES STEWART, London: Macmillan, 1986, p. 28.

individual, or small number of individuals, to erect and maintain, because the profit would never repay the expense, though it may frequently do much more than repay it to a great society".

Adam Smith also discussed extensively "the importance of social interdependence and the communal advantages of following 'rules of conduct', even when they go against what he called 'self-love'".[1]

This lecture is entirely in the spirit of Adam Smith. Collective defence and the administration of justice are generally agreed goods for which the state is responsible. The provision of certain public works and certain public institutions permits a wide range of public interventions. Infrastructure, public education and help for the poor were certainly in Adam Smith's mind. Arguments from free riders and externalities are used today to justify them. Modern theory and events have added other justifications for state intervention. The theory of the second-best has shown that if one price is not competitive, intervention with all other competitively determined prices may be justified. The world of small producers has given place to one of large corporations and trade unions. Modern industry has polluted the environment. At the same time, Adam Smith saw that market failure is not necessarily an argument for government intervention. There are, it is hardly necessary to say nowadays, also government failures. But equally, though less widely noticed, government failure is not necessarily an argument for the market. Only pragmatic experiments can show when and where intervention is the lesser evil. For we have to act in this least bad of all feasible worlds, in which everything is for the nth best. The challenge consists in designing institutions that combine an appeal to private initiative and enterprise with social objectives and public accountability.

Perhaps the most serious problems arise, as Michael Lipton has reminded us, not from market failure but from market success, not from government failure, but from government success. If it were just a matter of correcting failures, the task would be relatively easy. But if the signals propagated by the market are based

---

1. AMARTYA K. SEN, 'Economic Methodology: Heterogeneity and Relevance', *Methodus*, vol. 3 no. 1, June 1991, p. 74.

on a very unequal distribution of land, other assets, and income, it is *market success* in responding to these signals that causes the trouble. Amartya Sen has analysed famines and shown that often total food supply was adequate, but that the purchasing power (or, more generally, the entitlements) of a particular group of poor people had declined. In those conditions the market is all too successful in its signals, incentives and allocations, while people starve. Similarly, it is not government failure but *government success* (in pursuing the self-interested objectives of its officials) that produces the destructive results rightly deplored by the self-interest school and the state minimalists. What is needed then is fundamental structural change, a redistribution of assets and of access to power.

FIFTH LECTURE
The Political Economy of Reform

1. Introduction

Adjustment used to have a clear and narrow meaning. But gradually first growth, then poverty concerns, distribution, employment, public enterprises, the environment, women, and Uncle Tom Cobley and all, were creeping back in, until the term has become synonymous with development. Except that nobody will lay down his life for structural adjustment, or even salute the flag. Is there life after adjustment? You might think, at first, that life only begins after adjustment. But on reflection, you realize that all life is adjustment.

We have heard a lot about the need to get prices right, and to let the magic of the market work. But what Lance Taylor called Buchanan's heaven, or the combination of a weak, minimalist state and well working competitive markets does not exist. State minimalism and pricism do not go together. In South Korea and Taiwan the Invisible Hand is guided by a strong Visible Arm.

Another error is to think that the only thing that matters are macroeconomic policies. Of course, they are very important, but let us not forget in our enthusiasm for them that attention to projects and institutions is also very important. To overvalue the importance of a single component in a complex system (such as the exchange rate) can be worse than over-valuing the exchange rate.

My emphasis in this lecture is on policies in the *social* or *human* sectors of the economy, i.e. principally *public expenditure* on nutrition (food subsidies), health, and education; and it will be on the

235

political economy rather than on narrowly economic factors determining reform. The reason for discussing the political economy is that it is by now pretty well known what ought to be done in this area, yet not much is being done. True, there is still important work to be done on basic needs. The allocation of scarce resources between, say, health and education, and within each sector, between, say, textbooks and salaries for teachers, or the applicability of cost recovery in different situations remains to be explored. But the main question, why does human neglect continue, is important to anyone interested in reform, and points to political obstacles and inhibitions rather than economic or technical constraints.

2. Beyond Statistics

We devote financial and fiscal resources to the provision of education, health, nutrition, family planning. But in the supply of these social services the links between "inputs" of resources and "outputs" or results, reflected in a full, healthy and long life, are even more tenuous than the links between inputs of labour and capital and the production of turnips, shoes or sausages. There is a wide range of outcomes, as reflected in a healthy population, for a given amount of money spent on primary health care, or on a family planning programme for given resources devoted to it. Without money, hardly anything can be done. But even large amounts of money can have little impact. The ratio of public expenditure to national income (a guide to the available public resources), the ratio of social expenditure to public expenditure, and the ratio of priority social expenditure (in low-income countries on basic education and preventative primary health care) to social expenditure are guidelines to achievements in human development, but they are not sufficient for the desired results. What one should aim at is to get the best possible results from any given amount of expenditure. This is particularly important in times of financial stringency. But this will depend on a number of factors other than money. What then are these determinants of the effective use of funds for social purposes? They can be grouped under five headings.

1. Institutions
2. Skills and aptitudes
3. Attitudes
4. Levels of living
5. Policies

Institutions determine the organizational basis from which the energy, commitment and enthusiasm of the beneficiaries can be enlisted. Too much centralized decision-making may fail altogether or, if successful, will prove extremely expensive; too much reliance on "bottom-up" initiatives will be frittered away or be taken over by local power elites. It is the right combination of participatory and voluntary with central and local government institutions that will yield the best results.

The skills and the aptitudes of the teachers, village workers and health personnel will make all the difference in the delivery of these services. Education and training of the right type has to be provided, refresher courses should keep the workers up to date, and high wastage rates have to be avoided.

Attitudes are less easily measured than time spent on education, but the fact that they cannot be counted should not lead to the conclusion that they do not count. Human development is not just a question of literacy and numeracy, but of what might be called operacy, the skill and will of doing. They are concerned with choosing objectives and priorities, adopting valuations, developing alternatives, making decisions, resolving conflicts, accommodating other people's views. They spring from self-discipline, pride in work well done, willingness to cooperate.

Levels of living, normally considered to be consumption and not regarded as being productive, are at low levels crucial in determining the efficiency of work done. The dedication and commitment to work on a health or education programme is more likely to be forthcoming from a well nourished, alert, healthy group of people.

Policies are more fully discussed elsewhere in this lecture. It is plain that the right division of labour between different levels of government, NGOs, the market, and the family will be a crucial influence on the impact of social reforms.

Each of these five factors, which themselves interact, can be positive or negative from the point of view of human development. Positive institutions will draw on the enthusiasm and energy of the beneficiaries, negative will set a distant, distrusted, centralized, urban bureaucracy against them. Positive attitudes comprise a readiness to cooperate, to be self-reliant, to take a long view; negative attitudes are inhibitions by rulers to implement reforms, dependence of beneficiaries and reliance upon others doing the job. And so on.

These five variables are themselves largely a function of human development. A society that enjoys high and wide-spread levels of nutrition, health and education will tend to have institutions, skills, attitudes and policies conducive to human development. The effectiveness with which money for human development is used thus itself largely depends on human development. Progress in human development is both a condition and a result of human development. This explains why it is so difficult to get started on human development. But there is also a message of hope in it; for once the process does get started, it becomes self-enforcing and cumulative.

Whether the five variables work in a positive or negative direction will also depend on political pressures, political constituencies, political obstacles and political inhibitions. This lecture is concerned with these forces as they determine the shape and effectiveness of social services aimed at reducing poverty.

Expensive, heavily subsidized, urban hospitals for the middle class and the rich instead of low-cost, rural preventive health services; free university education for the children of the rich instead of primary village education for farmers' children; luxury flats instead of low-cost housing for the urban poor; subsidized food for urban officials, the military and the well-off instead of incentives for poor farmers and adequate wages for landless labourers; the support of monopolies and cartels instead of labour-intensive, informal sector micro-enterprises; these biases are the result of powerful and articulate interests. Those who benefit from these policies obviously form part of the pressures behind them. But there are also the professional interest groups – the doctors, the engineers, the university teachers – who claim privileges in the name of "excellence" and high professional standards. The medical and educational establishments tend to oppose attempts to restructure these services to the poor. The current period of restricted growth and debt burdens adds further difficulties to changing the direction of expenditure, compared with the earlier three postwar decades of rapid expansion. Even an altruistic government is faced with additional problems in promoting human development.

The picture of the state and the government painted by some contemporary writers is that of an instrument used ruthlessly to amass wealth and power by those in office, and for the benefit of those on whose support they depend, without regard either to efficiency or to the public interest. According to this view, reasonable men and women adopt policies that have harmful consequences for the societies they govern. The self-interest of bureaucrats, politicians and ordinary organized citizens leads the government to adopt policies that are neither in the public interest, nor in the interest of the poor, nor economically rational.

But surely this picture is at best incomplete. The principle of social impoverishment through competitive, short-term, self-interested political action by pressure groups that attempt to frustrate the working of Adam Smith's Invisible Hand has been aptly called the "Invisible Foot". The policy problem consists in finding ways to prevent the Invisible Foot (of political rationality) from trampling on and destroying the beautiful work of the Invisible Hand.

Governments, however, sometimes transcend individual and group interests and free themselves from the political pressures that make for allocation of scarce resources to the privileged and powerful. If there is one thing that is abundantly clear from historical evidence, it is that they can and do act in the common interest, or in the interest of the poor, the weak, the unemployed, and that they can act rationally. Otherwise, how can we account for the fact that measures are taken to protect children and future generations, who have no votes and no power? Such poor countries as Sri Lanka, Costa Rica, China and Jamaica have achieved spectacular results in longevity and health through public interventions.

Political action is not necessarily destructive but can be a way

239

of resolving conflicts. Action for the poor and for improving the human condition is certainly helped by democracy, a vigorous civil society and and a free press; and human development, even when it occurs in a dictatorship, eventually leads to the call for civil and political freedom, as recent events abundantly testify.

3. Successful Restructuring of Social Services

There are examples of successful restructuring of the social services towards the poor. Zimbabwe redirected public expenditure to primary education and health services after independence between 1979 and 1985. Although this was the result of a radical change of regime, the new regime was widely accepted. The ruling party, the Zimbabwe National Union, led by Mugabe, had a wide and largely rural support base. Political debate was intense and the press was relatively free and played an important role in keeping the government alert to social problems.

Free health care was available for those earning less than 150 Zimbabwean dollars a month and the immunization and diarrheal disease control programmes expanded rapidly. A children's supplementary feeding programme was instituted, providing a daily meal to undernourished children in rural areas. Similar restructuring took place in education, with communities participating in contributing labour. Health expenditure rose by 70 per cent between 1980 and 1982, a growing proportion of which was devoted to preventive rather than curative services.[1]

A quite different picture is presented by Chile under Pinochet. It enjoyed a rapid improvement in infant mortality and the health status of the poor. Chile had a long historical record of social services and benefited from continued expansion of female education and reduction in fertility. But there can be no doubt that government policy contributed to the success by expanding public support measures. Some have explained this as an attempt to check popular discontent at a time of political repression. "The expansion of targeted nutrition and health programmes also has an ob-

---

1. CORNIA, JOLLY AND STEWART, *Adjustment with a Human Face*, pp. 123-124.

viously populist ring in a country where popular expectations of public provisioning are very high, and the Chilean government has indeed consistently endeavoured to build political capital from its achievements in the area of child nutrition ".[1] Some critics have said that the programme was not so much targeted at the poor, as at a few indicators such as infant mortality, at the expense of the more broadly defined poor working class, whose wages fell and unemployment rose. Important lessons about political pressures and the search for popular support, even in an authoritarian regime, can be learned from Chile's achievements.

The political importance of a long history of social intervention is also illustrated by the success of Costa Rica. It has enjoyed an active democracy and social legislation since independence in 1821. Slavery was abolished in 1813 and capital punishment in 1882. Secondary education has been free and compulsory since 1869. As one can see, the foundations for the present success go back in history.

Indonesia in the 1980s restructured social expenditure to primary village schools, largely in order to reduce the risks of rural uprisings. Reforms in Morocco and Ghana also were intended to expand and improve rural primary education and to eliminate subsidies to middle-class university students, and in Ghana to pupils at the upper secondary level. Most of the resistance to these reforms was directed at the withdrawal of benefits from university students and limits on enrolment. In Ghana student protests occurred in 1987 and 1988, leading to a closing down of the universities. In Morocco enrolments were increased again in response to political pressures.[2] Both Ghana and Morocco continue to attempt restructuring in spite of middle-class opposition, which appears to be even stronger in this field than to eliminating food subsidies for the middle class. Plentiful external assistance helps such efforts. After 1988 Jamaica benefited from funds

1. See JEAN DRÈZE and AMARTYA SEN, *Hunger and Public Action*, Oxford: Clarendon Press, 1989, p. 239.

2. See JOAN NELSON, 'The Politics of Pro-Poor Adjustment', in *Fragile Coalitions: The Politics of Economic Adjustment*, Joan M. Nelson and contributors, Transaction Books, U.S.-Third World Policy Perspectives no. 12, Overseas Development Council, New Brunswick (USA) and Oxford (UK): Transaction Books, 1989, p. 108.

from the World Bank for a broad-based Social Adjustment Programme that had wide political support. Its small size was an advantage in getting aid. Larger countries have much greater difficulties in getting such support.

In addition to targeted subsidies and restructuring of the social services, there are numerous other measures a government can adopt to improve the condition of the poor. Clearly, they also raise problems of political economy. A land reform aiming at the redistribution of land, in many countries the most obvious policy for both equity and efficiency, is politically the most difficult.

Channelling credit to poor people has been highly successful and has met with less opposition. If the highjacking of subsidized credit by rich and powerful borrowers can be avoided, credit gives the poor access to productive assets, enabling them to earn higher incomes; it engages them in the productive process, thereby making them agents of change; and it enables them to acquire the education and skills for further raising their earning power. It also gives them self-esteem and the social recognition that is important to all of us. It is for reasons such as these that Professor Yunus, the founder of the Grameen Bank in Bangladesh, has written of credit as a basic human right.[1] The creation of efficient, small-scale, labour-intensive work opportunities is another promising area in which the interests of the better off and the poor can be made to coincide, if the activities are made complementary rather than competitive with the larger firms.

4. Normative Political Economy Again

I have said earlier that the idea of "political will" should be replaced by that of how to construct a political base for reform. A possible reason for the failure, in the past, to heed the recom-

---

1. There are arguments against credit as a top priority. First, at very low levels of development, food and health come first. At higher levels, education and training in vocational skills may make credit unnecessary, as the Carvajal Foundation in Cali, Colombia found. Micro-entrepreneurs have to undergo training in simple book-keeping and accounting in order to be entitled to credit after the course, but often find that they do not need it then. Credit, with its debt burden, can also blunt incentives to work, as the worker thinks he is earning for his creditor.

mendations of those advocating human development and poverty eradication, the main principles of which have been known for a long time, is the neglect of political constraints and of the need to create a constituency for reform.

Illustrations of such mobilization of interests for the benefit of poor people in developing countries can be found in the interest of bankers in advanced countries in liberalizing markets for labour-intensive imports from developing countries; or in the interest of independent retail chains or consumer groups in low-cost imports; or in the interest of US export lobbies in debt relief for the developing countries. Alliances of this kind can build on the interest of some groups in advanced countries to improve the lot of weaker and poorer groups.

Any attempt to include a political analysis is faced with a dilemma. Either recommendations are confined to what is regarded as politically feasible and end up in a sterile perpetuation of the status quo; or the recommendations, free of any political constraint and Utopian, end in frustration because of their lack of realism. There is, however, as I have already said in the context of Utopian thinking about global institutions, something to be said for Utopianism in policy analysis. For the reasons given,[1] it is useful to speculate about the kind of society we want, unencumbered by the inhibitions and obstacles of political constraints.

On the other hand, there is a danger that the best becomes the enemy of the good, the optimum an obstacle to improvements. To be successful, it is essential to have a feel for the politically possible, and more than a feel, to make a careful analysis of actual and potential power constellations, including the constraints to reform. It can be argued that past failures of human development are the result of the neglect of the analysis of how to mobilize pressures for its realization. A principal message of these lectures is to emphasize the need to include political feasibilities in the recommendations for human development, without losing the vision of a better society.

It is sometimes said that there is a trade-off between measures for the poor and economic growth; that it is the rich who save,

---

1. See pp. 120-121.

invest and take risks, and that poor countries cannot afford to forgo these benefits. But reducing poverty is also a form of investment, and in labour-surplus countries the best form. I have repeatedly emphasized that an alert, healthy, well-nourished, educated and skilled labour force is the best productive asset for a country. There is, however, a trade-off, at least in the short run; it is not that between the well-being of the poor and growth, but between the poor and non-poor, at least for a time. And since the non-poor frequently also have access to or exercise political power, and are vocal and organized, the question is one of politics or political economy. Although in the longer run this conflict often disappears, the opposition is not always foresighted and wise enough to realize this. Poverty and its eradication are ultimately not economic or technical, but political and power problems.

In the political economy of human development in general, in promoting and financing the well-being of the poor in particular, and in embarking on restructuring social services to the poor, six areas are worth exploring, as I have briefly indicated before:

1. Common or shared interests between rich and poor.

2. Mutual interests and bargains between rich and poor, including the payment of compensation.

3. Interest conflicts within the ruling groups that can result in benefits for the poor.

4. Empowerment of the poor and participatory forms of organization.

5. Organization of distinct "trustees for the poor" and "guardians of rationality".

6. International pressures and support.

These six sources of a political power base can be directed at three ratios, the product of which yields the ratio of priority social expenditure to national income. (If we multiply this ratio by income per head, we get the priority social expenditure per head of the population.) We might want to:

1. raise the ratio of public expenditure to national income, or

2. raise the ratio of social expenditure (all education and health) to public expenditure, or

3. raise the ratio of priority social expenditure (for low-income

244

countries basic education, primary health care, water for the rural poor) to social expenditure, or

4. make any given ratio more effective in achieving its objectives, by improving institutions, skills, attitudes, and levels of living.

Obviously, these goals should be achieved in the context of a growing national income, growing public expenditure, and growing social expenditure, or at least not declining ones.[1] In addition to the obvious reason that there would be no point in raising these ratios just by shrinking income, public expenditure or social expenditure (the three denominators), it is politically easier to raise tax rates and reallocate funds from, say, military to social expenditure, and from, say, higher education to primary education, when total income and public expenditure are growing than when they are constant or declining. In addition, much of public expenditure, such as interest payments, is committed and not available for reallocation. In the following sections some successes and failures are discussed under the six headings of political mobilisation.

5. Common Interests

It is fairly widely recognized that the government has to play a strong role in financing certain basic health and education services. Immunization and vaccination against infectious diseases and spraying to protect all residents from vector-borne diseases such as malaria are almost pure public goods.[2] So-called "merit goods", that is goods to which all citizens have a basic right (primary health and education), irrespective of their ability to pay, fall into the same category. The universal desire that no child should die of hunger or malnutrition can be similarly regarded as a public good, a concern of the whole community.

Some of these measures cost very little. For 10 cents per head

1. At the same time, in the face of declining denominators (national income, public expenditure, social expenditure), it is to be commended if priority expenditure on basic education and primary health care is maintained, so that the social priority ratio rises.

2. Amartya Sen wrote that he wished that poverty were like an infectious disease; it woud then soon be eliminated. Unfortunately, the rich might wish to put the poor into quarantine. Quarantine, however, is likely be much more expensive than the eredication of the disease.

oral rehydration can save children from dehydration, the result of diarrhoea, the biggest killer today. Instruction in the washing of hands, boiling water and sanitary practices prevents this illness. Immunization for life against the six leading child-killing diseases in poor countries can be achieved by spending 50 cents per child. In spite of this, these diseases kill 10,000 children a day.[1]

The pharmaceutical companies do not spend money on research into vaccines against malaria and other tropical diseases because these account for only 1 per cent of their profits. These diseases cause half the world's illness but receive only 3 per cent of medical research funds.[2] Neither common nor mutual interests can activate profit-seeking agents to devote efforts to the solution of these problems.

One reason for the neglect of relatively cheap, preventive health services in favour of expensive, curative ones has nothing to do with interest conflicts or special political or professional interest groups. The preference for curative over preventive health services is partly a matter of perception. A disease suffered is felt by some individual and those who care for him or her. An illness prevented is a mere shadowy statistic. The bias in favour of curative health services is, partly, a matter of human fallibility, especially where it could be shown that prevention would be in almost everyone's interest. Although the difference between a visible and felt ill and an invisible possibility remains, education and training can help to change such perceptions.

Even here political participation can overcome resistance. Intended beneficiaries of a health project in Lesotho were going to traditional healers rather than government health workers because the healers offered curative remedies whereas the health workers had prepared only lectures on preventive health. The traditional healers were then integrated into the formal health system and government health workers also provided curative remedies. As a result, the impact of the preventive service improved.[3]

1. James Grant, in *A World to Make, Development in Perspective,* edited by Francis X. Sutton, New Brunswick and London: Transaction Publishers, 1990, p. 115.

2. UNDP and WHO Reports, 1990.

3. Lawrence F. Salmen, 'Popular Participation and Development', The World Bank, mimeo, undated.

The interests of some non-poor groups can be enlisted for the benefit of the poor, if these groups gain from the pro-poor measures. For example, raising the productivity of small farmers and small businesses may lower the prices of the goods and services they produce. Of course, there should also be some increase in their incomes to avoid the productivity gains being too widely diluted. The buyers of these goods and services, and those who employ workers who buy them, will benefit and support the measures. Similarly, when the real incomes of the poor rise, the interests of those who gain from their higher purchases can be enlisted. Much of what the poor buy will be produced by the poor, and what the poor produce will be bought by them. To this extent, productivity-raising pro-poor policies will have multiplier effects. But some of these effects will spill over to the non-poor, and this will be a source of political support by the non-poor.

6. Mutual Interests and Compensation

As we have seen, *financing* a service must be distinguished both from its *provision* and from its *production*. Social services may be wholly privately, or wholly publicly, provided, financed and produced. But these services may also be financed by the state and provided privately; or they may be provided by the state but, through user charges, privately financed. Governments can issue vouchers for private schools to deprived parents unable to pay for them, who are then free to choose the school for their children. University students may receive loans which are repaid out of the higher income the education enables them to earn. In the USA states are now considering whether to subsidize private health insurance by poor people.

Some health and education programmes, as has been seen, are almost pure public goods. Others are almost entirely private goods, such as an appendectomy or a pain reliever. Most services combine features of public and private goods. A person treated for tuberculosis benefits, but the people who might otherwise have been infected also benefit. Family planning services benefit both the parents and the community. The public goods aspects fall under the previous heading of common interests, the private goods aspects imply that a benefit to one may mean a loss to someone else. Paying for services by those who can afford it does, of course, still leave benefits for those who pay and relieves the government of losses.

There are three ways of combining the virtues of markets and decentralization with those of the government in the finance and provision of public goods: the use of selective user charges (public provision, private finance); decentralization of health care (greater responsiveness and accountability of public provision and public finance to the needs of the poor); and government use of private-sector providers and producers (public finance, private provision), both profit-seeking and non-governmental organizations (NGOs). Each of these has merits and drawbacks. User charges which exempt the poor require means tests. Decentralization can be more responsive to needs and more accountable to the beneficiaries, but local tax capacity is often weak and central grants are required; these present a dilemma between automaticity and conditionality to prevent their use for local political purposes. Private providers paid for out of government revenue present problems of quality and cost control.

Compensation can take two radically different forms. First, in the process of implementing austerity measures or other policies that hurt the poor, particular groups of the non-poor may have to be compensated or "bribed" into accepting the policies; secondly, particularly vulnerable groups may be insured against deprivation, irrespective of their political power, as a matter of public policy.

Various "targeted" subsidies, food aid, employment schemes and the redirection of social services to these groups fall into the second category. In Costa Rica, during the stabilization policy 1982-83, the government set up a temporary food aid programme which distributed food to 40,000 families, about 1 in 12 households, designated as needy by local committees. In Chile employment programmes were expanded during the depression of 1983, and nutrition, health and subsidy programmes for poor children and mothers were strengthened.[1] During the Busia ad-

1. See NELSON, *op. cit.*, p. 101.

ministration in Ghana the devaluation of 1971 was accompanied by various "sweeteners," such as an increase in minimum wages and the price of cocoa. I shall discuss donors' programmes of compensating the poor later under "international support".

These palliatives, often temporary, can be interpreted in two different ways. They can be seen either as sops for the poor that keep them quiet and prevent the fundamental, structural measures that would permanently and substantially improve their lot. Or they can be regarded as part of a piecemeal campaign that, like numerous termites in the rotting woodwork, undermine the structure of an outdated system, or like pioneers demonstrate the way and build the constituencies that eventually lead to its replacement by an improved order. The chances of compensatory measures leading to long-term reforms are better if the measures protecting the poor are not, as it were, cosmetically stuck on after the event, but are built as an integral part into the adjustment programme from the beginning.

So far compensation to poor losers has been discussed. The other type of compensation may have to be paid to comparatively better off losers when progressive, pro-poor reforms are implemented, either because equity requires it, or, in spite of the fact that compensation would be inequitable, or otherwise undesirable, because political opposition has to be overcome. These compensation payments can be particularly important in periods of transition, in order to conciliate opponents, maintain coalitions and appease hostile antagonists. Since urban wage earners are often the losers in periods of adjustment, wage increases, redeployment payments or retraining schemes to these vocal and powerful groups may be necessary. When over-staffed bureaucracies have to be reduced, civil servants, particularly in Africa, also suffer from dismissal. Some of them have other sources of income, and can return to farming, but again for political reasons compensation may be necessary. Temporary subsidies for specific goods and services, investment in certain types of infrastructure projects, public housing, or, as in Turkey, rebates paid to consumers on value-added tax are other examples of compensation payments.[1]

1. See JOHN WATERBURY, 'The Political Management of Adjustment and Reform', in NELSON, *et al.*, *Fragile Coalitions: the Politics of Economic Adjustment*, p. 41.

In implementing compensation payments, policy makers will have to consider seven questions. First, are the losses for which compensation is considered real or only perceived? It was feared that the repeal of the Corn Laws in 1846 would lead to the death of British agriculture; in fact it flourished; the Factory Laws were thought to spell the death of British industry; in fact it prospered. As we have seen, the imposition of anti-pollution legislation has often led to the discovery of new, previously unexploited, profit opportunities that arise from the commercial use of substances previously discarded.

Second, are these payments politically necessary? Would not persuasion or weakening of the political opposition do? The answer will depend on the strength of the government and its commitment to the reform.

Third, is the compensation deserved? This is a moral or humanitarian question, the answer to which is likely to conflict with that to the previous one. It is the weak, powerless, poor and inarticulate who are likely to be the most deserving, though they are also most likely to benefit directly from the reforms.

Fourth, can the payments be afforded? Information and administrative costs may be excessive, or the effects on incentives and the allocation of resources may be undesirable. These costs can be reduced by deferring the payment of the compensation, e.g. by issuing government bonds to be cashed in some future year, when production will have increased.

Fifth, do they have undesirable side effects that cancel the benefits? In addition to the blunting of incentives and allocational distortions, they may lead to capital flight, to strikes, to sabotage, or even to coups d'état.

Sixth, can compensation be offered in non-economic forms? In Peru in 1976 President Morales Bermuda offered the restoration of civilian democratic rule for acceptance of his stabilization measures. Similar attempts were made in Argentina, Brazil and Algeria after food riots in October 1989 and in Jordan after riots in the spring of 1989. The Maharashtra Employment Guarantee Scheme in India, which transfers income from the urban middle class to the rural poor, has gained the political support of the urban groups because it reduces migration to Bombay; and the support of landowners, because it stabilizes the rural labour force and creates infrastructure in the countryside.

Seventh, can the policy makers rely on support by the international community? I shall discuss this question later.

The first type of compensation, targeting subsidies to the poor, and the second type, overcoming opposition of the non-poor, are combined when a targeted scheme is broadened. Narrow targeting of, say, food subsidies on low-income groups should aim at covering *all* the poor and *only* the poor. If it aims at achieveing this objective it has the advantage that it saves scarce budgetary resources and meets priority needs. But it has two great defects. First, while it avoids the leakage to the non-poor, it is bound to have another, possibly worse, leakage: some poor will be left out. Second, it does nothing to recruit the self-interested support of at least some non-poor. For both these reasons it is therefore better to err on the side of excess coverage than deficient coverage. In this way some of the beneficiaries who are not in dire need will support the scheme. Some of the benefits may then be recouped, e.g. by a tax on tobacco or alcohol, which does not hit children.

7. Some Country Experiences

Sri Lanka switched in 1978-80 from a general rice subsidy and ration scheme (including occasionally free rations) to a targeted food stamp programme aimed only at the poor. Previous attempts to reduce the heavy budgetary commitment to these subsidies had been disastrous. But the new government had been elected by a large majority; foreign aid was plentiful, the weather was good, international prices were low, and after years of stagnation growth was resumed. Rice farmers whose prices had been depressed, supported the elimination of the rations.

In spite of these favourable circumstances, the reforms showed both that political pressures led to many non-poor being covered, and that there was a failure to reach many poor. It also involved considerable administrative costs. In 1978 the subsidy was removed from the richest part of the population. In 1979 the rations were converted into non-indexed food stamps and an attempt was made to target somewhat larger benefits to the poorest third.

The share of food subsidies in total government expenditure was reduced from 15 per cent in the mid-1970s to 3 per cent in 1984. Their share in GNP fell from about 5 per cent to 1.3 per cent.[1] Subsidized rice rations were given to half the population. Subsidies to other food items, such as wheat and sugar, were available to all, and benefited the high-income households.

There was widespread under-reporting of incomes, especially rural incomes, which went unchallenged, in spite of attempts by the government, because members of parliament pressed against checks. As a result, it was later estimated that almost 30 per cent of households in the upper half of the income distribution received food stamps. At the same time, about the same proportion of households in the bottom half were *not* receiving them. Between 1978 and 1987 poverty rose from 23.3 per cent to 27.4 per cent of the population and income distribution became more unequal. In subsequent years inflation accelerated and by 1985 the real value of the food stamps had been halved. Nutritional status among the poor and other indicators of human welfare declined. A survey of 480 households showed that food stamps increased the calorie consumption of pre-school children by 5.4 per cent, while increasing the consumption of all other members of the household by nearly 10 per cent. Income transfers have to be much larger to affect pre-school children. At the same time, the calorie consumption per head of the bottom 20 per cent declined by about 8 per cent, from the already low level of 1,490 calories in 1978/9 to 1,368 calories in 1981/2.

The government attempted again to check the incomes of claimants, but once again parliament opposed it successfully, although special measures for the very poor were adopted. Aiding the poor is politically acceptable; cutting benefits to the middle classes is not. The objective of benefiting *all* the poor

1. See Neville Edirisinghe, *The Food Stamp Scheme in Sri Lanka: Costs, Benefits, and Options for Modification*, International Food Policy Research Institute, Research Report 58, Washington D.C., March 1987.

and *only* the poor is impossible to achieve; excess coverage is preferable, for both political and administrative reasons, to deficient coverage.

In Morocco as in Sri Lanka, subsidies on food items were removed between 1985 and 1988, and the impact on the poor softened by "food for work" programmes. Only the subsidies on flour, sugar and cooking oil remained. But the grade of flour that remained subsidized had accounted for about 80 per cent of all flour milled before the reforms. Again as in Sri Lanka, a good part of the middle income groups had to be included among those covered by the reduced subsidies. Covering *only* the poor proved politically unacceptable.[1]

In Argentina, Chile and Peru tax reforms that benefited the poor depended on the agitation of middle class professionals, white collar workers, small and medium-sized business men and bureaucrats, who shared in the transfers that were primarily intended for the poor.

In some cases narrow targeting has been more successful. The Colombian food stamp programme of 1978-82 and the Philippine food price discount of 1983 have successfully combined geographic targeting with additional indicator targeting based on the nutritional status of pre-school children. Indicator targeting refers to a method by which benefits are allocated according to correlates of poverty, such as region of residence, land holding, health and nutritional status, sex, race, and age, from sample surveys. Indicator targeting is also used in South Korea for those over 65, the disabled, children under 18 without parents or parents over 60, and people residing in welfare facilities. Programmes targeted to women can tackle the male-female disparities. Bangladesh has combined geographical targeting with sex targeting in a scholarship programme. Targeting by self-selection or self-targeting has also been used in Bangladesh for subsidies to sorghum, not much consumed by the better off. Although it is therefore possible, in some conditions, to overcome the technical defects of narrow targeting, the political support cannot be mobilized in this way.

1. See NELSON, *op. cit.*, pp. 106-107

The lessons from these experiences, particularly for attempts to restructure services to the poor, are four. First, the administrative costs of narrow targeting are high, and they rise as the targetting becomes narrower. In Colombia the administrative costs of food subsidies were higher than the value of the food distributed.[1] The less efficient the bureaucracy, the stronger the arguments against a targeted anti-poverty programme. Secondly, targeting is very difficult because the poor are heterogeneous and hard to identify, and their composition and location changes in time. There is therefore a substantial risk that some poor people will be left out. Thirdly, if small children in poor household are to benefit, the transfer to these households has to be substantial. Fourthly, and most importantly in the present context, the interests of at least some groups among the non-poor, especially the urban, middle income groups, must normally be mobilized or appeased, if measures intended to help the poor are to be successful. These conclusions point to the need for a broad coverage, unless special circumstances make narrower targeting advisable and feasible.

8. Interest Conflicts Within Ruling Groups

Conflicts within powerful groups can often be used for the benefit of the poor and powerless. The improvement of the living conditions of the British working class in the nineteenth century was the result of a conflict between Tory landlords and skilled operatives, who wished to remove the low-cost competition from women and children, on the one hand, and capitalist industrialists on the other. Before the poor were permitted to organize themselves effectively in trade unions and to strike and have secure funds, before they were given the vote in 1867, and before they had access to

1. See LANCE TAYLOR, SUSAN HORTON and DANIEL RAFF, *Food Subsidy Programs: A Survey*, Report prepared for the Ford Foundation, Cambridge, Mass.: MIT, December 1980, quoted in ALAIN DE JANVRY and ELISABETH SADOULET, 'Efficiency, Welfare Effects and Political Feasibility of Alternative Antipoverty and Adjustment Programs', mimeo. Against this, Mateus (1979) estimates the costs of Colombia's food stamp programme of 1978-82 at 3 per cent of the total cost of the food delivered. Pinstrup-Anderson in his book on food subsidies refers to the Colombian food stamp programme as a targeting success.

free public education through the Education Bills of 1870 and 1912, their fate improved as a result of the factory laws which introduced safety regulations, shortened the working day, and got women and children out of the mines, and of the repeal of the Corn Laws in 1846, which reduced the price of food for urban workers. The capitalists predicted that the factory laws protecting the poor would be the death of British industry; the landlords said that the repeal of the Corn Laws would be the death of British agriculture. In fact both industry and agriculture flourished for a quarter of a century. It shows how self-interest can be misperceived and how benefits can accrue from measures judged at the time to be harmful. The same is likely to be true for measures improving the condition of the poor in most developing countries. The long-term interests of the rich, properly perceived, are not likely to be harmed, quite apart from any gains in political stability.

Similarly, rich farmers have an interest in higher prices for their agricultural products, which benefit poor growers too, if they grow and sell the same crops, or if the higher prices affect all crops. There may be common interests in rural schooling and health services, rural infrastructure, and improved varieties of crops. On the other hand, the urban middle class, students, the military and civil servants want low food prices, from which the urban poor also benefit. The urban sector will gain strength in post-agrarian societies, although for reasons of collective action it can be very strong while its size is still quite small. When food prices are raised, protest movements comprise members of all these groups. Riots over food price increases have been common and fear of them has been an important motive for keeping them low. Reductions in food subsidies have led to riots in Egypt, Tunisia, Morocco, the Dominican Republic, Brazil, Bolivia, Peru and Zambia, among others; and to a coup in Liberia in 1980. But in spite of substantial reductions, they were tolerated in Sri Lanka in 1978 and 1980; and in Senegal in 1982 and 83. Important lessons in political economy can be learned from this.

Industrial employers have an interest not only in cheap food in order to keep wages down, but also in upgrading the skills of their work force. Their education and training adds power to previously weak workers. Such coalitions of interest of powerful groups with weak and poor people hold out promise for reforms.

The impact of some policies, such as tariff reductions or exchange rate devaluations or food pricing reforms, does not follow divisions between rich and poor, but cuts across them. Higher import prices benefit both rich and poor producers of domestic substitutes, lower import prices benefit both rich and poor consumers of these imports. In Ghana smallholder cocoa producers and other export cultivators have benefited from the devaluation and higher producer prices, although a widespread impression is that the gainers were foreigners, both resident and abroad.

Sometimes regional (or ethnic) lines can define interest alignments. Pressure for irrigation in a district in India, if successful, can raise the productivity and incomes of both rich and poor. An increased flow of resources to the northeast of Brazil benefits the landowners there and, with higher employment, also the landless labourers. A regional development programme for northeast Thailand was motivated by the fear of regional disaffection. Ethnic groups that cohere comprise both rich and poor, and the poor can benefit from benefits accruing to them.

There can be a harmony of interests between the providers of social services and their beneficiaries. Although it has been seen that some of these professional interest groups can interfere with basic needs, by insisting on over-qualification and excess standards, others can be recruited to the effort. Primary school teachers, paramedical personnel, nurses, social workers, extension workers, all stand to benefit from an expansion of services and are often better organized and more vocal than the recipients of their services. Kenya and Sri Lanka have powerful teachers' unions, both the result and the cause of the large amount of resources devoted to primary education in these countries. In Peru the expansion of primary education was largely the result of efforts by political parties to win teachers' votes.

In Costa Rica, which, incredible though it may sound, abolished its army in 1949, health workers and educators are favoured by policy, policemen are not. The political influence of the public sector employees has strengthened the welfare measures, just as the welfare measures have strengthened these groups.[1] Some regard the public sector as over-extended. It is ironical that President Rafael Angel Calderon, Mr Oscar Arias's successor, whose election promises included free housing and free food for the neediest and profit sharing for workers, created a new bureaucracy – the Ministry for the Reform of the State – in order to cut down the bureaucracy: a Ministry to reduce Ministries.[2]

9. Empowerment and Participation

The poor, like the rich and powerful, are a heterogeneous group. Action to reduce the poverty of one group, such as the urban poor, may increase the poverty of another group, such as the rural poor. One useful distinction among the chronically poor (as contrasted with those who are poor only temporarily) is that between the "working poor" and those who are excluded from the labour force. The "working poor", who sell the product of their unskilled labour and perhaps of a few, small assets, can organize themselves in order to raise the returns to these assets. The second category of poor cannot participate in the labour force either because they are old, infirm, chronically ill, or otherwise incapacitated, or because they are excluded by social or economic discrimination. The reduction of their poverty has to be sought through pressures for social services and transfer payments, and elimination of the discrimination. In the short-run conflicts may arise. In the long run, poverty reduction of both groups can be in the general interest of society, by both raising productivity and lowering desired family size (for an important reason for a large family is the need to be maintained if incapacitated).

The most obvious way in which political pressures can be used to benefit the poor is the vote in democracies. Although this may not help the poorest, coalitions between them and some better-off

---

1. See the excellent essay by LAURENCE WHITEHEAD, 'Political Explanations of Macroeconomic Management: A Survey', *World Development*, vol. 18, no. 8, August 1990.

2. See JAIME DAREMBLUM 'Costa Rica Needs Lower Taxes and a Leaner State', *The Wall Street Journal*, 5 October 1990, p. A 19.

groups, both self-interested and altruistic, are frequent, and the poorest 40 per cent have fared well in countries with multi-party systems and free elections: Costa Rica and Chile in the 1960s and early 70s in Latin America, Botswana, Mauritius and Zimbabwe in Africa, Sri Lanka in Asia.

The standard prescription for improving the condition of the poor is, of course, first, their combination in organized pressure groups for more vocal representation of their interests and concerns, and, secondly, self-help, "bottom-up" and "people-centred" development through participatory organizations. The former may be backed by withholding their labour in strikes as a bargaining weapon. For the latter various participatory forms of organization and self-help by the poor can also reduce their dependence, add to their power, help formulate policies, make them more self-reliant and provide some of the resources.

Participation and decentralization are sometimes used more as slogans than as a thought-out strategy. Participation can be both an end in itself and a means to the efficient provision of goods and services. It can take many different forms, such as co-determination (as in German factories), shop-floor participation in workers' councils, financial profit-sharing, collective bargaining, Swiss canton-like voting, representative elections, cooperatives, etc.

Some have claimed that even the market is a form of participation. And small village markets certainly can be, though large anonymous markets are less likely candidates for direct participation. On the other hand, it should be remembered that free, competitive markets, in conditions in which assets are fairly equally distributed and production is conducted in an efficient, labour-intensive manner, do create demand for labour and therefore raise its bargaining power. As the economy progresses, there is growing demand for upgrading skilled labour and this, again, adds to the power of workers.

Some forms of participation are incompatible with democratic government. Mussolini's and pre-Hitler Austria's fascist states took the form of corporate states, in which workers, employers, and farmers participated, being represented in separate chambers. Yugoslavia's Tito got the idea for his worker-managed enterprises from Mussolini's fascist state. Taiwan and South Korea, both authoritarian regimes, have practised successful participation. Democratic government, in which unrepresentative "representatives" are elected, can be a far cry from participatory government. Direct democracies have had short lives. The meetings of the Paris sections of the *sans culottes*, briefly, before Robespierre's fall, the Russian soviets for a brief period, Chinese villages briefly after the revolution, have enjoyed it. The Swiss cantons have lasted longer.

If participation goes together with decentralization, the result is often increased regional inequalities. This happened in Chile under Pinochet, and in China under the Communes. Poorer municipalities could afford only inferior services.

Most forms of participation require central government support. The paramedical personnel chosen from among the villagers need training at the centre. Central legislation is needed to get access to education, health, credit. Without it, local power elites tend to take over decentralized participatory organizations and central countervailing power may be needed to combat them. Finance for participatory institutions often depends on central government.

West Bengal has one of the more successful anti-poverty programmes. Its Communist state government maintained strong central control and replaced local leaders by its own cadres, while simultaneously pursuing a strategy of decentralization. It is a good example of the combination of centralized and decentralized state action.[1]

Another example is the civil rights movement in the USA. Here was indeed a grass-roots movement, with heavy involvement of volunteers. But it depended for its success on strong support by the central government and the Supreme Court. Anyone concerned with the fate of the Blacks in Mississippi would not want to decentralize power to the state of Mississippi. Control by local elites would not be a force for liberation or prosperity. But

---

1. See KAMLA CHOWDRY, 'Poverty, Environment, Development', in *A World to Make; Development in Perspective*, edited by FRANCIS X. SUTTON, New Brunswick and London: Transaction Books, 1990, pp. 137-150 and JUDITH TENDLER's comments, *Ibid.*, pp. 152-154.

mobilization of the Blacks themselves, with the support of central legislation and judicial rulings, can advance their cause.

Similarly in Pakistan the "basic democracies" instituted in the sixties were attempts to decentralize government and to mobilize local people. But the rich landlords took over, without improving the fate of the poor. In Nepal, where political parties were banned, the local elites used the system established under the 1982 Decentralization Act to benefit the richer farmers.

In other cases, however, the interests of local elites coincide with those of the poor, and decentralization then will lead to reform. In India, communities have joined forces to protect themselves against invasion by outsiders who wanted to denude their forests and pollute their rivers. Their defence cut across class lines and decentralization worked for the benefit of the poor.

In small-scale enterprises such as those that have grown up in the Third Italy, and in the informal sector of some developing countries interest alignments do not follow the lines of workers against employers, but buyers against sellers. What has come to be known as flexible specialization has presented quite new constellations of interest, different from those appropriate for the age of mass production.

A unity of interests also exists for educational and health reforms, from which the whole community benefits. But when the allocation of scarce goods is at stake, such as a land reform, agricultural credit, or the distribution of fertilizer, the local elites will tend to undermine the reforms. Even here, however, short-term interests of the rich and their long-term interests, or their perceived and real interests, may be in conflict. In the longer run the higher productivity and production of the poor can benefit the rich, just as an alert, educated, skilled, healthy labour force is beneficial to its employers. Empowerment of the poor can therefore be in the real (as opposed to perceived), and long-term (as opposed to short-term) interest of the rich and powerful.

The South Korean experience of financing universal primary education illustrates how parents, local institutions, the private sector and the national government can combine to produce good results. The government contributes to financing primary schools. Parent-Teacher Associations contributed initially up to

75 per cent of primary school expenses, more recently this has dropped to 28 per cent. (Parents finance the bulk of secondary and tertiary education.) They supplement teachers' salaries and participate in decision-making. Local government contributes 10 per cent.[1]

One of the most successful self-help projects in Africa is the Malawi Rural Water Supply Project. Again, it is based on strong government-community cooperation. It started in 1969 in two villages with 3,000 participants; it now benefits over a million people. The government provides equipment parts and assistance in training, the community the voluntary labour for construction and maintenance.

In the Dominican Republic small coffee farmers have pooled their resources and formed the Nucleus of Coffee Famers Associations. They do their own marketing, and provide credit and training. They are supported by Oxfam, an international NGO.

There is another area in which participation has to be modified. Highly technical decisions, such as those about whether to change the exchange rate (or leave it as it is), or about a weapons system, cannot be left to participatory organizations but must call on experts who, of course, should be accountable to the public.

But experts, doctors, scientists, engineers, bureaucrats, constitute also a power group that can be hostile to human development. The Mandwa project in India is a highly successful rural health care project which foundered on the resistance of the local power structure and medical professionals.[2] Semi-literate village women were selected by village leaders as part-time health workers. The success was striking: birth rates, death rates and infant mortality rates plummeted, and immunizations shot up. But the local richer and more powerful leaders joined hands with the government health services in open hostility and violence and demanded that the project be abandoned. The poor, who had

1. See LAWRENCE SALMEN, *Institutional Dimensions of Poverty Reduction*, Policy, Research, and External Affairs Working Papers, World Bank, May 1990, WPS 411, p. 22.
2. N. H. ANTIA, 'An Alternative Strategy for Health Care: The Mandwa Project', *Economic and Political Weekly*, vol. 20, nos. 51 and 52, December 1985, p. 2257-2260.

greatly benefited, were too dependent on the local power structure to oppose it.

Another qualification is that democracy and participation do not require all individuals to play the role of full-time political animals. There are the limits of time. Oscar Wilde remarked that the trouble with socialism is that it takes too many evenings. The time of women, an under-represented group on many political councils, is particularly scarce. Too much democracy can also kill off democracy. Compromises have to be made.

In spite of the above qualifications and limitations of participation, it is highly desirable to involve the beneficiaries of projects and policies in decisions that affect their lives and work, for at least three reasons, which are also three aspects of human development: participation is an end in itself and expresses the autonomy of the citizens; it makes the projects and policies more responsive to real needs; and it reduces the costs of constructing and maintaining them. A World Bank study found that of twenty-five completed agricultural projects only twelve appeared to be showing long-term benefits. The successful ones developed or strengthened institutional capacities for the participation in management by the beneficiaries.[1]

10. Success Stories

A good example of cost reductions comes from the Baglung district of Nepal. Local bridge committees working under village council auspices, with little outside help (steel cables supplied by UNICEF and a small grant from the central government), constructed 62 suspended bridges covering the whole district in five years. Local materials and artisans were used with unpaid labour and management. The bridges, some as long as 300 feet, cost only

[1]. See MICHAEL CERNEA, 'Farmer Organizations and Institution Building for Sustainable Development', *Regional Development Dialogue*, Nagoya, Japan: U.N. Centre for Regional Development, vol. 8 no. 2, Summer 1987, pp. 1-19. See also NORMAN UPHOFF's assessment of the World Bank's integrated rural development projects in Nepal, Ghana, and Mexico, 'Fitting Projects to People', in MICHAEL CERNEA, ed. *Putting People First: Sociological Variables in Rural Development*, New York: Oxford University Press, 1985, pp. 359-395.

one quarter of what the government had spent, and were built three to four times faster.[1]

A study conducted in the Philippines found that for the same levels of enrolment and quality, schools that relied more heavily on local funding were also more efficient. The savings were done mostly through reducing the costs of personnel.

There are now many examples of successful forms of centrally or externally assisted self-reliance, combining bottom-up and top-down forms of organization that have changed the lives of the villagers. Some of the most successful are in East Asia, such as the Farmers Associations and the Irrigation Associations in Taiwan, and the New Community Movement and the Village Forestry Associations in South Korea. In India the Amul dairy cooperative benefits 5.5 million mainly poor households in 16 states.[2] It is often cited as a highly successful non-governmental grassroots organization. But it was the government of India that drew on it and on the dynamic leadership of Verghese Kurien, for the design of the country's National Dairy Development Programme, known as "Operation Flood". The new programme also drew on people who had worked with the NGO.[3]

The Grameen Bank in Bangladesh has achieved world fame with its new approaches to credit for the landless and near-landless, and for women, its use of peer pressure for repayments, and its splendid 96 per cent repayment record. Within two years over 300,000 poor people have raised their incomes by 30 per cent on average. Although started in 1976 as a private voluntary organization, it was established by government order in 1983 and 25 per cent of its capital is owned by the government. The secret of its success is that it brings banking to the poor, often illiterate villagers,

1. See NORMAN UPHOFF, 'Assisted Self-Reliance' (below, p. 265, n. 1), and PRANCHANDA PRADHAN, *Local Institutions and People's Participation in Rural Public Works in Nepal,* Ithaca, N.Y.: Rural Development Committee, Cornell University, 1980.

2. See A. H. SOMJEE, *Development Theory: Critiques and Explorations,* New York: St Martin's Press, 1991; A. H. SOMJEE and GEETA SOMJEE, 'Cooperative Dairying and the Profiles of Rural Change in India', in *Economic Development and Cultural Change,* vol. 26, n. 3, April 1978 and A. H. SOMJEE and GEETA SOMJEE, *Reaching Out to the Poor,* London: Macmillan, 1989.

3. See SAMUEL PAUL, *Managing Development Programs: The Lessons of Success,* Boulder, Colorado: Westview Press, 1983.

instead of expecting them to come to the bank. Here again, as with the Amul Dairy project, the government replicated its success nationwide, leaving the leadership to its founder, Professor Yunus.[1]

Yet, the Grameen Bank covers only a small proportion of poor women. One reason for its slow rate of expansion lies in the scarcity of village workers. Even of those trained, many leave, and the recruitment of new staff is difficult. Another reason is to be found in the correct resistance by Professor Yunus to have the government's objectives imposed on him and his bank. While government backing in some areas is crucial to the success of NGOs, in others it can be a cause of failure.

Another successful NGO in Bangladesh is the Bangladesh Rural Advance Committee (BRAC), which has organized cooperatives for women and the landless, work projects for the poor, and education in basic literacy, numeracy and social studies for the children of poor households, in vocational training for women, in organizational training for local leaders, in specialized skills for paramedical personnel, and in literacy for adults.

In Nepal, the Small Farmer Development Programme has made credit and technical assistance available to 45,000 households. In northern Pakistan, the Agha Khan Rural Support Project has promoted self-help in over 500,000 communities, improving the lives of about 400,000 people in remote areas hardly served by the government. This was done through their own village organizations. In Sri Lanka, participatory irrigation management, rehabilitated with USAID assistance, has been extended to all major irrigation schemes.

Other examples can be cited from the Philippines, where the National Irrigation Administration, with Ford Foundation assistance, devised participatory irrigation management; from Thailand, where a national programme of evaluating data and participatory development for meeting basic needs has been designed by a provincial governor; from Malawi, where 2,000 villages are served by a gravity-flow system of piped water supply,

---

1. See MAHABUB HOSSEIN, *Credit for Alleviation of Rural Poverty: The Grameen Bank in Bangladesh,* International Food Policy Research Institute Research in collaboration with the Bangladesh Institute of Development Studies, Washington, D.C., Report 65, February 1988.

constructed and maintained by communities with assistance from the government and donors; from Zimbabwe, where a rural savings movement has mobilized deposits of over $ 2 million and farmers' associations have spread the new varieties of seeds and raised agricultural output; from Kenya, where the *harambee* self-help movement, with government contributions, mobilizes funds and labour in rural areas; from Burkina Faso, Mali, Senegal, where a network of grassroots organizations, based on traditional work groups known as *naams*, create jobs and incomes during the dry season, and from many other countries.[1]

Participation has frequently to be combined with help by central, provincial or local government, private firms and voluntary organizations. It is much to be preferred if there are several of these channels, so that the poor do not have to depend on a single agent and can exercise options between different institutions. These may also be strengthened by promoters, facilitators, animators, or similar agents of change, knowledge about whose role has been growing recently. The relationship between all these agents should be one of mutual learning and understanding.

An outstanding example of a successful participatory non-governmental organization that has politically organized very poor people is the Self-Employed Women's Association (SEWA), based in Ahmedabad, in Gujarat, India. It was founded in 1973 by Mrs Ela Bhatt who is its General Secretary. Its members are poor, illiterate women from the informal sector – junk dealers, street hawkers, domestic servants, artisans, sellers of scrap clothing, basket weavers, producers of handicraft, prostitutes – who have through self-help efforts and political action enormously improved their lot. It has established a cooperative bank and formed cooperatives for specialized activities. Its aims are both political and economic. The people the organization fought were not the conventional exploiters, capitalist employers, but money

---

1. See NORMAN UPHOFF, 'Assisted Self-Reliance: Working With, Rather than For, the Poor', in *Strengthening the Poor: What Have We Learned?*, John P. Lewis and contributors, U.S.-Third World Policy Perspectives, no. 10, Overseas Development Council, New Brunswick and Oxford: Transaction Books, 1988. See also for examples from Latin America ALBERT HIRSCHMAN, *Getting Ahead Collectively: Grassroots Experiences in Latin America,* New York, Oxford: Pergamon Press, 1984.

lenders, middlemen, merchants and the government. The government had discriminated against both the informal sector and women in providing credit, technology, and information. The local government and the police evicted them from the streets, or extracted bribes. SEWA also remained independent of, and was sometimes in opposition to, other large-scale organizations, such as trade unions, political parties and big firms.

Superficially, SEWA looks like a case of pure conflict between a poor people's organization and the government. But although elements of conflict are clearly present, SEWA also depended on the government for subsidized credit through the nationalized banks, for market outlets in government shops of their handicrafts, for purchases of their vegetables by government hospitals and prisons, and other services. At SEWA's suggestion, the government created a maternity benefit scheme and backed a life insurance scheme for self-employed women.[1] A state minister backed the fight for higher piece rates for scrap clothing sold to merchants, and the government responded to pressure to make the Plan more responsive to the needs of self-employed women and set up a commission on the subject. Mrs Ela Bhatt, the moving spirit behind SEWA, is now a member of the Indian Planning Commission. In spite of all these positive, unadvertised, links to the government, SEWA has remained autonomous and has not become an arm of the state.

The benefits of participation, and the need for government or donor support, are now beginning to be well understood. It is no longer believed that, for social reforms to occur, it is necessary and sufficient to seize the central power of the state. But the precise level for specific decisions (central, province, local or participatory), the combination of government, markets, NGOs and self-help organizations, the allocation between financing and providing the goods and services, and the precise division between central, external, and locally generated finance, the blend between cooperation and conflict, the need for accountability and democratic control, and the phasing of the decisions, all raise complex questions, the answers to which will vary from case to case.

1. See BISHWAPRIYA SANYAL, 'Sailing Against the Wind: A Treatise in Support of Poor Countries' Governments', typescript, October 1990, Cambridge, Mass.: MIT.

11. Guardians of Rationality and Trustees for the Poor

As we have seen, but it is worth repeating, the state is normally neither monolithic nor impervious to outside pressures (including pressures for rational and altruistic policies). Governments consist of many departments, ministries and agencies, and many layers, from central government via provincial (or in a federation state) government to village and town councils. Power is divided between the legislature, the judiciary and the executive. Each of these pulls in a different direction and the final outcome is the result of these forces. Pressure groups can influence these outcomes. Economists, and other professional groups committed to certain standards, action groups, the churches, voluntary organizations, can constitute themselves as both "guardians of rationality" and "trustees for the poor".[1] In the latter capacity they exercise influence on policies aiming at reducing poverty; in the former on policies that do not waste resources in an attempt to distort their allocation in favour of special interest groups. It is not their function to acquiesce in the results of the free play of market forces.

Sometimes showing that the interests of a group can be more effectively pursued by other, more benign, and fewer means can win acceptance. The military may not be convinced by the greater social value of village pharmacies than that of tanks, but they may be persuaded if its own objective, viz. security, can be shown to be achieved with fewer weapons. Channelling expenditure from swords to ploughshares, and from tanks to baby food, can be achieved by showing that national security is served better by a smaller military budget, and then redirecting the resources saved to the social sectors.

In a democracy, if all always acted and voted exclusively in their individual economic self-interest, the poorest 49 per cent of voters would lose. For in order to get a majority it is necessary to bribe only the middle 2 per cent of voters to vote with the top 49 per cent to achieve a majority of 51 per cent. And the top 49

1. See p. 219, n. 1.

per cent have more money for this purpose than the bottom 49 per cent.[1] Of course, the example is highly artificial, because people do not act like this, because people do not know to which percentile they belong, and because redistributive policies cannot be targeted precisely, and even if they could, because they have also indirect effects. Nevertheless, there is some evidence that in democracies there is, indeed, redistribution towards the middle, and little redistribution towards the poor, except in times of war. But the assumption of purely selfish voting is too unrealistic, and many quite well-off citizens, at least as voters, do show concern for the poor and vote for measures that reduce their poverty. "Welfare payments" may have acquired a bad name, but reducing the number of malnourished children or helping single mothers has great general appeal, as the 1990 UNICEF Economic Summit on children showed.

It is the middle income groups, including civil servants, military officers, workers in the urban organized sector, teachers, doctors, engineers, lawyers, university students, whose incomes may have to be reduced, or their growth slowed down, and who are also the most vocal and influential political groups. These groups are open to appeals to solidarity and patriotism, and they can be enlisted as trustees for the poor. In launching such appeals, it is helpful if any burdens that have to be accepted are seen to be equally and equitably shared, by the bureaucrats and the politicians as well as by the rest.

A free press is important in avoiding famines.[2] Starvation comes with autocracy. A. K. Sen has demonstrated this in his comparison of India and China. Zimbabwe also escaped famine during the drought of 1982-84 because of its relatively free press, one of the most active in Africa. On the other hand, submerged malnutrition, which over a longer period has demanded more victims than a famine, is not so eye-catching and newsworthy, and India has suffered from it more than China. And the Sudan had a famine when it still had a democratic regime.

1. See ROBERT NOZICK, *Anarchy, State and Utopia,* New York: Basic Books, 1974, pp. 274-275. As Nozick points out, other coalitions are possible.

2. See AMARTYA K. SEN, 'How is India Doing?', *New York Review of Books,* vol. 29, December 1982, and DRÈZE and SEN, *Hunger and Public Action.*

12. The Political Economy of Phasing the Transition

Should the transition from a wasteful, repressive, inhuman regime to a strategy of rational allocation and human concerns be sudden or gradual? Shock therapies have recently been recommended to East European countries in their transition from centrally planned to market economies. It has been said it would not be wise to attempt jumping over an abyss in two successive steps. It is certainly true that the shock approach can be appropriate in an economy that responds quickly and flexibly to changes in policies, in which signals are speedily heeded, incentives work in desirable directions, and the flow of resources responds quickly, that has provisions to look after its victims, in which external assistance is plentiful, and the demand for whose exports is high and expanding. If there is spare capacity in the sectors into which workers are to be redeployed, if foreign capital is rapidly repatriated, and if cuts in consumption can soon be reversed or in which those worst affected can be rescued, shock treatment may well be best. This is not the case in most African economies, nor in many others.

It is also true that sudden shocks may lend credibility to government intentions, without which the measures may not be sustainable, and that gradual and slow reforms provide more scope for oppositions to be formed, for hostile coalitions to be organized, and for opportunities for evasion to occur. But sometimes there is stronger opposition to sudden and large changes. There have been massive protests, riots and coups d'état in response to sudden and large cuts in consumption, employment, and output. Gradual change can be carried out with less pain and less opposition. In the context of a growing economy, resources can be reallocated between sectors without the need to dismiss workers; it is sufficient not to replace those that drop out as a result of age, death, or voluntary retirement. The same is true of capital equipment. There will be less need to scrap good machines; it will be sufficient not to replace them when they wear out. If general food subsidies are to be reduced in order to concentrate them on the poor, a gradual phasing out will be accompanied by increases in the supply of food, so that the sufferers from the price increase are somewhat cushioned. The avoidance of deprivation and extreme hardships will also reduce the chances of racial, ethnic and religious strife, and contribute to a more peaceful society. One of the great merits of economic growth is that it makes change and adjustments easier, less painful, to bear.

Restructuring for reform imposes strains and costs on some people. They may become unemployed and lose their source of income and self-respect, while the society loses their productive contribution. If the society does not have a social safety net to catch these victims of the reform process, suffering can be great, and political opposition to the reforms can mount. The effects of economic policies are never certain, and a gradual approach makes it easier to reverse course when errors are made. International support is often crucial in deciding on the speed of change. It has to be large enough to induce leaders to accept the risks of reform, but not so large as to make them avoid the necessary domestic measures. The reforms in Sri Lanka in 1977-1979 provide an example of how aid, combined with favourable economic conditions, can permit reforms towards more targeted policies to be carried out successfully.[1] The reforms in late 1980 in Jamaica under Prime Minister Seaga were less successful, in spite of international support, because of a failure in determination to implement painful domestic measures, such as devaluing the currency and reducing the civil service.

13. The Politics of Aid

Aid policies, just like domestic policies, are motivated by political pressures, national interests, idealism and human solidarity. Military security, altruistic and Machiavellian motives or profit-seeking export interests can inspire foreign assistance policies. It would be one-sided to criticize national policies for being subjected to political constraints without looking at international efforts in the same light. And it would be remiss in

1. See JOAN M. NELSON, 'The Political Economy of Stabilization: Commitment, Capacity and Public Response', *World Development*, vol. 12 no. 10, October 1984, pp. 1000-1005.

making recommendations about the redirection of aid, not to say anything about how political constraints can be overcome. Business interests are behind the provision of inappropriate, capital-intensive technologies, and the interests of consultancy and training firms behind the provision of inappropriate technical assistance. Denmark and Sweden have bought off the business lobby by earmarking a fixed percentage of the aid programme for programmes of interest to businesses and the donor country.[1] The answer to the pressures from consultancy firms and training institutions lies in decentralizing technical assistance programmes to the donor offices in the developing countries. The local representatives who are in continual touch with the needs of the people of the recipient countries are more likely to choose the right local people.

The interests of banks that have lent to developing countries and are eager to have their debts serviced are clearly partly behind the switch in donor policies from project aid to programme lending. The policy conditionality that accompanies such lending is, as I have already said, often based on the premature crystallization of flawed orthodoxies. Unfortunately or fortunately, depending on whose point of view one takes, policies, like projects, are substitutable for one another, and it is sometimes not difficult for the recipient country to evade the conditions imposed, particularly since the time period of the impact of policy changes is much longer than that of the disbursement of the loans.

It is often said that aid is inevitably given in the national self-interest of the donor country; it is just a branch of foreign policy. A lot depends, of course, on how narrowly or broadly national self-interest is interpreted. It is, however, noteworthy that countries like Holland, Sweden, and Norway, whose aid programmes are inspired by moral concerns of human solidarity, have given more aid, and of a better quality, than countries like the USA and the UK, which have defended aid in terms of national self-interest. Australia conducted a public opinion survey which showed that people regard aid as an expression of human solidarity.

1. See PAUL MOSLEY, 'Increased Aid Flows and Human Resource Development in Africa', UNICEF, International Child Development Centre, Innocenti Occasional Paper no. 5, August 1990.

Frequently NGOs and action groups agitate for more and better quality aid. Expanding the role of NGOs would help in reducing the bias in favour of large projects that create few jobs, and might raise aid effectiveness. To some extent this has occurred. But NGOs might object to becoming too dependent on government funds and government objectives. This objection might be met by expanding government contributions to NGOs more slowly, so that they can keep in step with non-governmental contributions, and by encouraging them to preserve their autonomy.

The obstacles to restructuring aid policies to the priority sectors often do not lie with outside pressure groups but have to be sought within aid ministries. Reducing conditionality would reduce the amount of work to be done by the donor, but would also reduce leverage. It could be replaced by actually giving aid only to those who have shown a commitment to human development policies. The news would soon spread. Quiet signalling can be more effective than ham-fisted conditionality.

An objection to supporting human development programmes consisting of primary education, primary health care, and family planning, that has sometimes been raised by aid ministries, is that they involve supporting recurrent expenditure, with the complaint that they present a bottomless pit, indefinite donor commitment. The answer should lie in designing strategies with gradually growing recipient contributions, or with self-liquidating cost-recovery over a specified period. This may be accompanied by jointly working out new sources of tax revenue to finance the human development projects, for which cost recovery would be wrong.

14. International Support

The international community can be mobilized both as a pressure group and as a source of finance for human development. Feeding and educating deprived children has a powerful appeal to human beings everywhere. A well-designed human development programme in a poor country can count on support by citizens from all countries. Eliminating hunger and starvation in the world can be regarded as a public good, and providing each hu-

man being born into this world with the potential for the full development of his or her capacities is part of the enlightened self-
interest of all mankind.

The United Nations Children's Fund (UNICEF) has been a
highly successful pressure group for protecting the poor, and
particularly children and pregnant women, in the adjustment
processes that had been initiated in the 1980s. Since 1985 it has
propagated the use of growth charts and growth monitoring,
oral rehydration, breast feeding and inoculation as cheap and
effective methods of dramatically reducing child mortality and
improving children's health. Through its book *Adjustment with a
Human Face*,[1] and through its dialogues with the International
Monetary Fund and the World Bank, its pro-poor advocacy
influenced the policies on conditionality of these two institutions
and other donors away from a merely technical, economic approach for stabilization and balance of payments corrections,
towards a more humane, compassionate approach, concerned
with the human and social dimensions of stabilization and adjustment. It also drew attention to the need and the political
advantages of protecting the poor (by a form of compensation)
from the burdens of adjustment. There were, of course, individuals and groups inside these institutions and in some developing
countries that had been responsive to pro-poor policies and that
had been continuing the traditions of the basic needs strategy of
the 1970s.

The success of UNICEF in getting governments to restructure
their expenditure has been due not only

1. to the general appeal of improving children's health, but
also

2. to the low costs at which substantial improvements can be
achieved,

3. to external financial support for these measures, and

4. to the fact that they included many children in the middle-
income groups.

On the other hand, the political benefits to governments of the
special campaigns that accompanied these drives may not be

---

1. CORNIA, JOLLY and STEWART, *op. cit.*

applicable to other areas with less public appeal, more narrow targeting to the poor, fewer resources contributed by other sectors such as the military, and less external finance.

Donors have funded programmes that compensate the poor during adjustment periods. The best known are the Bolivian Emergency Social Fund (ESF), started in 1986, and the Ghanaian Programme of Action to Mitigate the Social Costs of Adjustment (PAMSCAD), which started in 1988. These are programmes of employment creation through local public works, credit creation and social services. They are mainly intended to be temporary and for workers dismissed from the tin mines in Bolivia and from the over-staffed public sector in Ghana. Local communities and NGOs play an important part in proposing and designing these programmes. Bolivia's ESF in particular involved minimum government involvement and full delegation to local communities and private contractors. Another similar scheme is the Economic Management and Social Action Programme in Madagascar. It includes measures to provide drugs and support family planning. The projects are broadly targeted so as to gain wide political support. The World Bank is planning similar programmes for many other countries.

The Bolivian and Ghanaian programmes have been criticized because the foreign funds were not additional to other aid, and in any case quite small compared with Bolivia's debt service and the drop in the world price of Ghana's principal export, cocoa. A second ground for criticism is that the poorest among the dislocated did not benefit. However, in countries like Bolivia and Ghana, with so many poor people, it is hard not to benefit some poor people with almost any scheme. A deeper criticism is that both projects are remedial to adjustment measures, whereas the desirable policy would incorporate human concerns right from the beginning in the very structure of the adjustment process.

If a country that has in the past neglected human development intends to adopt reforms that promote it, it runs into short-term problems. These may take the form of heavy burdens on the budget and on administration, or of political discontent and riots by those who are likely to lose from the reforms. If there is redistribution of income to the poor, there is likely to be an additional impetus to inflation arising from the sectors producing goods (especially food) on which the poor spend their money, because their supply is inelastic in the short run. This may be accompanied by unemployment in the trades that had previously catered for the rich, because it takes time to shift resources. There may be a reduction in productive investment and balance of payments problems caused by additional food imports and capital flight, as the rich try to get their money out of the country. If a reform-minded government replaces a dictatorship, previously oppressed groups will assert their claims for higher incomes, with additional inflationary results. If some groups become disaffected they may organize strikes, sabotage or even coups d'état. All these are familiar troubles for reform-minded governments that wish to change the course of policy in favour of the poor.

In such critical situations the international community can help in making the transition less painful and disruptive, and more likely to succeed. It can help to overcome an important obstacle to reform – the fear that the cost of the transition to more appropriate policies is too high. It can add flexibility and adaptability to otherwise inert policies set on a damaging course. Structural adjustment loans have come to be accepted in other contexts, such as the transition to a more liberal international trade regime and more market-oriented domestic policies. By an extension of the same principle, adjustment loans, or, better, adjustment assistance in the form of grants, should be given to the transition to a more human development-oriented regime. They can take the form of financial or technical assistance to a land reform, or a tax reform, or of well-designed food aid or of international food stamps. An international economic order built on international support of domestic efforts for human development is more sensible and more likely to succeed than one built on the hope of trickle-down effects.

Combining development aid with conditions for policy reform, poverty alleviation, social objectives, reform of governance and political freedom has become popular among bilateral and multilateral donors. The concessionary component in the assistance buys, as it were, the policies that a purely commercial lender cannot insist on. It is controversial how desirable and feasible such conditionality is. Some observers have said that conditions can be imposed only if the recipient government is in any case committed to the policies. Complaints have been voiced that conditionality imposed by foreigners is intrusive, incompatible with national sovereignty, and can be counter-productive if it discredits domestic groups aligned with such reforms. It can also be evaded by substituting other undesirable policies for the ones eliminated by conditionality. The same objectives can be achieved by adopting a quieter style than imposing performance criteria, by supporting regimes determined to promote human development, withdrawing aid from those that do not, and thereby signalling unobtrusively to all the conditions for receiving aid.

15. The Struggle for Human Progress

It has taken the more enlightened advanced societies three centuries to achieve the civil, political, and social dimensions of human development. The eighteenth century established *civil* rights: from freedom of thought, speech and religion to the rule of law. In the course of the nineteenth century *political* freedom and participation in the exercise of political power made major strides, as the right to vote was extended to more people. In the twentieth century the welfare state extended human development to the *social* and *economic* sphere, by recognizing that minimum standards of education, health, nutrition, well-being and security are basic to the civilized life, as well as to the exercise of the civil and political attributes of citizenship. These battles had not been won easily or without resistance. Each progressive thrust has been followed by reactionary counter-thrusts and setbacks.[1]

The struggle for *civil* liberty was opposed, after the French Revolution, by those fearful that it could lead only to tyranny; the fight for *political* participation for fear that it would bring about enslavement to the masses. We are now witnessing one of

---

1. See ALBERT O. HIRSCHMAN, *The Rhetoric of Reaction: Perversity, Futility, Jeopardy,* Cambridge, Mass.: The Belknap Press of Harvard University Press, 1991.

these counter-attacks on the *economic* liberties of the welfare state, and on some fronts partial retreat. The arguments again are that the opposite of the intended results is achieved. Just as civil liberty was said to lead to tyranny, and political liberty to slavery, so compassionate public concern for the poor, it is now argued, can lead only to their pauperization. We know that human progress is possible, though not inevitable, on all three fronts.

DISCUSSION

JAGDISH BHAGWATI*

Paul Streeten's Lectures are to be applauded doubly. They are a worthy tribute to a gifted man. They are also an eloquent testimony to Streeten's own talents and accomplishments, both considerable. Here we have the richness of Streeten's ideas, evidence of an intellectually curious scholar reaching out into several disciplines and successfully blending insights from them and his enormous practical experience in the developing countries into a stimulating work.

How does one select from this menu of ideas, all interesting and worthy of debate? Perhaps I can focus on the central unifying theme which I believe underlies the many things that Streeten says. This, evidently, is the theme of the role of the state. Streeten considers this in relation to both domestic and international aspects of the question.

At the outset, I should note that there is a fundamental symmetry in the way domestic and international issues can be analysed. One can think of the international economy as consisting of interactions between nation states just as the nation state is composed of different domestic agents. This makes for a natural comparative advantage for trade theorists when questions of domestic income distribution are at stake. Since trade theorists quite naturally look at national impacts, positive and normative, their models and methods of analysis provide the natural general-equilibrium tools for analysing domestic income-distributional questions.[1] By constrast, the theorists of general equilibrium, outside of international economics, are not trained to think of constituent units or agents at all!

On the other hand, as Streeten argues, there is an asymmetry in his approach to the domestic and the international aspects of the role of the state as well. For the domestic arena, Streeten thinks that the state needs to play an active role. The bulk of his argumentation is directed against those who would like a

* Russel Sage Foundation, New York.
1. The parallels are not complete, of course. Thus, while trade theory has been extended to cases where a nation has within it, not just domestic but also foreign productive factors, there is no counterpart to such theoretical in the domestic context.

minimalist state. On the other hand, Streeten would like to disarm the state in favour of international cooperation, brought about in all kinds of ways and for all kinds of problems. In the international arena, Streeten sees sovereignty as perhaps an obstacle that one needs to surmount to achieve public good. A soft state abroad, but a purposive state at home, represents the kind of political-cum-economic preference that Streeten's analysis suggests.

I will focus mostly on the domestic aspect here. The key question for analysis is: why has minimalism surfaced as the fashionable viewpoint today, especially in relation to the developing countries? Of course, for those of us who have read beyond the technicalities of economics, it is not surprising that laissez faire was hardly ever the preferred position of even Adam Smith. Streeten cites Sen on how Adam Smith's greatness is diminished by suggesting that he was interested only in selfishness as the primary motivation of human beings and in laissez faire as the arrangement for human society. I believe that Sen misses the point. Adam Smith is justly celebrated for showing how selfishness could be harnessed by economic arrangement to provide public good. If he had shown instead that *altruism* was good for humankind, it is unlikely that he would have been applauded for saying the obvious: instead people have made their reputation by showing that the road to hell is paved with good intentions. The scientific world loves the counterintuitive! And it is well in this context to recall instead the wise saying of Alfred Marshall:

"Progress chiefly depends on the extent to which the *strongest* and not merely the *highest* forces of human nature can be utilised for the increase of social good".[1]

Adam Smith and Jeremy Bentham, the great utilitarian, were not for the abolition of the state; each saw a role for state action. Unlike the anarchist Bakunin, both saw the need for the state to provide the infrastructure of the military, the judical system *et al.* There is even the famous prescription of Adam Smith urging state provision of education to the masses who would be otherwise turned into automatons and morons by work in the new factories.

---

1. Quoted by Dennis H. Robertson in Robert Leachman, ed., *National Policy for Economic Welfare at Home and Abroad*, New York: Doubleday, 1955.

Except for the extreme fringe, therefore, the question has been, not whether the state should intervene, but how. In the developing countries, the debate has been particularly sharp because their very backwardness and their economic ambition to catch up have led to a great compulsion to intervene over a very wide range of activity: a phenomenon that the great economic historian Alexander Gerschenkron first identified clearly. By now, we have almost four decades of postwar experience with state action for development. And that experience has promted the minimalist position that Streeten critically opposes.

The problem is that, while economic theory suggests several reasons why the state should intervene, pratical experience appears to have been that the Visible Hand has often done worse than the Invisible Hand.

The theory of the Invisible Hand certainly shows that there are several reasons why markets will fail. Externalities and incomplete markets add up to an endless number of reasons why markets do not work efficiently. Economists have made their reputation since the time of Adam Smith, showing how the Invisible Hand is frail and needs to be held; or, as Joan Robinson used to say, the Invisible Hand often works by strangulation.

But now, especially after economists have studied how intervention works in reality, there is immense scepticism about the advisability of state intervention. At the theoretical level, prompted by these studies, there are two types of reactions: either that imperfections do not add up to a hill of beans and should be ignored; or that intervention will make things worse. The latter, because the state may be predatory, or ill-informed, or simply captured by special interests so that the intervention will be of a kind that has no relationship to the welfare-improving interventions divised by economists for benign governments that can do no wrong. All this adds up to a prescription for caution.

At the level of the experience in the developing countries, the caution about state intervention has been given a sharp focus because of the abundance of evidence of the perversity of such intervention and the costs imposed by it. Both the extent and the nature of the intervention have given us pause. In fact, there is so much state intervention in evidence in several of the developing countries and so little left to judicious use of markets that a wit has been led to observe that the problem has been that the Invisible Hand is nowhere to be seen. The result of these studies is a degree of shock for those of us (including myself) who recommended a variety of judicious interventions only to see the state mushroom into a Frankenstein's Monster that had no resemblance to what had been suggested.

The case of Indian development is perhaps the best illustration of this situation that has prompted a shift to minimalism. Indian planning was motivated by the early theories of investment allocation into creating a licensing machinery and a set of planned targets for industry and other activities that reflected some kind of "optimal" allocation of scarce resources. In reality, all this turned into a Kafkaesque control machinery, rigid in its economic conception and corrupting in its politics. Equally, we pushed for the growth of public enterprises on the ground that they would generate surpluses for the state for investment. In reality, given the nature of the state, they became a source of major losses that would hurt India's savings effort badly and help precipitate a crisis. Streeten argues that there is nothing *necessary* about this outcome. Yes, I agree. But in economics we must deal with "central tendencies": and here, surely, we must accept the fact that, while theoretically one can conceive of efficiently run public enterprises (as we in fact did in the 1950s), the state structure and the way in which these enterprises are going to be functioning in the political milieu make it highly probable that they will work exactly the way they turned out to.

Of course, the reaction of many economists, observing this experience with state intervention in the poor countries and reflecting on the matter thoeretically, has been to recoil altogether and often overshoot in the other direction, of an extremely minimalist state. Evidently, the pendum will swing again, restoring a more centrist view.

But, from a theoretical viewpoint, I must say that the experience of the postwar period has certainly activated a great deal of serious thinking about political-economy-theoretic argumentation in economics. We are now far more interested in questions of institutional design of policy intervention, for example, than before. Thus, in international trade policy, theorists are properly concerned now about questions such as: if quotas are permitted rather than tariffs to allow protection, will they lead to more or less excess protection; are the "fair trade" mechanisms which are usually captured for protectionist purposes, better insulated from such capture if they are within binational or multinational frameworks of adjudication than if they are in national jurisdiction as hitherto; and so on. Equally, there are issues of legislative design: the division of tariff-making resposibility between the executive responsive to national interest and the legislature responsive to constituency interest can critically affect the outcome of politics and import penetration in regard to free trade and protection. Clearly, this kind of "constitutionalism" is of importance in advising the old socialist countries that seek to construct new constitutions that would preserve freer trade.

Streeten's thoughts on the international issues are equally stimulating. His main focus is on how we are to achieve the cooperative solutions that an uncoordinated set of nation states would otherwise fail to achieve. There are doubtless a number of areas where public good requires the reaching of such cooperative solutions. According to the Kindleberger hegemonic theory, the hegemon provides the public good, as did Britain in the nineteenth century and the USA in the twentieth. Kindleberger is correct historically. But the experience does not prove, of course, that hegemons are *necessary* to create the cooperative outcome. In fact, much of recent political theory is addressed to the question as to how cooperation can develop under "anarchy".

It seems to me that the question of a hegemon is not altogether obsolete now. With the decline of the Soviet Union, the USA has emerged as a *de facto* unitary superpower. Undoubtedly it has diminished relatively, the rise of Japan and the EC certainly makes its economic dominance less. However, its consciousness that it has diminished thus makes the USA more eager to flex its muscle in a variety of situations, including the provision of public goods. By drawing on a immense array of incentives and disincentives, it can put together multilateral coalitions in favour of its own conceptions of what the public good is: as over the Uruguay Round multilateral trade negotiations and over the anti-Iraq UN action.

In this situation, perhaps the important question may well be not whether public goods will be provided under anarchy but whether in a new order where the USA has returned to being a political hegemon but a diminished economic giant conscious of its diminution, we will get public goods provided by the USA or public bads (which happen to be private goods for special interests in the USA).

The Uruguay Round illustrates this issue very well. The agenda of the Round includes several US demands, now conceded after US unilateral threats and bilateral sweetheart deals (e.g. with Taiwan on sanctions and with Mexico as part of the Free Trade Area negotiations, in the matter of intellectual property protection that goes well beyond what many economists think may be optimal), which are not necessarily in the international interest. This sort of question is hardly ever raised in the US discussions of trade policy; but it is central to worrying about the matter of the provision of public goods, especially when the very definition of what a public good is in an area is a matter of dispute and judgment.

If indeed there are legitimate differences of opinion on what a public good is, say on the nature and amount of intellectual property protection, then there is a real question: should not the international process of institution-building allow for greater continuity of diversity? Defining the problem simply as one of devising methods to provide a public good that is already agreed upon to be a public good may then not be enough.

I believe that an increasing number of problems will fall into this area in the future. For example, environmental issues that are of purely domestic jurisdiction (i.e. they do not involve physical spillovers into other nations as with acid rain or ozone layer depletion) are increasingly being forced into the framework of international regulation, with the advanced countries with economic and political power trying to use trade sanctions as instruments to impose their own views and policies of the "public good" on poorer nations.

Finally, I should mention one problem of nation sovereignty that Streeten does not address fully. This is the question of immigration. Since communities and nations tend to define themselves by exclusion, this is a hard area in which to get nations to surrender any degree of sovereignty. Yet, the enormous numbers of refugees, illegal immigrants and even legal migrants (growing at times due to family reunification imperatives) have made it imperative that the matter be brought increasingly under international monitoring. We have the IMF, the World Bank and the GATT. We need also a WMO: the World Migration Organization. The UNHCR is doing a splendid job. But we need to worry about the rights and obligations of legal and illegal migrants. A Code would be some way off. In the meantime, a WMO could write annual reports, just the way GATT has started doing with member countries' trade policies, simply putting together different nations' immigration polices in their entirety, so that we could both shame those who fall short by evolving moral and political criteria into doing more, and move over time towards evolving Codes of "best practice" to which nations may begin to adhere.[1] It is time to mount an assault on this last bastion of almost total sovereignty.

---

1. I have argued for Codes for nearly a decade and was pleased to see that the UN High Commissioner for Refugees, Madame Ogata, has recently begun to endorse them as well. The idea of a WMO to oversee the whole international scene of different types of flows is probably one that many have suggested. The idea of issuing annual reports is inspired by what GATT does and was developed by me recently in a *Christian Science Monitor* op. ed. article.

STUART HOLLAND*

I am personally much indebted to Paul Streeten. It was he who persuaded me to study economics after qualifying in – and already teaching – history and political theory at Oxford.

I tried to resist, telling him that I had already done an economics course at a university in the USA before coming to Oxford, and that I saw no point in spending my life pretending that the correlation of a handful of variables could explain the subtle interrelations which actually change the world.

But he was emphatic, stressing that the only way to challenge the already evident neoclassical bias of economics in the early 1960s was for historians, social theorists and others to qualify in economics, and then join the fray.

I had already read his first book, on economic integration.[1] I liked its style – not only that it was beautifully written, but that it challenged economic and social orthodoxy, and showed an overriding concern for practical outcomes which could benefit people, rather than prove some trivial theorem on artifical assumptions.

The style of the book, like these lectures, has been that of the man himself. They combine humanism with humour; intellect with imagination. Paul has the rare combination of an open mind and global range combined with subtle and close attention to detail. He is a leading scholar within the broad European humanist tradition.

In economics Streeten supports market forces where they work best, but also knows that they in no way guarantee the equation of social and private benefits. He knows that the market means freedom. But he is concerned with freedom *for* self-fulfilment and *to* achieve joint answers to common problems, rather than Hayek's or Friedman's monist concern for freedom *from* the state.

For Paul, as reflected in his early work with Gunnar Myrdal, this meant integrating *values* into economic analysis rather than pretending that economics was a science which was value free. It

*Istituto Universitario Europeo di Firenze.
1. PAUL STREETEN, *Economic Integration*, Leiden: Sythoff, 1962.

also meant strengthening *institutions* which can extend both markets and collective rights, rather than claiming that the state has no role but to diminish the choice of individuals to dispose of their personal income.

Such wide-ranging concern contrasts markedly with the modelling on limited and unreal assumptions in what passes today as mainstream economics.

If still in a minority in the profession, Paul Streeten is in good company in challenging the so-called mainstream.

For instance, the narrowing of the agenda of economics was highlighted some years ago by an analysis of a decade of articles in the *American Economic Review* by Wassily Leontief.

Himself an econometrician, Leontief deplored the fact that over half the *AER* articles were mathematical models without any empirical data and *less than half of one per cent* were articles containing models which used facts researched by the author.

Very similar results can be found from an analysis of the most recent decade of articles in the *European Economic Review*.

The economics acceptable to the so-called mainstream is not about Streeten's agenda of actual people in given societies with specific institutions. It is about a self-generating system of largely unsupported presumption.

It has for some time been conventional to equate such mainstream and "positive" economics, as if mainstream economics were empirically verifiable. However, while the neoclassical mainstream *assumes* that it is playing in an empirically verifiable world, it in fact rarely challenges its assumptions by empirical investigation.

In practice this not only prejudges – and thereby prejudices – perception of reality. It reverses what is supposed to be scientific method itself inasmuch as it does not base its premises on fact. Worse, it tries to change facts to fit its premises

For instance: (1) theoretical premises within the neoclassical model bear little relation to reality – *i.e. the theory does not fit reality;* yet (2) real policy implications have been drawn by some governments and international institutions from the unreal and unverified model – *i.e. policy tries to fit reality to the model.*

This is nowhere more apparent than in that arena in which

Paul Streeten has spent a major part of his professional life: development economics.

In the IMF and the World Bank in the 1980s, the aspirations of nine-tenths of humanity for a chance to join in the benefits of a market system were denied in terms of a dogmatic formula of structural adjustment.

For some time this meant two or more components of a catechism of devaluation, deflation and deregulation imposed on virtually any country irrespective of social needs, or the negative effects on other countries' trade.

The argument is not that no economies need to devalue and deflate for some of the time. But both the Fund and the Bank seemed to lose sight of Keynes's original concern in the note of April 1943 which first set out the case for the Bretton Woods system: i.e.

We need an orderly and agreed method of determining the relative exchange values of national currency units, so that unilateral action and competitive exchange depreciations are prevented.

We need a central institution of a purely technical and non political character, to aid and support other international institutions concerned with the planning and regulation of the world's economic life.

More generally, we need a means of reassurance to a troubled world, by which any country whose own affairs are conducted with due prudence is relieved of anxiety for causes which are not of its own making, concerning its ability to meet its international liabilities.

In particular the Fund and the Bank – through cross conditionality – have so often imposed both devaluation and the lowering of commodity prices as to result in precisely the competitive beggar-my-neighbour depreciations which Keynes wanted to avoid.

With structural adjustment packages introduced in some 90 countries – not least major economies such as Brazil, India and Russia – the results amount to beggar-my-neighbour deflation of world trade and payments.

This is not the place to enter into a detailed evaluation of all Fund and Bank policies. Nonetheless, as evident from the figures published in the Bank's own *Development Report,* the structural adjustment decade of the 1980s has seen a dramatic deterioration of the main economic indicators of Africa, Latin America and the Caribbean relative to the so-called failure years of the Keynesian consensus.

Table 1

The Slow-Down of Production

GDP average annual growth rate (per cent)

	1965–80	1980–90
Low- and middle-income countries	5.9	3.2
Sub-Saharan Africa	4.2	2.1
Middle East & N. Africa	6.7	0.5
Latin America & Caribbean	6.0	0.5
Severely indebted countries	6.3	1.7

Source: IBRD, World Development Report 1992 (Table 2) p. 220.

Table 2

Compressing Consumption

Average annual growth rate (percent)

	General Consumption Government		Private etc. Consumption	
	1965–80	1980–90	1965–80	1980–90
Low- and middle-income countries	7.0	3.5	5.4	3.2
Sub-Saharan Africa	6.8	1.0	4.2	0.8
Middle East & N. Africa	–	–	–	–
Latin America & Caribbean	6.5	4.2	5.9	1.2
Severely indebted countries	7.2	3.9	6.2	1.4

Source: *ibid.* (Table 8), p. 232

Table 3
Collapsing Investment
Average annual growth rate (percent)

	Gross Domestic Investment	
	1965-80	1980-90
Low- and middle-income countries	8.3	2.3
Sub-Saharan Africa	8.7	-4.3
Middle East & N. Africa	–	–
Latin America & Caribbean	8.2	-2.0
Severely indebted countries	9.3	-1.8

Source: *ibid.* (Table 8) p. 232

Moreover, since the early eighties the Fund and the Bank have in no way provided institutions *of a purely technical and non political character* such as Keynes advocated.

Rather, they have implicitly imposed a particular model of the economy and society on those countries in which they demanded structural adjustment packages. Deregulation and privatization were *de rigeur*.

Since the early 1980s the IMF and the World Bank have claimed that bureaucratized public sectors and vested interests obstruct a competitive, market clearing, equilibrium-tending, profit-maximizing system benefiting atomized but potentially sovereign consumers.

Bureaucracies and vested interests there undoubtedly are. Yet the *alternative* system ultimately imposed by the Fund and the Bank on many countries is not empirically or historically based. It only exists in the heads of the ideologues of neoclassical economic theory.

In many cases the Fund-Bank assault on the mixed economy and state welfare policies denies to the developing countries the means by which most of the G7 countries have themselves achieved their own economic development.

What happened in the Fund and the Bank in the eighties was not entirely an accident. In terms of ideas and ideology, it was the outcome of a 30 year journey by mainstream economics into a neoclassical cul-de-sac.

This not only has meant a waste of the best years of their youth for many of those students who wished to do economics in order to better the world.

More damaging still, it has meant a wasteland for those many economies which have been subjected to neoclassical and monetarist ideology in denial of their hopes for sustained development and welfare.

Ironically, it also negates the main concerns of the prophet whom neoclassical economists casually cite but have seldom read – Adam Smith.

It was Smith, rather than Marx or Keynes, who wrote in his *Theory of Moral Sentiments* that:

This disposition to admire and even to worship the rich and the powerful and to despise persons of poor and mean condition is the great and most universal cause of the corruption of our moral sentiments.

This does not deny the observation of Smith in the *Wealth of Nations* that it is not through altruism that the baker gives us bread. Smith knew well that wealth creation is based on self-interest and generates inequality.

But for him the story did not stop there, as it has with the *trickle-down* theorists. He deplored the social effects of such inequality. He also thought something should be done about it by individuals as citizens rather than simply consumers:

He certainly is not a good citizen who does not wish to promote by every means in his power the welfare of the whole society – the whole society – of his fellow citizens [*ibid*].

Smith also argues in the *Theory of Moral Sentiments* that:

It does not follow that a regard to the welfare of society should be the sole virtuous motive of action, but only that in any competition it ought to cast the balance against all other motives.

* * *

In challenging orthodox or mainstream economics for most of his professional lifetime, Paul Streeten's work has been within the grand European tradition of social and political economy: that of not only Smith and others of the Scottish enlightenment, but also of Marx and Veblen, of Schumpeter, Keynes and Kalecki and – not least – Myrdal.

Streeten's contribution enables us to recapture these very rich and very deep veins in the longer tradition of social and political economy, rather than the games – and game theories of models in mainstream economics.

In particular he has shown that abstract mathematical rigour can prove *rigor mortis* when transferred to bodies, institutions and societies to which its techniques and models are not appropriate.

Such an argument, widely made also by Thomas Balogh, is especially relevant in terms of the deflate, devalue and deregulate formula of the Fund and the Bank.

However, what I have always admired about Paul Streeten's work is the way that he is prepared not just to oppose sterile thinking but also to propose creative alternatives, constantly seeking to develop alternative models and paradigms.

This has been an immensely positive dimension of Paul's work. It also relates to the first substantive point of his lectures to which I want to refer, i.e. his unabashed testament for the so-called Utopians.

Paul recognizes that the pragmatists have too much detail and that the Utopians have too little. But in throwing his weight, on balance, in favour of the Utopians, he casts himself in the perspective of those who have contributed most to Western scientific culture.

It is not by sustained empiricism that economics has established its dubious credentials as a science. Nor is it by reference to fact alone that Hobbes, Locke, Rousseau or others have given us the framework of social contract theory, or the aspiration of individuals in society to be able to achieve a greater freedom through joint action than those more limited freedoms which they theoretically can gain as sovereign but atomized consumers in the market.

It is a combination of reaction to facts and aspiration for change which has marked each main step of human progress. In ignoring facts, and hypothesizing a false reality, economics in the last 30 years has regressed rather than progressed.

This is especially evident in the degree to which the new generation of economists trained in mathematics and the physical sciences dismiss social and political issues as unscientific.

Caught in their own mind sets on the virtues of particular techniques, they seem in most part ignorant of Voltaire's critique of the limits of the Leibnitz calculus on which their own neoclassical analysis so much depends.

In *Candide* Voltaire used the figure of Pangloss to parody Leibniz's presumptions that we live in the best of all possible worlds.

The Fund and the Bank admit that structural adjustment hurts, and claim that it has to do so in order to work. Adjustment today will give the best of all possible worlds tomorrow.

The fact that the results have been a scarcely mitigated disaster through the 1980s no more appears to shake their faith than the earthquake disaster in Lisbon shook that of Pangloss.

Moreover, mainstream economics, with its faith on the best possible long run outcome through market forces, either ignores or simply disregards the impoverishment of four-fifths of humanity in the global market economy.

By notable contrast, Paul Streeten has not been part of this mainstream. This has been most evident in the second aspect of his work which I want to stress on social indicators.

Because social indicators concern qualitative factors it is harder to get an agreed index than it is with certain quantitative data.

The work which Paul has done on social indicators with UNDP has been way ahead of most of what has been done so far in other institutions such as the European Community.

Under Keynes's influence, which was benign at the time, we have standardized certain categories of macroeconomic data – trade and output figures etc. – on a monthly basis. But social indicators have not yet been standardized. The work which Paul and others have been doing in UNDP has been genuinely pioneering. It has opened a new frontier which the World Bank – and to a lesser extent the IMF – recently has had to recognize.

If we can take over the mantle of Paul's own work in this area, we should be able to develop a new paradigm for development policy – that development assistance should not be concerned simply with the balance of payments adjustment of countries, but with the degree to which they manage to achieve actual performance in the realization of given social indicators.

Implicit in his argument, this would represent a counter-revolution relative to current IMF and World Bank policies, bringing them back to Keyness own concern that a system should be devised which should enable countries to adjust their payments without resort to deflation of domestic spending and welfare.

A third major point relates to Paul's reference during his second lecture on visible rather than invisible hands – or hand-in-hand rather than arm's length relations between firms.

For instance the relations between firms which work so well in Japan have little to do with the arm's length relations between anonymous units in an atomistic market so beloved of conventional neoclassical theory. In fact they have much more in common with what Albert Hirschman's has called *voice* and *loyalty* rather than a stimulus to efficiency from a threat to *exit* from the buyer-supplier relationship.[1]

Overall, in contrast with the neoclassical assumption that arm's length competition ensures the best of all possible worlds, Japanese economy and society is based on *cooperation* between producers and the state in order to be competitive in the world economy.

Neoclassical economics in a simplist way assumes that any cooperation must be collusive and therefore either economically or socially inefficient.

But for the Japanese, the whole dynamic of such cooperation is innovative, embodied in their term of *kaizen*, meaning constant improvement. The *kanban* just-in-time delivery, which has virtually abolished stocks – and with it the stock cycle – for Japanese producers and some leading distributors, is part of the *kaizen* philosophy.

Such real world models are not simply economic but also social and institutional. They have a historical basis partly in Confucianism but mainly in the manner in which Japanese firms after World War Two found that they needed to cooperate on a

---

1. ALBERT O. HIRSCHMAN, *Exit, Voice and Loyalty: Responses to decline in firms, organisations and states*, Cambridge, Mass.: Harvard University Press, 1970.

visible hand-in-hand basis in order to counter the Fordist economies of scale of the major US and European producers. In this
process they were aided and abetted by a range of national R&D
programmes and local innovation centres sponsored by the Japanese Ministry for Trade and Industry MITI.

Such a model is entirely different from the optimization models of microeconomic producers in an atomistic market assumed
by mainstream neoclassical economic theory.

In fact it is claimed that leading Japanese firms will not promote Western-trained economists over an intermediate level in
case they try to apply such theory in practice and thereby seriously compromise the economic prospects of the company.

But there is a major problem here also for international trade
and payments between countries.

Since relationships in the Japanese economy are based on *loyalty and voice*, there is hardly ever any *exit*. In other words Japanese
firms hardly ever break longstanding contractual relations.
Therefore there is much less chance for foreign firms to enter that
market than there would be if the relationships were based on the
arm's length transactions assumed in Western market models.

This is compounded by the fact that Japanese firms tend to
have their own exclusive distribution outlets. This may well have
meant that the producers concerned wished to exclude other
products by Japanese competitors, or it could be seen in Western
terms as simply wishing to maximize vertical scale economies. Alternatively, the own-product distribution outlet could be seen as
a way of gaining and retaining *loyalty* rather than threatening exit as a sanction to efficiency.

The result is that it is not only difficult but in many cases next
to impossible for many non-Japanese producers of intermediate
goods to penetrate the Japanese market.

The US and European Community may see this as non-tariff
barriers to trade. The Japanese see it not only as the way in which
they have always done business, but as how their culture and society work.

This relates to some of the key points which Paul Streeten has
made in his lectures, and in particular his reference to four different solutions or outcomes for world trading relationships:

1. the GATT solution on liberal trading lines and implying factor price equalization;

2. the Triad solution of negotiated outcomes between the USA, Europe and Japan;

3. alternate or successive hegemons taking over the previous role of the UK in the nineteenth century or the US in the twentieth century;

4. Balkanization and break up of individual economies and their relation to the global trade and payments system.

What concerns me – and I think concerns Paul – is that if one goes for a GATT type factor price equalization model on a global scale, this will not of itself eliminate major asymmetries between Japan and the United States, while it will Balkanize both the reforming and developing economies, neither of whom will be strong enough to enter the global trade and payments system on an equal basis with the companies of the Triad countries.

In other words, solution number one may actually aggravate solution number four. The underlying reasons are not only

i. the cultural, social and institutional barriers to trade such as those evident in Japan, but also

ii. the fact that old style comparative advantage and factor price equalization have by and large been superseded in multinational trade and payments, plus

iii. the inherent disequilibria and asymmetries in the market itself, of the kind brilliantly analysed by Myrdal as *circular and cumulative causation* or *spread and backwash effects,* as well as the fact that

iv. there is no clear alternative hegemon to the USA between Europe and Japan.

There might be an alternative to the USA as global hegemon if Europe and Japan could agree joint rules for mutual action in the international economy.

But so far they are inhibited from this by their different perceptions of the dynamics of the contemporary trade and payments system.

One problem for both the USA and the European Community is the degree to which they are caught in the paradigm of the liberal trade model. This in turn relates to the unscientific nature of most mainstream trade and payments theory.

Such theory as expounded not only in student texts, and by GATT, the IMF and the World Bank, seems simply unwilling to take account of what is actually happening in terms of the formation by the USA and the EC of regional trade blocs as the basis for regional institutions and regional cooperation rather than reliance on liberalization and factor price equalization.

It is crucial in this context to break beyond the bonds of neoclassical assumption and to recognize that Japan, NAFTA and the EC represent potentially positive rather than negative forces for international progress.

In this sense, the three international groupings should be *building blocks* for a new international economic order in which fewer actors or representatives have a better chance of dialogue leading to a positive sum outcome than do many wider voices simply protesting against the inequities of the prevailing international disorder.

The case is not that the future of the global economy should be left to the Triad or the G7 but that the onus for progress in the wider international economy should be thrown onto them, since their decisions will determine the global outcome.

Finally, one of the things that we should bear in mind in our debates on the role of the state and the mixed economy is that such roles can and do change over time.

There are parallels here with the arguments of Friedrich List on tariffs. List was not in favour of infant industry tariffs for ever. He recognized that infants could and should become adolescents and adults and stressed that tariffs should be reduced as they did so to maintain a competitive environment. The same should be the case on the role of the state's intervention in many other spheres such as public ownership of infant industries, or public assistance early in the product cycle.

There also are externalities. For example it has already been claimed that in India before the recent IMF backed liberalization, the state had 70 per cent of the capital stock, 30 per cent of the output and none of the profits.

One might with some reason ask: so what? It may well be argued that the Indian state sector had become bureaucratic, but this is not of itself proved simply by the claim that it is capital intensive and not making a given internal rate of return on such capital.

The illustration would be more effective if it were demonstrated that the state also was not providing external economies of any kind. And even in this case it may be that the state is serving other objectives or social economies which mean that people are under-employed who otherwise would be unemployed and either on susbsistence social welfare of a kind which also involves state expenditure or on the margins of existence with neither jobs, dignity nor welfare.

In practical terms these issues concern not simply economics but also social and political economy.

In analytic terms the dismissal in principle of public intervention and the institutions of the mixed economy needs to be founded on a case-by-case basis by actual analysis. When, as in the hands of the IMF, it amounts to the claim that private markets always are superior to public markets, it become not only dogmatic but an act of faith.

This is not only because the work of Wade and others has clearly shown that the newly industrializing economies of South East Asia – like Japan and most of the G7 – have employed public ownership, public regulation, tariffs, quotas, import controls and other devices to promote their own successful industrialization.[1]

It also is because only an dogmatist could dismiss the public sector out of hand as an institution in civil society.

Compare, for instance, the institutions of the public sector with another institution in civil society such as marriage. Marriage can be good, it can be bad, it can be indifferent, and sometimes you need divorce.

Sometimes, likewise you do need to privatize the state sector. But this of itself no more means that it *always* is right to abolish the public sector or the mixed economy than it would be right to argue that one should abolish marriage as an institution on the grounds that some marriages fail.

* * *

In summary let us be both analytic and synthetic in and between disciplines. Let us certainly be empirical. Let us recognize that

---

1. ROBERT WADE, *The Mixed Economy and Export Led Growth: Lessons from (Capitalist) East Asia*, 1991.

no one model or claimed paradigm should be an act of faith or *auto da fe*.

Above all, let us thank Paul Streeten not only for teaching several of us on the above grounds, but also for the way in which – not least during his period at the World Bank – he continued to argue the case for social and political economy, for building institutions and for investing in people, during a period in the 1980s where this was a minority view.

Some of Paul's own work has received less recognition in the wider public than it deserves. But this may be changing.

He will be aware, as we are, that many of the themes and issues for which he fought then in the eighties now are coming to the fore in the Bank in the nineties.

For instance, in an interesting and critical re-assessment of the dismissal of industrial policy and the mixed economy in its structural adjustment policies in the 1990s, a publication by the Operations Evaluation Department of the World Bank itself recently wrote that:

> A pragmatic view of the determinants of government success or failure should be based on the circumstances of each case. As one distinguished analyst[1] puts it:

> ... governments are neither monolithic nor impervious to outside pressures (including pressures for rational policies and altruism). If there is scope for a positive sum game and if a government can hold on long enough to tax the sum, rationality pays... Power is divided among the legislature, the judiciary and the executive. The obstacle to "correct" policy making is neither solely stupidity nor solely cupidity, neither solely ignorance nor solely political constraints or monolithic selfishness... There are large areas in which a better analysis and a clearer sense of direction would help, just as there are areas where it is fairly clear what should be done, but vested interests, whether those of the policy-makers or of pressure groups on whose support they depend, prevent it from happening.

In this major admission of *mea culpa* by the World Bank, Paul Streeten is the only economist to be cited in any quotation at all.

---

1. PAUL STREETEN, Review of T. Killick, A Reaction Too Far, *Economic Development and Cultural Change*, 39, 1991, p. 425.

Against the mainstream, he clearly has contributed to reversing the course of thought and action in one of the most important international institutions in the world.

Not least Paul's work, example and concern for others less distinguished than himself has embodied a genuine moral sympathy for individuals and for the human condition.

Adam Smith would clearly recognize and welcome in him the qualities which he advocated in his *Theory of Moral Sentiments,* and especially those of:

"A good citizen who wishes to promote, by every means in his power, the welfare of the whole society of his fellow citizens".

PAOLO SYLOS LABINI[*]

My comments refer to four of the many topics discussed by Paul Streeten in his lectures: 1) the complementarity between state and market; 2) the complementarity between large and small firms; 3) the question of institutional innovations to promote the development of backward countries and 4) Adam Smith and the theory of economic development.

Let us begin with the first topic.

1. Complementarity between State and Market

Paul Streeten points out that, under certain conditions, relations between the private and the public sector are largely conflictual or even – as the public choice school puts it – exploitive of citizens in general for the benefit of politicians and bureaucrats representing the state. However, for a variety of reasons – among which we find mutual interest, the search for consensus or the fear of popular revolt – in several circumstances state and market can fruitfully complement each other. To be sure, the optimum combination of state and market varies in the course of time and is more a question of quality than of quantity; but quantity is certainly an index that cannot be neglected. Thus, I would suggest reflecting not only upon the econometric study by Rati Ram quoted by Paul Streeten in his lecture on minimalism, but also upon the figures concerning the ratio between public expenditure and GNP in the United States. This country, which has the most consistent critical attitude towards state intervention in the economy, has seen that ratio jump from 7 per cent at the beginning of our century to 23 per cent in 1949 and to 34 per cent in 1989. The Reagan administration, so devoted to a programme of deregulation and to the reduction of public expenditures, was only able to stabilize that ratio, not reduce it: a clear indication, to my mind, that the forces pushing in the direction of state intervention are powerful indeed. This does not mean that we have to abandon a critical

[*] Università degli Studi di Roma "La Sapienza".

attitude towards state intervention; on the contrary, this attitude should become even more critical in order to combat the serious excesses and abuses so evident nowadays. Preliminarly, however, we must try to understand the reasons behind this expansion.

2. Complementarity between Large and Small Firms and the "Judo Trick"

Again, relations between large and small firms can be conflictual or, on the contrary, complementary; and, here again, the task of the economist is to distinguish between the two types of relations and point out how the complementary relations can be strengthened rather than take a black-or-white position supporting one category or the other. In this field, there is certainly a great variety of complementary relations, among which subcontracting is only one example. Here I wish to point out that two years ago, in a meeting concerning the growth of small firms in both the formal and informal sectors, a report was presented by an Italian research institute (CENSIS) showing that about 70 per cent of the small firms founded from 1978 to 1988 were created by people who were formerly dependent workers in relatively large firms. About a year ago, in a meeting concerning measures aimed at supporting the growth of small firms in their infancy – incentives, development agencies and business incubators – I posed a question regarding the possibility of not only supporting small firms in the first stages of their lives, but increasing their birth rate. The problem is how to stimulate large firms to give rise to new small firms by means of credit and fiscal and organizational measures. A few months ago, two young economists working in the Department of Economics at the University of Rome became convinced that this was a fruitful line of research and carried out a preliminary inquiry for the south of Italy; the results seem promising. Paraphrasing the title of the famous book by Piero Sraffa, we have called our project "Production of firms by means of firms". We hope that other researchers will follow this line of study.

On these topics, I would like to offer two further remarks.

First, to study how the two complementarities emphasized by

Paul Streeten can work efficiently in practice, we must study the experience of Japan. To be sure, the lessons that can be learned from Japan – especially those concerning the relations between large and small firms – reflect the peculiar social and cultural conditions of that country and cannot be repeated in other countries. As for the relations between state and market, it is important to clarify that Japan is by no means an example of laissez faire or of state minimalism; on the contrary, Japan is a very good example of how the social benefits arising from the complementarity between state and the market can be maximized.

Secondly, when we discuss relations between large and small firms, we must recall that, in developing countries, we find many people outside firms of any size. In this category we find pedlars and people that I would classify as "quasi beggars". These people can survive on their activities, but they are outside any process of growth and improvement. From this point of view, they represent one of the most serious problems in developing countries.

3. Institutional Innovations and Reforms

As you have noticed, my comments are not critical of Paul Streeten's views, but complementary, as are, in important circumstances, the relations between large and small firms and those between market and state. In the same spirit, I present my third comment concerning institutions and reforms. Paul suggests, among other things, the creation of an international central bank and of an international investment trust, within a multilateral scheme, to channel the surpluses of the surplus countries – like Japan – to the capital-hungry developing countries. I think that this is a reasonable proposal, but, for developing countries and especially for those of South America, I would give high priority to reforming their internal credit systems which – from what I have been able to see in Argentina, which is certainly not among the most backward countries – are in very bad shape. These credit systems, even apart from mistaken economic policy measures, are capable of channelling only a modest part of the surplus into productive activities. If we recognize that the credit system represents the way in which a part of the internal surplus can be *voluntarily* channelled away from its point of origin into diverse activities, while the fiscal system represents the way in which another part of the internal surplus can be *compulsorily* channelled into diverse activities; and if we admit that in developing countries the need for public expenditures in infrastructure and other productive purposes is not less but even greater, in proportion, than in advanced countries, the paramount importance of fiscal reform giving high priority to direct taxation becomes clear, especially, since increases in indirect taxes as well as in public service tariffs produce immediate or very rapid and significant increases in inflation.

4. Adam Smith and the Theory of Economic Development

My last point refers to what I consider the message emerging from the whole analytical work of Paul Streeten, that is, that in development theory we have to return to Adam Smith. I must say that Adam Smith was the intellectual love of my youth and that, in the course of time, this love, instead of declining, has increased. To return to Smith means that, in our theoretical analyses, we have to adopt an historical perspective and that we must make every effort to enlarge the scope of our interests. We have to realize that, even though we concentrate our attention on problems concerning the conditions of production and distribution of commodities and services, we cannot go on as if economic theory were an autonomous and purely quantitative discipline. The latter is precisely the standpoint of traditional economists, who almost always implicitly refer to the economy of advanced countries and take the institutional setup as given. But to economists studying developing countries it is evident that the institutional setup cannot be taken as given; for these economists it is vital to study the previous economic evolution – exactly as Adam Smith did systematically for England and other European countries and, less systematically, for several others. More generally, Adam Smith thought it was natural to analyse economic problems, not autonomously, but together with demographic, educational and institutional issues – to mention only three great categories of problems strictly related to economic life; for Smith, there was no cleavage between economic theory and economic history. To be sure, accepting this concept, it is much more difficult to be rigorous than if we assume that only quantitative aspects matter; yet, we have to try and be not only rigorous but also relevant, if we want to avoid our models lapsing into sterile exercises, rigorous yet irrelevant from the point of view of the interpretation of the real problems confronting us.

Paul Streeten points out that it is wrong to consider Adam Smith as an unqualified defender of state minimalism. In addition to the task of defending its citizens against external enemies and guaranteeing public order, the state has the task of "providing certain public works and certain public institutions, which can never be for the interest of any individual, or small number of individuals to erect and maintain". "This paper" – Paul adds after this quote – "is entirely in the spirit of Adam Smith". To my mind, this statement applies to the whole of Paul Streeten's work and not only to the lectures that he has presented here. It is high time to go back to the spirit and to the method of Adam Smith with modern eyes and by using modern analytical tools: this is the important message Paul Streeten is conveying to us. I hope that this message will be understood and absorbed by the young generation of economists, especially by those who intend to devote themselves to the study of the theory of economic development.

MICHAEL LIPTON*

I was lucky enough to have Paul Streeten as a teacher at Oxford; as a fellow-worker during my first job, on Gunnar Myrdal's *Asian Drama* in 1960-61; and as a colleague at the Institute of Development Studies in 1967-68. I have been learning from his writings for 35 years. In this dissection of the paradoxes of neo-liberalism, he is as perceptive and constructive as always.

His argument has seven strands. First, "human development" – not GNP, even real GNP per poor person – is the central goal of public policy; is usefully measured by the HDI; and (because literacy and life-expectancy are more equally distributed than income) refocuses development analysis upon the reduction of poverty and hunger. Second, "human development" is advanced by a liberal framework of prices and markets, but this requires a much larger, more active, and more efficient state than exists in most developing countries. Third, we can define the boundaries of what such a state should do. Fourth, state action can stimulate (a) private enterprise, through "crowding in", and (b) symbiotic (though not oppressive or cartel-like) relations between large, formal firms and small, informal firms, through the "Judo Trick". Fifth – in a "political economy" version of this – appropriate mixtures of private and state action can mobilize decisive pressures, even from the non-poor, for pro-poor reforms. Sixth, a world of Prisoners' Dilemmas requires the state or "the international community" to supply goods, services, or institutions. Seventh, these themes together illuminate the emerging relationships between countries in our strange new world of the Bankrupt Hegemon, and suggest improved international institutions.

1. Human Development

Alongside Amartya Sen and Dudley Seers, Paul Streeten has played a major role in redirecting development analysis away from GNP, via "basic needs", towards a broader concept of

* University of Sussex, Brighton.

"human development". GNP-based indicators exclude many items that humans value: longevity, safety, liberty, enlarged "capabilities". Also, relative prices (valuations) of items within GNP reflect scarcity and cash-backed demand, not need. But is the HDI a useful measure of comparative achievement? Could it unify the dispersed economic specializations, as each inquires how, when, and why its subject of study (trade, labour, property rights) explains changes in the HDI?

Unfortunately, Streeten's own objections to the HDI are decisive. Human development is a vector; the HDI is an arbitrarily weighted scalar.[1] There is no gain from knowing whether Tunisia has scored more on some composite health-literacy-GNP index than Algeria (and no objective way to weight, select, or reject components of such an index). But there is much gain in knowing that Tunisia has done better than similar countries on particular health or education indicators, and worse on others.

Streeten's discussions of poverty are fascinating and useful. For monitoring progress by appropriate measurement, he rightly recommends the Foster-Greer-Thorbecke poverty index P2. This does not – contrary to widespread belief – require more data than are produced by standard household surveys. On ways to help the poor, Streeten is rightly sceptical of direct targeting; but there is more scope for "self-targeting" on the poor via schemes that provide low-wage work, coarse grains, or services located in slums. Ultimately the problem of poverty will seldom be solved unless either work or work-enhancing assets (skills, land) are redistributed to the poor.

2. Pricism Versus State Minimalism

Streeten emphasizes that, for markets to work well, the state needs to undertake many direct stimulative actions involving infrastructure, education, etc. – and probably considerable direct

---

1. Streeten rightly points out that the "weights" among items in GNP, viz. market prices, have their problems too. However, unlike the weights in a PQLI or a HDI, market-price weights are not arbitrary. They measure the relative opportunity-costs of acquiring items within GNP.

commodity provision, financing, and/or production as well. So he is naturally surprised at the emergence of state minimalism alongside belief in a market agenda which, in fact, requires *more* state activity. He also points to several confusions: between state minimalism as political libertarianism, and as economic inaction; between *setting* the prices right (through public policy to alter incentives), and merely *letting* the prices come "right" via state inaction, as if the impact of income distribution on demand and hence on relative prices could be ignored;[1] and between "reducing public expenditure" overall, and *ad hoc*, devil-take-the-hindmost "cuts" that ultimately increase the cost of State security and social security: overall public expenditure in Reagan's USA and Thatcher's Britain rose to unprecedented proportions of GNP.

Streeten rightly criticizes some liberals for failing to see that much *more* state action is needed in many developing countries, in order to make markets work. But these liberals were not just being silly. They saw the state, notably in the swollen military bureaucracies of several African countries, and it did not work. Many politicians and bureaucrats, in order to prosper in societies that offered few non-state means of advancement, took actions that sabotaged markets. They set the prices deliberately wrong in order to profit therefrom, and/or imposed controls so as to create profitable corruption opportunities for themselves and their clients. State minimalism may indeed suffocate markets, but "big states" often strangle them; hence the minimalism of many marketeers.

The dilemma also applies the other way round. States need the market, both to obtain commodities competitively and efficiently, and to provide legal economic opportunities, thereby reducing the temptation for state agents to abuse the state to climb the

---

1. Other problems associated with pricism are (a) the fact that many countries are price-takers on international markets for most commodities, and that the prices that they "take" are heavily (but not reliably or predictably) distorted and destabilized, e.g. by the agricultural policies of developed Western countries; (b) that, especially but not only where particular developing countries are *not* pure price-takers, reducing price biases now affecting each producer may lead to market gluts, damaging the developing countries as *a whole* – most notably for beverage tree crop exports, which are in price-inelastic demand, and for which technical costs of adjustment (replanting) are very high.

economic ladder. Yet a growing state is readily destroyed by the market, if firms made powerful in the market place abuse that power to bribe or twist the state's arm to provide them with special favours.

This *state-market dilemma* can be resolved. There has to be, not only a network of NGOs (which Streeten rightly emphasizes), but a functioning civil society in the sense of Hegel and Gramsci.[1] Since both state and market must gain power for effective development – yet tend to destroy each other – that destructive power has to be held in check by numerous, peacefully and politically competing, individuals, firms and pressure groups (normally including political parties). These all seek to influence, expose, and change the behaviour of powerful agents of *both* the state *and* the private sector.

State, market and civil society are *rival* channels for the exercise of power. They can all increase in importance only if some fourth channel decreases in importance. That fourth channel is familial society: the network of family, ethnic group, etc. which currently dominates many decisions, especially in developing countries.

Streeten asks why state minimalists tend to assume that most, or all, harmful rent-seeking happens in the public sector. Probably, this belief depends substantially on the view that private firms operate in "contestable markets", where monopoly rents are constrained or eliminated by *potential* entry. This proposition is itself contestable; many privately owned natural monopolies do exist, e.g. water supply in Britain, and in other cases the capital costs of entry are prohibitive. Moreover, public-sector rents are themselves often contestable indirectly. The market to supply a licence to import a particular commodity is not directly contestable – the government enforces its monopoly; but private producers respond (1) by changing their output-mix so that they need the import no longer, or (2) by changing their input-mix so as to substitute for the import. In both cases, the market is quasi-contestable.

---

1. See my 'The State-Market Dilemma, Civil Society, and Structural Adjustment', *The Round Table*, no. 317, January 1991.

State minimalists argue that market failure need not justify government intervention; state failure may follow, with worse results. Streeten retorts that, similarly, state failure need not justify privatization; the private sector may fail even more expensively. We need to deconstruct these notions of success and failure: to do what? Many of the worst outcomes in developing and developed countries alike have been due neither to the failure of markets to communicate correct signals to optimizing individuals, nor to the failure of the state to meet its leaders' objectives.

For example, unemployment (and slow formal-sector growth) can arise from transactions costs, not from "market failure". The cost, for a firm, of shifting from informal to formal activity – of screening and supervising a substantial labour force, rather than family labour plus a few known employees; of learning to operate effectively in broader capital and product markets – is often too large to be worth bearing. This underpins two distinct sorts of labour-market dualism. One is specified in Dandekar's completely decomposable, two-block Sraffa model of India – with a *non-communicating* equilibrium wage in each block. The other type has two *communicating* labour markets, in which the informal sector does outwork, especially at critical stages of the business cycle, for the formal sector, as in the "Third Italy".[1] Neither type involves market failure.[2]

Most alleged "state failures" are so described because of the illusions about Platonic states that Streeten exposes. Many governments artificially underprice foreign currency, not because of state failure to perceive the consequences, but because of state *success* in doing so. It is not stupidity; is it just cupidity? Indeed, these politicians correctly believe that, by creating opportunities for their families, clients or dangerous rivals to make money by obtaining foreign exchange cheaply and selling it at the equilibrium

1. S. BERGER and M. PIORE, *Dualism and Discontinuity in Industrial Societies*, Cambridge: Cambridge University Press, 1980.

2. Nor do the cycles of over-capacity and under-capacity in steel and fertilizers – which casts some doubt on Streeten's remedy, international investment agreements. Experienced businessmen are well aware that these cycles happen. Modern economic theory, in seeking micro-foundations in intelligible theories of expectations, has blown away the cobweb theorem, which asserted that businessmen learn from experience, but never learn that their learning process is failing.

price, they can achieve something: on a cynical reading, can get rich or keep power; on a kinder reading, can keep the state functioning. Even then, the results of state success by such methods are bad. Corruption empowers, but also corrupts.

Streeten is rightly wary of the concepts of market and state success and failure. These do not exist in the abstract: there is success-in and failure-to. Moreover, many of the least socially desirable outcomes of political and economic behaviour are the consequences, not (*pace* Oxenstierna) of state or market failure, but of their *success* – in providing signals that tell private firms and households how to maximize, and state agents how to get more power.

It is worth spelling out why Sen and Streeten are right that most famines are the appalling consequences of state or market *success*. Consider the Irish famines of the late 1840s. Massive deaths were caused because the potato blight, via low harvests, slashed the demand for harvest labour, and hence the labourers' cash demand for food in Ireland. Combined with relatively healthy demand levels in England, this caused food to flow from Ireland to England, even as the Irish were starving and the English were not. This was a tragic "market success". Then consider the Bengal famine of 1943. The state achieved *success* in moving more food staples to Calcutta. But – because the rural non-poor have a price-inelastic demand for food staples – the (rather small) reduction in rurally retained food supply induced a big rise in rural food prices. This "rationed out" the rural poor, many of whom starved as a result of state success.

The implication of all this is much more radical than that of "failures" of functioning states or market mechanisms. If an operation fails because of some error or wrong specification, it can be put right for the next patient. But if systematically "the operation is successful and the patient dies" then a new *structure* – at least of treatment, possibly of a branch of medicine – is needed. This applies to much treatment of the ills of underdevelopment. (This is partly why "structural adjustment programmes" should be called "non-structural adjustment programmes" – and why they often fail.)

3. What Should The State Do?

Three prior remarks are needed, before I address Streeten's remarks on this question (secs. 4-6 below). First, Streeten and I (and most analysts) usually read the question as "What should the state do *for the best*?" Yet we do not believe that such motives alone determine state decisions: only that state agents should face rules or incentives that lead them to act *as if* they were Platonic guardians. We continue with the "Platonic-state" convention only in order to juxtapose that norm against the realities.

Second, as Streeten points out, crowding-in tends to exceed crowding-out. However, this does not meet the *fiscal* objections of many who oppose state expansion. With a finance constraint, the fact that extra state investment crowds extra private investments *in* makes it even worse, since what is required is to *reduce* total claims on scarce saving. On this pre-Keynesian approach, extra state investment in India might briefly crowd private investment in – but later, *following* adjustment in the fiscal (or foreign) balance, public investment must crowd out private, as a rival claim on the savings fund. The relevant question, then, is: does the state investment add more to social welfare than would the private investment activities, which would have taken place out of the same savings fund, had the state investment (and the temporarily crowded-in private investment) not happened? If its pre-Keynesian formulation makes sense, then this is indeed the question raised by the "crowding" debate.

Third, the distinction between "public" and "private" commodities is *not* useful in deciding what should be done by the state, and what by the private sector. A public commodity is normally non-price-excludable, and always non-rivalrous: you do not have less if I have more, at least in the short run. However, many public commodities are most efficiently supplied (1) by small groups of people – e.g. farmers who jointly provide the "public good" of common control over common grazing rights; or (2) under contract to the state, but by the private sector. If the public sector has persistently failed with a problem in agricultural research (assuming the output to be a piece of knowledge that is non-rivalrous and non-price-excludable), then perhaps it should offer a contract, or a prize, for private researchers or research companies to solve the problem. Conversely, some pure private goods are under-supplied by the private sector. "Merit goods" are, by definition, socially affordable yet undersupplied – in the sense that some people are almost universally agreed to be "entitled" to them, but cannot afford them. Also, the products of non-contestable monopolies are all too price-excludable, and highly rivalrous; yet it may well be more cost-effective for the state to produce them than to (purport to) regulate a private monopoly that does so.

The distinction between "public" and "private" commodities, therefore, is simply *neither necessary nor sufficient* to tell us which commodities are likely in practice, or desirable in principle, to be candidates for public-sector production, provision or financing. The distinction – while analytically of the highest importance – is *completely useless* for that purpose.

4. State-Private, and Resulting Formal-Informal, Relations

Streeten especially seeks to crowd in joint formal-informal activ-ity, in the spirit of the "judo trick".[1] What policies will induce big formal, and small informal, enterprises to behave symbiotically (yet competitively) rather than separately?

It is important to adapt such policies to the *sort* of informal sec-tor one wishes to encourage. Its advantages lie in those types of activity, and of informal firm, that feature labour-intensity of the sort that benefits from the low costs of a largely family-staffed en-terprise in screening, recruiting, search and supervision. A less fa-miliar advantage of informal-sector enterprises associated with family production is that certain critical inputs – supervision, storage, vehicles, cash – can be shunted, not only among lines of production, but *between the firm's production and the family's consump-tion*, according to the pressure of demand and the flow of the sea-

---

1. Can we think of a better expression than the "judo trick"? In judo, the smaller and weaker partner seeks to use the strength of the stronger partner, so that the latter self-destructs and loses. The formal firm will never want to be symbiotic with informal firms, while it believes that it thereby helps them to destroy it. *Both* parties must expect to gain.

sons.[1] Where family and such "extended fungibility" do most to enhance efficient and flexible resource use, large formal-sector firms are often at a disadvantage. Hence farming, retailing, and construction – often characterized by advantages to "extended fungibility" – have substantial family sub-sectors.

However, formal enterprises use the state – via its quasi-political paraphernalia of zoning, licenzing, "health" rules, harassment of hawkers, etc. – to protect themselves against such otherwise well-adapted informal-sector competition. The political reaction, all too often, is to support the small against the smallest: the urban semi-formal against the rural, family, fungible and informal. Thus "industrial estates", and other attempts to create "small" entrepeneurship out of thin air by subsidizing it, usually do so against (for the most part) even smaller, family-based enterprise. The concentration of both political support and economic research on *urban* informal enterprise illustrates the pressure to neglect those largely rural activities, locations, and types of families, in which informality and fungibility have the greatest economic advantages. Yet it is not clear how small family enterprises, often dispersed and illiterate, are *either* to influence a state dominated by "great families" interlocked with formal-sector firms, *and/or* to attract such firms economically. How is the informal, small family firm to be "baled in" via the judo trick – and via state policies that favour it – rather than excluded?

Even if this trick is brought off, Streeten himself stresses the danger that the large formal enterprise may exploit or entrap small informal family enterprises, leaving them worse off than before the judo started, and unable to extract themselves. There are many examples of this in the history of outwork. The danger, however, can be reduced. Household lace workers in southern India can organize as a union, bargaining with the large purchaser about the price of their craftwork. Several substantial purchasers may compete for the informal-sector product, as when small tea growers in Kenya or Sri Lanka have the choice among

1. M. LIPTON, 'Family, Fungibility and Formality: Rural Advantages of Informal Non-Farm Enterprise versus the Urban-Formal State', in S. AMIN, ed., *Human Resources, Employment and Development*, vol. 5: *Developing Countries*, London: Macmillan (for the International Economic Association), 1984.

estates to process their leaf. Or – perhaps least desirable, because so readily diverted to bad ends – the state can set up a regulatory review system.

Success in such areas seems to be relatively *un*likely, if we insist on looking first to multinational corporations as the formal-sector partner in judo. One such corporation, Brown and Polson, was the predecessor, indeed the proximate cause, of the dairying co-operative in Anand that was the seed of India's National Dairy Development Board. This Board, as Streeten mentions, has achieved a successful "judo trick"; the many poor family-farm buffalo-owners sell milk, for reliable collection at a reasonable price, to the Board's large formal processing concerns. However, before the advent of the cooperative, judo was not played. The multinational had found it more profitable to provide processing on conditions dictated by market power, and highly exploitative of the buffalo-owners.

How should competitive, or at least equal-exchange, relationships between informal and formal enterprises be promoted? First, as Streeten (like Berger and Piore) emphasizes, the informal sector, in flexible contractual relationships with formal firms, can both *provide* and *require* seasonal or counter-cyclical stabilization of employment for the poor. Second, the sector can sometimes compete effectively against the high-wage formal "labour aristocracy".

One potential formal-informal symbiosis cries out for exploration. The deracializing land reform now needed in South Africa might become less contentious if some of the large white farmers of underutilized land could see themselves as being transformed into processors, bulkers-up, marketers, and even extension agents for black family farmers. These could then obtain a rapidly increasing share of total land, while the white ex-farmers increasingly became (competitive but still profitable) input suppliers, marketers, or processors.

5. The Optimum State-Private Mix: its Role in Pro-Poor Reform

Why have optimum-mix questions been so little regarded, amid the war between unreal paradigms of maximal and minimal state actions? Part of the answer is the high prestige of formal model-building. The state-minimalist model was originally perfect competition. This creature proved as rare as the Arabian phoenix. Next, we were presented with conventionalist strategems to shore up the model. First came the argument that the evidence was "not inconsistent with" the proposition that agents acted "as if" there were perfect competition. More recently, we have the view that markets with free entry and exit are "contestable" however monopolistic they may be. At the other extreme, the shaky model of the optimal plan was similarly shored up by Barone-Lange-Lerner strategems.

Central-planning models are discredited now, for reasons largely exogenous to rational economic debate. However, these models may again acquire prestige, as the capacity of modern computing grows – alongside the social wastes (and crime costs) of massive unemployment, even where the unemployed are not very poor. Models, not just facts, kick. Yeats wrote: "The best lack all conviction, while the worst / Are full of passionate intensity". In this case it is not simply a matter of best and worst. The polar extremes of state and market provide intensely beautiful models (though in economics truth is *not* beauty) that embody "the fascination of what's difficult". Commonsense mixture or juxtaposition of state and market provides no beautiful models, and much inelegant, even casual, empiricism. Yet we all know well – outside the world of academic and political posturing – that a sensible combination of public and private, plan and market, *must* be sought.

In seeking it, Streeten spells out six routes to pro-poor reforms. What is the role of a state – Platonic or self-interested – in each of them? We assume that society can be divided into "rich and powerful" households and "poor and weak" households; and that there is an agreed index of poverty – say P2. Will the rich accept a policy likely to reduce P2?

In the first case, no rich household loses from the policy. Then government needs only to explain this. In Streeten's second case, some rich households lose, but can be compensated out of extra GNP, leaving everybody better off. This still requires that efficient compensation be organized, financed and (like the anti-poverty benefits themselves) targeted. However, by assumption, governments can draw on extra GNP, pay for all this, and leave no net losers.

The third case raises more problems for government. The rich are split; but rich gainers from poverty-reducing government action can overcome rich losers. If the conflict is close, careful government steering is needed to bring off the pro-poor change. But who are the steerers, and what are their goals and powers? Can one design a "constitution of anti-poverty" that would induce governments to take pro-poor actions in these circumstances, and to win over, or alternatively win against, rich opponents? This might be done in several ways – including reallocation of activities between public and private sector. Sometimes (as with health care), state provision is indicated; in other cases (grain marketing?) privatization often benefits the poor. However, as shown above, useful pro-poor actions by the state do *not* correspond to the provision of all, or of only, "public goods". For example, health care, while usually not a true public good, is normally grossly undersupplied to the poor by private providers. In such cases – given potential competition, and overview by civil society – an ingenious state, by providing, producing, and/or financing the commodity itself, *can* help the poor, detach powerful rich gainers, and satisfy its own functionaries with the same set of tolerably efficient actions.

In Streeten's fourth case, the poor have enough power to ally themselves with rich gainers from the proposed pro-poor legislation, and thus to overcome other rich people – who would, in the absence of "poor power", have frustrated it. This political counterpart of the "judo trick" is how many pro-poor measures are implemented in democracies, but it depends on the capacity of the poor to wield power and influence. Two factors are crucial in this. Are the poor dispersed, weak, rural, illiterate, so that the costs of organizing pressure by them are high? Are the poor an out-group, an underclass, discriminated against, or otherwise stigmatized by factors they cannot themselves change, so that the productivity gains from "mobilizing" the poor (and hence the funds from which to compensate, or bribe, potential losers) are small? Good pro-poor politics – both within the state and acting

322

upon the state – in "case four" requires identification of appropriate coalitions of the poor, and between poor and non-poor, that can bring off the necessary trick.

In Streeten's fifth case, the "trustees of the poor, guardians of rationality", possibly combined with potential rich gainers and with organized poor, bring about a change which the last two groups on their own could not have achieved. Some NGOs – e.g. the descendants of the Gandhian movement in India – are important here. Influences in and on the state merge: through "moral" landowners (and businessmen) in the Shaftesbury tradition; through academe; through the media; and through localized pressure groups.

Streeten's sixth route to pro-poor reform invokes donors *ex machina*: foreigners who, in combination perhaps with rich gainers and "trustees" as well as with the poor, induce states to take pro-poor actions. The World Bank's courageous, coherent, but as yet unimplemented manifesto at the end of the 1990 *World Development Report* presages such "poverty conditionality". It depends heavily on how far donors (i) possess "acceptable power" in the political context of the recipient country, (ii) see it as in their interest – economic, political or moral – to use that power to supplement pressures within the recipient country for pro-poor changes. In the 1960s, the "Alliance for Progress" for land reform in Latin America was such an example. In many countries now, an analogy would require donors to press for the privatization of bureaucratically managed and elite-benefiting state and collective lands, not to big farmers or yeoman politicians, but to the rural poor.

The last four routes all presuppose a functioning Hegelian "civil society". Yet this public good is undersupplied not only by the private sector – partly because of Olson's "contributors' dilemma", in which we each leave it to our neighbours to organize pressures on our joint behalf – but also by the state itself. Why should a State support pressures upon it to change, let alone to reduce its command over power and resources? Some enlightened despots in eighteenth-century Europe did recognize that they stood to gain if at least the intellectuals argued among themselves, challenged their leaders, and hence improved social and particularly agricultural organization. Yet, in general, self-preserving state authorities undersupply – even undermine – the institutions of competitive civil society.

We also need more exact specification of gains and losses. Streeten identifies two main dimensions. Will the rich accept (1) short-run but smallish losses, to achieve long-run but biggish gains; (2) sure but small sacrifices, to reduce the risk of big losses? Changes in the world economy in the 1980s have made the rich less likely to respond to these trade-offs in ways that help the state towards pro-poor actions. If the rich emphasize long-run gains, they will often support taxes to improve the education or health of the poor, since that will accelerate economic growth, from which the rich themselves will eventually benefit. But the tripling of world real interest rates around 1979 – persisting ever since – sends the wrong signal: that future gains, due to the reduction of poverty by state action, matter much less to rich people than previously, as compared with the immediate costs to them of such action.

Similarly, if the rich are concerned with security rather than income, they are more likely to accept some redistribution, so as to keep the poor sufficiently contented to avoid massive disaffection. Again unfortunately, the risk-aversion of the rich, and therefore their likely willingness to accept pro-poor changes that reduce their current incomes, has in the 1980s been greatly reduced by (a) better insurance markets; (b) for the financially or educationally rich, more possibilities for international migration; (c) above all, the collapse of most external support for domestic revolutionary movements such as the Hukbalahap in the Philippines, or the Farabundo Marti Front in El Salvador. Risks from such movements were earlier instrumental in reconciling the rich to bearing the costs of pro-poor interventions in Malaya (to which Streeten refers) and Korea.

6. Prisoners' Dilemmas and Public Action

In deciding about the proper role of non-private action, we need to know where private actions would produce "unacceptable" results. There are two subsets of such actions. First, some actions may produce Pareto-superior results today, but at the cost of distributions, or compositions, of GNP that endanger (a) poor people now or (b) well-being later. Streeten concentrates on the second subset: individually competing behaviour that is agreed by all to produce Pareto-inferior outcomes to cooperation, yet that is adopted by individuals because they fear to be "suckered", as in "paradoxes of isolation" or Prisoners' Dilemmas (PDs), and "paradoxes of assurance". As Streeten shows, such cases often provide excellent arguments for public or collective enforcement. However, as Platteau stresses,[1] such state enforcement of contract-keeping and other forms of cooperative virtue – while often essential if markets are to work properly – requires "sufficient" internalization of contract-observing values by individuals. Otherwise, the cost of enforcement becomes too great. Moreover, the "collectivity", over which values are internalized, has to be agreed by citizens. If *national* cooperation in observing contracts – an essential precondition for nationwide markets – is forced on, or rushed into, a *familial* society whose collective values are to maximize kin welfare even if that means cheating strangers, the consequences, especially among ethnic groups in one nation, can be disastrous.

Let us assume that – once moral norms sanctioning cooperative behaviour are internalized – national loyalties override sub-national collectivities. Then two questions arise for the state. First, what norms induce appropriate cooperation (without stifling appropriate competition)? Can I will the maxim of my non-defecting (cooperative) action in a PD to become a universal law, if I know that some people sometimes will defect? Axelrod[2] has shown experimentally that *repeated* Prisoners'-Dilemma games tend to be played cooperatively, but with each participant starting to defect (play competitively) against those participants who have defected on the previous turn. This "tit-for-tat" teaches

1. J.-P. PLATTEAU, 'The Free Market is not Readily Transferable', mimeo, 25th Anniversary Conference, IDS, Brighton, 1991.

2. R. AXELROD, *The Evolution of Cooperation*, New York: Basic Books, 1984. The stability of tit-for-tat outcomes depends on sufficient players being prepared, in game $n+2$, to punish (by not cooperating with them) not only defectors in the previous game $n+1$, but also players who in game $n+1$ have failed to punish defectors in game n.

defectors that cheating does not pay in the long run. That shows that people work out for themselves a neat solution to the Kantian problem. They cooperate, gain by doing so, occasionally find that someone else cheats, punish him by themselves starting to cheat him – and gain by doing so, because potential cheats learn that if they defect so will their next opponents, leaving then worse off that if they had cooperated.

Second, how are appropriately defined Kantian norms[1] to be internalized, in a society increasingly permeated by, and overtly justifying, the unbridled pursuite of economic self-interest? The Victorian novelists – George Eliot in *Middlemarch*, Trollope in *The Way We Live Now*, Dickens almost everywhere – took it for granted that businessmen cheat. For decades, such views have been regarded as naively populist. More recently, however, the self-interest craze may have undermined its own foundations. Where is the border between fair trading and cheating, in a society where private self-enrichment is increasingly the overriding public norm, requiring the pursuit of self-interest rather than the internalization of cooperative priorities? Complete self-interest "if you can get away with it", and what is half-admiringly called "sailing close to the wind", blur the boundary between economic behaviour and economic crime – and the *respect for contract* on which markets depend. (The London Stock Exchange has the motto *verbum meum pactum*: my word is my bond.)

Some enforcement is usually needed to prevent cooperative solutions from deteriorating. But constant recourse to law enforcement is costly and harsh, and can undermine the markets it purports to underpin (as with medical litigation in the USA). Hence respect for cooperation (including cooperation *not* to rig or fix supposedly competitive markets) must come mainly from shared norms or values. Rampant self-interest destroys those values; yet market-based development requires substantial, rewarded pursuit of self-interest.

---

1. In view of Platteau's point about the costs of enforcement, such norms – and shame about breaking them – are essential if the Axelrod-Akerlof repetition-reputation outcomes are to generate cooperative behaviour, e.g. where needed to sustain markets and to uphold contracts. See G. AKERLOF, *An Economic Theorist's Book of Tales*, Cambridge: Cambridge University Press, 1984.

Taine wrote, "Ignorance of history makes us libel our times; things have always been like this". Yet, in the aftermath of Michael Milken, Charles Keating, BCCI, Robert Maxwell, and several major scandals in Japan, is it mere casual empiricism to suggest that since, say, 1975 economic crime, relative to GNP, has risen dramatically? If it has, it reflects the transvaluation of values in the 1980s. Our business (and televised) values now instil the norms of defection; even in laboratory PD games, I suspect, it is no longer only economics graduates who defect automatically. Our *reluctant* admission of this is signalled by hypocrisy, "the tribute that vice pays to virtue": by the absurd pretence, in the early years of the US savings-and-loan scandal, that only a tiny proportion of the collapses was due to theft or fraud; by the absurd claims that insider dealing is (a) victimless and (b) therefore ethical.

Given the propensity to defect, what happens in *many-person* PD games? Streeten says that, with many other players, enforcement becomes more expensive and difficult, so that each player becomes more likely to defect. However, whereas in a one-shot two-person PD detection destroys co-operation, this need not be true with many players. If a few small countries ignore international agreements on CFCs, it may not matter much. A PD in which a few defect (and in which it may not be worth securing 100 per cent compliance) can produce a "sufficiently cooperative" outcome to prevent the commons from becoming overgrazed.

This is a dangerous argument. If wrongdoing spreads, so does the perception that one can get away with it. Also, the argument fails in some contexts: if there is an international agreement on nuclear restraint, and just one country starts dropping hydrogen bombs, the result is disastrous. But often the presence of many participants cuts both ways – raising the costs of enforcement, but also permitting (perhaps via coalitions) a "sufficiently cooperative" outcome despite some defection.

7. International Action, Bankrupt Hegemons, and PDs

However decent people's values are, some enforcement is usually needed to prevent a cooperative solution from deteriorating.

This may be a weakness in proposals for stabilizing energy prices. Rather as with the International Coffee Agreement (or with Locke's objections to laws fixing the rate of interest), it will always pay a low-cost provider and a needy demander – of oil, coffee, or money-to-lend – to make a transaction outside the rules, therefore undermining the agreed prices. This is especially important with oil – see the refusal of Mexico, Britain and other countries to join OPEC, and the flouting of OPEC rules by some of its members. It is hard enough to detect this, let alone stop it.

Proposals for international organizations, e.g. to safeguard the global environment, need to be clear just what problems are due to defecting behaviour in PD games. Most environmental problems are not. They are due to policies, technologies, or incentives that encourage rapid depletion (or pollution) for *any* agent managing resources – private, collective or public. Consider the effect of population growth on resource depletion. Normally,[1] growing population, by pressing upon certain scarce resources, raises the rewards to discovering more of them; to finding ways of producing with less use of them; or to changing the product-mix away from those items which use up many of them. This incentive affects individuals, families, firms, collectives, and states alike. However, when (as since 1978) world real interest rates are artificially tripled due to Western macroeconomic mismanagement, then signals are given to all agents – private, collective, state – that the future does not matter, relative to current benefits from resource use. Thus *the transmission is broken*: events that normally, by threatening to accelerate depletion, would change incentives and technologies (and thus reduce depletion, by inducing resource-saving, inventions, and resource discoveries) now fail to do so, because exogenous factors have shifted incentives the wrong way.[2] If we try to tackle these problems by changing the

1. W. BECKERMAN, *In Defence of Economic Growth*, London: Cape, 1974.

2. M. LIPTON, 'Accelerated Resource Depletion by Third World Agriculture: Made in the West, in the Commons, or in Bed?' in S. A. VOSTI, T. REARDON and W. VON URFF, eds., *Agricultural Sustainability, Growth, and Poverty Alleviation: Issues and Policies*, Proceedings of the Conference held 23-27 September 1991, Feldafing, IFPRI/DSE/ZEL: Feldafing, 1992.

rules, or enforcement procedures, for national or global commons, we shall not get far.

That is especially the case since developments making resources scarcer (and tending to deplete or pollute them) – *of themselves* tend to lead to such resources being moved from common to private or state management.[1] Many people object to this, but it removes the "dilemma of the commons" by putting the costs of depletion into the same hands, or pockets, as the benefits from it. This militates against the likely value of proposals such as that for an international environmental protection agency. The partial success of international environmental action on particular issues such as CFCs show that where a global commons (and a PD) is a big part of the problem nations already cooperate to defend such commons. The deeper problem arises from artificial incentives to evade such defences – or from drains on the public purse that deplete funding for technologies to create profitable alternatives to depletion.[2]

Persistently high real interest rates are the environmental equivalent of AIDS. They destroy the *immune response* to depletion. This they do by reversing the price changes, caused by threats of resource depletion, that otherwise lead economic agents – individuals, communities, states – to respond to those threats.

Not all international problems involve PDs. But many do. For such cases Streeten is to be congratulated for "Utopian proposals"; for clarifying their justification (e.g. macroeconomic rather than microeconomic, for commodity price stabilization); and for emphasizing that rules and frameworks for enforcement, rather than buildings and international civil servants, are the "new institutions" required. However, there are problems. Does the framework for progress exist (or how can it be created)? What are the likely areas for progress?

On the framework, Streeten writes that "technologically we

1. N. S. JODHA, 'Population Growth and the Decline of CPRs in India', *Population and Development Review*, vol. 2 no. 2, June 1985.

2. The proportion of non-oil developing-country central governments' expenditure (plus lending, minus capital repayments) that was used in repaying interest rose fairly steadily from 5.6 per cent in 1972 to 18.7 per cent in 1988, the latest available year. See IMF, successive *Yearbooks of Government Finance Statistics*, Washington, D.C.

have moved toward a global community". Indeed, new techniques accelerate cross-border decisions, especially cash transfers; but this need not create global community. For example, it prevents enforcement of most agreements on exchange controls. Leave aside whether such agreements are desirable (if their enforcement greatly reduced drug trafficking, even many liberals might stomach them). Anyhow, technological unification of business decisions has here *retarded* global community.

The other side of this coin is that "there is no world government to set the rules" or to enforce them. An international community needs a "PD Interpol" to create credible respect for global commons – *especially* because of the greatly eased facilities for international movement and transfer that constitute part of Streeten's case for the growing globalization of the community.

Underlying proposals for better "global community" must be a view of the present nature of the world polity. Streeten sees US hegemony as dying, and Japanese or European hegemony as powerless to be born. Lacking a hegemon, the world requires some international public authority to avoid the "chaos of the 1930s", the last interregnum between hegemonies (British and US). Yet US power – in the Gulf, Israel, and Mexico-Canada – seems pretty formidable still. The USA is a *bankrupt hegemon*; so what's new? The UK increasingly lurched into that position from around 1880 to 1939. So, regionally, did successive Chinese dynasties, and the Mughals in South Asia. It would not require much modernization of Gibbon to write the history of Roman decline in these terms.

History teaches that a bankrupt hegemon can long remain a hegemon, while it can extract imperial tribute (as the UK found increasingly costly, but as Rome, and the Mughals, managed to do long after they became apparently bankrupt). Today, there is a new twist: flourishing non-hegemons, such as (until very recently) Japan, want to, or are locked into, lending the hegemon money to conceal its bankruptcy. It is Japanese cash flows that sustain the USA's "bankrupt hegemon" posture – increasingly so, as US net debtor positions mount. Probably "Japan Inc." will ultimately – in adversity or otherwise – cease thus throwing good money after bad, and weather the resulting short-term disruptions. But perhaps, especially in view of the large share of Japanese exports that (as Streeten points out) go to the USA, Japanese public and private sectors will, for many years yet, see cash-flow support of the bankrupt hegemon as being in their own medium-term interests. Thus a *pax Americana*, financed by Japan, could last some time. As the problems with the Uruguay Round suggest, this augurs badly for the success of international institutions *not* dominated by the hegemon. Yet only these would be acceptable to other countries as a "PD police" for such global commons as avoiding "strategic" trade.

A prolonged Japanese-financed *pax Americana* would imperil one of Streeten's proposals. You cannot recycle the same cash twice, any more than you can sell the same pig. If Japan's surpluses are needed to make up for low saving in the USA, they cannot be recycled to developing countries. Streeten does not propose to recycle all of them to the developing world. Some would be left for the USA. However, the US public-sector deficit ratchets steadily upwards; and the private sector does not run a correspondingly increasing surplus. So the share of available Japanese surpluses, required to meet the US deficit alone and maintain the bankrupt-hegemon posture (and defend returns to *past* Japanese lending to, and investment in, the USA, in part by defending the dollar) would increase. That will reduce Japan's capacity to recycle surpluses to poorer countries.

Uncertainty about the status of the hegemon also affects Streeten's proposal for a world central bank. The principal role of a national central bank is to act as the government's bank, smoothing its accounts; historically other roles have grown from that. On this model – lacking a world government – a full-fledged world central bank must be, at least, banker to the hegemon government. But the Fed is that. Also, to the extent that the USA is a bankrupt hegemon, key transactions are bilateral with Japan, rather than requiring the existence of a multilaterally oriented world central bank. Similarly the "bankers' bank" functions, which such a bank would exercise, are currently assigned to other, quite defensively oriented, institutions: national central banks. Streeten is therefore right to start off the "world central bank" with something for which there is already a great head of steam: an international lender of last resort (ILLR).[1] National central banks perform this function in crisis – but, if commercial banks are not to be encouraged by ILLR provision to over-lend in good times, must then also limit lending to or by any particular institution. Such a stabilizing function is needed at international level, as the huge swings in bank sentiment (and hence cross-border lending) – alongside the big rise in multi-country and interbank loans and guarantees – demonstrate. The failure of the Bank of England to protect even small BCCI depositors shows how lack of an ILLR imperils even *national* LLR functions. Once again, to avoid moral hazard, restraint needs to be exercised by the ILLR in good times, as well as insurance provided in bad. Over time, such an ILLR may acquire more of the range of functions of a world central bank.

The same problem of moral hazard may require modification in Streeten's proposals for debt forgiveness. The problem is twofold. Debt forgiveness encourages countries and borrowers that have so far repaid their debts, not to do so in future. It also encourages individual banks, now marginally persuaded to be "baled in" as renewed borrowers to emerging and just-creditworthy developing countries, to get out quickly, for fear that they will be punished for having behaved properly in the past.

Furthermore, the gainers from debt forgiveness include many a not-so-poor developing country, whose government knowingly took on debt to enrich its (or its clients') immediate families, well knowing that they would take the money and run, not to mammy but to Miami. In interbank competition, the losers from debt forgiveness would be banks who loaned to the countries now forgiven; hence, competitively, the beneficiaries would be those banks which had refrained from lending to developing countries. Most seriously, capital to pay for debt forgiveness would, in part, be diverted from some very poor developing countries that did not (or could not) borrow privately – or that borrowed, and strained every sinew to repay. That is not the sort of international income redistribution we should be looking for. Nor is invest-

---

1. M. Lipton and S. Griffith-Jones, *International Lenders of Last Resort: Are Changes Required?*, Midland Bank Occasional Paper in International Trade and Finance, March 1984.

ment in drug-running and Miami real-estate the sort of "Third World demand for commercial bank lending" that we ought to encourage by forgiving debts incurred through it. Surely, international institutions need to address this problem. However, redirecting scarce flows of developed-country capital into debt forgiveness for relatively non-poor Latin American countries – so that Bangladesh becomes the international lender of last resort – cannot be the right answer.

I shall not end on a disagreement. Streeten's important lectures redirect our attention to some basic inconsistencies in current advice to developing countries. Fortunately the consensus that threatened the international institutions in the mid-1980s – around naive state minimalism, accompanied by almost total reliance on price mechanisms as opposed to price policy – has now been vigorously challenged from within those institutions themselves, as well as from outside. Streeten has provided an essential prologomena – both nationally and internationally – to a reconstruction of state intervention to reduce poverty, instability, and resource depletion, as well as to provide necessary infrastructures for growth. His methods rely upon, instead of futilely attempting to fight against, competitive markets, incentives that reflect factor and product scarcities and individual and family goals.

SIRO LOMBARDINI*

1. Complementary Remarks

I have always appreciated Streeten's contributions to the theory of development because he has been able to reconcile the peculiarity of development problems with the goal of economical analysis aiming at producing not contingent statements. Therefore my remarks will be complementary rather than critical.

Streeten has rightly asserted that we can not assess economic development on the basis of the mere rate of growth of Gross National Products. Human beings are both means and goal of economic development. Such a statement has not only a theoretical relevance, but also empirical implications. I shall mention only one.

Expenditures for education have to be considered both as investments (in human capital) and as expenditures required to reach a fundamental social goal (more educated people). The attainment of such a goal has positive feedback effects on the preconditions for economic development. The role of human capital in development has been analysed in models of endogenous growth. Even if the function of production is homogeneous of first degree in labour and capital, growth is possible also for economies characterized by stationary population.

Streeten's more appropriate conception of economic development helps us in understanding why investments in human capital are the more productive among those that can be realized in underdeveloped countries.

Their rentability is threefold: the direct effect on the quality of labour, the satisfaction of the social goals, the feedback on the propensity to develop of society. If economic development is conceived in terms of the mere growth of GNP, only the first effect can be envisaged.

* Università degli Studi di Torino.

2. Order and Progress

The main point I want to offer to the debate are some remarks on economic development being irreducible to growth. In the growth models of the Harrod-Domar type, growth is the result of external factors (that was also Pareto's conception). Such a theoretical limitation (of these models as compared with classical theory, Smith theory in particular) has been removed by the recent *models of endogenous growth*.

These models have clarified how *some structural features of the economy* (as for instance the already recalled accumulation in human capital and the operation of monopolistic competitive markets) can produce growth process. But they cannot be considered *models of economic development*.

In fact economic science was born out of two fundamental conceptions of Enlightenment philosophies: *order and progress*. In Smith the two concepts have equal dignity. Later the former superseded the latter. Neither concept can be reduced to the other. Order (being interpreted by a static or a dynamic model) entails conservative laws (the assumption of a structurally stable system); why development is by its nature destructive of the structure by which the system has been interpreted before innovations occurred (being a theoretical structure – for instance a system of competitive markets – or an empirical structure arrived at through empirical analyses).

In Smith as well as in Marx and, later on, in Schumpeter, the analyses of the *economic order* (in Smith the theory of normal prices, in Marx the theory of value and for Schumpeter Walras's equilibrium model) are not integrated in their theory of development that are properly conceived as theory of structural changes. They could not be. In the middle of the last century it was because of the prevailing conception of science (Kant's conception) that the order analysis superseded the analysis of economic development; in our time the maintenance of such a state is due to the epistemological shortage of quite a few economists.

3. Macroeconomics

The dilemma – order or progress – has been by-passed – or at least some economists thought it could be – by macroeconomics. In fact macroeconomics has became a veil hiding all problems relating to the structure of global variables. Therefore most of the effects of economic development cannot enter into the analysis.

Macroeconomics has been useful in dealing with some problems of monetary and fiscal policy. Yet even the analysis of these policies has been distorted. Macroeconomics cannot explain why big state budget deficits have been associated with stable prices in the United States contrary to what has happened in Italy.

The reason why economists have mostly failed in explaining the long boom of the eighties and seem incapable of assessing the present recession is that changes in the structure of global variables have been disregarded because of the kind of theories and models that have been used. The reasons behind the fall of the propensity to save could not be discovered; the impact of the change in income distribution on the level and the structure of demand could not be properly assessed.

4. The Preconditions for Development and its Multi-objectives

Economic development requires some preconditions and can and must pursue several objectives. It is for these reasons that most economists think that argument about development does not belong to economic science, but can be the object and the result of historical assessments. Economists can only throw light on the mechanism accounting for growth that is associated with *the* market economy.

It is a curious position. In dealing with market we admit various market forms. Some theories of takeover mechanism as well as the theory of contestable markets have proved that monopolistic markets can produce effects similar to those of competitive markets. Yet most economists think of *the* market economy, in spite of the essential differences between Japan's market economy

337

and that of the United States. Having disregarded the preconditions for both market economy and economic development (mostly the cultural preconditions), they have converted the main economic theory, that is a theory of the *adjustments* that can occur *in specific conditions* in a market economy already established, into *the* theory of the market economy. Our Russian colleagues who believed in such a theory have unconsciously contributed to the economic disaster of their country.

Economic development not only postulates multi-objectives but can also make them contradictory. Growth of income is certainly an objective, as well as an equitable distribution of welfare. Yet in some countries – of Latin America in particular – when economic development was fostered, income distribution has become more unequal. The order approach suggests trade-off functions. A real development approach requires the investigation of possible development scenarios to find out those that reduce (eventually eliminate) the contradiction, the scenarios being different mostly according to the different role of the state.

Contradictions among objectives must be analysed in association with conflicts arising in society. We do not live either in the paradises or in the hells Streeten has commented on. We live on earth where societies are characterized by conflicts and the state is neither the neutral *deus ex machina* assumed by some students of welfare economics nor the devil that contractualism wants to get rid of.

Parallelisms that can occur among some contradictions and some social conflicts may help us to visualize positive scenarios for economic development. The interest of producers of durable consumption goods is a factor in explaining the increase in wages that has occurred in some phases of economic development. I hope that when Brazilian industrialists and bankers become aware of the need of a sustained increase of internal demand a land reform can be implemented.

5. State and Market

Historical analysis may help building theories of economic development. The converse is also true: theories of economic development may help historical analysis. Perhaps the most interesting investigation's of the economic history of the United States have been stimulated by Schumpeter's theory of economic development. Some reflections of the economic history of quite a few countries have led me to suggest a possible double theme for scientific reflections: There cannot be a sustained development without a positive role by the state (think of the effects of some of the public expenditure projects of the US government on the industrial structure); development cannot be maintained if market mechanism does not work.

Smith was well aware of the role of the state whose function was not the mere satisfaction of some collective needs. He pointed out the reasons why the state has to create some conditions for economic development: in particular to produce those infrastructures the productivity of which cannot be properly assessed in the too short horizon of entrepreneurs. More radical is Mill's position on this point.

Smith was also convinced that the pressure on the government by merchants are against public interest. Competition can frustrate entrepreneurs' search for rent provided the state operates properly (not once for all, by issuing an anti-trust law, but in all decisions of economic policy).

In Smith's view market cannot rely only on self-interest as some superficial interpreters of his thought have asserted. Sentiments of sympathy are necessary as much as self-interest. If we go into the question we can more precisely say that some feeling of common interest must exist for social cohesion to be sufficient to yield a market democracy. Buchanan's conception of a weak state being associated with a competitive market entails a strong assumption about social cohesion. There is no spontaneous constitution that can create the required social cohesion. The reverse is true. It is a pre-established social cohesion that makes it possible to arrive at a democratic constitution.

The erosion of social cohesion due to the evolution of the economic and political system has come to such a critical point that the need for a strong state has become a crucial issue. In fact pressure on the government comes not only from merchants – as Smith has pointed out – but from all social groups. A strong state is required to subordinate the various contrasting interest to some common interest (*public good*). Two inter-related problems arise: how can public good be defined and how can a strong state be reconciled with a democratic system. That is not a juridical-technical problem: it is a social-cultural problem (concerning in particular the role of political parties).

While domestic need points towards a strong state, a worldwide cohesion required to avoid disruption of international political and economic systems is possible if national states agree to renounce some of their powers. For the international order to be rebuilt and maintained, weak states are required.

6. Some Shortcomings of the Order Approach

The order approach superseding the development approach had some drawbacks. I want to mention only two.

The first is the identification of efficiency criterion with the Pareto criterion of optimality. It may be worth while remembering that Pareto himself was well aware of the limitations of his criterion.

The second drawback is linked with the first. Most economists are convinced that the relations between ethics and economics are a meaningful problem. Unfortunately it is usually analysed in the context of the order approach (whereas the problem is relevant only in the development approach). The results are trivial statements. Yet they satisfy people who are morally motivated but ignorant of economic processes as well as those businessmen who are interested in these problems for a mere public relations point of view.

COMMENTS ON THE DISCUSSION
Paul Patrick Streeten

I AM DEEPLY grateful to the commentators for their remarks. I have learned much from them. Perhaps this is not surprising, since the speaker is encouraged to suggest names, and each of the commentators is not only a brilliant scholar but also a dear friend; two of them were my students. Let me reply to some of their comments.

I was a bit shaken (and welcome this condition) by Michael Lipton's assertion that "the distinction between 'public' and 'private' commodities . . . is simply neither necessary nor sufficient to tell us which commodities are likely in practice, or desirable in principle, to be candidates for public-sector production, provision or financing. The distinction – while analytically of the highest importance – is *completely useless* for that purpose."

Of course, one can think of many public goods that can be produced, provided and financed by other institutions than the state, or by no institution. Lipton gives as an example a group of farmers with common control over common grazing rights. We might add a common language, which nobody controls, and a common currency, which some would take away from state control and put under the control of an independent central bank and such valuable public goods as trust, loyalty and truth-telling. Occasions like the Mattioli Lectures partake also in the nature of public goods. But given the two characteristics of public goods of non-rivalry in consumption, and, normally, non-excludability in charging for them, is the government (central and local) not one of the institutions (among others) that is particularly fit to produce, provide or finance some of these goods and services, particularly if no other institution will? Mass education to a certain age when education is compulsory, roads and highways, police and army protection, public health facilities such as vaccination campaigns, sewers and drainage are examples. The power to tax, at the local, regional and national level, make the state a peculiarly fit institution for this purpose. Of course, various combinations of producing, providing and financing these goods and services can be used to achieve maximum effectiveness. State schools may charge fees, or free vouchers can be issued to choose a private school. Public activities can be subcontracted to private firms, like the management of jails in the USA. Highways often charge

343

tolls. In Singapore payment of a tax is a condition for cars to enter the city. Private security guards are hired by residents and firms (though such private armies constitute their own threat to civil liberties), and the services of a public police force may be made available against the payment of a fee. The disposal of solid waste can be done by public authorities or by private firms. But, fundamentally, the decision which goods and services to leave to private organizations and which to the state is itself a political decision which governments must make.

Lipton defends the GNP against the HDI on the ground that "unlike the weights in a . . . HDI, market-price weights are not arbitrary. They measure the relative opportunity costs of acquiring items within GNP." But this is true only for any single purchaser (or for a group with identical tastes and incomes). The opportunity cost of a rich man to buy whisky cannot be brought to the same denominator as that of the poor mother to buy milk. The price of whisky is high, partly because the higher incomes of the rich bid it up. I think Lipton will agree that this prevents us from using the GNP as a measure of welfare. But it cannot be used as a measure of production and productivity either. For this would assume constant unit costs, so that the factors allocated to the production of whisky could be transferred at constant unit costs to that of milk. This assumption clearly has to be dismissed.

I am grateful to Paolo Sylos Labini that he has added further examples to the need for complementarity between (a) states and markets, (b) large and small firms, (c) self-interest and altruism. The Sraffaesque notion of the "production of firms by means of firms" is most attractive. It is evident that complementarities exist not only between state and market, between large and small firms, and between morality and self-interest in Adam Smith (self-interest works only in the context of trust), but also between Paolo Streeten and Paolo Sylos Labini.

I agree with him on the wide gap between rhetoric and reality in the Reagan administration (and also, by the way, Mrs Thatcher's). The rise in public expenditure in governments that are committed to reducing the public sector is to be attributed to national and social security, and in the USA to interest payments on the rapidly rising national debt.

344

Siro Lombardini raises the interesting question of the returns on (the right kind of) education, or investment in human capital, or the development of human resources. It seems to me that we can distinguish between five different aspects of the process of being educated and its final results.

First, education is (or can be) like a non-durable consumption good, like an apple. While we are being educated we enjoy it, reading books, writing essays, even attending classes, in the process of consuming it.

Second, it is also like a non-durable production good, like coal that fires the engine. It is used up in the process of producing a durable good.

Third, its end-product, the result of studying, is like a durable investment good. It is like a machine or a knitting frame. It yields a stream of higher salaries, profits, rents and other forms of income, both to the educated person and to other members of the society. Such externalities justify subsidizing it.

Fourth, it is like a durable investment good for non-marketed activities, like a refrigerator or vacuum cleaner. For example, educated women are better wives, mothers and housekeepers than uneducated ones. They carry out unpaid intra-family activities more efficiently.

Fifth, it is like a durable consumption good, like a television set. The educated person can enjoy literature, art and science more fully.

The characteristics pertaining to the likenesses to an apple, a heap of coal, a piece of equipment, a television set, and a refrigerator can either all be combined in harmony, or they can give rise to conflicts. Humanists and human resource developers are not known for peaceful coexistence.

What is, however, often forgotten is that education and skill creation, the cultivation of aptitudes, have to be combined with the creation of the right attitudes. For the income maximizer these are different from those for the contemplative navel-gazer, for the nurturing, breast-feeding mother from those for the employment-seeking woman. If education is combined with the wrong attitudes (e.g. contempt for manual work), or with inadequate physical investment in complementary equipment, the

345

result is disaffected intellectuals, the educated unemployed, a source of rebellious rather than productive activity. Aspirations beyond opportunities cause unemployment and misery. If each of us wanted to be Pope, and we were not prepared to accept any other job, there would be a lot of unemployment.

Jagdish Bhagwati could have said, not only that reputations are made by showing that selfishness promotes the public good, but also that altruism can produce bad results. O. Henry's story of the two lovers who sacrifice the things dearest to them, only to find that the sacrifice has been futile, illustrates this. But Adam Smith knew that selfishness has to be embedded in a system of morality and trust in order to work for the common good, just as the Invisible Hand has to be attached to a strong Visible Arm.

I was moved and touched by Stuart Holland's generous tribute. I can only say that the devotion, admiration and loyalty are mutual.

BIOGRAPHY
of Paul Patrick Streeten

1. Biographical Note

I was born in 1917 in Vienna, still but barely into the k. & k. Austro-Hungarian monarchy. Growing up in this post-imperial city, fleeing to England in 1938, spending most of my life in post-imperial Britain, and coming to post-Watergate, post-Vietnam America in 1976, I have become something of an expert in imperial decay. In particular, I am aware of the lag between technological advance and institutional inertia. Our institutional imagination is much more inert than our scientific one. I believe I occupy a good vantage point from which to criticize the nostalgic dreamers of imperial glory and to preach the virtues of humility.

My earliest childhood memory – I must have been about four or five years old – concerning economics is overhearing a conversation in a shop about "die Krone wird aufsteigen" (the Crown will rise) during a period of hyper-inflation. I imagined a distinguished, queenly elderly lady climbing up a mountain.

As a young man in Vienna I was interested in psychology, sociology and the history of art. I organized study groups and we had endless discussions on country hikes and round camp fires. These were combined with political activism, that had become illegal after 1934. The Austro-Marxism of Otto Bauer had much in common with the Keynesianism that was brewing in England in the late 1930s and to which I was introduced later as an undergraduate at Oxford. We engaged almost full-time in political activities, and I remember the eminent cosmologist, chief scientific adviser to the British government and Master of Churchill College, Cambridge, Sir Hermann Bondi, when he was still an adolescent, dropping in at our flat at all times of the day with messages and ideas. He scored some bad marks with my stepfather, who hated being interrupted at meals. But politics did not exhaust my interests. I attended lectures in the Urania by Erich Vögelin on the spread of culture by Genghis Khan, read the writings of the psychoanalytical art historian Ernst Kris, and attended stimulating talks on Renaissance art by Paul Deri.

When I came to England as a refugee in 1938 and was given the opportunity to continue my studies, I wanted to study sociology. Aberdeen, the first university to offer me a place, had no sociology department, so I was steered into economics. Aberdonians are renowned for their stinginess, even meanness. Yet, it is due to their generosity that I am not a sheep farmer in South Africa, the alternative suggested by many friends at the time.

My studies of law in Vienna had been interrupted by Hitler's march into the city. My studies at Aberdeen were interrupted on a sunny Whitsun morning in May of 1940. Two kind policemen woke me up to arrest me. I was technically an enemy alien. Although I had been cleared by tribunals and accepted to join the armed forces, the mass internment of refugees was a panic measure. The friendly policemen said I should pack a few things, for it would be only a few days. But internment was a big break in my life, lasted for nearly a year, and included exile in Canada. In the various camps we used the considerable talent gathered together to set up universities. Heinz Arndt, Radomysler (who later committed suicide) and Leser were among the camp's economics faculty. Radomysler was encouraging in destroying the belief, widely held among us internees, that we should all have to become farmers, by saying that the income elasticity of demand for intellectual services is much higher than for farm products.

After release from internment came service in the British army, Commando training in Wales and Scotland, the invasion of Sicily, and being severely wounded south of Taormina. After about a year in various hospitals in Sicily, Egypt, Scotland and Sussex in the winter of 1944 I was able to resume my studies for the third time; this time at Oxford. Even though I had to wear a large metal contraption to hold up my left arm, Oxford was a wonderful experience. The combination of philosophy, politics and economics suited my interests. I was most attracted to philosophy, but thought it would be easier to earn my living with a training in economics. I believe that Oxford-trained economists, though they have spent less time on economics than their Cambridge equivalents, are better economic theorists for having had to study philosophy (Cambridge-trained ones had a hard time distinguishing between the identity and the equality of savings and investment), and better applied economists for having had to study politics. After Finals in 1947 I was elected to a Lectureship, and the next year to a Fellowship, at Balliol College.

The genuine Athenian democracy of an Oxford College, the college spirit, and the daily contact with brilliant colleagues from many areas and with excellent undergraduates provided a heady mixture. These were the happiest years of my life.

I was also awarded a Studentship at the newly founded Nuffield College, whose Warden, Henry Clay, was very kind to me. I was supposed to embark on graduate studies and my supervisor was John Hicks. International trade theory assumed then largely perfect competition. I wanted to apply the theory of monopolistic (and oligopolistic) competition to international trade: to the relations both between governments (say in tariff war or exchange rate devaluations) and between firms. It was admittedly an ambitious proposal. Hicks would not tolerate it. Young men must do empirical work, and, by implication, only Hicks should do theory. He wanted me to write a thesis on tramp freights. I found that too boring. (G. M. Meier inherited tramp freights from me and wrote his B. Litt. thesis on the subject.) Having been meanwhile elected to a Fellowship with full tenure, and being busy with teaching, there was no need for acquiring another degree and I dropped it.

As a Tutorial Fellow of Balliol College in the late forties and fifties I had to cover a wide area of economics. My teaching load was heavy, sometimes up to 25 hours a week. It may be that for this reason, and the fact that I never had to engage in graduate studies, I have never acquired a taste for specialization. I find the question, "What's your field?" embarrassing. Many of my colleagues cultivate patches, knowing more and more about less and less. I have always liked to jump from topic to topic. Methodology, welfare economics, public finance, international trade, monopolistic competition, human resources, development studies, have at different times engaged my interest. But I was fortunate in my Balliol teaching in being able to divide the teaching with Thomas Balogh, who taught applied economics, while I could concentrate on theory.

My interest in development sprang from four sources. First, in the late 1950s I wrote critically on the doctrine of balanced growth as expounded by Paul Rosenstein Rodan and Ragnar Nurkse. It was at about the same time as Albert Hirschman advocated unbalanced growth. Secondly, Gunnar Myrdal called on me again to help him with the monumental Twenty Century study *Asian Drama*. Third, my social concern for poverty eradication combined with objections to nationalism and a feeling of solidarity with the world community pointed to development. Fourth, the multi- and inter-disciplinary character of development studies attracted me. For it is not a sub-branch of economics, but a field of study much wider than economics. Theory preceded practice, for my contributions to *Asian Drama* preceded my having set foot in a developing country. I visited India for the first time in 1963, after the bulk of my work for the book was finished.

I have always been sceptical of a certain kind of economic model. They tend to neglect the role of institutions, history, politics and valuations in the analysis of economic problems. In my early work on welfare economics, international trade, public finance and flexible exchange rates I had seen the importance of discontinuities, asymmetries, irreversibilities and indivisibilities.

In my first book, *Economic Integration*, I criticized the economic claims for European integration and the doctrine of balanced growth. Work with Gunnar Myrdal on *Asian Drama* and later as Deputy Director-General of the Economic Planning Staff in the UK Overseas Development Ministry changed my interest from theory to policy. I wanted to know how to bridge the gap between thinkers and doers. Experience in advising policy makers in a very small country (Malta, with Dom Mintoff) and a very large one (India with Pitambar Pant) led me to think about different kinds of interaction between domestic and international forces. At the same time, I never lose any sleep over policy makers not accepting my advice.

Work in the Ministry of Overseas Development between 1964 and 1966 with Dudley Seers, Barbara Castle and Sir Andrew Cohen made me aware of the political and practical constraints of implementing policies, and drew my attention to the question of how to mobilize interests and concerns for support of desirable policies. Although aware of the thick, syrupy flow of history, and the difficulties of swimming against it, I have never ceased to believe in the usefulness of making Utopian blueprints. Like the giant Antaeus, who gained his strength from contact with the earth, and who was killed by Hercules by being lifted off his mother earth, I have since then felt the need to keep in touch with practical affairs from time to time, and in the late 1970s spent a few years in the World Bank, at the invitation of Hollis Chenery. I gained other practical experience from service on the Board of the Commonwealth Development Corporation, the Royal Commission on Environmental Pollution, in College administration, in India working with the charismatic Pitambar Pant, the head of the Perspective Planning Division of the Planning Commission, and in other capacities. It is from these practical experiences that I acquired my admiration for the rare quality of *Zivilcourage*, inadequately translated as moral courage, the courage to speak up for your convictions even if in a minority of one, surrounded by hostile antagonists. This impressive character feature is not correlated with physical courage.

Among the intellectual influences of my childhood that of my uncle Ludwig Neumann is outstanding. My father having died before I was two, my mother moved with her two sons into the household of her sister, who had two daughters, and my uncle took the place of my father. He stimulated our imagination with magical stories and made us socially and morally sensitive and responsible. Then there was our youth leader Heinz Trampusch, who was also our tutor at home, and who aroused my curiosity in science (he was a zoologist and taught us to dissect mice) and politics. Later, in my youth, important influences were a lawyer friend of the family, and an admirer of my aunt, Walter Fröhlich, whose Manchester liberal convictions, applied to both economics and politics (he defended in court socialists arrested by the Dollfuss-Schuschnigg regimes) contrasted sharply with the socialism of my uncle (he emigrated and taught economics at Marquette University); my school teacher Häussler, who carried membership cards of all political parties as an insurance, the idealist sociologist Max Adler, who tried to combine Kant and Marx; the philosopher Moritz Schlick who was shot dead by a student in the University of Vienna and Edgar Zilsel, who lectured on hero worship at the People's High School in Vienna and, after emigrating, committed suicide in California. In Aberdeen I was taught by the economist Lindley Macnaghten

353

Fraser (his Christian names, the names of two British judges, are significant) and the dour and kindly philosopher John Laird. I also enjoyed the flamboyant style of the psychologist Rex Knight.

At Oxford Thomas Balogh and Maurice Allen provided a well balanced team of tutors, combining intuition with critical analysis, and radicalism with conservatism. The philosopher Donald Mackinnon was not only kind but also famous for his effortless and unselfconscious eccentricity and very stimulating ideas. The Master, A. D. Lindsay, taught me political theory. I attended the lectures of Michal Kalecki and Frank Burchardt. I also liked Harry Weldon, bachelor Fellow of Magdalen, who is the model for the devilish villain in C. S. Lewis's science fiction novels.

With Balogh I formed a close friendship and we collaborated on several articles, including a critique of the neoclassical calculations of "returns to education" and an essay showing that high interest rates can contribute to inflation. We were critical of the hopes built on flexible exchange rates (40 years later I still regard our critique as valid) and of the economic promises of the European Common Market (where I am less certain that we were right). I regarded it as my task to put Balogh's brilliant intuitions into shapes more acceptable to the economics profession.

A year in the United States on a Rockefeller Fellowship brought me in touch with Paul Baran and Tibor Scitovsky (as well as Paul Samuelson, Gottfried Haberler, Alvin Hansen, Edward Mason, James Tobin and Carl Kaysen), reunited me with my family who had migrated to America, and, above all, led to the discovery of the young woman who became my wife.

In the late 1940s I got to know Gunnar Myrdal, who had asked me to translate and edit his youthful, iconoclastic book *The Political Element in the Development of Economic Theory* into English, and with whom I collaborated on several other projects throughout his life. I collected his methodological writings in *Value in Social Theory*, and wrote a long Introduction to it. I still think it contains a valid critique of welfare economics. It was widely praised, and completely ignored, sometimes even by myself. When I worked with Myrdal on *Asian Drama* he thought my critique of planning models and the production function excessively detailed and called it slightly contemptuously "filigree work".

354

Among scholars whose ideas and work I admire for their combination of brilliant insights and range with human and moral concerns are Albert Hirschman, Amartya Sen, Tibor Scitovsky, Nicholas Kaldor, Jagdish Bhagwati, George Richardson, Thomas Schelling, Ronald Dore, and the historian turned economist Hugh Stretton. Among younger economists, my favourites, for different reasons, and friends are Frances Stewart, Sanjaya Lall, Michael Lipton, Robert Klitgaard, Michael McPherson, Stuart Holland, Mohan Rao, Gillian Hart and Jeffrey James. Among more action-oriented men I admire Mahbub ul Haq and Nurul Islam. A longer list of my favourite scholars is contained in the list of members (and ex-members) of the board of the journal *World Development*.

I have been a better critic than apologist or advocate. My first two published articles contained a critique of the theory of the firm and of the theory of profit. During my years in the World Bank in the late 1970s I was put in charge of the work on basic needs. I never felt comfortable in that role. After having left the Bank I felt liberated when I could return to a more critical stance.

I have always wished I had learned more mathematics. Without this grounding, one feels like a handloom weaver in the days of the power loom. But the thought is made bearable by the fact that most of the power loom weavers seem to be weaving the Emperor's clothes. The rigour achieved by much mathematical modelling is all too often a rigor mortis. And the models, shapely and elegant though they may be, too often lack the vital organs.

All thinking calls for structure and abstraction. Models can serve as scaffolds, or as crutches for better access to an incoherent, highly complex reality. And it has often been said that practical men and women use crude implicit models. A sharp focus illuminates a small area, but excludes what lies outside it. At any given time there is only one orthodoxy, but many heterodoxies.

I regard the principal function of the dissenter as being to produce an alternative paradigm only in order to serve as an intellectual muscle therapist, who, by engaging us in intellectual finger exercises, cures us of intellectual cramps, who prevents the premature crystallization of flawed orthodoxies. His function is more therapeutic than substantive.

355

The heterodox dissenter stands for humility, modesty and tolerance. For the orthodox the worst offence is fuzziness. If I had to choose I would rather be accused of fuzziness than of reductionism. The heterodox dissenter prefers, I think, to be accused of fuzziness. He prefers, like Amartya K. Sen, to be vaguely right to being precisely wrong. The orthodox insist that reductionism is not the occupational disease of economists, it is their occupation. But if in the process they throw the baby out instead of the bathwater, the reduction loses its point.

2. Bibliography

'The Theory of Profit', *Manchester School*, vol. XVII, No. 3, September 1949, pp. 266-96.

'The Theory of Pricing', *Jahrbücher für Nationalökonomie und Statistik*, Band 161, Heft 3/4, October 1949, pp. 161-87.

'Mängel des Preismechanismus', in *Vollbeschäftigung*, Cologne: Bund Verlag, 1950, pp.149-72.

'Exchange Rates and National Income', with T. BALOGH, *Banca Nazionale del Lavoro*, No. 3, October/December 1950, pp. 249-54; reprinted in *Bulletin of the Oxford University Institute of Statistics*, vol. XII, No. 4, March 1951, pp. 101-8.

'The Inappropriateness of Simple "Elasticity" Concepts in the Theory of International Trade', with T. BALOGH, *Banca Nazionale del Lavoro*, No. 3, October/December 1950, pp. 583-95; reprinted in *Bulletin of the Oxford University Institute of Statistics*, vol. XIII, No. 1, February 1951, pp. 65-77.

'Economics and Value Judgements', *Quarterly Journal of Economics*, vol. LXIV, No. 4, November 1950, pp. 583-95.

'Reserve Capacity and the Kinked Demand Curve', *Review of Economic Studies*, vol. XVIII (2), No. 46, 1950-51, pp. 103-13.

'La théorie moderne de l'économie de bien-être', *Economie Appliquée*, Tome V, No. 4, October 1952, pp. 429-53.

Translation, editing and appendix on 'Recent Controversies' (pp. 208-17), Gunnar MYRDAL, *The Political Element in the Development of Economic Theory*, London: Routledge & Kegan Paul, 1953.

'The Effect of Taxation on Risk-Taking', *Oxford Economic Papers*, vol. V, No. 3, October 1953, pp. 271-87.

'Keynes and the Classics', in K. KURIHARA, ed., *Post-Keynesian Economics*, New Brunswick, N.J.: Rutgers University Press, 1954, pp. 345-64.

'Elasticity Optimism and Pessimism in International Trade', *Economia Internazionale*, vol. VII, No. 1, February 1954, pp. 85-112.

'Programs and Prognoses', *Quarterly Journal of Economics*, vol. LXVIII, No. 3, August 1954, pp. 355-76.

Revision, editing and two additional chapters 'Opium Eaters and Opi-

um Abstaines' and 'The Planned World of Today', R. L. HEIL-
BRONER, *The Great Economists,* London: Eyre & Spottiswoode, 1955;
published in the USA as *The Wordly Philosophes*; German translation
Wirtschaft und Wissen, Cologne: Bund-Verlag, 1955.

'Productivity Growth and the Balance of Trade', *Bulletin of the Oxford
University Institute of Statistics,* vol. XVII, No. 1, February 1955, pp.
11-17.

'Two Comments on the Articles by Mrs. Paul and Professor Hicks', *Oxford Economic Papers,* vol. VII, No. 3, October 1955, pp. 259-64.

'Some Problems Raised by the Report of the Royal Commission on the
Taxation of Profits and Income', *Bulletin of the Oxford University Institute of Statistics,* vol. XVII, No. 4, November 1955, pp. 321-61.

'The Taxation of Overseas Profits', *Manchester School,* vol. XXV, No. 1,
January 1957, pp. 89-105; reprinted in *Studi in Memoria di Benvenuto
Griziotti,* Milan: Giuffré, 1959.

'Government and the Economy in the U.S.A.', *Rivista di Diritto Finanziario e Scienza delle Finanze,* vol. XVI, No. 1, March 1957, pp.
34-51.

'The Economic Consequences of Overseas Trade Concessions', *Bulletin
of the Oxford University Institute of Statistics,* vol. XIX, No. 3, August
1957, pp. 279-83.

'Growth, the Terms of Trade and the Balance of Trade', with J.
BLACK, *Economie Appliquée,* vol. X, No. 2/3, April/September 1957,
pp. 299-322.

'Sviluppo economico, stabilità e altri fini della politica fiscale', *Rivista
internazionale di scienze sociali,* Serie III, vol. XXVII, No. 5, October
1957, pp. 414-23.

'A Reconsideration of Monetary Policy', with T. BALOGH, *Bulletin of the
Oxford University Institute of Statistics,* vol. XIX, No. 4, November 1957,
pp. 331-39.

Editing and 'Introduction' (pp. ix-xlvi), Gunnar MYRDAL, *Value in Social Theory,* London: Routledge & Kegan Paul; New York: Harper
& Brothers, 1958.

'Taxation and Enterprise', *University of Toronto Quarterly,* vol. XXVII No.
2, January 1958, pp. 137-47.

'Tassazione e iniziativa privata', *Rivista internazionale di scienze sociali,* Serie III, vol. XXIX, No. 1, January 1958, pp. 19-29.

'A Note on Kaldor's "Speculation and Economic Stability"', *Review of Economic Studies*, vol. XXVI, No. 1, October 1958, pp. 66-8.

'El Principio de Compensación', *Revista de Economía Política*, vol. X, No. 1, January/April 1959, pp. 5-23.

'Unbalanced Growth', *Oxford Economic Papers*, vol. XI, No. 2, June 1959, pp. 167-90.

'Déséquilibre et croissance', *Cahiers de l'institut de science économique appliqée*, No. 85, Hors Série 3, July 1959, pp. 71-108.

'Tax Policy for Investment', *Rivista di diritto finanziario e scienza delle finanze*, vol. XIX, No. 2, June 1960, pp. 117-37; reprinted in a shortened version in *Mercurio*.

'Domestic vs. Foreign Investment', with T. BALOGH, *Bulletin of the Oxford University Institute of Statistics*, vol. XXII, No. 3, August 1960, pp. 213-24.

Economic Integration: Aspects and Problems, Leyden: A. W. Sythoff, 1961; Second revised and enlarged edition, 1964.

Contribution to *Théorie et Politique de l'expansion régionale*, Brussels: Les Editions de la Librairie Encyclopaedique, S.P.R.L., 1961, pp. 333-49, pp. 421-31, pp. 473-87.

'Socialist Economics' in *Collier's Encyclopaedia*, New York: Crowell-Collier, 1962, pp. 124-32.

'Commercial Policy', in G. D. N. WORSWICK and P. H. ADY, eds., *The British Economy in the Nineteen-fifties*, Oxford: Oxford University Press, 1962, pp. 76-113.

'Wages, Prices and Productivity', *Kyklos*, vol. XV, No. 3, October 1962, pp. 723-31; reprinted in R. J. BALL and P. DOYLE, eds., *Inflation*, Harmondsworth: Penguin, 1969, pp. 177-85.

The Crisis of Indian Planning, joint editor with Michael LIPTON, Oxford: Oxford University Press for the Royal Institute of International Affairs, 1963; Second edition, 1968.

'Values, Facts and the Compensation Principle', in E. von BECKERATH and Herbert GIERSCH, eds., *Probleme der normativen Ökonomik und der wirtschaftspolitischen Beratung*, Berlin: von Duncker & Humblot, 1963, pp. 164-79.

'More Care about Capital Use', *Yojana*, vol. VII, No. 5, March 1963, pp. 17-18.

359

'Unbalanced Growth: A Reply', *Oxford Economic Papers*, vol. xv, No. 1, March 1963, pp. 66-73.

'The Case for Export Subsidies', *All India Congress Committee Economic Review*, vol. xiv, No. 21, April 1963, pp. 1-2.

'Common Fallacies About the Common Market', *Weltwirtschaftliches Archiv*, Band 90, Heft 2, April 1963, pp. 276-89.

'Problems of Economic Integration', *Weltwirtschaftliches Archiv*, Band 90, Heft 2, April 1963, pp. 49-54.

'The Coefficient of Ignorance', with T. BALOGH, *Bulletin of the Oxford University Institute of Statistics*, vol. xxv, No. 2, May 1963, pp. 97-107; reprinted in Mark BLAUG, ed., *Economics of Education*, Baltimore: Penguin, 1968, pp. 383-95; also reprinted in Ronald A. WYKSTRA, ed., *Human Capital Formation and Manpower Development*, New York: The Free University Press, 1971, pp. 194-204; as well as in Ian LIVINGSTONE, ed., *Development Economics and Policy: Readings*, London, Boston and Sidney: Allen & Unwin, 1981, pp. 25-9.

'Economic Equilibrium', 'Wealth' and 'Welfare', in Julius GOULD and William L. KOLB, eds., *A Dictionary of the Social Sciences*, London: Tavistock Publication for UNESCO, 1964.

'The Use and Abuse of Models in Development Planning', in K. MARTIN and J. KNAPP, *The Teaching of Development Economics*, Proceedings of the Manchester National Conference on Teaching Economic Development, April 1964, London: Frank Cass; Chicago: Aldine Publishing Co., 1967, pp. 57-84.

Contribution to *Bergedorfer Protokolle: Economic Aid - A Way to Growth or Decline?*, Protokolle No. 15, Hamburg: Bergedorf, 1964, pp. 70, 81, 98, 122, 128.

'Programmes and Prognoses, Unbalanced Growth and the Ideal Plan', *Banca Nazionale del Lavoro Quarterly Review*, No. 17, June 1964, pp. 115-29.

'Teaching the Cool', *The Oxford Magazine*, New Series vol. v, No. 2, October 1964, pp. 33-34.

'Hilfe, Handel and Entwicklung', *Schmollers Jahrbuch*, Band 84, Heft 6, November 1964, pp. 676-90.

'Educational Planning for Development', *Overseas Universities*, August 1965.

'Programme und Prognosen', in G. GÄFGEN, ed., *Grundlagen der Wirtschaftspolitik*, Cologne: Kiepenheuer & Witsch, 1966, pp. 53-76.

'The Objectives of Economic Policy', in P. D. HENDERSON, ed., *Economic Growth in Britain*, London: Weidenfeld and Nicolson, 1966, pp. 29-53.

'Rich and Poor Nations', in P. D. HENDERSON, ed., *Economic Growth in Britain*, London: Weidenfeld and Nicolson, 1966, pp. 261-89.

'Studying To Make Overseas Aid More Effective', *The Times*, 16 September 1966.

'International Monetary Reform and the Less Developed Countries', *Banca Nazionale del Lavoro Quarterly Review*, No. 20, June 1967, pp. 157-77.

'Development and the Institute of Development Studies', *Journal of Administration Overseas*, October 1967.

'The Frontiers of Development Studies', *The Journal of Development Studies*, vol. IV, No. 4, October 1967, pp. 2-24; reprinted in I. LIVINGSTONE, ed., *Economic Policy for Development*, Harmondsworth: Penguin, pp. 418-46.

Collaboration with Gunnar Myrdal, *Asian Drama - An Inquiry into the Poverty of Nations*, Appendixes, New York: Twentieth Century Fund, 1968.

'Economic Development and Education', *Educational Encyclopaedia*, Israel: Ministry of Education and Culture and Bialik Institute, 1968.

'Counselling in British Stabilisation Policy', in Hans K. SCHNEIDER, ed., *Grundsatzprobleme wirtschaftspolitischer Beratung*, Berlin: Duncker & Humblot, 1968, pp. 103-17.

'International Capital Movement', in Ernesto D'ALBERGO, ed., *Essays in Honour of Antonio de Viti de Marco*; reprinted in Ernesto d'Albergo, ed., *Studi in memoria di Antonio de Viti de Marco*, Bari, 1972.

'A Poor Nation's Guide to Getting Aid', *New Society*, February 1968.

'European Development Policy and Development Concepts', *Rivista internazionale di scienze economiche e commerciali*, vol. XV, No. 5, May 1968, pp. 405-32.

'Improving the Climate', *Ceres*, vol. II, March/April 1968.

'EEC Membership: Impact on the British Balance of Payments', *Intereconomics*, No. 10, October 1968, pp. 298-302.

'Die EWG ist gar nicht so anziehend', *Wirtschaftsdienst*, vol. XLVIII, No. 12, December 1968, pp. 695-703.

'Education and Development', in K. HUFNER and J. NAUMANN, *Economics of Education in Transition*. Festschrift für Professor Dr. Friederich Edding, Stuttgart: Ernst Klett Verlag, 1969, pp. 183-98.

'The Case for Export Subsidies', *The Journal of Development Studies*, vol. V, No. 4, July 1969, pp. 270-73.

'A New Commonwealth', *New Society*, July 1969; reprinted in *The Frontiers of Development Studies*, Basingstoke and London: Macmillan; New York: Wiley, 1972, 403-7.

'Nouvelles manières d'aborder le probleme de l'investissement privé dans les pays en voie de developpement', *Revue de la Société d'Etudes et d'Expansion*, vol. LXVIII, No. 238, November/December 1969, pp. 909-24; reprinted in *Mercurio*, vol. XIII, No. 9, September 1970; also reprinted in J. Dunning, ed., *International Investment*, Harmondsworth: Penguin, 1972, pp. 434-54.

Unfashionable Economics. Essays in Honour of Lord Balogh, ed., London: Weidenfeld and Nicolson, 1970.

'Two Worlds: Problems of Integration', *History of the 20th Century*, vol. VIII.

'An analysis of the factors that militate against or are conducive to the formation of international trade groupings', in *International Trade Groupings*, London: Ministry of Overseas Development, 1970.

'An Institutional Critique of Development Concepts', *Archives Européenes de Sociologie*, Tome XI, No. 1, January 1970, pp. 69-80.

'Linking Money and Development', *International Affairs*, vol. XLVI, No. 1, January 1970, pp. 23-9.

'The Role of Private Investment', *Venture*, January 1970.

'Principles and Problems of a Liberal Order of the Economy', *Weltwirtschaftliches Archiv*, Band 104, Heft 1, January 1970, pp. 1*-5*.

'Obstacles to Private Foreign Investment in the LDC's', *Columbia Journal of World Business*, vol. V, No. 3, May/June 1970.

'Enoch Powell, the Churces and Aid', *Study Encounter*, vol. VI, No. 2, 1970.

Capital for Africa: The British Contribution, with Helen SUTCH, London: Africa Publications Trust, 1971.

Commonwealth Policy in a Global Context, joint editor with Hugh CORBET, London: Frank Cass, 1971.

Diversification and Development: The Case of Coffee, with Diane ELSON, London and New York: Praeger, 1971.

'New Approaches to Private Overseas Investment' in Peter ADY, ed., *Private Foreign Investment and the Developing World*, Praeger Special Studies in International Economics and Development, New York and London: Praeger, 1971, pp. 51-85.

'The Development Process: Comment', in A. A. AYIDA and H. M. A. ONITIRI, eds., *Reconstruction and Development in Nigeria*, Proceedings of a National Conference (Ibadan, Nigeria), New York and London: Oxford University Press for the Nigerian Institute of Social and Economic Research, 1971, pp. 81-3.

'Economic Development and Education', in A. R. DESAI, ed., *Essays on Modernization of Underdeveloped Societies*, Bombay, 1971.

'Costs and Benefits of Multinational Enterprise in Less Developed Countries', in John H. DUNNING, ed., *The Multinational Enterprise*, London: George Allen &Unwin, 1971, pp. 240-58.

'Trade and Liquidity: the Indian Subcontinent', with Akbar NOMAN, in Barbara WARD, Lenore D'ANJOU and J. D. RUNNALS, eds., *The Widening Gap*, New York and London: Columbia University Press, 1971, pp. 185-213.

'Aid to India', *Year Book of World Affairs 1970*, London: Stevens & Sons, 1971, pp. 138-52.

'The Developing Countries in a World of Flexible Exchange Rates', *International Currency Review*, vol. II, No. 6, January/February 1971, pp. 21-7; reprinted in *The Frontiers of Development Studies*, Basingstoke and London: Macmillan; New York: Wiley, 1972, pp. 246-53.

'Development Investment', *Venture*, June 1971.

'Conflicts between Output and Employment Objectives', with Frances STEWART, *Oxford Economic Papers*, vol. XXIII, No. 2, July 1971, pp. 145-68; reprinted in Ronald ROBINSON, ed., *Prospects for Employment Opportunities in the Nineteen Seventies*, 1971; also reprinted in Richard JOLLY, Emanuel DE KADT, Hans SINGER and Fiona WILSON, eds., *Third World Employment*, London: Penguin, 1973; as well as in M. P. TODARO, *The Struggle for Economic Development: Readings in Problems and Policies*, New York and London: Longman, 1983, pp. 164-81;

also reprinted in *Bangladesh Economic Review*, vol. 1, No. 1, January 1973, pp. 1-24.

The Frontiers of Development Studies, Basingstoke and London: Macmillan; New York: Wiley, 1972.

Aid For Africa, New York and London: Praeger, 1972.

'Overseas Development Policies', with Dudley SEERS, in Wilfred BECKERMAN, ed., *The Labour Government's Economic Record, 1964-1970*, London: Duckworth, 1972, pp. 118-56; reprinted in *The Frontiers of Development Studies*, Basingstoke and London: Macmillan; New York: Wiley, 1972, pp. 254-96.

'A New Look at Foreign Aid', in T. J. BYRES, ed., *Foreign Resources and Economic Development*, A Symposium on the Report of the Pearson Commission, London: Frank Cass, 1972, pp. 183-94; reprinted in *The Frontiers of Development Studies*, Basingstoke and London: Macmillan; New York: Wiley, 1972, 297-306.

'The Political Economy of the Environment: Problems of Method', in C. F. CARTER and J. L. FORD, eds., *Uncertainty and Expectations in Economics. Essays in Honour of G. L. S. Shackle*, Oxford: Basil Blackwell, 1972, pp. 276-90; reprinted in *The Frontiers of Development Studies*, Basingstoke and London: Macmillan; New York: Wiley, 1972, pp. 367-80.

'Balanced versus Unbalanced Growth' in W. L. JOHNSON and D. R. KAMERSCHEN, eds., *Readings in Economic Development*, Cincinnati and Brighton: South-Western, 1972, pp. 230-40.

'Regional Integration in Asia', *Foreign Trade Review*, January/March 1972.

'Little-Mirrlees Methods and Projects Appraisal', with Frances STEWART, *Bulletin of the Oxford University Institute of Economics and Statistics*, vol. XXXIV, No. 1, February 1972, pp. 75-91.

'Economic and Social Rights and the Developing Countries', *Revue Européenne des Sciences Sociales*, Tome X, No. 26, February 1972, pp. 21-38.

'Terms of Trade Are Not Made On Paper', *Ceres*, vol. V, No. 2, March/April 1972; reprinted in a shortened version as 'Self-help for Poor Nations', *New Society*, April 1972.

'The Effects of Asian Economic Integration on Private Overseas Direct Investment', *Foreign Trade Review*, April/June 1972.

'Santiago in Retrospect', *Third World*, vol. I, No. 2, October 1972.

'Technology Gaps between Rich and Poor Countries', *Scottish Journal of Political Economy*, vol. XIX, No. 3, November 1972, pp. 213-30; reprinted in P. K. GOSH, ed., *Technology Policy and Development: A Thrid World Prospective*, International Development Resource Book, No. 3, Westport, Conn. and London: Greenwood Press, 1984, pp. 7-26; a shorter version was in *Royal Central Asian Journal*, 1971 and in *Kajian Ekonomi Malayasia*, June 1971.

'Cambridge Conference on Trade and Development', *Journal of World Trade Law*, vol. VI, No. 6, November/December 1972, pp. 703-6.

'To Back Moral Appeals by Power', *Bulletin of Peace Proposals*, vol. III, 1972.

Trade Strategies for Development (ed.), Papers of the Ninth Cambridge Conference on Development Problems (September 1972), Basingstoke and London: Macmillan, 1973.

'Industrialization and Trade Trends: Some Issues for the 1970s: Comment', in H. HUGHES, ed., *Prospects for Partnership: Industrialization and Trade Policies in the 1970s*, Baltimore and London: Johns Hopkins University Press for the International Bank for Reconstruction and Development, 1973, pp. 35-9.

'Some Comments on the Teaching of Economics', in I. LIVINGSTONE, G. ROUTH, J. F. RWEYEMANU and K. E. SVENDSEN, eds., *The Teaching of Economics in Africa*, Report of a Conference (April 1969, Dar es Salaam), London: Chatto & Windus for the Sussex University Press, 1973, pp. 46-50.

'An Institutional Critique of Development Concepts', in I. LIVINGSTONE, G. ROUTH, J. F. RWEYEMANU and K. E. SVENDSEN, eds., *The Teaching of Economics in Africa*, Report of a Conference (April 1969, Dar es Salaam), London: Chatto & Windus for the Sussex University Press, 1973, pp. 82-94.

'Probleme internationaler Kooperation in Forschung und Technologie aus der Sicht der Europäischen Gemeinschaften', in Burkhardt RÖPER, *Technischer Fortschritt und Unternehmensgrösse*, Düsseldorf: 1973.

'Research: A Comment', *Food Research Institute Studies in Agricultural Economics, Trade and Development*, vol. XII, No. 1, January 1973, pp. 59-61.

'Trade Strategies for Development: Some Themes for the Seventies', *World Development*, vol. I, No. 6, June 1973.

'Money: The Root of All Good ?', *Third World*, vol. II, No. 7, July/August 1973.

'The Multinational Enterprise and the Theory of Development Policy', *World Development*, vol. I, No. 10, October 1973.

'Preface to "Earned International Reserve Units"', *World Development*, 1973.

The Limits of Development Research, Oxford: Pergamon Press, 1974.

'The Multinational Enterprise and the Theory of Development Policy', in John DUNNING, ed., *Economic Analysis and the Multinational Enterprise*, Praeger International Studies in International Economics and Development, New York and London: Praeger, 1974, pp.252-79.

'World Trade in Agricultural Commodities and the Terms of Trade with Industrial Goods', in Nurul ISLAM, ed., *Agricultural Policy in Developing Countries*. Proceedings of a Conference Held by the International Economic Association at Bad Godesberg, West Germany, Basingstoke and London: Macmillan; New York and Toronto: Halsted Press, 1974, pp. 207-23; reprinted in Hans SINGER, Neelamber HATTI and Rameshwar TANDON, eds., *International Commodity Policy*, New Delhi: Ashish Publishing House, 1987, pp. 198-218.

'Alternatives in Development', *World Development*, vol. II, No. 2, February 1974, pp. 5-8.

'The Limits of Development Research', *World Development*, vol. II, Nos. 10-12, October/December 1974; reprinted in P. J. LAVAKARE, A. PARTHASARATHI and B. M. Udgaonkar VIKAS, eds., *Scientific Cooperation for Development: Search for New Directions*, New Delhi, 1980.

'Social Science Research on Development: Some Problems in the Use and Transfer of an Intellectual Technology', *Journal of Economic Literature*, vol. XII, No. 4, December 1974, pp. 1290-300.

'The Use and Abuse of Models in Development Planning', in Y. RAMATI, ed., *Economic Growth in Developing Countries - Material and Human Resources: Proceedings of the Seventh Rehovot Conference*, Praeger International Studies in International Economics and Development, New York and London: Praeger in cooperation with the Continuation Committee of the Rehovot Conference, 1975, pp. 395-402.

'Industrialization in a Unified Development Strategy', *World Development*, vol. III, No. 1, January 1975, pp. 1-9; reprinted in Sir Alec CAIRNCROSS and Mohinder PURI, eds., *Employment, Income Distribution and Development Strategy, Essays in Honour of H. W. Singer*, Basingstoke and London: Macmillan; New York: Holmes & Meier, 1976, pp. 90-105.

'Policies Towards Multinationals', *World Development*, vol. III, No. 6, June 1975, pp. 393-7; reprinted in C. Díaz ALEJANDRO, S. TEITEL and V. E. TOKMAN, eds., *Política económica en centro y periferia, Essays in Honour of Felipe Pazos*, Mexico City: Fondo de Cultura Económica, 1976, pp. 389-97.

'Why Interdisciplinary Studies?', in Glynn COCHRANE, ed., *What Can We Do For Each Other - An Interdisciplinary Approach to Development Anthropology*, Amsterdam: B. R. Gruner, 1976.

'The Dynamics of the New Poor Power' in G. K. HELLEINER, ed., *A World Divided: The Less Developed Countries in the International Economy*, Perspective on Development, No. 5, New York, London and Melbourne: Cambridge University Press, 1976, pp. 77-88; reprinted in an expanded version in *Resources Policy*, vol. II, No. 2, June 1976, pp. 73-86.

'The Meaning and Purpose of Interdisciplinary Studies', *Interdisciplinary Science Reviews*, vol. I, No. 2, 1976.

'Bargaining with Multinationals', *World Development*, vol. IV, No. 3, March 1976, pp. 225-9.

'The Meaning and Purpose of Interdisciplinary Studies as Applied to Development Economics', *Interdisciplinary Science Reviews*, June 1976.

'It *Is* A Moral Issue', *Crucible*, vol. XV, July/September 1976, pp. 108-12.

'New Strategies for Development: Poverty, Inequality and Growth', with Frances STEWART, *Oxford Economic Papers*, vol. XXIIX, No. 3, November 1976, pp. 381-405; reprinted in C. K. WILBER, ed., *The Political Economy of Development and Underdevelopment*, 1979.

Foreign Investment, Transnationals and Developing Countries, with Sanjaya Lall, Basingstoke and London: Macmillan, 1977.

'New Strategies for Development: A Comment', with Frances STEWART, in *Hommage a François Perroux*, Grenoble: Presses Universitaires de Grenoble, 1977.

'The Distinctive Features of a Basic Needs Approach to Development', *International Development Review*, vol. XIX, No. 3, 1977, pp. 8-16; reprinted in P. K. GOSH, ed., *Third World Development: A Basic Need Approach*, International Development Resource Books, No. 13, Westport, Conn. and London: Greenwood Press, 1984, pp. 29-40.

'Changing Perceptions on Development', *Finance and Development*, vol. XIV, No. 3, September 1977, p. 14; reprinted in *Challange*, vol. XX, No. 5, November/December 1977, pp. 63-6.

'Labour-intensive Technologies for the Caribbean Area', with Jeffry JAMES, *The Seoul National University Economic Review*, vol. XI, No. 1, December 1977, pp. 147-76.

'Development Ideas in Historical Perspective - New Interest in Development', *Internationales Asienforum*, vol. IX, Nos. 1/2, January/May 1978, pp. 27-40; reprinted in I. ADELMAN, ed., *Economic Growth and Rescources*, Proceedings of the Fifth World Congress of the International Economic Association Held in Tokyo, Japan, vol. IV, *National and International Policies*, New York: St. Martin's Press, 1979, pp. 56-68; also reprinted in *Toward a New Strategy for Development, A Rothko Chapel Symposium*, New York and Oxford: Pergamon Press, 1979; reprinted as well in *Regional Development Dialogue*, vol. I, No. 2, Autumn 1980; also reprinted in R. P. MISRA and M. HONJO, eds., *Changing Perceptions on Development Problems*, Nagoya, Japan, 1981.

'Basic Needs: Some Issues', with S. J. BURKI, *World Development*, vol. VI, No. 3, March 1978, pp. 411-21.

'Editor's Introduction', *World Development*, Special Issue 'Poverty and Inequality', vol. VI, No. 3, March 1978, pp. 241-3.

'Transnational Corporations and Basic Needs', in Mary Evelyn JEGEN and Charles K. WILBER, eds., *Growth with Equity: Strategies for Meeting Human Needs*, New York: Paulist Press, 1979, pp. 163-74.

'Growth, Redistribution and Basic Human Needs', in K. LASKI, E. MATZNER and E. NOWOTNY, eds., *Beiträge zur Diskussion und Kritik der neoklassischen Ökonomie*. Festschrift für Kurt W. Rothchild und Josef Steindl, Berlin, Heidelberg: Springer Verlag, 1979, pp. 105-21.

'Self-reliant Industrialization', in Charles K. WILBER, ed., *The Political Economy of Development and Underdevelopment*, 1979; reprinted as 'Eigenstandige Industrialisierung', in Khushi M. KHAN, ed., *Self-reliance als nationale und kollektive Entwicklungsstrategie*, Munich: Weltforum Verlag, 1980; also reprinted in Saeed Ahmad QURESHI and Muhammad ARIF, eds., *Strategies of Planning and Development*, Punjab, Pakistan: Planning and Development Board.

'Basic Needs: Premises and Promises', *Journal of Policy Modeling*, vol. I, No. 1, January 1979, pp. 136-46.

368

'Multinationals Revisited', *Finance and Development*, vol. XVI, No. 2, June 1979, pp. 39-42; reprinted in Robert E. BALDWIN and J. David RICHARDSON, eds., *International Trade and Finance: Readings*, Second Edition, Boston and Toronto: Little, Brown, 1981, pp. 308-15.

'Indicators of Development: The Search for a Basic Needs Yardstick', with Norman HICKS, *World Development*, vol. VII, No. 6, June 1979, pp. 567-80.

'From Growth to Basic Needs', *Finance and Development*, vol. XVI, No. 3, September 1979, pp. 28-31; reprinted in *Poverty and Development*, Washington, D.C.: World Bank, pp. 5-8; also reprinted in James L. DIETZ and James H. STREET, *Latin America's Economic Development: Institutionalist and Structuralist Perspectives*, Boulder and London: Rienner, 1987, pp. 33-41.

'On Setting Investment Priorities for Portugal: The Long Run Point of View: Comment', in Fundação Calouste Gulbenkian and the German Marshall Fund of the United States, *Segunda Conferência Internacional Sobre Economia Portuguesa: 26 a 28 de Setembro 1979*, vol. I, Lisbon: Fundação Calouste Gulbenkian, 1980, pp. 483-8.

'Can Basic Human Needs be Met by the Year 2000?', in K. HAQ, ed., *Dialogue for a New Order*, Pergamon Policy Studies on International Development, New York, Oxford, Toronto and Paris: Pergamon Press, 1980, pp. 219-31.

'Development: What Have We Learned?' in J. PAJESTKA and C. H. FEINSTEIN, eds., *The Relevance of Economic Theories*, Proceedings of a Conference Held by the International Economic Association in Collaboration with the Polish Economic Association at Warsaw, Poland, New York: St. Martin's Press; London: Macmillan, 1980, pp. 181-99.

Contribution to John Sewell and the staff of the Overseas Development Council, eds., *The United States and World Development: Agenda 1980*, New York: Praeger, 1980.

'Basic Needs and Human Rights', *World Development*, vol. VIII, No. 2, February 1980, pp. 107-11.

'Development Choices for the 1980s and Beyond - The Choices Before Us', *Development - The International Development Review*, vol. XXII, Nos. 2/3, 1980, pp. 3-12.

'Comment on Benjamin Higgins "The Disenthronement of Basic Needs"', *Regional Development Dialogue*, vol. I, No. 1, Spring 1980, pp. 117-20.

'Basic Needs in the Year 2000', *The Pakistan Development Review*, vol. XIX, No. 2, Summer 1980, pp. 129-41.

'The New International Economic Order: Development Strategy Options', in *Development and Peace*, vol. I, No. 2, Autumn 1980, pp. 5-25; reprinted in Christopher T. SAUNDERS, ed., *East-West-South: Economic Interactions between Three Worlds*, East-West European Interaction Workshop Papers, vol. VI, New York: St. Martin's Press, 1981, pp. 219-45.

Development Perspectives, Basingstoke and London: Macmillan; New York: St. Martin's Press, 1981.

First Things First: Meeting Basic Human Needs in Developing Countries (with S. J. BURKI, Mahbub ul HAQ, Norman HICKS, Frances STEWART), Oxford: Oxford University Press for the World Bank, 1981.

Recent Issues in World Development, joint editor with Richard JOLLY, Oxford, New York, Toronto and Sidney: Pergamon Press, 1981.

Contribution to Friedrich Ebert Foundation, ed., *International Responses to the Brandt Report. Towards One World?*, London: Temple Smith, 1981.

'Foreword', in Danny M. LEIPZIGER, ed., *Basic Needs and Development*, Cambridge, Mass.: Oelgeschlager, Gunn & Hain, 1981, pp. xi-xxii.

'Constructive Responses to the North-South Dialogue', in Edwin F. REUBENS, ed., *The Challenge of the New International Economic Order*, Boulder: Westview Press, 1981, pp. 71-89.

'Reply [Indicators of Development: the Search for a Basic Needs Yardstick]', with Norman HICKS, *World Development*, vol. IX, No. 4, April 1981, pp. 374-97.

'Comment on T. R. Lakshmanan's "Technical Change and Income Distribution in Regional Development"', *Regional Development Dialogue*, vol. II, No. 1, Spring 1981.

'Issues for Transnational Corporations in World Development', *CTC Reporter*, vol. I, No. 10, Spring 1981, pp. 19/22.

'Basic Needs and the New International Economic Order', in T. E. BARKER, A. S. DOWNES and J. A. SACKEY, eds., *Perspectives on Economic Development: Essays in the Honour of W. Arthur Lewis*, Washington, D.C.: University Press of America for the Department of Economics, University of the West Indies, Cave Hill Campus, Barbados, 1982, pp. 110-34; reprinted in *Mondes en Developpement*, Tome X, No. 39, 1982, pp. 317-31.

'Growth, Redistribution and Basic Human Needs', in Claes BRUNDE-SIUS and Mats LUNDAHL, eds., *Development Strategies and Basic Needs in Latin America*, Boulder: Westview Press, 1982, pp. 31-54.

'The Conflict between Communication Gaps and Suitability Gaps', in Meheroo JUSSAWALLA and D. M. LAMBERTON, eds., *Communication Economics and Development*, Policy Studies on International Development Series, Elmsford, N.Y.: Pergamon Press in Cooperation with the East-West Center (Hawaii), 1982, pp. 16-35.

'The Limits of Development Research', in Laurence D. STIFEL, Ralph DAVIDSON and James S. COLEMAN, eds., *Social Sciences and Public Policy in the Developing World*, Lexington, Mass.: Lexington Books, 1982, pp. 21-56.

'Thoughts in Progress: Development', *Development - Seeds of Change*, vol. 1, No. 1, 1982, pp. 76-7.

'What New International Economic Order?', *Pakistan Journal of Applied Economics*, vol. 1, No. 2, Winter 1982, pp. 123-56; reprinted in *Schriften des Vereins für Socialpolitik*, Band 129, 'Ordnungspolitsche Fragen zum Nord-Süd-Konflikt', 1983, pp. 79-112

'Approaches to a New International Economic Order', *World Development*, vol. x, No. 1, January 1982, pp. 1-17; reprinted in John ADAMS, ed., *The Contemporary International Economy*, New York: St. Martin's Press, Second Edition 1985, pp. 495-524; also reprinted in Hans SINGER, Neelamber HATTI and Rameshwar TANDON, eds., *Economic Theory and New World Order*, New Delhi: Ashigh, 1987, pp. 15-52.

'Environmental Aspects of Development', in *Wirtschaft und Gesellschaft*, vol. VIII, No. 2, 'Expansion, Stagnation and Demokratie - Festschrift für Theodor Praeger und Philipp Rieger', Vienna: Kammer für Arbeiter und Angestellte, 1982, pp. 415-28.

'Thoughts on North-South and Cancun', *Third World Quarterly*, vol. IV, No. 3, July 1982, pp. 526-9.

'The New International Economic Order', *International Review of Education*, Special Issue 'Education and the New International Economic Order', vol. XXVIII, No. 4, 1982, pp. 407-29.

'A Cool Look at "Outward-Looking" Development Strategies', *The World Economy*, vol. V, No. 2, September 1982, pp. 159-69; reprinted in *Essays in Honour of A. N. Damaskenides*, 1982.

'Trade as the Engine, Handmaiden, Brake or Offspring of Growth?', *The World Economy*, vol. V, No. 4, December 1982, pp. 415-7.

Human Resources, Employment and Development, Proceedings of the Sixth
World Congress of the International Economic Association held in
Mexico City, 1980, vol. II, *Concepts, Measurement and Long-Run Per-
spective*, joint editor with Harry MAIER, New York: St. Martin's
Press; Basingstoke and London: Macmillan, 1983.

'Twenty-one Arguments for Public Enterprise', in Khadija HAQ, *Global Development: Issues and Choices*, Washington, D.C.: North-South
Roundtable of S.I.D., 1983, pp. 124-36.

'Food Prices as a Reflection of Political Power', *Ceres*, vol. XVI, No. 2,
March/April 1983, pp. 16-22.

'Development Dichotomies', *World Development*, vol. XI, No. 10, October 1983, pp. 875-89; reprinted in G. M. MEIER and Dudley SEERS,
eds., *Pioneers in Development*, Oxford: Oxford University Press for the
World Bank, 1984, pp. 337-61.

'Direct Private Foreign Investment, Transnational Corporations and
Development', in *Commonwealth Economic Papers*, vol. II, No. 18, 'Towards a New Bretton Woods - Challenges for the World Financial
and Trading System', Selected background papers prepared for a
Commonwealth Study Group, November 1983.

'Why Development Aid?', *Banca Nazionale del Lavoro Quarterly Review*,
No. 147, December 1983, pp. 379-85; reprinted in *International Journal of Development Banking*, vol. II, No. 1, January 1984.

'È possibile uno sviluppo indipendente?', *Politica Internazionale*, Nuova
Serie, vol. XI, Nos. 11/12, November/December 1983, pp. 131-41.

'The New International Economic Order', *Occasional Paper*, No. 3,
1983, Center for Advanced Study of International Development,
Ann Arbor: Michigan State University.

'Comments on Albert O. Hischman's Chapter', in G. M. MEIER and
Dudley SEERS, eds., *Pioneers in Development*, Oxford: Oxford University Press for the World Bank, 1984, pp. 115-8.

'La Interdependencia desde una perspectiva Norte-Sur', *Información
Comercial Española*, No. 605, January 1984, pp. 53-7.

'Basic Needs: Some Unsettled Questions', *World Development*, vol. XII,
No. 9, September 1984, pp. 973-8.

'Development Economics in Retrospect and Prospect', *Middle East
Technical University Studies in Development*, vol. XI, Nos. 1/2, Ankara,
1984, pp. 29-40.

'Dall'antagonismo alla cooperazione', in Ugo LEONE, ed., *Le organizzazioni internazionali e la cooperazione allo sviluppo*, Rome: F.lli Palombi, pp. 33-45.

'Comment on Anne O. Krueger's paper', in Ernest H. PREEG, ed., *Hard Bargaining Ahead: U.S. Trade Policy and Developing Countries*, New Brunswick and Oxford: Transaction Books, 1985, pp. 58-60.

'Balliol Men in Fact: An Autobiographical Fragment', *Balliol College Record*, Oxford, 1985, pp. 44-56.

'Ideas, Not Money, Wave of the Future', *EDI Review*, April 1985, pp. 1-3.

'In Memory of Thomas Balogh', *World Development*, vol. XIII, No. 4, April 1985, pp. 465-6.

'A Problem To Every Solution', *Finance and Development*, vol. XXII, No. 2, June 1985, pp. 14-16.

'Gaps, Inequalities and Absolute Poverty', *Futures*, vol. XVII, No. 3, June 1985, pp. 292-4.

'Development Economics: The Intellectual Divisions', *Eastern Economic Journal*, vol. XI, No. 3, July/September 1985, pp. 235-47.

'Come vincere la povertà entro il 2000', *Cooperazione*, Nuova Serie, vol. X, No. 55, October 1985, pp. 11-14.

'Basic Needs: The Lessons', in Irma ADELMAN and J. Edward TAYLOR, *The Design of Alternative Development Strategies*, Rohtak, India: Jan Tinbergen Institute of Development Planning, 1986, pp. 27-37.

'Suffering from Success', in Alejandro FOXLEY, Michael MCPHERSON and Guillermo O'DONNELL, eds., *Development, Democracy and the Art of Trespassing, Essays in Honour of Albert Hirschman*, Notre Dame, Ind.: University of Notre Dame Press for the Helen Kellog Institute for International Studies, 1986, pp. 239-46.

'What Price Food?', in S. GUHAN and Manu SHROFF, *Essays on Economic Progress and Welfare*, in Honour of I. G. Patel, Bombay, Calcutta, Madras: Oxford University Press, 1986, pp. 142-58.

'The United Nations: Unhappy Family', in David PITT and Thomas G. WEISS, eds., *The Nature of United Nations Bureaucracies*, London and Sidney: Croom Helm, 1986, pp. 187-93.

'Changing Emphases in Development Theory' in Udo Ernst SIMONIS, ed., *Entwicklungstheorie - Entwicklungspraxis: eine kritische Bilanzierung*, Berlin: Duncker & Humblot, 1986, pp. 13-39.

373

'Basic Needs: Some Unsettled Questions' in *Challenge of Development and Basic Needs in Africa*, Nairobi: Oxford University Press, 1986.

'Notes on Development Planning: Problems and Solutions', *International Journal of Development Planning*, vol. I, No. 1, January/March 1986, pp. 1-18.

'What Do We Owe the Future?', *Resources Policy*, vol. XII, No. 1, March 1986, pp. 4-16.

'Intergenerational Responsibilities', *Asian Journal of Economic and Social Studies*, vol. V, No. 2, April 1986, pp. 103-18.

'Aerial Roots', *Banca Nazionale del Lavoro Quarterly Review*, No. 157, June 1986, pp. 135-59.

'Mankind's Future: An Ethical View - Duties Towards Our Descendants', *Interdisciplinary Science Reviews*, vol. XI, No. 3, Autumn 1986, pp. 248-56.

'Old Aberdonians: An Autobiographical Fragment', *Aberdeen University Review*, No. 176, Autumn 1986, pp. 395-409.

'Intergenerational Responsibilities', *Razvoj Development International*, vol. I, No. 1, 1986, pp. 21-39.

What Price Food? Agricultural Price Policies in Developing Countries, Basingstoke and London: Macmillan, 1987.

'Balogh' and 'Myrdal', in John EATWELL, Murray MILGATE and Peter NEWMAN, eds., *The New Palgrave: A Dictionary of Economics*, Basingstoke and London: Macmillan, 1987, pp. 181-2 and pp. 581-3.

'Interdependence' in John DUNNING and Mikoto USUI, eds., *Structural Change, Economic Interdependence and World Development*, Proceedings of the Seventh World Congress of the International Economic Association Held in Madrid, Spain ,vol. IV: *Economic Interdependence*, Structural Change, Economic Interdependence and World Development Series, Basingstoke and London: Macmillan; New York: St. Martin's Press, 1987, pp. 19-29.

'Transition Measures and Political Support for Food Price Policy Reform', in J. Price GITTINGER, Joanne LESLIE, and Caroline HOISINGTON, eds., *Food Policy: Integrating Supply, Distribution and Consumption*, Baltimore and London: John Hopkins University Press for The Economic Development Institute, the World Bank, 1987, pp. 277-81.

'Approaches to a New International Economic Order', in Hans

SINGER, Neelambar HATTI and Rameshwar TANDON, eds., *Economic Theory and New World Order*, New Delhi: Indus Publishing Company, 1987, pp. 15-52.

'Interdependence: A North-South Perspective', in Hans SINGER, Neelambar HATTI and Rameshwar TANDON, eds., *Economic Theory and New World Order*, New Delhi: Indus Publishing Company, 1987, pp. 271-82.

'World Trade in Agricultural Commodities and the Terms of Trade with Industrial Goods', in Hans SINGER, Neelambar HATTI and Rameshwar TANDON, eds., *International Commodity Policy*, New Delhi: Indus Publishing Company, 1987, pp. 198-218.

'The International Economic System', *Journal of Economics and Administrative Studies*, vol. I, No. 1, Winter 1987, pp. 1-23.

'New Directions for Private Resource Transfers', *Banca Nazionale del Lavoro Quarterly Review*, No.160, March 1987, pp. 61-76; reprinted in *Development and North-South Cooperation*, vol. III, No. 4, June 1987, pp. 93-109.

'International Cooperation and Global Justice', *Journal für Entwicklungspolitik*, Band III, No. 3, 1987, pp. 5-15.

'The Case for Dual Exchange Rates', *Journal of Foreign Exchange and International Finance*, vol. I, No. 2, April 1987, pp 177-80.

'Structural Adjustment: A Survey of Issues and Options', *World Development*, vol. XV, No. 2, December 1987, pp. 1469-82; reprinted in Simon COMMANDER, ed., *Structural Adjustment and Agriculture: Theory and Practice*, London: James Currey, 1989, pp. 3-18.

'Structural Adjustment', *Asian Journal of Economics and Social Studies*, No. 3, 1987, pp. 173-96.

'The Contribution of Non-Governmental Organizations to Development', *Development: The International Development Review*, No. 4, 1987, pp. 92-5; reprinted in *Asian Journal of Economic and Social Studies*, vol. VII, No. 1, January 1988, pp. 1-9.

Beyond Adjustment: The Asian Experience (ed.), Proceedings of a Conference sponsored by the Indian Council for Research on International Economic Relations and by the International Monetary Fund (Bombay, 1986), Washington, D.C.: International Monetary Fund, 1988.

'Intergenerational Responsabilities or Our Duties to the Future', in

Sidney DELL, *Policies for Development, Essays in Honour of Gamani Corea*, London: Macmillan, 1988, pp. 3-21.

'Lord Balogh', in *Dictionary of National Biography*, Oxford: Oxford University Press, 1988, pp. 25-6.

'Gains and Losses from Trade in Services', in Khadija HAQ, ed., *Linking the World: Trade Policies for the Future*, 1988, pp. 117-25.

'Conditionality: A Double Paradox', in C. J. JEPMA, ed., *North-South Cooperation in Retrospect and Prospect*, London and New York: Routledge, 1988, pp. 107-19.

'International Cooperation and Global Justice', in Hans SINGER, Neelambar HATTI and Rameshwar TANDON, eds., *Challenges of South-South Cooperation*, part 2, New Delhi: Indus Publishing Company, 1988, pp. 911-27.

'Surpluses for a Capital-Hungry World', in Paul STREETEN, ed., *Beyond Adjustment: The Asian Experience*, Washington, D.C.: International Monetary Fund, 1988, pp. 256-61; reprinted in Hans SINGER, Neelamber HATTI and Rameshwar TANDON, eds., *Resource Transfer and Debt Trap,* part 1, New Delhi: Indus Publishing Company, 1988, pp. 217-22; also reprinted in H. W. SINGER and Soumitra SHARMA, *Economic Development and World Debt*, Basingstoke and London: Macmillan, 1989, pp. 23-6.

' "New" Directions for Private Resource Transfers', in Lee A. TAVIS, ed., *Rekindling Development, Multinational Firms and World Debt*, Notre Dame, Ind.: University of Notre Dame Press, 1988, pp. 294-311.

'The Double Paradox of Conditionality', in Lee A. TAVIS, ed., *Rekindling Development, Multinational Firms and World Debt*, Notre Dame, Ind.: University of Notre Dame Press, 1988, pp. 294-311.

'Stabilization and Adjustment', *Labour and Society*, vol. XIII, No. 1, January 1988, pp. 1-18.

'The Universe and the University', *Salzburg Seminar Newsletter*, No. 16, 1988.

'Let's Recycle the Japanese and German Surpluses to Help the Third World', *The International Economy*, January/February 1988, pp. 20-1.

'Private Foreign Investment for Africa: The Judo Trick', *Razvoj Development International*, vol. III, Nos. 1/2, January/December 1988, pp. 173-6.

'Reflections on the Role of the University and Developing Countries', *World Development*, vol. XVI, No. 5, May 1988, pp. 639-40.

Mobilizing Human Potential: The Challenge of Unemployment, New York: United Nations Development Program, 1989.

'International Cooperation and Global Justice', in Irma ADELMAN and Sylvia LANE, eds., *The Balance between Industry and Agriculture in Economic Development*, Proceedings of the Eighth World Congress of the International Economic Association, Delhi, India, vol. IV, *Social Effects*, Basingstoke and London: Macmillan, 1989, pp. 3-17.

'Accelerating Development in the Poorest Countries', in Robert J. BERG and David F. GORDON, eds., *Cooperation for International Development: The United States and the Third World in the 1990s*, Boulder: Lynne Rienner Publishers, 1989, pp. 142-63.

'International Cooperation', in Hollis CHENERY and T. S. SRINIVASAN, *Handbook of Development Economics*, vol. 2, Amsterdam: North Holland, 1989, pp. 1153-86.

'A Survey of the Issues and Options', in Simon COMMANDER, ed., *Structural Adjustment and Agriculture in Theory and Practice in Africa and Latin America*, London: James Currey for the Overseas Development Institute, 1989, pp. 3-18.

'Disguised Unemployment and Underemployment', in George R. FEIVEL, ed., *Joan Robinson and Modern Economic Theory*, New York: New York University Press, 1989, pp. 723-6.

'Joan Robinson: Utter Fearlessness', in George R. FEIVEL, ed., *Joan Robinson and Modern Economic Theory*, New York: New York University Press, 1989, pp. 861-2.

'The Politics of Food Prices', in Nurul ISLAM, ed., *The Balance between Industry and Agriculture in Economic Development*, Proceedings of the Eighth World Congress of the International Economic Association, Delhi, India, vol. V, *Factors Influencing Change*, Basingstoke and London: Macmillan, 1989, pp. 61-71.

'The Judo Trick', in Lionel ORCHARD and Robert DARE, eds., *Markets, Morals and Public Policy*, Sidney: Federation Press, 1989, pp. 77-103.

'A Comment', in Bernard SALOMÉ, ed., *Fighting Urban Unemployment in Developing Countries*, Paris: Development Centre of the OECD, 1989, pp. 99-101.

377

'National Food Security and Commodity Agreements', *International Journal of Development Planning Literature*, vol. IV, No. 2, April 1989, pp. 91-103.

'The International Economic System', *Asian Journal of Economics and Social Studies*, vol. VIII, No. 1, January 1989, pp. 1-20.

'The Impact of the Changing World Economy on Technological Transformation in the Developing Countries', *Razvoj Development International*, vol. IV, No. 1, January/June 1989, pp. 23-42.

'Interest, Ideology and Institutions: A Review Article of Bhagwati on Protectionism', *World Development*, vol. XVII, No. 2, February 1989, pp. 293-8.

'The Interdisciplinary Role of the University', *Interdisciplinary Science Reviews*, vol. XIV, No. 2, June 1989, pp. 107-9.

'Dudley Seers (1920 - 1983): A Personal Appreciation', *IDS Bulletin*, vol. XX, No. 3, 'Dudley Seers: His Work and Influence', July 1989, pp. 26-30.

'Global Institutions for an Interdependent World', *World Development*, vol. XVII, No. 9, September 1989, pp. 1349-59.

'International Cooperation', *Asian Journal of Economic and Social Studies*, vol. VIII, No. 4, October 1989, pp. 265-94.

'Program vs. Project Aid: a Role Reversal', *Methodus*, December 1989, pp. 14.

'Lord Balogh', in Philip ARESTIS and Malcom C. SAWYER, eds., *Biographical Dictionary of Dissenting Economists*, Aldershot: Edward Elgar Publishing, 1990, pp. 14-21.

'Paul Streeten', in Philip ARESTIS and Malcom C. SAWYER, eds., *Biographical Dictionary of Dissenting Economists*, Aldershot: Edward Elgar Publishing, 1990, pp. 555-62.

'Intergenerational Responsibilities', in Salvino BUSUTTIL, Emmanuel AGIUS, Peter SERACINO INGLOTT and Tony MACELLI, eds., *Our Responsibilities Towards Future Generations*, Malta: The Foundation for International Studies (in cooperation with UNESCO), 1990, pp. 157-71.

'Gunnar Myrdal', in Gilles DOSTALER, Diane ETHIER and Laurent LEPAGE, eds., *Gunnar Myrdal et son oeuvre*, Montreal: Les Presses de l'Universite de Montreal, 1990, pp. 11-24.

'Comparative Advantage and Free Trade', in Azizur Rahman KHAN and Rehman SOBHAN, eds., *Trade, Planning and Rural Development*, Basingstoke and London: Macmillan, 1990, pp. 36-54.

'The Impact of the Changing World Economy on Technological Transformation in the Developing Countries', in H. W. SINGER, Neelambar HATTI and Rameshwar TANDON, *Joint Ventures and Collaboration*, New World Order Series, vol. x, New Delhi: Indus Publishing Company, 1990, pp. 39-55.

'Comparative Advantage and Free Trade', in H. W. SINGER, Neelambar HATTI and Rameshwar TANDON, *North-South Trade in Manufactures*, New World Order Series, vol. VII, New Delhi: Indus Publishing Company, 1990, pp. 35-51.

'Gunnar Myrdal', *World Development*, vol. XVIII, No. 7, July 1990, pp. 1031-7.

'Poverty: Concepts and Measurement', *The Bangladesh Development Studies*, vol. XVIII, No. 3, September 1990, pp. 1-18.

'How Economic Institutions Affect Economic Performance in Industrialized Countries: Lessons for Development', with Peter DoERINGER, *World Development*, vol. XIIX, No. 9, September 1990, pp. 1249-53.

'Basic Needs: Some Unsettled Questions', in K. AMAN, ed., *Ethical Principles for Development Needs, Capacities or Rights*, Proceedings of the IDEA / Montclair Conference, Upper Montclair, N.J.: Institute for Critical Thinking, 1991, pp. 24-34.

'Stabilization and Adjustment', in H. W. SINGER, Neelambar HATTI and Rameshwar TANDON, *Adjustment and Liberalization in the Third World*, New World Order Series, vol. XII, New Delhi: Indus Publishing Company, 1991, pp. 303-26.

'Structural Adjustment: A Survey of the Issues and Options', in H. W. SINGER, Neelambar HATTI and Rameshwar TANDON, *Adjustment and Liberalization in the Third World*, New World Order Series, vol. XII, New Delhi: Indus Publishing Company, 1991, pp. 93-120.

'The United States, Britain and International Development', in H. W. SINGER, Neelambar HATTI and Rameshwar TANDON, *Adjustment and Liberalization in the Third World*, New World Order Series, vol. XII, New Delhi: Indus Publishing Company, 1991, pp. 451-66.

'The Role of Direct Private Foreign Investment in Poor Countries', in H. W. SINGER, Neelambar HATTI and Rameshwar TANDON, *For-*

eign Direct Investment, New World Order Series, vol. XI, New Delhi: Indus Publishing Company, 1991, pp. 171-99.

'The Impact of the Changing World Economy on Technological Transformation in the Developing Countries', in D. VAJPEYI and R. NATARAJAN, eds., *Technology and Development Public Policy and Managerial Issues*, Jaipur, India: Rawat Publications, 1991, pp. 11-26.

'The Implication of Industrial Adjustment for Developing Countries', in I. YAZAMAWA and A. HIRATA, eds., *Industrial Adjustment in Developed Countries and its Implications for Developing Countries*, Tokyo: Institute for International Development, 1991, pp. 240-61.

'Global Prospects in an Interdependent World', *World Development*, vol. XIX, No. 1, January 1991, pp. 123-33.

'Social Development in Africa: A Focus on People', *Development: Journal of the Society for International Development*, No. 2, 1991, pp. 33-9.

'What's Right with GATT', *The New Leader*, May 1991, pp. 17-18.

'The Judo Trick, or Crowding In', *Small Enterprise Development*, vol. II, No. 2, June 1991, pp. 24-34.

'A World to Make: Development in Perspective', *Economic Development and Cultural Change*, vol. XL, No. 1, October 1991, pp. 209-14.

'Globale Aussichten in einer interdependenten Welt', *Wissenschaftliche Zeitschrift der Humboldt-Universität zu Berlin, Reihe Geistes und Sozialwissenschaften*, Heft 4/5, 1991.

'The Spread of Keynesianism', *Economics and Politics*, vol. III, No. 3, November 1991, pp. 279-86.

REFERENCES

Antia N. H., 'An Alternative Strategy for Health Care: The Mandwa Project', *Economic and Political Weekly*, vol. 20, Nos. 51 and 52, December, 1985, pp. 2257-2260.

Arrow Kenneth, 'Political and Economic Evaluation of Social Effects and Externalities', in Michael D. Intriligator, *Frontiers of Quantitative Economics*, Amsterdam: North-Holland, 1971.

Arrow Kenneth, *Information and Economic Behavior*, Stockholm: Federation of Swedish Industries, 1973.

Arrow Kenneth, *The Limits of Organization*, New York: W. W. Norton, 1974.

Arrow Kenneth (ed.), *The Balance Between Industry and Agriculture in Economic Development*, Basingstoke: Macmillan/IEA, 1988.

Atkinson Anthony Barnes, *The Economics of Inequality*, Oxford: Clarendon Press, 1976.

Atkinson Anthony Barnes, 'Original Sen', *New York Review of Books*, vol. 34, No. 16, October 1987, p. 43.

The Atlantic Monthly, October 1990.

Axelrod Robert M., *The Evolution of Cooperation*, New York: Basic Books, 1984.

Bardhan Pranab K., *Pattern of Income Distribution in India: A Review*, Calcutta: Statistical Publishing Society, 1974.

Bardhan Pranab K., *Rural Economic Change in South Asia: Methodology of Measurement*, forthcoming.

Barro Robert, *A Cross-country Study of Growth, Saving and Government*, NBER Working Paper No. 2885, Cambridge, Mass.: National Bureau of Economic Research, 1989.

Barry Brian, 'Claims of Common Citizenship', *The Times Literary Supplement*, vol. 47, No. 4, 20-26 January 1989, p. 52.

Bayoumi Tamim, *Saving-Investment Correlations*, IMF Working Paper 89/66, Washington D.C.: International Monetary Fund, August 1989.

Berg Alan, *The Nutrition Factor*, Washington D.C.: Brookings Institution, 1973.

Bhagwati Jagdish, 'Directly Unproductive Profit-Seeking Activities', *Journal of Political Economy*, vol. 90, No. 5, October 1982, pp. 988-1002.

BHAGWATI Jagdish, 'International Trade in Services and its Relevance for Economic Development', Xth Annual Lecture of the Geneva Association, Oxford: Pergamon Press, 1985.

BHAGWATI Jagdish, *Protectionism*, Cambridge, Mass.: MIT Press, 1988.

BLEJER Mario and Mohsin KHAN, 'Government Policy and Private Investment in Developing Countries', *IMF Staff Papers*, vol. 31, 1984, pp. 379-403.

BLOMSTROM Magnus, Irving KRAVIS and Robert E. LIPSEY, *Multinational Firms and Manufactured Exports from Developing Countries*, NBER Working Paper No. 2493, Cambridge, Mass.: National Bureau of Economic Research, January 1988.

BROOKNER Anita, *Latecomers*, New York: Pantheon Books, 1989.

BROWNE Stephen, *Foreign Aid in Practice*, London: Pinter, 1990.

BUCHANAN James M., *Liberty, Market and State: Political Economy in the 1980s*, New York: New York University Press, Brighton: Wheatsheaf, 1986.

BUCHANAN James M., *Economics: Between Predictive Science and Moral Philosophy*, compiled by Robert D. TOLLISON and Viktor VANBERG, College Station: Texas A&M University Press, 1987.

CERNEA Michael (ed.), *Putting People First: Sociological Variables in Rural Development*, New York: Oxford University Press, 1985.

CERNEA Michael, 'Farmer Organizations and Institution Building for Sustainable Development', *Regional Development Dialogue*, Nagoya, Japan: U.N. Centre for Regional Development, vol. 8, no. 2, Summer 1987, pp. 1-19.

CHAKRAVARTI Sukhamoy, *Development Planning: The Indian Experience*, Oxford: Clarendon Press, 1987.

CHAMBERS Robert, *Poverty in India: Concepts, Research and Reality*, Brighton: Institute of Development Studies Discussion Paper No. 241, January 1988.

CHAMBERS Robert, 'Editorial Introduction: Vulnerability, Coping and Policy', *IDS Bulletin*, vol. 20, No. 2 (Brighton, Sussex: Institute of Development Studies), April 1989.

CHOWDRY Kamla, 'Poverty, Environment, Development', in Francis X. SUTTON, *A World to Make: Development in Perspective*, New Brunswick and London: Transaction Books, 1990.

CHUTA Enyinna, and Carl LIEDHOLM, *Employment and Growth in Small-Scale Industries*, London: Macmillan, 1985.

CLAIREMONTE Frederick F. and John CAVANAGH, 'Transnational Corporations and Services: The Final Frontier', in *Trade and Development*, UNCTAD Review No. 5, Geneva: LLN, 1984, pp. 215-273.

COLANDER David (ed.), *Neoclassical Political Economy*, Cambridge, Mass.: Ballinger, 1985.

COLCLOUGH Christopher, 'Are African Governments as Unproductive as the Accelerated Development Report Implies?', *IDS Bulletin*, vol. 14, No. 1, January 1983, pp. 24-29.

COLCLOUGH Christopher and J. MANOR, eds., *States or Markets? Neo-Liberalism and the Development Policy Debate*, Oxford: Clarendon Press, 1991.

COMMANDER Simon (ed.), *Structural Adjustment and Agriculture in Theory and Practice in Africa and Latin America*, London: Overseas Development Institute, 1989.

COOPER Richard N., 'Panel Discussion: The Prospects for International Policy Coordination', in William H. BUITER and Richard C. MARSTON, *International Policy Coordination*, Cambridge: Cambridge University Press, 1985, pp. 369-370.

COOPER T. C., 'Poverty', unpublished note, 1972, quoted in Amartya SEN, *Resources, Values and Development*, Oxford: Basil Blackwell, 1984.

CORDEN Max, 'The Theory of Debt Relief', *Journal of Development Studies*, vol. 27, No. 3, April 1991, pp. 135-145.

CORNIA Giovanni A., Richard JOLLY and Frances STEWART, (eds.), *Adjustment with a Human Face*, Oxford: Clarendon Press, 1987.

DANDEKAR V., and N. RATH, *Poverty in India*, Poona, 1971.

DAREMBLUM Jaime, 'Costa Rica Needs Lower Taxes and a Leaner State', *The Wall Street Journal*, 5 October 1990, p. A 19.

DASGUPTA Partha, 'Power and Control in the Good Polity', in Alan HAMLIN *et al.*, *The Good Polity*, Oxford: Basil Blackwell, 1989.

DASGUPTA Partha and Debraj RAY, 'Inequality as a Determinant of Malnutrition and Unemployment: Theory', *Economic Journal*, vol. 96, December 1986, pp. 1011-1034.

DASGUPTA Partha and D. RAY, 'Inequality as a Determinant of Malnutrition and Unemployment: Practice', *Economic Journal*, vol. 97, March 1987, pp. 177-188.

385

DATTA Gautam and Jacob MEERMAN, *Household Income or Household Income per Capita in Welfare Comparisons*, World Bank Staff Working Paper No. 378, Washington D.C.: World Bank, 1980.

DATTA-CHADHURI Mrinal, 'Market Failure and Government Failure', *Journal of Economic Perspectives*, vol. 4, No. 3, Summer 1990, pp. 25-40.

DE SOTO Hernando, *The Other Path; The Invisible Revolution in the Thirld World*, New York: Harper & Row, 1989.

DEATON Angus, 'On Measuring Costs', *Journal of Political Economy*, vol. 94, No. 4, August 1986, pp. 720-744.

DEATON Angus and John MUELLBAUER, *Economics and Consumer Behaviour*, Cambridge: Cambridge University Press, 1980.

DIAZ-ALEJANDRO Carlos, 'Latin-American Debt: I don't Think We're in Kansas Anymore', *Brookings Papers on Economic Activity*, No. 2, 1984, pp. 335-388.

DORE Ronald, *Flexible Rigidities, Industrial Policy and Structural Adjustment in the Japanese Economy 1970-80*, Stanford, Calif.: Stanford University Press, 1987.

DORE Ronald, *Taking Japan Seriously: A Confucian Perspective on Leading Economic Issues*, Stanford, Calif.: Stanford University Press, 1987.

DORFMAN Robert, 'Protecting the Global Environment: An Immodest Proposal', *World Development*, vol. 19, No. 1, January 1991, pp. 103-110.

DOWNS Anthony, *An Economic Theory of Democracy*, New York: Harper & Row, 1957.

DRÈZE Jean and Amartya SEN, *Hunger and Public Action*, Oxford: Clarendon Press, 1989.

DRUCKER Peter, 'Japan's Choices', *Foreign Affairs*, vol. 65, Summer 1987, pp. 923-941.

DUNN John (ed.), *The Economic Limits to Modern Politics*, Cambridge: Cambridge University Press, 1990.

East Africa Economic Review, Special Issue on Contract Farming and Smallholder Outgrower Schemes in Eastern and Southern Africa, Economics Department, University of Nairobi, August 1989.

The Economist, September 16, 1989.

EDIRISINGHE Neville, *The Food Stamp Scheme in Sri Lanka: Costs, Benefits, and Options for Modifications*, Research Report No. 58, Washington D.C.: International Food Policy Research Institute, March 1987.

FOSTER James, Joel GREER and Erik THORBECKE, 'A Class of Decomposable Poverty Measures', *Econometrica*, vol. 52, No. 3, May 1984, pp. 761-766.

FOXLEY Alejandro *et al.*, *Development, Democracy and the Art of Trespassing; Essays in Honor of Albert O. Hirschman*, Notre Dame, Ind.: University of Notre Dame Press, 1986.

FRANK Robert H., 'Review of Amartya Sen: *The Standard of Living*', *Journal of Economic Literature*, vol. 27, No. 2, June 1989, p. 666.

GEERTZ Clifford, 'Myrdal's Mythology', *Encounter*, July 1969, pp. 34-54.

GLEWWE Paul and Jacques van der GAAG, *Confronting Poverty in Developing Countries*, Living Standard Measurement Working Paper No. 48, Washington D.C.: World Bank, 1988.

GLOVER David J., 'Contract Farming and Smallholder Outgrower Schemes in Less Developed Countries', *World Development*, vol. 12, Nos. 11-12, November-December 1984, pp. 1143-1157.

GLOVER David J., 'Increasing the Benefits to Smallholders from Contract Farming: Problems for Farmers', *World Development*, vol. 15, No. 4, April 1987, pp. 441-448.

GOLDSMITH Arthur, 'The Private Sector and Rural Development: Can Agribusiness Help the Small Farmer?', *World Development*, vol. 13, Nos. 10-11, October-November 1985, pp. 1125-1138.

GORMAN W. M., 'The Demand for Related Goods', *Journal Paper* J3129, Ames Iowa Experimental Station, 1956.

GREER Joel and Erik THORBECKE, 'A Methodology for Measuring Food Poverty Applied to Kenya', *Journal of Development Economics*, vol. 24, No. 1, January 1986, pp. 59-74.

GREER Joel and Erik THORBECKE, 'Food Poverty Profile Applied to Kenyan Smallholders', *Economic Development and Cultural Change*, vol. 35, No. 1, October 1986, pp. 115-141.

GRINDLE Merilee S. and John W. THOMAS, *Public Choices and Policy Change; The Political Economy of Reform in Developing Countries*, Baltimore: The Johns Hopkins University Press, 1991.

GUISINGER Stephen, 'Host-Country Policies to Attract and Control Foreign Investment', in Theodore H. MORAN *et al.*, *Investing in*

Development: New Roles for Private Capital?, Overseas Development Council, New Brunswick: Transaction Books, 1986.

HAYAMI Yujiro and Vernon W. RUTTAN, *Agricultural Development: An International Perspective*, Baltimore: The Johns Hopkins University Press, 1971, 2nd revised edition, 1984.

HEILBRONNER Robert L., 'The Murky Economists', *New York Review of Books*, vol. 33, No. 7, 24 April 1986, pp. 46-48.

HICKS John R., *Value and Capital*, 2nd edition, Oxford: Oxford University Press, 1946.

HIRSCH Fred, *Social Limits to Growth*, Cambridge, Mass.: Harvard University Press, 1978.

HIRSCHMAN Albert O., *Getting Ahead Collectively: Grassroots Experience in Latin America*, Oxford: Pergamon Press, 1984.

HIRSCHMAN Albert O., *The Rhetoric of Reaction: Perversity, Futility, Jeopardy*, Cambridge, Mass.: The Belknap Press of Harvard University Press, 1991.

HOSSAIN Mahabub, *Credit for Alleviation of Rural Poverty: The Grameen Bank in Bangladesh*, Research Report No. 65, Washington D.C.: International Food Policy Research Institute, 1988.

HUNTINGTON Samuel P., 'The U.S. — Decline or Renewal?', *Foreign Affairs*, vol. 67, Winter 1988-9, pp. 76-96.

IFR Report 1986, Washington D.C.: International Food Policy Research Institute.

ILO, *Employment, Incomes and Equality: A Strategy for Increasing Productive Employment in Kenya*, Geneva: International Labour Office, 1972.

JODHA N. S., 'Poverty Debate in India: A Minority View', *Economic and Political Weekly*, Special Number, November 1988.

KALDOR Nicholas, 'The Role of Commodity Prices in Economic Recovery', *World Development*, vol. 15, No. 5, May 1987, pp. 551-558.

KASHYAP S. P., 'Growth of Small-Size Enterprises in India: Its Nature and Content', *World Development*, vol. 16, No. 6, June 1988, pp. 667-681.

KENNEDY Paul, *The Rise and Fall of the Great Powers: Economic Change and Military Conflict, 1500-2000*, New York: Random House and Unwyn Hyman, 1988.

KLITGAARD Robert, *Controlling Corruption*, Berkeley: University of California Press, 1988.

KLITGAARD Robert, 'Incentive Myopia', *World Development*, vol. 17, No. 4, April 1989, pp. 447-459.

KRUEGER Anne O., 'The Political Economy of the Rent-Seeking Society', *American Economic Review*, vol. 64, June 1974, pp. 291-303.

LAL Deepak, *The Poverty of Development Economics*, Cambridge, Mass.: Harvard University Press, 1985.

LALL Sanjaya, *Multinationals, Technology and Exports*, London: Macmillan, 1985.

LALL Sanjaya and Frances STEWART, *Theory and Reality in Development; Essays in Honour of Paul Streeten*, London: Macmillan, 1986.

LANCASTER Kelvin J., 'A New Approach to Consumer Theory', *Journal of Political Economy*, vol. 74, No. 2, 1966, pp. 132-157.

LANDES David S., 'Rich Country, Poor Country', *The New Republic*, November 20, 1989, pp. 23-27.

LANDES David S., 'Why Are We so Rich and They so Poor?', *American Economic Review*, vol. 80, No. 2, June 1990, pp. 1-13.

LEWIS John P., *et al.*, *Strengthening the Poor: What Have We Learned?*, U.S.-Thirld World Policy Perspectives, No. 10, Overseas Development Council, New Brunswick: Transaction Books, 1988.

LEWIS William A., 'Economic Development with Unlimited Supplies of Labour', *Manchester School*, vol. 22, No. 2, May 1954, pp. 139-191.

LIEDHOLM Carl and Donald MEAD, *Small Scale Industries in Developing Countries: Empirical Evidence and Policy Implications*, International Development Paper No. 9, East Lansing, Mich.: Department of Agricultural Economics, Michigan State University, 1987.

LIPTON Michael, *Poverty, Undernutrition and Hunger*, World Bank Staff Working Paper No. 597, Washington D.C.: World Bank, 1983.

LIPTON Michael, *Demography and Poverty*, World Bank Staff Working Paper No. 623, Washington D.C.: World Bank, 1983.

LIPTON Michael, 'The Prisoner's Dilemma and the Coase's Theorem: A Case for Democracy in Less Developed Countries', in R. C. O. MATTHEWS, *Economy and Democracy*, New York: St Martin's Press, 1985, pp. 49-109.

LIPTON Michael, 'Who Are the Poor? What Do They Do? What

Should They Do?', Lecture to the Center for Advanced Studies in International Development, Michigan State University, East Lansing, Mich., March 13, 1988.

LIPTON Michael, 'Agriculture, Rural People, the State and the Surplus in Some Asian Countries: Thoughts on Some Implications of Three Recent Approaches in Social Science', *World Development*, vol. 17, No. 10, October 1989, pp. 1553-1571.

LIPTON Michael, 'The State-Market Dilemma, Civil Society and Structural Adjustment', *The Round Table*, No. 317, 1991, pp. 21-31.

LIPTON Michael and Stephany GRIFFITH-JONES, *International Lenders of Last Resort: Are Changes Required?*, Midland Bank Occasional Paper in Trade and Finance, March 1984.

MARX Karl, 'Wage, Labour and Capital', in KARL MARX and FREDERICK ENGELS, *Selected Works*, Moscow: Foreign Language Publishing House, 1958, vol. 1, pp. 930-994.

MEIER Gerald M., *Emerging from Poverty; The Economics that Really Matters*, Oxford: Oxford University Press, 1984.

MORRIS Morris D., *Measuring the Condition of the World's Poor: The Physical Quality of Life Index*, London: Frank Cass, 1979.

MOSLEY Paul, 'Increased Aid Flows and Human Resource Development in Africa', Innocenti Occasional Paper no. 5, Florence: UNICEF International Child Development Centre, August 1990.

MULLINEUX Andrew W., 'Do We Need a World Central Bank?', *Royal Bank of Scotland Review*, No. 160, December 1988, pp. 23-35.

MYRDAL Gunnar, *Asian Drama: An Inquiry into the Poverty of Nations*, Harmondsworth: Pelican Books, 1968.

NAYYAR Deepak, *International Trade in Services: Implications for Developing Countries*, Exim Bank Commencement Day Annual Lecture, 1986.

NELSON Joan M., 'The Political Economy of Stabilization: Commitment, Capacity and Public Response', *World Development*, vol. 12, No. 10, October 1984, pp. 983-1006.

NELSON Joan M. *et al.*, *Fragile Coalitions: the Politics of Economic Adjustment*, U.S.-Thirld World Policy Perspectives No. 12, Overseas Development Council, New Brunswick: Transaction Books, 1989.

The New York Times, 9 November 1989, p. A 17; 15 May 1991, p. D 11.

NOZICK Robert, *Anarchy, State and Utopia*, New York: Basic Books, 1974.

NUSSBAUM Martha, 'Women's Lot', *New York Review of Books*, vol. 33, No. 1, January 1986, pp. 7-12.

NYE Joseph, 'No, The U.S. Isn't in Decline', *New York Times*, October 7, 1990.

ORTIZ Guillermo and Carlos NORIEGA, *Investment and Growth in Latin America*, Washington D.C.: International Monetary Fund, 1988.

PAUL Samuel, *Managing Development Programs: The Lessons of Success*, Boulder: Westview Press, 1982.

PEATTIE Lisa, 'An Idea in Good Currency and How it Grew', *World Development*, vol. 15, No. 7, July 1987, pp. 851-860.

PERROUX François, *L'Europe sans rivages*, Paris: PUF 1954.

PHELPS BROWN Henry, *Egalitarianism and the Generation of Inequality*, Oxford: Clarendon Press, 1988.

PLATTEAU Jean-Philippe, 'The Free Market is not Readily Transferable: Reflections on the Links Between Market, Social Relations and Moral Norms', Paper prepared for the 25th Jubilee of the Institute of Development Studies, Brighton, Sussex, 1991.

PRADHAN Pranchanda, *Local Institutions and People's Participation in Rural Public Works in Nepal*, Ithaca, N.Y.: Rural Development Committee, Cornell University, 1980.

RAM Rati, 'Government Size and Economic Growth: A New Framework and Some Evidence from Cross-Section and Time-Series Data', *American Economic Review*, vol. 76, No. 1, March 1986; and vol. 79, No. 1, March 1989, pp. 191-203.

RAO Bhanoji, 'Measurement of Deprivation and Poverty Based on the Proportion Spent on Food', *World Development*, vol. 9, No. 4, April 1981, pp. 337-353.

REUTLINGER Shlomo and Harold ALDERMAN, 'The Prevalence of Calorie-Deficient Diets in Developing Countries', *World Development*, vol. 8, No. 4, April 1980, pp. 399-411.

RIDING Alan, 'Peruvians Combating Red Tape', *New York Times*, 24 July 1988, p. 3.

ROBINSON Joan, 'Disguised Unemployment', *Collected Economic Papers*, vol. 4, Oxford: Basil Blackwell, 1973.

SABEL Charles F., *Changing Models of Economic Efficiency and Their Impli-*

cations for Industrialization in the Thirld World, Department of City and Regional Planning, Cambridge, Mass.: MIT, 1987.

SALMEN Lawrence, *Institutional Dimensions of Poverty Reduction*, Policy, Research and External Affairs Working Papers, WPS 411, Washington D.C.: World Bank, 1990.

SALOMÉ Bernard (ed.), *Fighting Urban Unemployment in Developing Countries*, Paris: Development Centre of the OECD, 1989.

SAMSTAG T., 'Pollution Prevention Pay Handsomely', Science Report of *The Times*, October 15, 1984.

SANDMO Agnar, 'Buchanan on Political Economy: A Review Article', *Journal of Economic Literature*, vol. 28, No. 1, March 1990, pp. 50-65.

SANYAL Bishwapriya, 'Sailing Against the Wind: A Treatise in Support in of Poor Countries' Governments', typescript, Cambridge, Mass.: MIT, 1990.

SEEBOHM ROWNTREE B., *Poverty: A Study of Town Life*, London: Macmillan, 1901.

SEERS Dudley, 'Life Expectancy as an Integrating Concept in Social and Demographic Analysis and Planning', *Review of Income and Wealth*, vol. 23, No. 3, September 1977, pp. 195-203.

SEN Amartya K., 'Poverty: An Ordinal Approach to Measurement', *Econometrica*, vol. 44, No. 2, 1976, pp. 219-231.

SEN Amartya K., *Poverty and Famines*, Oxford: Clarendon Press, 1981.

SEN Amartya K., 'How is India Doing?', *New York Review of Books*, vol. 29, 16 December 1982, pp. 41-46.

SEN Amartya K., *Resources, Values and Development*, Oxford: Basil Blackwell, 1984.

SEN Amartya K., *Commodities and Capabilities*, Prof. P. Hennipmen Lectures in Economics, Amsterdam: North-Holland, 1985.

SEN Amartya K., *The Standard of Living; The Tanner Lectures*, edited by G. HAWTHORNE, Cambridge: Cambridge University Press, 1987.

SEN Amartya K., *Hunger and Entitlements*, Wider Research for Action, Helsinki: Wider, 1987.

SEN Amartya K., 'Gender and Cooperative Conflicts', Working Paper No. 18, Helsinki: Wider, 1987, to be published in I. TINKER (ed.), *Persistent Inequalities*, New York: Oxford University Press.

SHAPIRO Helen and Lance TAYLOR, 'The State and Industrial Strategy', *World Development*, vol. 18, No. 6, June 1990, pp. 861-879.

SINGER Hans W. and Simon MAXWELL, 'Food Aid to Developing Countries: A Survey', *World Development*, vol. 7, No. 3, March 1979, pp. 225-247.

SINHA Radha *et al.*, *Income Distribution, Growth and Basic Needs in India*, London: Croom Helm, 1979.

SMITH Adam, *An Inquiry into the Nature and Causes of the Wealth of Nations*, London: Everyman, Home University Library, 1776.

SOMJEE Abdulkarim H., *Development Theory: Critiques and Explorations*, New York: St Martin's Press, 1991.

SOMJEE Abdulkarim H. and Geeta SOMJEE, *Reaching Out to the Poor*, London: Macmillan, 1989.

STEWART Frances and John WEEKS: 'Raising Wages in the Controlled Sector', *Journal of Development Studies*, vol. 16, no. 1, October 1979.

STIGLITZ Joseph E. *et al.*, *The Economic Role of the State*, Oxford: Basil Blackwell, 1989.

STONE Richard, *An Integrated System of Demographic, Manpower and Social Statistics*, Paris: UNESCO, 1970.

STONE Richard, *Towards a System of Social and Demographic Statistics*, United Nations Statistical Office, Series F, No. 18, New York: United Nations, 1975.

STREECK Wolfgang, 'The Social Dimensions of the European Community', Paper prepared for the 1989 Meeting of the Andrew Shonfield Association, Florence, 14-15 September 1989.

STREETEN Paul, 'More on Development in an International Setting', in Dudley SEERS and Leonard JOY, *Development in a Divided World*, Harmondsworth: Penguin Books, 1971.

STREETEN Paul, *The Frontiers of Development Studies*, London: Macmillan, 1972.

STREETEN Paul, 'Dynamics of the New Poor Power', in Gerald K. HELLEINER, *A World Divided: The Less Developed Countries in the World Economy*, Cambridge: Cambridge University Press, 1975.

393

STREETEN Paul, 'From Growth to Basic Needs', *Finance and Development*, vol. 16, No. 2, June 1979, pp. 39-42.

STREETEN Paul, 'Development Ideas in Historical Perspective', in *Toward a New Strategy for Development; A Rothko Chapel Colloquium*, New York, Oxford: Pergamon Press, 1979.

STREETEN Paul, 'Development: What Have We Learned?', in Josef PAJETSKA and C. H. FEINSTEIN, *The Relevance of Economic Theories*, London: Macmillan, 1980, pp. 181-199.

STREETEN Paul *et al.*, *First Things First*, Oxford: Oxford University Press, 1981.

STREETEN Paul, 'Development Dichotomies', *World Development*, vol. 11, No. 10, October 1983, pp. 875-889.

STREETEN Paul, 'A Problem to Every Solution', *Finance and Development*, vol. 22, No. 2, June 1985, pp.14-16.

STREETEN Paul, 'What Do We Owe to the Future?', *Resources Policy*, March 1986.

STREETEN Paul, 'Suffering from Success', in Alejandro FOXLEY *et al.*, *Development, Democracy and the Art of Trespassing*, Notre Dame, Ind.: University of Notre Dame Press, 1986.

STREETEN Paul, 'Structural Adjustment: A Survey of Issues and Options', *World Development*, vol. 15, No. 12, December 1987, pp. 1469-1482.

STREETEN Paul, *What Price Food?*, London: Macmillan, 1987.

STREETEN Paul, 'Disguised Unemployment and Underemployment', in George R. FEIVEL, (ed.), *Joan Robinson and Modern Economic Theory*, London: Macmillan, 1989, pp. 723-726.

STREETEN Paul, 'A Survey of the Issues and Options', in Simon COMMANDER (ed.), *Structural Adjustment and Agriculture in Theory and Practice in Africa and Latin America*, Overseas Development Institute, London-Portsmouth: Heinemann,1989.

SUTTON Francis X. (ed.), *A World to Make: Development in Perspective*, New Brunswick: Transaction Books, 1990.

SVEDBERG Peter, *Undernutrition in Sub-Saharan Africa: A Critical Assessment of the Evidence*, Helsinki: Wider, 1987.

TAYLOR Lance *et al.*, *Food Subsidy Programs: A Survey*, Report prepared for the Ford Foundation, Cambridge, Mass.: MIT, 1980.

TENDLER Judith, 'The Remarkable Convergence of Fashion on Small Enterprise and the Informal Sector', mimeo, 1987.

TIMMER Peter C. *et al.*, *Food Policy Analysis*, Baltimore: The Johns Hopkins University Press, 1983.

TOWLE Philip, 'Last Days of the American Empire', *London Review of Books*, 19 May 1988, p. 8.

TOWNSEND Peter, *Poverty in the United Kingdom*, Harmondsworth: Penguin Books, 1979.

UNDP, United Nations Development Programme, *Human Development Report*, 1990 and 1991.

WADE Robert, *Governing the Market*, Princeton, N.J.: Princeton University Press, 1990.

WARREN Bill, 'The Postwar Economic Experience of the Third World', in *Toward a New Strategy for Development; A Rothko Chapel Colloquium*, Oxford: Pergamon Press, 1979, pp. 144-168.

WATERBURY John, 'The Political Management of Adjustment and Reform', in Joan NELSON, *Fragile Coalitions: The Politics of Economic Adjustment*, U.S.-Thirld World Policy Perspectives, No. 12, New Brunswick: Transaction Books, 1989.

WCED, World Commission on Environment and Development, *Our Common Future*, Oxford: Oxford University Press, 1987.

WEBER Max, *The Theory of Social and Economic Organization*, A. M. HENDERSON and Talcott PARSONS, trs., New York: The Free Press, 1947.

WHITEHEAD Laurence, 'Political Explanations of Macroeconomic Management: A Survey', *World Development*, vol. 18, No. 8, August 1990, pp. 1133-1146.

WHO Report 1990, Geneva: World Health Organization.

WILLIAMSON John, and Donald R. LESSARD, *Capital Flight: The Problem and Policy Responses*, Washington D.C.: Institute for International Economics, Policy Analyses in International Economics, November 1987.

INDEX

INDEX

RAFFAELE MATTIOLI LECTURES

RAFFAELE MATTIOLI FOUNDATION
Fondazione Raffaele Mattioli
per la Storia del Pensiero Economico

Published

RICHARD F. KAHN, *The Making of Keynes' General Theory* (First edition: May 1984; Japanese edition, Tokyo: Iwanami Shoten, Publishers, April 1987).

FRANCO MODIGLIANI, *The Debate over Stabilization Policy* (First edition: July 1986).

CHARLES P. KINDLEBERGER, *Economic Laws and Economic History* (First edition: December 1989; Italian edition, Bari: Laterza, 1990; Spanish edition, Barcelona: Editorial Crítica, December 1990).

ALAN PEACOCK, *Public Choice Analysis in Historical Perspective* (First edition: March 1992).

SHIGETO TSURU, *Institutional Economics Revisited* (First edition: January 1993).

KARL BRUNNER - ALLAN H. MELTZER, *Money and the Economy. Issues in Monetary Analysis* (First edition: June 1993).

PAUL P. STREETEN, *Thinking About Development*.

To be published

ERIK F. LUNDBERG, *The Development of Swedish and Keynesian Macroeconomic Theory and its Impact on Economic Policy*.

HERBERT A. SIMON, *An Empirically Based Microeconomics*.

NICHOLAS KALDOR, *Causes of Growth and Stagnation in the World Economy*.

RICHARD STONE, *Some British Empiricists in the Social Sciences*.

DESIGN, TEXT IN BASKERVILLE VAL AND PRINTING
BY STAMPERIA VALDONEGA, VERONA
MAY MCMXCV